MY ADVENTURES IN THE
GOLDEN AGE OF MUSIC

Da Capo Press Music Reprint Series

GENERAL EDITOR

FREDERICK FREEDMAN

VASSAR COLLEGE

MY ADVENTURES IN THE
GOLDEN AGE OF MUSIC

HENRY T. FINCK

DA CAPO PRESS · NEW YORK · 1971

Library of Congress Cataloging in Publication Data

Finck, Henry Theophilus, 1854-1926.
    My adventures in the golden age of music.
    (Da Capo Press music reprint series)
    Reprint of the 1926 ed.
    1. Musicians—Correspondence, reminiscences, etc.
2. Music — New York (City) I. Title.
ML423.F46   1971   780.15   70-87496
    ISBN 0-306-71448-5

This Da Capo Press edition of
My Adventures in the Golden Age of Music
is an unabridged republication of the
first edition published in New York and
London in 1926.

MY ADVENTURES IN THE
GOLDEN AGE OF MUSIC

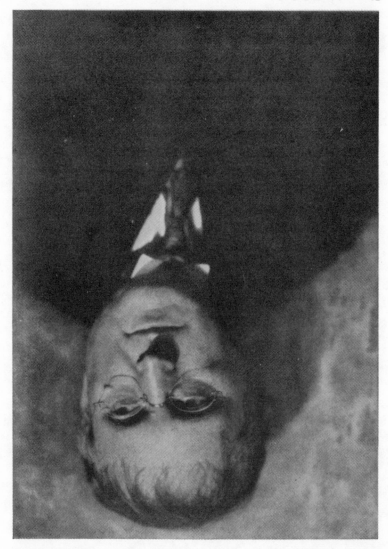

HENRY T. FINCK

Photograph by F. E. Geisler

MY ADVENTURES IN THE
GOLDEN AGE OF MUSIC

BY

HENRY T. FINCK

Author of "Musical Laughs," Etc.

ILLUSTRATED

FUNK & WAGNALLS COMPANY

NEW YORK AND LONDON

TO

MY LIFE-LONG FRIEND

CHARLES F. THWING

AND THE OTHER SURVIVORS

IN 1926 OF THE HARVARD

CLASS OF 1876

H. T. F.

CONTENTS

PAGE

I Offer No Apology xiii

PART I

In Missouri During the Civil War Period . 1

Near Mark Twain's Birthplace, 1—Druggist and Music Lover, 2—Glimpses of a Happy Family, 3—A Busy Father, 4—Pork and Corn Bread, Et Cetera, 7—Catfish, and Girls, 9—In War Time, 11—Covered Wagon or Panama?, 12

PART II

In Wild and Woolly Oregon—1862–1872 . . 17

Oregon Apples at Home, 19—From Stage to Railroad, 23—Chinook Wind and Salmon, 25—Oregon a Great State for Epicures, 26—A Shameless Pleasure-Seeker, 29—Hunting for Pretty Girls, 30—A Musical Oasis, 33—Doctor Keil and His Colony, 38—What a Wolf Did for Me, 41—Longing for Harvard, 44—Climbing Mount Hood, 47—Up the Columbia River, 53—Poor Bruno, 55

PART III

Four Years at Harvard 61

By Way of St. Louis, 63—Unpleasant Surprizes, 64—Disgraceful Failure and Triumphant Success, 66—Professors Lane and Greenough, 68—Professors Bartlett and Norton, 70—President Eliot and Professor Paine, 73—Student Music and Pranks, 80—Eating in Memorial Hall, 82—Longfellow and Howells, 84—Emerson, Holmes, and Lowell, 89—Agassiz, John Fiske and William James, 91—Professors Child and Peabody, 95—Professors Palmer and Bowen, 98—More Student Pranks, 103—Writing for College

Papers, 105—My Failure as Book-Agent, 106—Climbing Mount
Washington, 108—Woodberry and I, 110—Olmsted's Amusing
Reminiscences, 113—The Centennial Class, 115

PART IV

PAGE

LISTENING, LOAFING AND STUDYING IN EUROPE . 117

Off for Bayreuth, 119—How I Met Wagner, 122—Munich, Beer,
and Music, 126—I Win a Harvard Fellowship, 133—Two Winters in Berlin, 135—In Romantic Heidelberg, 146—A Winter in
Gay Vienna, 153—Uncle Edward and the Prussian Octopus, 158

PART V

THE GOLDEN AGE IN MUSICAL NEW YORK—AND
AFTER 163

A Marriage of Two Papers, 165—In the Editorial Den, 166—
Carl Schurz, 169—Wanted by the Tribune, 170—Night Work
and Pleasures, 172—Theodore Thomas, 173—Adelina Patti, 180
—William Steinway, 185—Campanini and Mapleson, 188—The
Great Opera War, 192—Seidl the Great, 197—Overthrow of
German Opera, 202—The DeReszke Miracle, 204—Emma Eames
and De Gogorza, 208—Materna, Brandt, and Lehmann, 212—
Niemann, Alvary, Fischer, 215—Emma Calvé, 217—Nellie
Melba, 222—Marcella Sembrich, 225—Lillian Nordica, 232—
Schumann-Heink, Homer, Fremstad, 236—Grau's All-star Casts,
242—Seidl's Death and Funeral, 246—Colonel Ingersoll, 250—
Godkin and Walter Damrosch, 251—Romantic Adventures, Nar-
row Escapes, 256—A Typhoid Episode, 259—A Winter in Cali-
fornia, 263—The Villard Family, 264—Not A Mary After All,
270—Mrs. Thurber's National Conservatory, 274—Dvořák and
the "New World" Symphony, 277—Edward MacDowell, 282—
Paderewski, 287—Ernest Schelling and Granados, 302—Josef
Hofmann, 304—Fritz Kreisler, 305—Maud Powell, 311—Guiomar Novaes of Brazil, 315—How I Made Conried Manager, 318
—My Fight for Parsifal, 320—Strauss Versus Strauss, 325—
Geraldine Farrar, 327—Enrico Caruso, 335—An Evening Post
Happy Family, 339—The Astonishing Oscar Hammerstein, 349
—A Champion of French Music, 352—Campanini's Triumphs,
354—Maurice Renaud, 356—Mary Garden, 362—Victor Her-
bert, 364—Rosa Raisa and Polacco, 368—Gatti-Casazza and

CONTENTS

Toscanini, 370—End of the Golden Age, 375—Maria Jeritza, 377—Bori, Easton, and Galli-Curci, 380—A Bunch of Singers, 383—Kahn and Gatti as Humorists, 386—War-time Opera, 388 —Percy Grainger, 391—Three Millionaires, 396—Three Boston Critics, 400—My New York Colleagues, 403—Huneker in His Letters to Me, 413—Presser, Cooke, and Kelley, 415—Why I Took to Jesting, 418—Philharmonic Drives and Musical Politics, 420—Gustav Mahler in New York, 424—Ossip, Clara, Hildegarde and John, 426—Summers in Maine, 430—A New Psychology of Eating, 433—From Lust to Love, 436—Luther Burbank and John Muir, 441—Doctor Kellogg and Battle Creek, 446— Postscript, 449—Good Bye to New York, 452

INDEX 459

ILLUSTRATIONS

	FACING PAGE
HENRY T. FINCK . . . . *Frontispiece*	
THE FINCK FAMILY	14
H. C. FINCK, FLORA, REGINE, JOSEPHINE, HENRY, AND EDWARD	
THE AUTHOR AS A STUDENT AT HARVARD	78
THEODORE THOMAS	174
ADELINA PATTI	182
ITALO CAMPANINI AS "MANRICO" IN "IL TROVATORE" . .	190
ANTON SEIDL	198
JEAN DE RESZKE AS "ROMEO"	202
EDOUARD DE RESZKE	206
EMMA EAMES	210
LILLI LEHMANN AS "BRÜNNHILDE"	214
EMMA CALVÉ	218
MELBA AS "MARGUERITE" IN "FAUST"	222
MARCELLA SEMBRICH	226
LILLIAN NORDICA	234
ERNESTINA SCHUMANN-HEINK	238
HENRY T. FINCK AT FIFTY	254
ABBIE HELEN CUSHMAN FINCK	270
EDWARD MACDOWELL	286
IGNACE J. PADEREWSKI	292
FRITZ KREISLER	306
MAUD POWELL	314
GUIOMAR NOVAES	318
GERALDINE FARRAR	330
CARUSO AS "DON JOSE" IN "CARMEN"	338
MARY GARDEN IN "THAÏS"	362
GIULIO GATTI-CASAZZA	370
ARTURO TOSCANINI	374
JERITZA AS "TOSCA"	378
GALLI-CURCI AS "GILDA" IN "RIGOLETTO"	382
PERCY GRAINGER	394

EDITOR'S NOTE—On the eve of publication word was received of the sudden death of Mr. Henry T. Finck, at his summer home in Maine. Painful as this news was to his many personal friends and to those associated with him in his long career as author and musical critic, it is nevertheless gratifying to his publishers to be able to announce that Mr. Finck had finished within a few days of his death the final revision of the proofs of these memoirs. *My Adventures in the Golden Age of Music* thus reaches the public in carefully matured, complete form fashioned by its author. Critics generally have recognized the active part taken by Mr. Finck in the evolution of musical art and criticism in this country during the last fifty years. It is thus of quite incalculable importance, historically, to have from him his own record of the great and stirring events in which he himself stands out as a leading and always influential figure during a picturesque period which he has well described as the Golden Age of Music.

An editorial writer in the New York *Times* thus indicates some of Mr. Finck's outstanding qualities as a man and a critic:

> He had fancy and imagination and a gift of humor. Yet withal he was a man of amazing industry. The list of volumes which came from his pen bespeaks a worker who let no interval of time go to waste. His long activity as a musical critic in New York made him with a multitude of music-lovers a name either to swear by or swear at, and he will be remembered for his distinct personality as well as for his gifts as a writer.

CLIFFORD SMYTH

I OFFER NO APOLOGY

SINCE I am not "adding one more to the long list of books on this topic" I do not offer the usual apology. This is the only genuine and original autobiography of Henry T. Finck and will remain so forever. Some readers, nevertheless, may think I ought to apologize for the unblushing way in which I have quoted pleasant things said about me by celebrities. They should bear in mind that I have been equally frank and naïve in calling attention to the many occasions when I made a fool of myself.

My witty colleague and friend, Deems Taylor, once wrote for the *New York World* a very unbiased article on a juvenile piece of his that had been played at an orchestral concert. In view of the physiological doctrine that a man's body is entirely made over every seven years, he felt at liberty to treat a piece of his that was over seven years old as if it were composed by another man.

Adapting this notion to my own case I call attention to the alarming fact that this world has been afflicted with no fewer than ten Henry T. Fincks within the last seventy years. I, Henry T. Finck No. 11, discourse herein about my ten predecessors as if they were different persons; this has enabled me often to write unegotistically as if I were at work on a biography instead of an autobiography.

From one point of view I claim that my memoirs are a model of modesty. My ego is not usually in the limelight. I simply appear as the guide who takes you to interesting places or brings you face to face with famous women and men. The number of these included in the present volume may seem surprizingly large. I never had any difficulty in adding a celebrity I admired to the list of my friends. How did I do it? By winning his or her affection.

If you wish to win a woman's love or admiration you do not compliment her on those of her attributes or charms which are so conspicuous that any fool can see them. You discover some subtle traits that others have overlooked and dwell on those. That's what I have done habitually with the celebrities I have been called upon to discuss as a newspaper critic, and that's why they have taken me to their hearts. "I saw your little bird," one painter said to another who had put it in to emphasize the solitude of a scene, and you may be sure that this pleased the artist more than a string of adjectives would have done.

My wife aided me in the search for "birds," especially in the case of great French artists like Renaud and Muratore (the pages on Renaud in this volume are mostly by her) and that's why the greatest of the great were always glad to come and lunch with us or invite us to lunch or dine with them, and why I have plenty of personal gossip and new anecdotes to offer. Many critics love to dwell on flaws in the work of the great and the greatest. I heard those flaws but ignored them, dwelling instead on the things that raised these artists above the level of dull mediocrity on which most musicians and other mortals dwell.

From my boyhood I was an epicure—a pleasure-seeker and only the best of everything gave me real pleasure. In accepting a position as musical critic I became a professional pleasure-seeker, making a business of what to others is entertainment. As the season for critics is short, I thus had plenty of time to seek for diverse pleasures during long vacations in the country; in writing books on various subjects; in gardening and in travel at home or abroad. Fate brought it about that the story of my life presents a greater variety of scenic backgrounds and "atmosphere" than the records of most writers of memoirs: first, Missouri in the Civil War period; then wild and woolly Oregon before there was a railroad; then five years at Harvard, the home of many celebrities at that time; next, three years in German and Austrian university towns: Heidelberg, Berlin, Vienna; a year in Wagnerian Munich; finally New York, where I became a musical editor almost at the beginning of the cult of high-brow music and remained so to the end of the Golden Age and beyond.

Goethe called his autobiography "Truth and Fiction." Mine differs from his in that it is all truth and nothing but the truth. Not the whole truth, I confess. No mention is made in it of my frequent narrow escapes from the gallows or the electric chair or lynching. No reference is made to my hold-ups of California stages, my bold burglaries and midnight murders, my outrageous conduct at petting parties, my frequent elopements with other men's wives, and so on. Concerning such incidents there is so much in the daily papers that I feared my readers would yawn if I told them all my criminal adventures. Should there be an unexpected call for these scandalous details it will be easy to supply them in a second volume, same size as this, to be called "The Whole Truth" or "The Real Henry T. Finck."

There are two kinds of autobiography: one which, like the present volume, relates an author's adventures among his fellow men and women, and a second which tells the story of his ideas, ideals, aims and achievements. This second kind I provided in a volume entitled "Musical Progress," which includes the sum and substance of my mental activity in music. It might be called the psychic, or esthetic, complement to the present volume, as supplements to which I may name the three books which tell of my adventures in Spain, Japan, and on our own Pacific

Slope; also my books on gardening and on Success in
Music, both of which are replete with autobiographic incidents and adventures.

What impresses me most in reviewing the story of my
life, is that it covers practically the whole of the Golden
Age of Music in New York. There will never be another age like it. The radio is making terrible havoc
in the activities and earnings of professional musicians
(ask them!) while the cacophonists, sarcastically dubbed
"futurists," are doing their level best, with their insane
cult of dissonances, to assassinate whatever interest is left
in the divine art. They are greater enemies of music than
the jazz bands. "Paradise Lost" might be an appropriate sub-title for my reminiscences of The Golden Age of
Music.

H. T. F.

New York, Sept. 30, 1926.

PART I

IN MISSOURI DURING THE CIVIL WAR PERIOD

IN MISSOURI DURING THE CIVIL WAR PERIOD

NEAR MARK TWAIN'S BIRTHPLACE

THE first time I met Mark Twain I made a fool of myself.

It was at one of the Friday evening receptions given at the hospitable home of Mr. and Mrs. Richard Watson Gilder, which approximated the literary salons of Paris more nearly than any other social function in New York.

As editor of the *Century Magazine* Mr. Gilder was intimate with all the prominent writers and artists of his day. No formal invitations for special dates were issued; hence you never knew whom you might meet at these weekly receptions. It was pot luck.

My duties as musical critic of the *Evening Post* kept me pretty busy evenings, but once in a while I shirked my task and, in search of pleasure, piloted myself to the Gilder salon.

One evening, as I entered the parlor, I was delighted to see that Mark Twain was there. He was talking with Edmund Clarence Stedman. Mr. Gilder was surprized when I told him I had never met the great humorist. Promptly he introduced me, and then came the aforesaid foolishness.

"Mr. Clemens," I remarked, "probably you don't know that you and I are the two great Missouri authors. To be sure," I added idiotically, "*I* don't amount to much but you make up the average."

1

If I had had any sense I would have said "To be sure *you* don't amount to much but I make up the average."

That would have made him think I, too, had a sense of humor.

However, being kind at heart, he forgave me, and when I told him that I, too, was born near Hannibal, Missouri, he told me how he had recently visited that place after an absence of years.

"Of course they received you with brass bands and that sort of thing," I said.

"No," he replied, "I didn't give them a chance." And then he talked about the changes he had noted in his natal place.

My birthplace was at Bethel, Shelby county. Store-keepers in our village went to Hannibal to buy their goods. One of them had his shop in our block and I never failed to be there when he came back from that town and opened his boxes.

Generally, he brought a present for me. I remember particularly a noisy pipe he once gave me.

Was I happy? Much more so, I fear, than anybody else in the neighborhood. For weeks I mourned and wondered what had become of that pipe after the second day of my ownership. I searched and searched, but no trace of it could be found.

Druggist and Music Lover

My father was a professional apothecary and an amateur musician. That is, he made his living selling drugs—also sugar, coffee, and tobacco—and gave his leisure time to training a village band and a choir.

This seemed to be the chief delight of his life. Like Liszt, he refused to accept a cent from any one for music lessons. He learned to play nearly every instrument in the band—just for fun—and his enthusiasm did wonders in getting the young men and women of the village interested and proficient in playing or singing together.

Their meeting place was in our house and thus I grew up from the start in a musical atmosphere.

The instrument chosen for me was the violoncello, which was considerably taller than I when at the age of seven I first began to draw a bow across its strings.

GLIMPSES OF A HAPPY FAMILY

When my cousin Fernande Fink, daughter of the mayor of Böblingen in Wurttemberg, some years ago, sent me a batch of letters that had been written in the forties and fifties of the nineteenth century by my father and mother to their families, I eagerly scanned them for mention of my noble self in my august childhood. I was rewarded by the following glimpse (date: February 27, 1855; I was born on September 22, 1854); a glimpse which also includes my sisters Flora and Regine and my brother Edward, who were, respectively, six, two, and four years older than I. My mother wrote:

"I hardly know where my head is, the children are all shouting and laughing around me. Flora and Edward have in their arms large dolls. Edward shouts: 'Flora, I am your grandfather,' and Flora answers, 'Yes, and I am your grandmother; you must now pay me a visit.' Whereupon Edward rides to her on his hobby horse and asks, 'Are the children behaving themselves?' At this, Regine cries 'I am no child, I am a man.' She is about right, for she often bosses the game; she's a tomboy. They are all, thank heaven, in good health, and are hugely pleased with dear little Henry; he is getting along splendidly and gives us all much pleasure; often he entertains himself by the hour with the toys his father makes for him on the turning

TxU

lathe he bought not long ago. Every day the children are surprized with some new toys he turns out for them: mortars, cups, rolling pins, salt- and sugar-shakers, eggs of diverse colors—all this he does in his hours of recreation. What I do with my time I can hardly tell: sometimes only the most important things can be attended to, only now and then can I do a little mending or knitting—it all depends on how my little son behaves himself."

Here is another snapshot of my mother from one of her letters: "You wish to know what I do with myself besides attending to the things my dear mother taught me, such as cooking, baking, washing, ironing, sewing, knitting, mending, etc. Well, I can milk a cow, which gives me special pleasure; also I can make trousers, vests, and coats. There is no work I dodge and I am not ashamed to perform the humblest tasks; however, you also have no occasion to be ashamed of your daughter; I am withal the same merry Beatrice, I often sing from morn to night. Among my greatest joys is churchgoing, and when I feel like reading I take the Bible or Arnd's 'True Christianity.' "

A Busy Father

When my mother married my father all she had to do was to add a c to her maiden name, which was Fink (Beatrice). My father's full name was Henry Conrad Finck. He was born at Murrhardt, a few miles on one side of Stuttgart; my mother, at Sindelfingen, a few miles on the other side of that city. They did not know each other in Europe but came over on sailing vessels separately, in their early youth, so I may consider myself as practically an American of the second generation. How they got married is told very briefly in one of mother's letters, dated November 24, 1847:

"The best news I can give you to-day is that I am, since November 18, back in Cincinnati, the happy wife of Henry Finck, son of merchant Finck in Murrhardt. Let me tell you what he is and how I came to know him.

"Last year he came, with several boxes of musical instruments, to New Orleans, where he remained several weeks with his uncle, Consul Finck, and then went up to St. Louis. There he became acquainted with Christopher Giesy and heard from him that he would be able to sell some of his instruments in Bethel. In May he came to Bethel and remained there teaching music. I also took lessons of him in singing and playing the guitar.

"I was well, contented and happy, when suddenly, in August, I was stricken with malarial fever, which no one escapes here. I was homesick, too, and in the delirium of fever I spoke much about you, my dear parents, and incessantly begged mother for raspberry-shrub.

"During this illness I made up my mind to return to Cincinnati as soon as I was well again. The date for my departure was already fixed when my dear Henry asked me—well, you know what. On October 14 we were betrothed and proceeded joyously to St. Louis, where pastor Grell united us in marriage at the home of Cousin Kurfiss. My only sorrow was that my dear parents could not be present to witness my bliss.

"Two days ago we moved into our home. My husband has secured a position in the musical department of the National Theater. He will also give music lessons—on any instrument. I am very happy in my own home and I venerate the parents who could rear a man like my husband. I believe I am the luckiest woman in Cincinnati and the happiest."

It has already become apparent that my father had other strings to his bow beside the profession of an apothecary, for which he had a thorough four-years' training in

Germany. As a matter of course he also became a physician.

What this meant may be learned from the following paragraph taken from a letter written by my mother in February, 1858. By that time there had been another addition to the family, a daughter named Josephine. All five of us were down with scarlet fever at the same time. Hardly were we out of danger when mother's turn came. "Although I was not dangerously ill," she wrote, "I suffered much anguish and shed many tears when I looked at my children; Josephine suffered most because she was teething at the same time, but she improved two weeks ago and is now learning to walk. I alone am still weak and can do very little, but I am able to be up."

It was an exceptionally severe epidemic, and it kept my father busy day and night. "My dear husband," mother continues, "has had a very hard winter. Patients in nearly every home; often he was called five times in one night, and his days were spent at the bedsides. In three weeks before I fell ill there were fifteen deaths in the village from scarlet fever."

Contagious diseases are not the only dangers to which doctors are exposed. I remember two incidents connected with father's medical ministrations which nearly cost him his life. He was called to a patient on a very dark night. He had to cross a river on a bridge which was rickety, but he did not know that during a storm some of the planks had been torn away. He was just about to put his foot on one of the spaces thus left—which would have meant sure death in the water below—when a flash of lightning revealed the danger and saved him.

Missouri was a Slave State then and one of the slave-holders had his farm not far from our village. Covered with a new fur-lined overcoat which afforded him much comfort, my father was passing by this place on a winter

day when several bloodhounds, excited by the smell of the
fur, rushed at him, and had not an overseer called them
off at that moment, the wearer of the coat would have been
attacked and possibly killed.

I remember hearing the jubilant shouts of the slaves
late in the afternoon when their daily task was over.
Theirs was hard work, yet they were not too tired to play
and caper in the evening. The strings for their banjos
they got from my father. As he refused payment for
them they used to bring us apples and nuts.

PORK AND CORNBREAD ET CETERA

As the child is father to the man it is hardly necessary
to say that the future author of "Food and Flavor" and
"Girth Control" was already in his boyhood particularly
fond of good things to eat. It was therefore a great griev-
ance that Dr. Finck did not approve of pork but followed
strictly the laws of Moses, though there was not a drop of
Jewish blood in his veins. As he wrote in one of his home
letters: "Pork we never have, I allow none to come into
the house, although it is here, in Missouri, the staple food,
and a family of the size of mine usually disposes of half-
a-dozen hogs a year."

In one of my father's letters written in the year of my
birth he gives some interesting details regarding the gastronomic and agricultural habits of Missourians in 1854.
"You will laugh when I tell you about farming here-
abouts: six successive years of wheat on the same ground
and then six fallow years. No trace of manuring except
in the gardens of the Germans here. The Americans let
their cattle roam about outdoors all the year; here in
Bethel we keep ours in the stable at least in the winter and
feed them. If a farmer wants to slaughter a hog he takes
his rifle and shoots one in the woods. If it happens that

he shoots one belonging to a neighbor he simply has to pay for it. He may be well off, owning hundreds of acres, yet contents himself with a fare of smoked pork and corn-bread three times a day. Some have fifteen or twenty cows, yet never have a drop of milk in the house or cream for their coffee, so great is the indifference, frivolity, and indolence of the women."

In the same letter, as in others, I find evidence that my love of gardening is also an inherited trait. I cannot suppress the vain wish that father could have been told by a fairy that his infant son would some day write "Gardening With Brains," which the most famous gardener of all times, Luther Burbank, would pronounce the best of all books on its subject.

It was fortunate for Burbank that we did not live near his gardens in Santa Rosa.

In our neighbor's garden there was a young dwarf-apple-tree bearing two apples which the owner watched with much interest. They were just about ripe when one night they disappeared. I alone knew what had become of them.

For some reason or other father did not want us to attend a certain wedding to which we were all invited. The bride's family was wealthy and there was sure to be a sumptuous dinner. When the hour arrived, I prowled around the festal house and odors from the viands in the kitchen were wafted to my nostrils. That settled it. Though not dressed for a wedding, I made a bee-line for the dining-room, where I was pleasantly received, and dined like a prince. No reprimand followed at home; perhaps my escapade never became known there.

Father was a great smoker. He had a huge pipe bowl with a long stem which, Turkish fashion, cooled the smoke before it entered the mouth. When writing letters or composing music (his favorite occupation) he had this long pipe at his side, leaning against the table, and now and then took a whiff. I did not envy him and have always regarded smoking as an incomprehensible habit.

For one thing I have always been grateful to my paternal ancestor. He obliged us to eat every course at table if we wished any of the following courses. There was one soup—"burnt soup" we called it—which I particularly disliked. One day we had it at the noon meal. I refused it—and left the table. In the evening, there it was again —for me. I ate it—and the rest of the supper. This method taught us to eat 'most everything—a very useful accomplishment. Thanks to it I have never been embarrassed when dining out, for I refuse nothing—except blancmange; *that* I would rather starve than eat.

Every mortal has juvenile disappointments which he or she never forgets. To this day, in my seventy-third year, I still feel sorry for what I did one afternoon. Walking up the street I saw two boys busy carrying a pile of firewood into the kitchen, armful after armful.

"Come and help us," one of them shouted. As carrying wood was not one of my favorite amusements I declined and walked on. Afterwards I heard that when the boys got through they were rewarded with huge pieces of gingerbread—mind you, old-fashioned Southern gingerbread.

The loss of that gingerbread treat was, as you can easily understand, one of the tragedies of my eight years in Missouri. Another was a fishing episode—even now I cannot talk about it without being "mad at myself" for having been so careless.

Catfish and Girls

There were plenty of catfish of good size in the river flowing past Bethel. As a matter of course I often went fishing. I had no basket but just a string with a stick at each end; into this I inserted each fish as caught, and then stuck one stick into the mud near the water so as to keep the fish alive. On the tragic day I remember, I had a dozen fine fellows on my string, and then caught a whopper much over a foot long. How he did wiggle as I took him off the hook and how desperately he tried to stick his cruel "thorns" into my flesh! At last I got him on the string and stuck it into the mud again. A big flutter and flash—and the big strong fellow, with a dozen on the same string, floated down the river into deep water. Oh, oh, oh! The unlucky thirteen!

In that same river we boys of course often went swimming. One day I was with two schoolgirls of sixteen, far away from the village. It was a very warm afternoon and the girls longed for a swim. They had no bathing suits but talked the matter over and decided that I was so young that I might be ignored. So we all went in together à la Adam and Eve.

Yes, I was young then—only seven—but I had already fallen in love with two girls. One was some years older than I; a black-eyed beauty who sometimes took care of me. One day she was in the garden with several other girls. Looking out of the window I shouted: "Martha, come in, it's raining."

Whether or not the others got wet did not worry me.

But my first real love was a schoolgirl named Catharine. She seemed to me quite unlike all other girls—a different species altogether. And the proof of my genuine romantic love lay in my actions.

During recess in school one afternoon there was a tremendous, typically Missourian hailstorm. It was in summer but the ground was soon white as with winter snow. Some of the hailstones were as big as hickory-nuts and Catharine wished she had one of them. At the risk of

having my skull cracked I ran out like a medieval knight
and chivalrously brought in the biggest stone in sight.

In War Time

In the old days, when St. Louis was the starting point
for adventurous souls seeking homes or a fortune in
the Wild West, Missourians were called border ruffians.
When the Civil War came, Missouri was a frontier State
in another sense of the word. Our village, in particular,
seemed to be a dividing line between the Northern and
Southern forces. Union troops might pass through our
Main Street one day, Confederates the next.

While mostly favoring the North, our men had to
observe neutrality as well as they could. I remember seeing them drill, but nothing in particular was done.

Of course we boys all played "soldiers." Belonging to
a musical family I felt that I had a right to be in the front
as bugler. When that job was given to an older boy I set
up a howl and kept it up till the post was assigned to me.

The schoolgirls also played "soldiers." Of course they
knew less about it than we boys did, and we had a good
laugh when we learned that my "tomboy" sister Regina,
who was Captain, deposed the General for not obeying her
orders.

Of course we all longed for real guns and swords in
place of the wooden ones we made for ourselves. Imagine
my joy when, one day, after some soldiers had been camping near the village, I discovered a genuine, life-size mus-
ket, with cartridge belt and all!

Triumphantly I took them home, but father most cruelly, as I thought, took them away from me and gave them
to the headman of the village. Fathers are so tyrannical!

There was one consolation. We had also found a half-
emptied barrel of crackers—hard-tack; these we were

allowed to keep. They were new to us and we thought them very good to eat. As a tit-for-tat my father gave me a basket of apples to distribute in the street to the next troop of Union soldiers that came along. They seemed very glad to get them.

These were some of the harmless and comic aspects of the conflict. Bethel was fortunately spared the direct proof that "war is hell"; but a horrible confirmation of Sherman's aphorism that war is hell was furnished in Palmyra, not far from Bethel, where there was a horrible butchery of seven soldiers by their enemy. The victims were taken to the place of execution, each one seated in the wagon on his own coffin. The details of the butchery are too grewsome to relate, nor need I dwell on the guerilla warfare carried on in all directions.

Covered Wagon or Panama?

The region where such things could happen was obviously not the best place for a widower with five young children. Yes, a widower, for my mother had died in the meantime.

It is pathetic to read my father's words in a letter dated March 25, 1859: "The children are getting along very well but they are without what is the greatest of all blessings, a loving mother. I do my best to be both mother and father to them but my many duties keep me from doing all I would like to."

I should add here that, in addition to the manifold duties already mentioned, my father held the position of postmaster. And he was also a sort of *alter ego* to Dr. Keil, the clergyman who had founded the local community—a socialistic experiment in Bethel, concerning which I have told in Part II. Dr. Keil had gone to Oregon, and whenever a letter for his congregation came from him, it was addressed to my father, who read it aloud in church.

As I was only five years old when my mother died, I recall her only dimly. I remember being distressed on seeing her lying on a bed in a shroud and asking: "Why doesn't mother wake up?"

Let me say it again, Missouri at this time was not a desirable place for a widower with five young children. Can you blame Henry Conrad Finck for being eager, under the circumstances described, to emigrate from the seat of war to the far-distant, peaceful, primitive State of Oregon, two thousand miles away?

This plan, to be sure, antedated the war. In one of father's letters written as far back as March 25, 1859, I find a reference to friends in Oregon who were trying to persuade him to join them. One of these was the same Christopher Giesy who had induced father to go to Bethel. He himself, poor man, did not live to welcome us when we finally came. In crossing a turbulent river his boat capsized and as he had not learned to swim he was drowned.

There were other friends, however, in Oregon, and, to join them, my father finally made a firm decision. The only question was: "Covered wagon or Panama?"

I have often thought how interesting it would be if I could recall among the adventures of my childhood a trip across the plains with a caravan of ox-drawn white-canvassed wagons, encountering Indians, fording dangerous torrents, thirsting in the desert, seeing buffaloes, antelopes, coyotes, prairie-dogs and a hundred other interesting things.

A covered-wagon caravan was joined by a number of men and women in our Bethel colony, but it was of course impossible for my father to think of such a thing with five children aged six, eight, ten, twelve, and fourteen, and no mother to help take care of them.

Panama was the alternative, and via Panama we went, thence to San Francisco, and from there to Portland. There was, of course, no transcontinental railroad, so we had to travel first, nearly a thousand miles in the wrong direction to New York, where we took the steamer going south, still farther away from Oregon.

Crazy journeying, this may seem—like going from Boston to New York by way of Chicago; but even thus we reached our goal in five weeks instead of the five months required by the covered wagons.

We had to wait for the steamer several days in New York but I was too young to remember now what that town looked like in 1862. We stopped at what was then an "uptown" hotel—on Barclay Street! We heard a concert, and I was allowed to taste beer. One mouthful was quite enough.

The boat which took us to the Isthmus of Panama was of course the first ocean steamer I had ever been on. But we had been on a ferryboat at Quincy, Illinois, where we crossed the Mississippi. The funny thing about this was that I did not dare to stay outside, because I had read about the rocking and pitching of ships, and of the waves dashing over them. When my brother came to ask me to come out I said I was afraid, whereupon he told me laughingly that we were almost over. The motion was so gentle I didn't know the boat had started!

My Mexican recollections are also meager. At Acapulco, where our ship stopped a few hours, I remember the brown naked boys diving into the deeps around the ship for coins thrown into the water by passengers.

At Aspinwall I had a glorious time picking up empty sea-shells on the beach. I was simply dazed by their countless number, the variety of shapes and the iridescent colors, each seeming more beautiful than the others. After filling all my pockets with choice specimens I threw most

THE FINCK FAMILY
H. C. FINCK, FLORA,
REGINE, JOSEPHINE, HENRY AND EDWARD

of them away again because I found others that seemed still more exquisite.

The cry of "Five cents a glass, ice-lemonade" was new to me, as was the lemonade itself. And then the oranges— the first I had ever tasted or even seen! Imagine what a treat to a born epicure like myself. So deep was the impression made on me by their fragrance and flavor that to this day, more than sixty years later, the scent and flavor of an orange recall Panama-land to my olfactory memory.

A little less vivid are my recollections of coconut palms and orange-trees seen while crossing the fifty-mile isthmus; of big-leaved banana-trees; of naked children at the stations, and fruit-women with baskets of bananas or oranges on their heads and a baby fastened with a sling on the back.

No canal, of course, in those days; nobody had even dreamt of such a ludicrously impossible thing. But there was a railroad which carried us across the isthmus to Panama through the tropical jungle and past thatched huts with scantily-clad natives. Then came the steamer which at last took us north to our destination. Of this trip I recall only that somebody stole a large metal flask of port wine my father had bought for medicinal use; also, that the meals were good and that I was wofully disappointed one day when I wanted more of the dessert and the waiter said: "Pudding all gone." Another juvenile tragedy.

PART II

IN WILD AND WOOLLY OREGON
1862-1872

IN WILD AND WOOLLY OREGON

OREGON APPLES AT HOME

IT HAS always been a matter of special satisfaction and pride to me that my early life, from my eighth year to my eighteenth, was associated inseparably with Oregon apples.

If there is anything in all the wide world better to eat than an Oregon apple I have not found it though I have been an indefatigable traveler on four out of the five continents of this globe of ours.

The term "Oregon apples" includes, of course, those grown in the State of Washington, which formerly was a part of Oregon Territory, the grandest corner of the United States, because of its glorious snow-peaks and forests.

When once a foolish notion is spread abroad it is almost impossible to annihilate it. All my life I have been fighting the outrageous lie that the highbred Oregon apples, while large and beautiful to look at, are inferior in flavor to the underbred, puny Eastern apples. During every one of the forty-three years I spent in New York City, the greatest apple market in the world, I compared the Oregon fruit with the Eastern, and almost invariably found the Western better.

My testimony is of exceptional weight because I have always been an ultra epicure, almost like a dog in the keenness of my olfactory sense, on which our discriminating enjoyment of fruit and all food depends chiefly.*

* For proof and explanation of this assertion see my "Food and Flavor" and "Girth Control."

Nor is this superiority of Oregon fruit due chiefly to the greater and more scientific care bestowed on orchard-culture on the Pacific Coast. It is largely due to soil and climate, just as the quality and aroma of choice wines like Chambertin, Chateau Yquem, Barolo or Budai are dependent on climatic and soil peculiarities in France, Italy, and Hungary.

Oregon apples can be grown only in Oregon. Hence my aforesaid pride. My youth was spent in the midst of a large orchard which supported our family and, later on, paid for my education at Harvard. It came about in this way:

When we came from Missouri via New York and Panama to Portland, situated some hundred miles up the Columbia and Willamette rivers, we did not stop at this metropolis of Oregon, which, with its view of five giant snow-peaks, is undoubtedly the most picturesquely situated city in the United States, but took the stage for a village named Aurora Mills, twenty-nine miles south of Portland. Here Dr. Keïl had made his home—apparently because he could buy there a flour-mill and a saw-mill—and was gradually importing his colony from Missouri.

We did not exactly belong to this colony, yet we shared certain of its socialistic advantages, while the colony benefited by my father's musical endeavors to help make life worth living.

By rare good luck, which I shall never cease to chuckle over, he was able to buy a house with a fine apple orchard on a hill only half-a-mile from the village. It was, as I have since discovered, one of the very first and best of the many commercial orchards for which Oregon soon became famous. I find in my diary that we harvested up to two thousand bushels in one year.

What did we do with them? My first impression is that

we ate most of them; but there were plenty left to ship to San Francisco. There they were sold at auction, and the proceeds paid our living expenses, with a margin for other things.*

Harvest-time for the saleable apples began after the middle of September and lasted into November. When the proper date arrived the whole Finck family turned out, each of us with a basket and a stepladder. A double hook was attached to each basket so that it could be hung upon the branches and leave both hands free for picking the ripening fruit, which we soon learned to do with lightning rapidity while carefully avoiding bruises.

My father was a scrupulously honest man. In winter, when he and Edward packed the fruit in boxes, every apple that was in the least bit damaged or undersized was rigidly excluded. Thus it came about that we always got the best market-price. Honesty, we had been told, is the best policy, and we saw that it was so. Only—we were not always sure the other fellows were honest.

Circumstances alter cases. Those fellows—I mean the commission merchants who shipped our boxes and sold them in San Francisco—got rich very much quicker than we did. Some of them became millionaires; we didn't. Did they really sell our apples at auction or did they make a deal? We had grave suspicions when we got only $1.50 a box. At other times, to be sure, we got $3 and more.

What my brother and I didn't know about apples wasn't worth knowing. We had in our orchard dozens of varieties. Some of them we would no more have thought of eating than raw potatoes or pumpkins. There

---

* The interesting fact is mentioned in Bancroft's work on Oregon (vol. ii, p. 257) that in 1853—only nine years before we bought our orchard—four bushels of Oregon apples were sold in San Francisco for $500. The following year forty bushels brought $2,500 in the same market. "In 1861 the shipment of apples from Oregon amounted to over 75,000 bushels; but they no longer were worth their weight in gold." Too bad!

were too many good kinds to waste our appetite on the poor stuff.

The man who had planted our orchard had shown such good taste on the whole that we wondered why he had overlooked the Red Astrachans. Of course we had the luscious Gravensteins (one tree, for which I made a bee-line when I returned to Aurora after a quarter of a century East and in Europe); winesaps (very good but not equal to the Stayman variety which then did not exist), excellent yellow Newtown pippins; with other favorites of our time, like Baldwins and greenings, for which I never cared much except baked or as sauce.

We doted on white winter pearmains and on the russets, both golden and Roxbury which, alas, have become so scarce. We had green Newtowns which were even more juicy than the yellow. What has become of them and what of the mealy bellflowers, and the unique West-field seek-no-further and others worth perpetuating? The criminal aim of fruitmen to reduce the number of varieties in our markets should be stopped by law and the police.

There were rambos, too; you never can get them now. Yet the rambo is worth its weight in cider—the best cider ever made. It is practically all juice, with just a peel around it. We took wagon-loads of them to the cider-mill, eating a dozen on the way, and afterwards sucking a quart or two of cider out of the barrel with a straw. Ever do that? No? Then you don't know what a boy *can* do. Sick? Why it kept away every doctor in the world without exception. Rambo cider is, in my opinion, a specific against doctors.

Not all of this cider was consumed in liquid form. Much of it was boiled in huge kettles all night till most of the water had disappeared as steam, leaving an apple but-ter which we all relished on bread, especially when, in the

last stage, plums or sliced pears had been cooked in with
the thickened cider. Aurora apple butter became famous
all over the State.

But I must not allow this favorite topic of mine to take
up too many pages of my autobiography.   One word more
I must add about our Oregon orchard. You may not
believe it, but it is a positive fact that we never needed
to spray against pernicious insects and we never had it
plowed! No need of these things. Lovely cornflowers
(bachelor's buttons) of all colors grew all over the
unplowed orchard, sowing themselves year after year for
more than half a century.

Surely, Oregon is the natural home of the apple—and
the cornflower!

From Stage to Railroad

When we traveled from San Francisco to Portland in
1862 we took, of course, the weekly steamer. There was
another way: by stage; but that took much more time
besides being arduous and uncertain. That is to say, we
heard that when the stage got stuck in the mud the mail-
bags containing the newspapers were simply cast out into
the mire. How could we feel sure that we would not come
next in the lightening process?

Imagine a whole big State like Oregon without a single
railroad! On June 4, 1870, I made this entry in my diary:
"The Oregon and California Railroad is coming right
through the middle of town; to-day they commenced to
move an old shop. The store and a stable must likewise
be removed." On July 14: "R.R. men leave town now
and it will be quiet again till the track-layers come."

For some years after the trains began to run between
Aurora and Portland passengers who had more time than

money still used the steamboat on the Willamette River, the nearest stop of which was four miles from our village. This had always been our way of shipping apples and continued to be so after the railroad came because of the considerable difference in freight rates.

Before the iron horse came, the Aurora band, which was started by my father, and which was in great demand for political meetings and other festive occasions, was waiting at this stopping-place one day, bound, I believe, for Oregon City. When the boat came near, the leader told us to get ready and welcome it with a march. To this our humorist objected, with mock solemnity, on the ground that the boat might shy at the music and leave us behind. I thought this was awfully funny, laughed immoderately, and thus made myself popular with the humorist.

He was our postmaster, and one of his side employments was to cut my hair whenever necessary. He had done this sometimes rather grudgingly, but after I laughed so heartily at his joke he was more than willing to give me even a State-prison cut if I asked for it.

The magnate to whom we felt particularly indebted for our first railway was Ben Holladay. "How this man," I wrote in my diary on August 24, 1870, "has changed the whole country! Our town looks quite unlike what it was last year."

Holladay's most important achievement was that he opened up the Puget Sound region. Having unlimited means he hired a large steamer in San Francisco and took a number of prominent persons from that city and Portland into those amazingly interesting waters which have since enabled Washington to forge ahead of her placid twin sister, Oregon. For this excursion Holladay engaged the Aurora band.

Chinook Wind and Salmon

The object of these pages is not so much to accumulate details regarding my juvenile doings as to provide glimpses of Oregonian local color of half a century ago. In such an attempt, a conspicuous spot must be occupied by the Chinook wind.

How I used to enjoy that exhilarating wind! We had a pet lamb which, when that wind blew, used to put its four hoofs together and hop around like a crazy kangaroo till the whole Finck family was doubled up with laughter. And we all felt like joining in the lamb's capers. I well remember how madly Bruno, my dog, and I used to chase one another through the orchard, he barking and I shouting like a wild Indian.

Afterwards I learned a few hundred words of Chinook speech, which was enough to get along with, at least so far as the girls were concerned. The men didn't interest me particularly. Why should they? I had not yet begun to study anthropology but material for studies in primitive love was at hand. Indian and half-breed girls used to come to our house for music lessons. They usually came on horseback, and I often accompanied them when they left. Some of them were quite pretty and they were not excessively coy.

If you have never before heard of the adorable Chinook winds which melt the mountain snows at unexpected moments and make everybody feel that life is decidedly worth living (the exact opposite of the African sirocco, which makes Europeans commit suicide or wish they had never been born) you surely have heard epicures rave over Chinook salmon.

Excepting the Channel sole, as you get it grilled in London or fried in Paris, I know of no fish equal to the

salmon which enters the Columbia river at the Chinook
end. It is as superior to ordinary salmon in richness and
delicacy of flavor as American shad is to German carp or
Channel sole to our flounder. The salmon wheel and other
methods of wholesale slaughter have sadly reduced their
numbers—we Americans are horrible wasters—but when
I was a boy the Chinook salmon were as abundant as
blackberries in the woods. Everybody caught them;
wagon-loads were peddled around. For fifty cents I used
to buy a specimen as heavy as I could lug home. Fish
weighing fifty or sixty pounds and more were not uncom-
mon. We never tired of them.

Whenever I brought home a salmon I promptly
chopped off its head and buried it. That was because I
had been made to believe that the blood of a raw salmon
kills a dog. Great was my consternation one day when
I found Bruno placidly gnawing at a salmon head I had
buried an hour before. Evidently this kind of "blood-poi-
soning" is very slow in its action for Bruno did not die
till several years later!

OREGON A GREAT STATE FOR EPICURES

As a matter of course in those wild and woolly days
there were plenty of trout—if you knew where to look for
them. Sometimes, to be sure, they were annoyingly coy.
No bait seemed to tempt them. But I found one that
usually fetched these finny epicures: salmon roe. Another
sure bait was crawfish eggs or tails. These were always
at hand. Our mill creek was black with crustaceans and
they were easily caught with a bit of raw meat on a line.

We could watch this in the shallow water and see the
crawfish creep up to it, grab hold and smile with satisfaction. We waited till half a dozen or more were fastened

to the meat and then gently lifted and landed the bunch on the grass. In later years they got more wary, often let go, and sometimes a landing net had to be used. But not when I was a boy.

Crawfish parties were the most popular of all our picnics. We took the girls along, all were welcome; also, we took a pan and salt and matches. When our tin pails were full we killed and cleaned the crawlers—it took some skill to avoid their claws—and made a fire. In a few minutes they were ready and—well, I cannot say more for them than that they were as delicious as Chinook salmon.

Oregon was indeed a great state for epicures. I might add pages about salmon-berries, strawberries perfuming the whole neighborhood, luscious blackberries, unique service- and thimble-berries and so on, but will refrain. I have, however, some more interesting things to tell about birds and beasts of a period now gone, alas! forever, thanks to civilization.

As a boy I used to deplore the lack of civilization in primitive Oregon. To-day I say in italics, *civilization be hanged*.

Passenger pigeons used to thicken the air so they could be knocked down with poles. In my day they had already been thinned out so that a shotgun had to be used. Not far from Aurora there were two mineral springs. They were about half a mile apart, if I remember right. I used to go with another boy, he firing at the poor pigeons from one of the springs, I at the other when they sought refuge there. It was a mean thing to do, but boys are experts in the shameless pursuits of pleasure.

Grouse shooting—in which there was lots of "local color"—seems to me to have been less objectionable because the birds had a better chance.

The Oregon grouse was (I don't know if I might still write "is") a most interesting and unique bird. Sitting near the top of the tall fir-trees it made, with intervals of silence, a peculiar hooting sound which, if I heard it now, would carry me back to my old home as inevitably as the fragrance of an orange recalls Panama to me.

As the trees were close together it was difficult to tell on which the bird sat unless one had a pheasant-dog to bark up the right tree. The bird felt so safe in its hiding place that this bark did not scare it away. It was so high up that a shotgun could not be used, and to find it and hit it with a rifle took some skill; so the bird had a good chance of escaping; which reminds me of an amusing incident.

Among the members of Dr. Keil's colony was an old German soldier who had fought in the Napoleonic wars. He was very proud of his record as a rifleman, and a great boaster about past performances. One day a friend of mine (himself unseen) happened to see this warrior fire at a grouse. Shot followed shot till there were ten; then the old soldier shook his fist at the fearless bird and shouted: "Had I but one more bullet I'd have you sure!"

Among our domestic animals was a lamb to which I have already referred. This pet accompanied our pigs into the woods every day and in the evening they all came back together. After a few years we got half a dozen more sheep. We naturally expected that our lamb would promptly join them, but oh no! It kept on going with the pigs, same as before.

I used to boil for them huge kettlesful of potatoes, which I mixed with bran. They also got apples by the basketful. They went around biting these in two and eating the best ones first; which showed discrimination but wasn't wise. A real epicure keeps the tidbits for the end.*

* If you are interested in this subtle problem, read the chapter "Are Pigs Genuine Epicures?" in my "Gardening With Brains."

A Shameless Pleasure Seeker

I cannot tell a lie, so I confess that I was a thief. Not
that I stole other people's umbrellas, as most civilized men
and women do, or kept borrowed books for good and all;
these were too ordinary misdemeanors to appeal to me.
No, all of my thefts (and there were lots of them) were
of the gastronomic persuasion. If I wanted a good thing
to eat and could get it without being caught in the act I
took it *prontissimo,* no matter to whom it belonged.

Oregon offered an opportunity so delightfully tinged
with local color that this perhaps ought to excuse my
doings. Have you ever eaten smoked venison-ham? If
you have you won't feel like throwing stones at me.

Smoked venison-ham is not a thing you can buy. If it
were known how good it is there would not be a deer left
on this globe in five years. In my day deer were as
plentiful in Oregon as jack-rabbits in California. Every
autumn the young men of Aurora went off into the Cascade Mountains repeatedly, with two or three wagons and
brought them back, loaded with choice venison. Everybody got steaks and chops and ribs, but the hams went to
the smoke-houses.

The largest and best of these was that of our neighbor
Dr. Keil, head of the colony. He always had the best of
everything for he was the boss. Not my boss, to be sure,
but that didn't worry me. I often went to his smoke-
house when nobody was around. It was a very tall building and the sausages and hams—pork and venison—were
way up where there was no heat but plenty of cool fragrant smoke from the smoldering fires below. I mounted
to the top, selected a choice venison-ham and with my
pocket knife cut out a generous slice which I carried to
the dense woods and devoured at leisure.

There were encores galore. In those days, before I
became a musical critic, I approved of encores. And
I always obeyed the eleventh commandment which, according to the German student code, is "Thou shalt not
allow thyself to be detected." Anyhow, there was more
of the venison-ham than the Doctor and his family could
eat. He preached communism; he was good-natured; had
I been caught in the act he probably would have smiled
and said: "Boys will be boys."

HUNTING FOR PRETTY GIRLS

One of my juvenile occupations was hunting for pretty
girls. It is natural that the future author of "Romantic
Love and Personal Beauty" and "Primitive Love and
Love Stories" should have preferred this kind of hunting
to gunning for deer and grouse.

In looking over the four volumes of my Oregon diary
I am amused at the frequency of the allusions to pretty
girls who swayed my susceptible heart to love, sometimes
primitive, but usually just romantic.

On page 83 of the first volume of the diary I suddenly
dropped English and began to write in Latin. The reason for this was that I did not wish anyone who might
come across these manuscript books to read what I wrote
about the girls. Usually I did not mention their names,
as those would not be disguised in Latin script; so, whenever I did name them, I used Greek letters.

At that time I wrote Latin almost as fluently as English. I had the sense of humor to point out myself that
some of the sentences were "Oregon Latin." But most
of them were correct if not Ciceronian, and I read them
easily now at seventy.

My mind was thoroughly saturated with classical
notions, so I am not surprised to find that I hunted for

girls even in the water: "Tertia hora post meridiem cum fratre et duobus aliis juvenibus in pluvium me immersi et corpus ablui. Sed nullas nymphas invenire potui ibi. Credo eas omnes terram reliquisse!"

It was certainly odd to mix up Greek ideas about nymphs with these waters coming from the melting snows in the Cascade Mountains seven thousand miles away from Attica. Pudding River is the poetic name of this torrent, in which we naked boys—like white Indians—used to while away summer afternoons, hiding our clothes, chasing each other in canoes and then basking in the hot sand to warm up again.

A perplexing dilemma confronted me one day. There was to be an excursion from Portland which would bring hundreds of men and women—and girls—to Aurora. On the same day there was to be a spiritualist meeting at Butteville, some miles away. I prayed to Apollo and Cupid to advise me: in which place would I be likely to find the greater number of pretty girls?

Finally I decided to remain in Aurora to wait for the excursion. It was frustrated by a railway accident and nobody came—only two carloads of Chinamen, who naturally thought the two brass bands at our station were there to greet them. Much vexed I hastened to Butteville, but got there too late to make a conquest.

One day I found in my garden an eight-pound watermelon "as sweet as a girl's kiss." Then I remembered that, at the age of sixteen, I really did not yet know how sweet a girl's kiss is: "Ego quidem non adhuc facultatem ni fortunam habui talem recipere, sed sensus latens me admonet eam dulcissimam omnium rerum esse, et spero tempus non procul abesse quum experiri possum an ita sit."

Soon I found out. I am not going to commit what the Scotch poet says is "the greatest sin 'twixt heaven and hell, first to kiss and then to tell," for I shall not mention names. But I visited three sisters and the youngest of them "gave me kisses sweeter than honey" (osculas melle dulciores mihi dabat).

As so often happens to boys, the object of my deepest passion was a young married woman. She was a brunette of the most pronounced Spanish type, with large, glorious black eyes—eyes such as you see only in Spain which, as an enthusiastic admirer of feminine beauty once exclaimed, "is not a peninsula but an eyeland."

Her husband having gone East on business, she was spending the summer in the Aurora hotel and often came to our house. She was the most refined and highly educated young woman I had ever met, and that had a good deal to do with my adoration of her. After she left, I waited three days, all told, for the letter she had promised me and then gave way to utter despair. "After all the things we talked about it seems incredible that she should have forgotten her promise. All joy has left my soul and my only consolation lies in reading my most serious books."

Seven months later she, "whom I had loved more than myself," came back. She had been with her husband and both had been ill. She was far from well now. "O God," I prayed, "if I ever have done a good deed, reward me by saving her life." She felt sure she would die; "she begged me to decorate her grave with flowers from my garden and to visit it occasionally."

Before I got interested in girls I thought nothing in the world was as delectable as flowers. The change came in July, 1871. On the ninth of that month I find this entry in my diary: "The drought continues and my flowers are dying. But never mind, I now have something sweeter than flowers."

Was there anything fickle and objectionable in my falling in love with so many pretty girls? Not at all. To me girls have always been like flowers. If I dote on pansies, have I not a right to love poppies, too, and roses and sweet peas?

Girls are like music, too. If I am thrilled by a Schubert song, why should I not glow with heavenly joy over a Chopin nocturne too?

When I was reading *Harper's Magazine* in those days, I never dreamed that the time would come when its editor would frequently ask me to write articles for him, among them one on "The Evolution of Girlhood." A queer title this may seem, for were there not girls always?

Children, yes, but girls of sweet sixteen to twenty-six or thirty did not exist. Everybody married early and had a lot of children and there was no girlhood such as you find to-day in any high school. That girlhood is a product of modern civilization, as I was the first to point out. In paying so much attention to the pretty girls of Oregon I was therefore simply studying modern civilization.* I always *was* a great student!

A Musical Oasis

Perhaps you have heard of the naval officer who was sent to study the manners and customs of certain cannibal islanders and whose report was summed up in one sentence: "Customs, disgusting; manners, none."

That "manners, none" occurred to me on reading the repeated lamentations in my diary over the absence of musical culture in early Oregon, and the extraordinary conduct of those who were impervious to the delights of the divine art. One day two young men, friends of ours, called. "After hearing Edward play a piece on the

---

* The article on "The Evolution of Girlhood" which Mr. Alden asked me to write for his magazine I consider the best and most important of my many magazine articles.

piano"—and he played well—"they abruptly leave, without giving any reason."

On another occasion a "young rowdy began, while we played, to whistle a comic song—yes, *while we played!* But I soon had him quieted."

The worst was yet to come; it made me explode with indignation and wrath. Summing up the situation I referred scornfully to persons "who do not care for music unless it is a gallop or a polka, who are entire strangers to those emotions of profound happiness and ecstasy which fill the soul of a refined person on hearing music of a higher order; yes, when you play a sonata of Beethoven or an overture by Mozart for them, they listen a few moments then start up from their chairs, whistle 'Marching Through Georgia,' and show their ill breeding in all other possible ways (this has actually happened several times); and, when you get through, they ask immediately if you can't give them 'something with a tune in it,' 'something that can be called real music,' such as 'Captain Jinks,' till it takes an amount of patience bordering on the incredible and becomes difficult to suppress your ardent and passionate desire to fling them headlong outdoors and treat them in such a manner that they will carry the consequences of their barbarous conduct to their graves."

Brass bands were, of course, much in favor with the whistling boors who aroused my juvenile indignation. And how I hated them! Read this as a sample: "Brass band music has this peculiarity that it always reminds me of a threshing machine through which live cats are being chased." It must have been very jazzy, for on another page I wrote: "It would have been a pleasant affair, had it not been for the workmen and farmers blowing into their confounded horns as if they were going to scare the devil himself out of his domains." And again—I may as well quote the original: "Duo societates musicales (?) tibiis metalli canentes aerem implevere horribili ululatu."

How then was it that I myself belonged to a band? Well, it wasn't a brass band but had wood wind-instruments too, and it played civilized music. The Aurora Band was one of my father's creations. At the Salem State fair it always got the first prize in contests with bands from Portland and elsewhere, and it was, as I have previously stated, in much demand throughout the State for fairs and political rallies.

The snare-drum was my chosen instrument because I could learn that in a few weeks. When I chose it I did not know that I would be the most popular member of the band. In remote regions where most of the settlers and their young folks had never heard any real music, the rhythmic rattle of the side-drum appealed to them even more than the cornet. I was therefore always surrounded by a gaping multitude who greatly admired my deft manipulation of the drum-sticks. I felt as proud as if I had been a Caruso or a Chaliapin.

Of course the highest peaks of music were not reached by this band. These we scaled at home, which was a veritable oasis in the howling wilderness of surrounding unmusicality.

Nearly every day we had home-made music, usually of a high order and often of the highest. My father was an excellent violinist and he had a splendid instrument which, many years later, came within one inch of persuading the great Franz Kneisel that it was a genuine Stradivarius. My brother played the flute and the piano; I, the violoncello and the piano. Everybody sang, and young girls often came to join our choir. Father composed for them and was very happy. He was also the best guitar player I have ever heard. He composed many pieces for that unjustly neglected instrument which, well played, is so much better than a piano played indifferently (as it usually is); and I shall never forget how he used to thrill me with some of his own pieces played with the guitar tuned the Spanish way.

Two young men, Lawrence Ehlen and William Schwaderer, often came to help us play string quartets. We began with the easy, insipid works of Pleyel, then passed upward to Haydn, Mozart, and Beethoven. Franz Kneisel, leader of the best string quartet in America, used to tell me in New York that he always looked forward to my *Evening Post* criticisms of his concerts because they were by one who knew what he was writing about—one who had himself played all these things and therefore knew them thoroughly.

The two young men who played quartets with us were real enthusiasts. Nothing could prevent their coming even when the rain poured down in torrents and their wagon had to be dragged through mud more than a foot deep. I hope they had the intense musical thrills that enthralled me. You may be interested in a few sample extracts from my diary showing how a sixteen-year-old boy in Oregon was overwhelmed by high-brow music, when the vast majority of those about him passionately preferred the low-brow kind.

"Nothing in the world exercises so great an influence on me as the divine art. I am greatly moved sometimes when I read poetry or a pathetic description by a good prose writer, or when I watch a thunderstorm, in which I find an extraordinarily great pleasure, but all these things are unimportant in their effect on me when compared with music, my element, which attracts me as water does a duck."

We had our chamber music at home, but I longed insanely to hear an orchestra play the great symphonies and to help play them: "I am only afraid that I shall not be able, at least at first, to play these on account of the intensity of the emotion which will perhaps make me forget that I am playing, or even make me faint away. For if my own playing is capable of bringing tears to my eyes and to make a thrill run through my whole frame, what will be the effect when I hear the great master musicians?"

Father sometimes told us of the effect of an orchestra of sixty playing a Mozart overture or some other great work. Concerning this I wrote: "The mere thought of this is sufficient to overwhelm my feelings and ennoble my whole character. When I think of such an orchestra an indescribable thrill runs through my heart—such a strange, mysterious but delightful feeling that in such a moment I feel myself brought nearer to the immortal God by one-half the distance that separates us from him; I feel inclined to fall on my knees and adore the Great Power, of whatever nature it may be, that could create music, the most divine of all gifts to man. Now if the mere thought of such a thing can thus overwhelm my soul, what an inconceivably ecstatic delight will be mine when I actually shall hear such music."

One of the most violent emotional "brain storms" I remember was one afternoon when Edward—who had an agreeable tenor voice—first sang a group of Schubert's songs, then new to me. I happened to be petting Bruno, who was curled up under an apple tree near the house. I buried my face in his beautiful soft fur and wept and sobbed in a woful ecstasy of heavenly joy.

Many years later I came across a German book on this curious "Ecstasy of Woe," which so overwhelms emotional individuals on hearing sad music.

Here is a confession written when I was eighteen: "Often when I play, tears of joyful emotion steal into my eyes, sometimes so profusely that I cannot see the notes and have to stop. To weep over the beauties of music is a pleasure which I would not give for all the treasures in the world."

Is it a wonder that the pleasure-seeker who wrote these things ultimately became a musical critic, adopting a profession which enabled him to hear music every afternoon and every evening? But that was not till eight years later, and many things happened in between.

While my father was always giving music lessons to other young folks he never gave us any. He took it for granted that nature would teach us, as it teaches chicks to scratch and ducks to swim; and we justified his faith. In my diary I find a number of pages telling how I gradually mastered the problem of the violoncello till, at eighteen, I could play a concerto. I had nothing but Romberg's instruction book to guide me.

Dr. Keil and His Colony

Dr. Keil, though personally rather unprepossessing, short and heavy, had a pleasant manner and an undoubted gift of leadership, and he managed to blind his followers to his own selfishness. The colonists gladly gave him the lion's share of their best without questioning his right to it, and he died the rich man of Aurora.

His church stood on a hill-top and there he preached to his attentive congregation. Although ignorant he had considerable eloquence and knew how to key up his hearers emotionally. Occasionally a hysterical or nervous young woman would rise suddenly, fling up her arms and with shrill cries rush up toward the preacher.

Evidently it was Dr. Keil's eloquence rather than what he said that moved his congregation. He had little knowledge of any kind. When my father gave him our copy of

Rotteck's "History of the World" (written for young folks) he was tremendously interested, and thenceforth had more substance in his sermons. We attended his church now and then; there was no paternal compulsion.

The colonists who made up Keil's congregation were "poor but honest" persons, mostly without higher education, but extremely kind, good-natured, sensible and mutually helpful. If the whole world were made up of such there would be no need of locks and keys and safes. I would have trusted my bottom dollar to any one of them. They wore their best clothes on Sundays and the flowers in their gardens showed that they loved beautiful things. And they liked to eat good meals; indeed they did. Aurora cookery became famous all over Oregon.

It was not strange that in the pre-railroad days the stage always stopped for a meal at Aurora, for stages travel slowly and make many stops. But why did trains stop for meals at Aurora when the Portland terminal was only twenty-nine miles away? Because the trainmen wanted the better meals they could get at Aurora—better meats, better vegetables, better pies and puddings.

At the Salem State Fair the meals used to be wretched till an Aurora restaurant was started. It was a huge success from the start. It needed a regular circus tent to accommodate all who crowded in at meal-time; and nearly the whole Aurora Colony, men, women and children, were in Salem for a week, cooking and serving meals.

Our "butcher frolics" were great affairs. Each family had its day when its fat porkers were slaughtered and converted into divers delicacies. I always looked forward to the day when Mike Rapps came with his unerring rifle and started the affair. Mike was an epicure. He refused to eat anything except the brains of the pigs he had just killed. I suspected those must be particularly delicious, so I tried them, fried, and—well, after that, Mike always had to share them with me. Pig's brains are, in fact, infinitely better (if properly cooked) than calf's brains; yet in our idiotic markets you cannot buy them.

There were few "butcher frolics" I did not attend. Bruno always went with me and there were so many bones and scraps for him that he gradually swelled up till he looked more like a football with legs than a dog. "For shame, Bruno!" I used to say to him on the way home, but he didn't care a damn. He would have probably ignored my book on "Girth Control" (as some foolish bloated persons do now) could I have read an advance copy to him.

Five years after I left Aurora the impending disintegration of the colony was hinted at in a letter from my father, dated December 13, 1877: "Yesterday afternoon Jonathan Wagner, Keil's prime minister, came to Portland to buy some beer for Keil who fell ill a few weeks ago in consequence of the annoyance caused by divers revelations. In the evening came a telegram announcing Keil's sudden death. This will make a nice mess! I am sure that if I still lived in Aurora I would have a house full of people asking me what to do. But I haven't the least intention to mix myself up with this affair. I had not seen Keil for four or five years. Dissatisfaction had been rife for a long time and it is probable that there would have been a village revolution in the Spring, partly because of the extravagance of spending $20,000 for a needless mill-race. Jacob Findling, Adolf Pflug and others of the Doctor's old adherents had died lately and the more recent members of the colony would have gone away were they not held by their houses, barns, and gardens. The papers will now be filled with a lot of nonsense about the death of the communist leader, but in his heart he never was a communist any more than was Ben Holladay."

WHAT A WOLF DID FOR ME

His full name was Christopher W. Wolf. He was one of the bachelors who lived in a house built for them opposite Keil's, a house which also had a large hall for entertainments and Wolf's schoolroom. He was a highly educated man, a graduate of the University of Göttingen. He was a clergyman but gave up preaching because of growing doubts. For a time he devoted himself assiduously to sawing wood and astonishing the natives with odd practises, one of which was to take a cold bath in the river in the early morning, even if he had to cut a hole in the ice— which, to be sure, was not often necessary in the mild climate of Oregon.

When he heard that I got up before five o'clock in the morning in order to prepare myself for college by learning Latin and Greek all by my lonely self, he took pity on me and kindly offered to teach me—free, of course. He felt that such ambition ought to be encouraged. I gladly accepted his offer.

It was the most fortunate thing that ever happened to me in all my long life. For Wolf not only taught me the old languages, but he helped to open my eyes to the countless beauties of nature about us.

As a born gardener I naturally loved flowers, wild as well as cultivated, but it was he who revealed to me the lure of botany, the scientific side of plant-life. I soon found it great fun to be able to discover the name of any strange plant I came across by comparing its leaves and roots and stems and corollas and stamens and pistils with the classified descriptions given in my botanical text-book.

By the time I was fourteen I had already gathered over four hundred different kinds of plants growing in our neighborhood, all of them carefully dried and put away, with their names, in old almanacs and magazines. This herbarium was afterwards enlarged to over five hundred. How fragrant it was when I came across it many years later!

Dr. Wolf also made me familiar with the enchantments of mineralogy, and soon I began to keep my eyes open for specimens of rare kinds.

Astronomy was one of his hobbies and he found me a most willing companion in the study of it. Even before I came under his influence I was often in the mood to recite to myself the familiar

"Twinkle, twinkle little star
How I wonder what you are—"

It was, I think, a rather unusual thing for a boy of sixteen to write in his diary as I did when I was suffering from a bad cold: "Passed a miserable night; could not sleep till nearly eleven. It is a most horrible feeling, which I shall never forget, to seem to be every moment on the verge of suffocating. Though, when I think it over clearly, I am not afraid to die, for I long to understand the great mysteries of astronomy and other things that no one on earth can discover."

This longing for knowledge of the stars—we now know there are at least three *billions* of them—has haunted me, I might almost say tormented me, all my life. It made me forgive Wolf even when he came up the hill to wake me at two or three o'clock at night to show me some constellation or star-group visible only at that time. Of course, he provided me with an atlas of the constellations, and this led to a funny incident.

My sisters had invited a dozen girls to one of the crazy-quilt parties then in favor, each girl bringing her own silk patches to sew on. While they were chatting away like magpies I came through the room with a lighted lantern.

"Where are you going?" they shouted in chorus.

When I said "Star-gazing," they exploded with laughter:

"Do you need a lantern to see the stars?"

"Not the stars but the atlas," I explained; and they agreed that I wasn't such a fool as I looked.

In those days I might have almost seen the stars without getting out of bed, for Edward and I, and father too, slept right under the roof, and the shingles were so loosely put together that, though the rain was kept out, a driving snowstorm, such as occurred once in a long while, would deposit a layer of snow right on our beds. Those were days of glorious health!

Festina lente was not one of Wolf's maxims. He believed in losing no time. He taught me French, *beginning* by having me read to him Voltaire's "History of Charles XII"! This may seem absurd, but so many French words come from the Latin, and I knew Latin so well, that I really could guess the meaning of most French sentences at first sight. Grammar came later. But it was with Greek grammar and literature that my studies with Wolf were chiefly concerned.

In my diary I find frequent complaints that Wolf hurried me too much. Once I intimated plainly that if he wasn't a free teacher I'd give him a piece of my mind! But we got results. Soon I became so proficient that I began to dispute the proper translation of certain sentences with him. Nothing could have pleased him more than that, for it showed what an intense and genuine interest I took in my studies.

Wolf was proud of this pupil; I remember his satisfaction when, one day, another teacher was visiting us and Wolf asked him to choose any page in Herodotus for me to translate, and I read it off as easily as if it had been English.

Longing For Harvard

When Heine as a youngster called on Goethe he was so
abashed at being in the presence of the great man that he
could not think of anything to say except to mutter that
it was a fine day. The eminent novelist, W. D. Howells,
was greatly amused when I told him this story one day
while talking with him in his Cambridge home.

In the early pages of this book I related how I made
a fool of myself the first time I met Mark Twain. And
now I blush to relate how incredibly silly I was in presence of the august Dean of Harvard University when he
had sent me a request to come to his office.

So far as I have been able to find out, I was the first
boy who ever came to Harvard from Oregon. It was
therefore natural that Dean Gurney should be interested
in me. "What made you come all the way from Oregon
to Harvard?" he asked.

"I don't know," I stammered timidly, "there are some
others."

Anything more stupid than that answer cannot be
imagined. There was, in the first place, no other boy
longing to go to Harvard that I knew of; and, as for the
"I don't know"—why, I could have read to Dr. Gurney
whole pages from my diary telling about my eagerness for
an academic education and my reasons for choosing Harvard. The best was always just good enough for me,
and Harvard was reputed the best—that's what I should
have told Dean Gurney.

As far back as June 4, 1870, I find this entry in my
diary: "Can scarcely wait for the time when I shall go
to Harvard University and have so many chances of seeing and learning things. I don't see why we should sit
here at the 'end of the world,' where there is scarcely a

civilized and refined human being to be found, when we might as well be elsewhere and have the benefit of good music and education, and innumerable things."

A few weeks later: "Sometimes I build magnificent castles in the air of being a distinguished scholar in college," etc. On another page, after referring to "this miserable, uncivilized, barbarous Oregon" I add: "Father always remonstrates" (and a wise father he was!) "when we talk of going to some other State, assuring us we shall never have better times than at present. I believe he is right as far as bodily enjoyment is concerned but not so far as concerns the mind. Hurrah for college!"

Poor fellow! I did not know how foolish I was, how infinitely more interesting were my surroundings in Oregon than my environment would be in Cambridge, and how superior the open-air nature education I got was to the school-bench drilling I should have later on at Harvard, Heidelberg, and Berlin. But that's the way in this world; we don't know we are living in Paradise till it's become Paradise lost.

While swearing at wild and woolly Oregon I was enjoying everything *hugely,* including my studies, which gave me no end of pleasure. "Cicero," I wrote in my diary, "asserts that our greatest delights (summa voluptas) come from learning. He was right as I can attest from my own experience. If I had the choice between a life of ignorance, such as is led by many, and no life at all, I would choose the latter."

In copying this, I recall what Mary Schüle, who knew me as a small boy, once told me. When I first went to school I came home one day and shouted angrily: "If I could get at the man who invented learning I would roast him alive."

All beginnings are difficult, as the old proverb says. Even Beethoven is said to have shed tears over his first

music lessons. The more deeply I got "under the skin"
of my studies the more I loved them; I find myself wishing in my diary that the days were not so short so that I
might study more than twelve hours out of twenty-four.
Sometimes I allowed myself only six hours of sleep, which
was very foolish indeed. Except during gardening and
apple-picking time, I did not get any physical exercise,
hence headaches and occasional blues. "Worked in the
field for the first time in three years" is an entry in my
diary, which doesn't show me in a favorable light. I did
not yet realize that perfect health is the one thing in this
life compared with which all others are airy trifles.

Headaches, blues and lack of physical vigor might have
been avoided had I known that more than half of the
things I was studying so hard were not needed for entering Harvard. In the Eastern preparatory schools the
boys were taught by tutors who knew exactly what their
pupils would be examined in. But neither Wolf nor I
knew that my knowledge of botany, astronomy, chemistry,
mineralogy, physical geography, history and other topics
would not help me to get into the portals of Harvard. I
am very glad now that I did learn all these things in my
most impressionable years and under such favorable outdoors conditions, but I have to thank the bracing Oregon
climate that I did not break down under the strain.

My diary shows that besides attending to all these
studies, academically required or otherwise, I also did a
good deal of miscellaneous reading. Novel reading I was
at first inclined to regard as a waste of time, but later on
looked on it more indulgently. History I did not dote
on because it was chiefly a record of wars, and for the same
reason I did not care much for Homer's *Iliad* or Cæsar's
works. I was, however, keenly interested in the Franco-
Prussian war, and it is with tremendous satisfaction that

I record the fact that my heart was instinctively on the right side.

While my ancestors came from Germany, that did not incline me to approve of the Prussian habit of "shooting up Europe" once every few decades. "For the good of mankind," I wrote, "I hope France will win this war; if the Prussians won they would become insufferable." "I wish the war were over and all Prussians in hell, where they belong," is another specimen of "my sentiments."

CLIMBING MOUNT HOOD

While I was counting the months and weeks when I would be able to start for Harvard, I began to feel more and more intensely that it would be tragedy to leave Oregon, and my family, my friends, and my dog. In fact, something like a panicky feeling came over me gradually. There were things I *must* see before I left Oregon, for who could tell when I would be able to come back?

It worried me particularly that I had never been up the Columbia River or made closer acquaintance with Mt. Hood, the idol of Oregonians, which is to them what the sacred Fuji is to the Japanese. We saw Hood from our house and there were viewpoints near-by where we could behold the monarch of the eternal snows from foot to summit. Whenever I did thus see it, on a clear day, I felt like getting on my knees and worshiping fanatically.

Oh, how I pitied those of my acquaintances who could not enjoy the thrills given by this sublime spectacle, or who were not frantic with joy during a sublime storm, as I was when the rain beat violently against the windows and the wind shrieked and shook the house to its foundations.

The feelings aroused by the beautiful are delicious but

are not the thrills given by sublimity even more soul-stir-ring?

I had not at that time read Kant's definition of the "Sublime" but I think my own juvenile description (I wrote it in Latin) is quite as good: "When I listen to such a storm, a secret terror pervades my whole body, while at the same time my mind is affected by an incred-ibly delicious feeling." It is this mixture of terror and delight that constitutes the feeling of sublimity as dis-tinguished from the beautiful which is not alloyed with a sense of danger.

Hood, Oregon's monarch mountain, combined the sub-lime with the beautiful, and with it I longed passionately to become more intimately acquainted. At the proper moment the opportunity presented itself. I have always been a lucky fellow.

"Saw a grand spectacle at 7 P. M. The sky was, W. and E., of a reddish and bluish-gray hue, and directly above Mount Hood there was a very bright stripe which for a moment seemed like a volcanic eruption, but soon proved to be a rainbow."

This was one of the earliest entries in my diary (May 19, 1870). Two years later I started to chase that rain-bow. It was Dr. Wolf who originated the plan of at-tempting an ascent of Mt. Hood. I had gone into the forest one day, as was my wont, to prowl around for wild flowers and then to sit on a moss-covered log listening to the music made by the lofty tree-tops when stirred by a breeze. Suddenly I saw Wolf standing on a rock, lost in admiration of the scene before him. I approached so that we could share our feelings and to hear his poetic encomiums on the Holiness of Nature. As soon as he saw me he beckoned me to come to his side; then point-ing at the Cascade range and its mighty monarch, the majestic Hood, he gloated with me over the snowy fields

tinged by the golden rays of the setting sun before it
finally disappeared behind the lofty summit.

"Would you like," he asked, "to wander some day on
those ivory fields surrounded by the golden halo of the
setting sun? I have decided to make the ascent. Several
of my young friends have promised to go with me. Will
you join us?"

I ought to have said "No" for I was in no condition for
climbing a snow mountain rising to a height of more than
two miles. In my eagerness to prepare for Harvard and
to store my mind with knowledge of every kind I had
criminally neglected physical exercise. I had been suffering also from a cold which was so stubborn that I decided
it was wise, even in July, to give up my daily swim in the
turbulent Pudding River. Yet I promptly and eagerly
replied "Yes" to Wolf's question.

Neither he nor any of the young men who came along—
Fred Will, George Wolfer, and John Will—had ever had
the slightest experience in mountain-climbing, but we
cheerfully and recklessly started off in a covered wagon
drawn by two mules, followed by Bruno and another dog.
We realized it would take us a full week to make the round
trip.

Details regarding this trip have some historic interest
because all the conditions half a century ago were so entirely different from what they are now, when anyone
with a pair of strong legs can go by boat or train from
Portland to Hood River (of apple fame), thence by stage
to the excellent Cloud Cap Inn and from there in a few
hours to the summit in charge of a guide who has made
the ascent more than a hundred times and has a lot of
interesting stories to tell about fires and avalanches and
deer and butterflies and panthers and other details in
Hoodian local color.

I have been on the mountain in this up-to-date fashion

too, and enjoyed it very much indeed, for Hood is a wonderfully interesting peak, no matter how approached; but
I feel that it is not solely the magic of youth that makes
me remember the earlier ascent as the more romantic. Fortunately I took my diary along so I need not rely on my
memory for details. The first day's uneventful record
ends with "am writing this on foolscap (to be copied into
my diary later) on a *Harper's Magazine,* kneeling by the
camp-fire."

In place of steamboat, railway and stage, *we* had nothing but a very bad emigrant road and often we had to get
off and walk. That gave us a better chance to shoot grouse
and other game for supper, which we usually did. Fred
Will proved to be an excellent cook; his soup, in particular, was so good that it made me record my opinion
that all young men ought to learn to cook.

I used to prepare meals at home when my sisters (all
of them wonderful cooks) were away; but Fred didn't
know that, and a little judicious (and honest) flattery
made him cheerfully attend to all the culinary duties while
I rested after the day's hard tramp. Being an epicure—
that is, a pleasure seeker—is a subtle art of divers aspects.
It has been the key-note of my whole life. Flattery will get
you most anywhere, but it should be *honest;* mine always
was. I have made a specialty of discerning people's best
points and focusing their attention on those. Thus I
learned to talk about girls themselves in a way to interest
them, and that's what made them like me. *Ars Amandi!*

On the second day of our trip I stood aghast looking
down and up on miles upon miles of burnt giant firs—
branchless stems standing around like blackened straw
stubble in a mowed field. Poor forests! Here in the
wilderness fires destroyed them, and in the valleys below
man chopped and sawed them by the thousands to make
way for the plow.

I am amused to read that the camp that night was, to cite a few adjectives from the diary, "the most confounded, infernal, horrible, insupportable place in the world." Mosquitoes, of course.

At four P. M. on the fourth day we reached the snow-line. Here we camped. The diary says: "Find some difficulty in cooking at this height. We always get up at three, so I feel tired and sleepy." Worst of all, "our provisions are giving out so we cannot feed the dogs" (poor Bruno) "till we come back to the wagon. Weather very hot but a strong wind blows up here."

At five o'clock on the fifth day we started on the snow slope for the summit. The mules and the dogs were left in camp tied to logs. Some way or other Bruno managed to get free, but fortunately I had told him sternly to stay right there so he did not try to follow us. Near this camp I had found a rock-fissure from which issued a strong sulfurous smell. On the way up we came across others of these reminders of the fact that we were on the face of a volcano which used to hurl rocks many miles in all directions.

And now, as we are nearing the top, let me make a frank confession. There have been men—thousands of them—men of the highest type, who underwent incredible fatigue and freely risked their lives for the sake of making a record in climbing difficult peaks. They were guided by the sporting instinct. This instinct, I regret to say, was never part of my make-up. I have always climbed mountains solely for the sublime scenery they commanded. No scenery, no climbing, so far as I was concerned.

That's what happened on Hood. My diary frankly records my failure to reach the summit and the reasons. Not being used to physical exercise I became dead tired. We hadn't had enough to eat, which helped to weaken me.

My feet were ice cold from the snow-water that had got into my shoes. We were within a few hundred feet of the top, but the slope was discouragingly steep. The main trouble, however, was that the wind had changed and blown over the smoke from a forest fire, completely obliterating the scenery. That settled it. No scenery, no H. T. F.

"Revolving all these things in my mind, I tell my companions abruptly that I shall go no further—they might go wherever they pleased. At first they remonstrated, but I had made up my mind! Should I proceed to the summit when I was almost dead with fatigue, just for the sake of being able to say I had been on the top of Mount Hood? Never! That is not my nature. So I lay down on the snow and took a splendid nap lasting an hour."

When the four men came back they told of the difficulties they had had to overcome, by far the worst of the whole ascent, including the cutting of steps in the ice. On the summit they had found a flag, some money and other things left there by men who had been up before them. But no scenery.

Can you imagine anything more utterly insane than my lying down in the snow to sleep an hour, after my recent dangerous cold? Of course the cold came back; when we returned to Aurora I was voiceless for several days.

The entire ascent from the snow-line had taken eight hours. We came down in two. I brought back home the account of our trip, part of it written at the spot where I slept and waited for the men to come down. I also brought back some valuable additions to my herbarium. And another thing, thus referred to shamelessly: "Took stones along from top. Great demand for them at home. Supply soon exhausted and I had to go down to Pudding River to get some more to satisfy all my friends."

Up The Columbia River

In those days everybody read the daily or weekly *Oregonian,* as a matter of course. I can see myself sitting on the counter in the Aurora post-office-grocery, eagerly perusing its columns.

We used to laugh over the advertisements in the *Oregonian* informing the readers that a certain store was "directly opposite Mount Hood." We also enjoyed the story about the old settler who, after explaining that volcanoes grow gradually by the addition of stones brought up during eruptions, added: "I remember the time when Hood was a mere hole in the ground."

The easiest and best way to see Mount Hood in its full majesty was in those days, as it is to-day, a trip up the Columbia by boat. For hours the sublime peak is in sight from many different points of view, seeming so near at times that it looks as if one might jump onto it from the steamer.

"While looking with admiration at the beautiful landscape on both sides of the river," I wrote in my diary, "a bright idea suddenly entered my head. I hastened to the very foremost part of the steamer where I saw a board nailed on just behind the flagpole. To my great joy I found I could use this board as a seat. With my left arm I held on to the flagpole and then bent my head down so that I lost sight of the boat completely and saw nothing but the foamy waters beneath and the scenery on both sides. I imagined myself detached from the ship, flying through the air over the waves.

"I had chosen the most favorable moment for this experiment. We were nearing the point called Cape Horn because of the great turbulence and wildness of the waves due to the strong wind that blows steadily across the water in this region, sometimes so violently as to prevent the smaller boats from going upstream. Of course this gale contributed much to the beauty and wild romance of my situation. I took off my hat and let the wind play with my hair. The billows ran as high as in the ocean. The keel of the boat, dividing these wild waves, threw up the water in a thousand drops of all sizes and glittering in all the colors of the rainbow, occasionally sending a shower of fine spray over me. This lasted about two hours, till I was chilled through and had to go back."

Another sentence throws further light on why I so hugely enjoyed such experiences: "The sight of all this quite inspired me and I made several additions to my number of 'New Ideas' which I write down in a little book I always carry in my pocket—ideas on philosophy or anything that may occur to me at such moments."

When our boat had got to within about ten miles of the Dalles it was hailed, at a place where there was no village nor even a house, by "an elderly, pleasant-looking gentleman in company with a lady and several children, who had motioned to the pilot to stop. He brought on board several boxes filled with plants and minerals. I soon learned from a fellow passenger that he was the distinguished Oregon geologist, Mr. Condon, whose invaluable collection of fossilized animals and plants is the first thing all educated persons who come to the Dalles go to see. I managed to obtain the pleasure of a talk with this very kind and affable gentleman. On being told in the course of our conversation that I would shortly start for Harvard College he kindly invited me to come and examine his collection, remarking that I might be questioned in Cambridge and Boston as to the geology of Oregon, and that he could, in half an hour, give me a better idea and knowledge of it, than I could get by months of book-study."

Of course I accepted his invitation and was much impressed by his collection, which was piled up in two rooms, partly on shelves, but many specimens lying pell-mell on the floor, among them not a few which would occupy the places of honor in other museums. Among the objects that impressed me most were "some plates of clay with impressions of ferns and other vegetation as distinct as if they had been engraved on them with supreme skill."

POOR BRUNO

For obvious reasons I had not taken my dog along on this river trip—poor Bruno, who was so soon to be deserted by his heartless master, destined never to see him again. To this day I cannot think of that cruel desertion without having my vision dimmed by tears. For the sake of a mere college education, how *can* I have left that most intimate friend of mine?

Bruno was the most wonderful dog ever known on this planet, with the possible exception of Shep and Laddie, my two Maine pets of later years. Now, I know that nearly every man who owns a fine dog thinks he is the most remarkable animal ever seen—I say he *thinks* so; but I *know* mine were, which makes all the difference in the world, don't you see?

Never having studied the Napoleonic code of morals and therefore not knowing that "la recherche de la paternité est interdite," I tried hard to find out, in the canine "Who's Who" of Oregon, what dog had the honor of being Bruno's father, but in vain. Nor do I know just what kind of a dog his mother was. She was much smaller than Bruno and was called a pheasant dog; she never failed to spot and bark up the exact tree on which a grouse was hooting.

Bruno was born in a—but let me cite his own words from an autobiographic sketch he once began: "I was born in Aurora, Oregon, and spent the first weeks of my life in a basket under the counter in the post-office. One day a boy came along and carried me off in his arms to a house on a hill about half a mile from the village. Here I was fed on bread and milk till I was old enough to eat meat.

"My 'master'—as I will call him in deference to custom —was about twelve years old. I heard afterwards that I was not at all intended for him, but he just carried me off in a high-handed way and refused to return me. He said I was too beautiful for anyone else to have, as he enjoyed beauty in dogs more than anyone else. I now consider myself very lucky in having fallen into his hands because there was no one in the community who would or could have done so much to make a superior dog of me.

"Every morning he went to the room of a private teacher named Wolf who gave him lessons in French, Latin, and Greek, as well as in botany and other sciences. I always went with him to this place and either waited for him outside, or, when the weather was wet or cold, I went in and lay in front of the chimney fire; the kind old man did not object.

"In this manner I got accustomed to the sound of several languages and gradually my intelligence expanded with that of my master, who seemed to take a special pleasure, outside of school hours, in teaching me sentences in all of the five languages he knew or was learning. Not being able to hold a pen, I never learned to write, but my master, from daily and hourly association with me, learned to understand all my thoughts and feelings and he has kindly offered to act as my amanuensis—I believe that's the right word."

The autobiographic sketch unfortunately ends here; but my diary makes frequent reference to Bruno—as the preceding pages show—and I also recall my adventures with him as if they had happened a year instead of more than half a century ago. The most vivid incident in my memory is what happened in the forest one day, when we came across a big snake.

There were many snakes in Oregon at that time. Some of them were as beautifully colored as humming-birds. They were harmless, but Bruno hated them. Every time he saw one he rushed up, grabbed it in the middle and shook it till it was dead.

On the occasion just referred to I did not wish him to do this because the snake was so large and of an unknown kind—it may have been poisonous. Bruno did not see it at once. I ordered him back, seized a big stick and advanced to kill the snake. The moment I lifted it up Bruno saw the snake and darted at it, so that the stick intended for the ophidian came down on the poor dog's head. With a loud cry he fell over and seemed to be dead.

You can imagine my feelings when I lifted him into my arms and ran for home in the hope that father might be able to revive him. Coming to a brook I bathed his head with the cool water; a moment later he opened his eyes, then got on his feet and trotted off as if nothing had happened.

In warm weather Bruno slept by himself in a cool place, but when it was cold he slyly curled himself up for protection behind our pet lamb. He was extremely fussy about the green daybed I made for him daily under an apple tree in front of the house. If I forgot it he came to me, put his head on my knee and looked at me till I went and gathered an armful of fresh ferns for him to lie on.

And now we come to the tragedy of Bruno's life. The day was approaching when I must leave him and the rest of the family. In a reminiscent mood I wrote about him in my diary: "Ever since I got him (about six years ago) he has been continually at my side, never leaving me for a moment unless compelled to. When I studied, he lay under my table. When I played the piano he lay under it."

A foreshadowing of what would happen when I was gone was given during a visit at the Case farm seven miles from our house, where I went for a final week-end visit. When I was on my horse ready to go back, I called for Bruno, but he failed to appear. After waiting an hour I concluded he had gone home alone and rode away. But he had not come home. I waited a day, with ever-increasing anxiety, and the following morning I rode back to the farm.

To my great joy when I arrived in sight of the house a dog came running toward me barking furiously. He had not recognized me at once—of course it was Bruno—but when he saw it was I he leaped over the fence in a bound and would have jumped up to me on the horse had I not dismounted instantly. For ten or fifteen minutes he would not allow me to speak to anyone else. The diary continues:

"The girls then told me that Bruno had returned an hour after I had left. He searched for me everywhere. They had to open every door in the house for him, as he persisted in scratching and whining till his wish was gratified. Even the kitchen and the pantry were searched by him. Finding nothing he lay down in a corner and refused to notice anybody. Three times a day savory meat was offered him but he paid no attention to it. Not till he heard my horse did he stir from the place.

"Is it to be wondered at that I reciprocated the attachment of this dog? My constant companion from morning till night, he would accommodate all his actions to mine. ... And then he has such beautiful, clear faithful eyes, so expressive as to seem almost human. He makes me al-

most believe in the old Greek notion about the transmigra-
tion of human souls into animals."

July 31, 1872, arrived. When I woke up at seven I
could hardly believe that at 2:30 the train would carry me
away from all that was dear to me, including Oregon
itself. "I got up, went to father's bed and wept bitterly.
I then went outdoors to Bruno's bed and there gave my
tears, for a long time, free course. Bruno was quite astonished at my conduct; he looked at me with his faithful,
loving eyes, and then, as if vaguely understanding the
cause of my grief, he kissed away the tears and tried to
show his sympathy." It was lucky that I could not tell
him. What would he have done?

They took him along to the station. When he saw me
get on the car he tried to jump on too and had to be held
back. It was hard to leave my family and my friends who
had gathered to see me off. But I would see them again
after a few years and I could communicate with them by
letter.

With Bruno I could not do that. He would never know
what had become of me, why I had so cruelly deserted
him. Poor Bruno! If he acted so disconsolately at that
farmhouse when he lost me for a day what would he do
on failing to find me day after day and week after week?

They wrote to me about it at Harvard; told me that
he hunted for me all over the village. Every morning,
precisely on the hour when I used to take my books and
go to Wolf's, he started off by himself. On the way he
took his swim at the usual place, then lay down at Wolf's
and when the hour was up he trotted back home. "Poor
Bruno Finck!" my friends said among themselves.

There was some consolation. Members of the family
still remained in the house on the hilltop, so he had his
home. But not long afterwards the family moved to Portland. It was not believed that Bruno would be happy in

a city, so he was left behind, in the same house to be sure, but with a difference! No one cared for him.

How he missed us was shown when Josephine, some months later, visited Aurora, staying with several friends in succession. Where she remained Bruno remained, day and night. After she returned to Portland he was again alone. One day he disappeared.

What had become of him? I never could find out. Had he committed suicide? Had somebody shot him out of pity? I almost hope so. He was only six years old, the age when dogs are at their best: Poor Bruno!

PART III

FOUR YEARS AT HARVARD

FOUR YEARS AT HARVARD

By Way of St. Louis

THE world had moved in the ten years since we had come to Oregon from Missouri via New York, Panama, and San Francisco. It was still necessary to go from Portland to San Francisco, but there a railroad was waiting to take me straight across to New York or Boston. To be sure, it was only a few years old and it came near not being built then because a transcontinental railroad was considered such a reckless absurdity that the courageous financiers who backed this scheme kept mum about it for fear that panicky depositors would start a run on their banks.

At that time the Union Pacific trains were still held up sometimes by herds of buffaloes stubbornly refusing to leave the track in spite of frantic blowing of whistles. I did not see such a holdup, I am sorry to say, but remember the well-trodden buffalo trails along the track. Indians there were aplenty at the stations. I woke up one night and found a man fumbling all over my body in search of the money I was taking along to Harvard. He did not find it, for it was safely sewed up (gold coin) in a leather bag that clung to my skin under all my clothes. There were no Pullman sleeping-cars at that time, I believe.

If I had gone straight to Cambridge I would have arrived a month too soon for the examinations, so I took this opportunity to visit my uncle Conrad (John C. Finck) in St. Louis. The first thing I asked for was a bath. When I saw the muddy-looking Mississippi river water in the tub, I looked so dismayed that my uncle burst into a roar of laughter. He explained that it wasn't as bad as it looked—just sediment washed down from the Missouri river and perfectly harmless.

Unlike my father, my uncle was a real business man, practical and prosperous, a wholesale dealer in cement. He made me promise to spend the whole of the following summer with him, and I did so, teaching his children as a slight return for his hospitality. I can hardly say, however, that I enjoyed St. Louis as a summer resort, either in 1872 or 1873. The heat was terrific most of the time, 100 in the shade being of frequent occurrence. Oh how I longed for the mountain breezes and the cool nights of Oregon!

I found a comparatively cool corner in the garden, where I read all day long the fine collection of books in my uncle's library, including the complete works of Goethe, which I enjoyed hugely. "You are the most indefatigable reader I have ever seen," uncle remarked. I wrote letters too, when the varnish did not make the table sticky—it was as hot as if there had been a stove under it.

Unpleasant Surprizes

After leaving Oregon I did not keep up my diary; but once in a while I jotted down a few remarks. Among the most diverting of these are my comments on the site of Harvard University. I was terribly disappointed. No Mount Hood, no Cascade range, no Columbia river, no big trees—how absurd to choose such a site for a big educational institution! I would have never done it! Read what I wrote:

"Surely no one will deny that it would have been impossible to find a more uninteresting, dreary locality for a university than that chosen for Harvard. To be sure, the college yard in summer presents a very pleasant appearance. But when, tired of study and confinement, we students wish some recreation or long for an excursion to some attractive locality, we discover that there is no such place. The stony hills surrounding us are anything but inviting. The Charles river may be romantic at some place near its source but certainly is not so in this neighborhood, while Mount Auburn, after all, is not a park but a cemetery." I remember how I used to walk and walk and walk trying to get away from the suburban homes out into the wilds of nature, but in vain.

The site of Harvard being my first unpleasant surprise, the second was the kind of people I met—or most of them —during my first weeks in Cambridge. My Oregon diaries are full of glowing visions of the marvelously civilized humans I should meet in Boston and Cambridge, all of them highly educated, bright, sympathetic, and *enthusiasts for the best music*—for was not Boston reputed the musical center of America? Imagine my indignation on finding that no one I met cared any more for music than he or she did for Chinook Indians; and that in Boston, during August and September, the only musical entertainment offered was an occasional organ recital!

Monstrous! Unbelievable! Had I been unjust to my "uncivilized" neighbors in Oregon? Were the Bostonians, musically speaking at any rate, just as wild and woolly?

Homesickness in its most virulent form developed under these conditions: "Often have I shed tears of gratitude that I never seriously incurred the displeasure of my father, and thus insured his blessing, which is worth more to me than all the treasures in the world. Oh, how happy, how enviable I was at home—and I did not realize it!

Give me back the old times, in home sweet home! The images of the dear ones at home rise up before me and my tears drop on the paper."

If I had only had a piano to give vent to my feelings. But even that consolation was denied me for the moment.

Luckily I soon found that my first impressions of New England folk were misleading and that the fault was largely my own. I was like a transplanted tree, bound to suffer until my roots had got a grip on the new soil. In particular, I soon discovered that there was a widespread interest in good music. My skill in playing the violoncello became a bridge by means of which I entered the best society in Cambridge, including the home of the great poet, Longfellow, at which I spent many happy evenings playing with one of his daughters.

Before I could call myself a Harvard student I had to pass a formidable set of examinations for which I was only partially prepared, for Wolf had had rather vague ideas of what would be expected of his pupil. Many things I knew that I need not have known; but, also, there were needful things that I had neglected to learn. If I failed—horrible thought!—would I dare to return to Oregon? Bruno would be delighted, but what would my friends think of me? Would I ever be able to look them in the face again?

DISGRACEFUL FAILURE AND TRIUMPHANT SUCCESS

I did fail dismally. The mathematical examiners were unanimous in voting me unprepared for college. They gave me three "conditions."

This result might have been predicted. I had no gift whatever for mathematics. To this day I do not trust myself in adding up a column of figures; my wife always has to verify it. Algebra and geometry are repeatedly referred to in my Oregon diary as the studies I liked least of all. I gave them little attention and Wolf did not help me for the simple reason that he didn't know much about mathematics himself.

The Harvard examiners in Greek and Latin were, on the other hand, hugely delighted with my answers to their questions. These answers, indeed, ripened in their minds a plan they had been discussing of giving young men entering the Freshman class a chance to try for "advanced standing" in the classics.

This meant that those who tried these extra examinations and succeeded would be allowed to enter the Sophomore class at once so far as the classics were concerned, thus escaping the more or less elementary drilling inflicted on the poor "Freshies."

Naturally I was eager to try for this honorable distinction. I was told I would have to do some translating into Latin and Greek and translate at sight from those languages. The professors were considerate enough to ask me what authors I felt best prepared to read from. Without the least desire to boast, I answered that any writer would suit me. "Plato, Xenophon, Herodotus, Thucydides, Homer, Cicero, Horace, Ovid, Vergil, Tacitus or anything you like."

The professors looked astonished. They had never had an experience like that before. One of them told me afterwards that they put their heads together and decided that if I was bluffing they would give me a chance to regret it. So they selected some of the most difficult pages they could find. Some of these I had not seen before but I translated them all swimmingly and the delighted examiners promptly promoted me to the Sophomore classics.

PROFESSORS LANE AND GREENOUGH

Here is an illuminating page from my Harvard diary:
"Usually we got nothing but the anatomy—the bony
skeleton—of a language; the beautiful body and the soul
were ignored. Thanks to our excellent Latin professor,
Greenough, I got a good insight into the spirit and beauty
of the Satires of Horace; but still a thousand striking
thoughts of this inimitable poet did not receive at my
hands more than a small part of the attention they deserved. Every line is a little essay. . . But I shall read
Horace for myself . . . and who knows but that I shall
become one of the few college graduates who in their old
age still read Latin and Greek writers in the original
tongue."

Professor Greenough had a funny way of stopping his
lecture the moment the college bell began to ring at the
end of the hour. He might be in the middle of an important sentence, but the first stroke of the bell cut it short,
and the sentence was never completed, for he did not
return to it at the next lecture!

My other Latin professor, Lane, did me a tremendous
service in helping to develop my style in writing. His
specialty was Tacitus, and he never tired of pointing out
to us that this master of a concise style *always puts the
emphatic word in the emphatic place.*

Thousands of times in my later career as journalist and
author did that italicized sentence come into my mind
when momentarily hesitating over the construction of a
sentence.

I never ceased studying the beauties of literature and
literary style. My best teacher was Bartlett's "Dictionary of Familiar Quotations." I bought two copies of this,

one for my library, the other for tearing off leaf after leaf and carrying it in my pocket for reading and re-reading at spare moments till I knew the contents by heart. Thus I became thoroughly familiar with the world's best thoughts expressed in the most elegant and forcible style. At some of these thoughts thus expressed, I felt like shouting for joy. They affected me like exquisite music. But no secular literature—not even the inspired pages of Shakespeare—has ever given me such quasi-musical thrills of delight as the first chapter of the Biblical Ecclesiastes. I have read it hundreds of times: "All is vanity" . . . and the older I get the more I gloat over its wonderful perfection of style and thought.

In one respect Professor Lane was like his philological colleagues, as I found out to my cost. He made us translate, in the classroom, paragraphs from the Latin here and there, and then commented on them in a more or less grammatical vein. Again my *bête noire,* grammar. These comments seemed to me of no special importance and I was surprized to see the other students copying them carefully in their note books. I didn't.

When examination day came I found to my dismay that about half the questions related to the professor's notes, most of which I did not remember. Consequently I got only 84 per cent. and was lucky to get that.

It was not only wounded vanity or pride that hurt me; it was the fact that I had applied (this was in my Senior year) for a position as Latin tutor at Cornell after leaving Harvard. With only 84 per cent. to show, I knew that that plan was knocked on the head. I am glad, very glad, that it was, for I have had an infinitely more interesting life than I would have had teaching Latin in what Dr. Alexander McKenzie of Cambridge would have called a "freshwater college." But all the same——

Professors Bartlett and Norton

My knowledge of German served me a good turn, thanks to the fact that Professor Bartlett was a rational man. I called on him and had a long talk in German, during which I tried to convince him that it would be a waste of time for me to attend the German classes. "Grammar," I argued, "is only a means to an end. I speak German as fluently as English. In neither language could I pass even an elementary examination in its grammar. Why should I bother with the scaffolding when the house is already completed?"

He quite agreed with me and excused me from the recitations. The examination I had to attend, but it was understood that my refusal to answer the grammar questions would not count against me provided I explained my point of view in German on the examination paper. I did so, pointing out that children often learn two or even three languages at once, speaking them all equally well, without any grammatical drilling, whereas those who learn a language the grammatical way seldom speak it well.

I got 100 per cent.—but not till after a talk with the professor, who summoned me to his room. "I fear I can give you only 99," he said, "because there is an error in one of your translations. You used the expression *der See* instead of *die See*."

I looked at the passage. *Der See* means a lake, while *die See* means the ocean. "True," I answered, "but please remember that I had not read the book from which a page was on your examination paper for translation, and the context on this page does not show whether the reference is to a lake or to the ocean."

"You are right," he answered, seemingly relieved. "I'll give you 100."

Once I had a narrow escape from getting a low figure
where I was particularly anxious to have a high one.   It
was at one of Professor Norton's examinations.   I had
been extremely interested in his lectures on the history
and true inwardness of the fine arts, particularly painting
and architecture in Italy, and I had taken copious notes
while he was talking.   Owing to temporary indisposition
I had missed two important lectures and had foolishly
neglected to copy another student's notes.   At the examination, four out of the twelve questions related to these
two lectures!

Fortunately they came last on the paper.   That saved
me from disaster.   Usually the Norton examinations began
at 11.   This one began at 10.   I did not know it till I
got to the hall at 11 o'clock.

The Professor was indulgent: "I cannot expect you
to answer all these questions in one hour.   But I shall
make allowance for your late arrival."   He did so, giving
me a high mark.

Charles Eliot Norton was one of the Harvard professors to whom I look back with the warmest gratitude for
benefits received.   My subsequent travels in Italy would
have been far less enjoyable but for his illuminating talks.
He was, I believe, the first instructor who introduced
the refining spirit of art in these academic circles.

He was very kind, too, in inviting the students to come
to his house on certain evenings, when he chatted with
us and showed us his art treasures.   Most of the students
were embarrassingly bashful on these occasions, scarcely
daring to open their mouths.   I felt ashamed of them.
They reminded me of the timid divinity student who
escorted a young lady home after a reception and whose
only conversational effort on the way was to say: "Quite
a moon to-night!" to which she replied: "Yes, very."

One evening the professor brought me an old book

beautifully illustrated by medieval monks, with Latin text. "Here is a page," he said, "I have tried hard to translate, but in vain. Perhaps you, with your second-year honors in the classics, can help me."

I looked it over and shook my head. I took it home and pored over it an hour, then brought it back and said: "I am afraid Cicero himself could not have understood that monk's Latin."

Professor Norton had a daughter, Sallie, who played the violin, and played it well. I was engaged to bring up my 'cello twice a week and play duos with her. One day, when I referred to a Haydn piece as "jolly," she said it was so, "but papa doesn't like that word."

Professor Norton was the most intimate friend of Ruskin and he taught me to share his enthusiasm for that wonderful writer on the "Stones of Venice," the beauties of cloudscape and other wonders of art and nature. No matter how good your eyes may be you simply cannot know what clouds are till you have read Ruskin's "Modern Painters." It helped me to enjoy doubly the wondrous cloudscape as well as the mountains of Switzerland —I was going to call them indescribable, but Ruskin *has* described them.

I kept in touch with Norton after leaving college. The following letter dated March 6, 1877, is printed here because it illustrates his kind interest in his pupils: "I was pleased to receive a few days since your letter from Munich, and your account of Wagner's 'The Mastersingers'. I put your article at once into Mr. Godkin's hands, and am glad to say that it will appear this week (or next week) in the *Nation*. I read it with much interest and thought it was well done.

"Your account of your life at Munich is very pleasant. It is a rare chance to get such an opportunity for culture . . . I trust you are making some study of the method of instruction and discipline in the gymnasia and the University at Munich. A thorough acquaintance with them would be of great advantage to you should you come back to take a place in one of our colleges. Our methods are capable of great improvement, and we need to know the foreign standards of education in order to raise our own to their level.

"No great changes have taken place this year in Cambridge. The body of scientific teachers are making one of their periodical attempts to advance the interests of their studies at the cost of those of the 'humanities', but I think they will fail. The advantages of a liberal education must not be sacrificed for those of a narrow special training.

"My room is just now blue with examination books. Their number is legion, the task of reading them unwelcome and wearisome.

"I wish you would give my kind remembrance to Mr. Wheeler. I am glad to hear that he is well. I shall be glad to hear from you, or from him, if at any time I can be of service to you.

"I am

Very truly yours,
C. E. NORTON."

As this letter shows, Prof. Norton built the bridge across which I went four years later to become one of the editors of the New York *Nation*.

PRESIDENT ELIOT AND PROFESSOR PAINE

Everybody has seen, or heard of President Eliot's "Five-Foot Shelf of Books." He chose a limited number of volumes the reading of which would be the equivalent of a liberal education, and thousands have found it so.

The rare acumen and the liberal spirit exhibited in this choice of books in his later years were manifested by Charles W. Eliot from the start of his career as President of Harvard University. I cannot sufficiently thank my stars for having made my college term coincide with his first years at the head of that institution. 'Twas my usual good luck!

He became president in 1869. After forty years of service he retired. He was even then called "America's first citizen." When he reached the age of ninety, the man who ranks next to him as an educational authority, my classmate Charles F. Thwing, ex-president of the Western Reserve University in Cleveland, wrote: "His primacy has received full recognition. He stands alone."

As Dr. Thwing has pointed out, President Eliot's mind was from the start both microscopic and telescopic. No detail was too small for him, yet he had the far vision which looks to the future. He was an educational warrior, not afraid to fight obsolete practises. He never shrank from taking the unpopular side when he felt sure he was right, even when his actions might result in a temporary decline in the number of students. He had the courage, as in the cases of Langdell and Royce, of appointing to responsible positions men he believed in, though they had not yet made a name for themselves. He reorganized the medical department in the face of much opposition. And he was, in the words of Thwing, "a mighty believer in liberty."

Personally, I was concerned particularly with this passion for liberty—it meant the elective system of studies—and with the President's fostering of the department of music under John K. Paine.

Thanks to the elective system, I was able to drop the loathed mathematical studies after the Freshman year, and choose subjects in which I was interested and able to do something worth while. To be sure, a certain class of students abused this privilege by electing what were known as "soft" courses; easy subjects treated by kind-hearted professors and resulting in high marks. But after all, it did not greatly matter what that class of youths chose as long as the real students could follow their natural inclinations, classical, mathematical, scientific, artistic, or what not, and this paved the way to their life work.

As for the fine arts, I don't know if Professor Norton had a predecessor elsewhere, but it is certain that music received its first academic recognition in American colleges at Harvard under the fostering protection of President Eliot. His father, who was Mayor of Boston before 1840, devoted part of his time to promoting the introduction of music into the public schools of that city, so the matter was hereditary. In an address delivered some years ago Dr. Eliot said:

"When I became president of Harvard University there was no organized department of music in it and it was not customary in New England for highly educated, long-trained men to adopt the profession of music. There were many amateurs but few professional devotees. I remembered that in the oldest curriculum known to us for the Bachelor's degree—nearly 500 years old"—(Oxford had a professorship of Music in the ninth century)—"there stood among the seven subjects music. I knew how fine an element in culture music was, and I did my best with admirable supporters to develop a department of music at Harvard University, hoping that the influence of that department might spread through all the walks of life; and in the thirty-five years past the influence of that department has spread and associated itself with many other forces."

While President Eliot "knew how fine an element in culture music is" he was not aware of certain important facts that have recently come to light and which show how shrewd, how very shrewd indeed, was the instinct which made this chief of American educators (and his father before him) plead and fight for music as a factor in general education, and how accurately he hit the nail on the head when he wrote that "music, rightly taught, is the best mind-trainer on the list"; adding that "we should have more of the practical subjects like music and drawing and less grammar and arithmetic."

Positive proof that music is "the best mind-trainer" has come from Magdalen College, where all the musical instruction at Oxford is given. There are many prizes and scholarship. Only ten per cent. of the students at Magdalen take music, yet this ten per cent. take seventy-five per cent. of all those prizes and scholarships, leaving only twenty-five per cent. for the other ninety per cent. of students. And this is not the record of one year but the average of *thirty successive years.*

Three cheers for music! And three cheers for President Eliot, whose example has made it fashionable in American universities.

Three more cheers, if you please, for John Knowles Paine, a man from Maine (he was born in Portland), who exhibited the holy zeal and perseverance of a true missionary for the divine art. He made up his mind, as early as 1862, to become a Harvard professor of music and he won, after a severe struggle.

Needless to say that after Charles W. Eliot came on deck as captain of the ship, it was easy sailing for him. For some years, to be sure, there were not many students, nor were the accommodations for them satisfactory; good recitation rooms were scarce.

When I studied harmony and the history of music with Paine the class gathered in a large room in the basement of University Hall. A piano was provided. Occasionally, by way of diversion, Paine and I played a Beethoven sonata for piano and violoncello. I also frequently played with him at his residence, where I had the privilege of meeting some persons noted then and, more so, later on; among them John Fiske, Rose Hawthorne (daughter of the great novelist), and Amy Fay, just back from her studies with Liszt. She had described these studies in her letters to friends at home and was preparing her letters for issue in print under the title of "Music Studies in Germany"—a book which gives a more vivid picture of Liszt among his pupils at Weimar than any other book does in any language.

In our Oregon home Liszt was unknown—we did not have the right kind of a piano or the necessary technique for his pieces. What is much stranger is that we did not know about Chopin! One day, in Boston, I saw, at Ditson's, a collection of his nocturnes in a bright red paper cover. A glance showed me—for I could hear music with my eyes—that here was something rich and strange that would enchant me.

It was a red-letter day in my musical life. That night, when everything was quiet in the college yard, I went into our basement music room, placed the nocturnes on the piano with feverish haste and began to play. It was like an opium dream, a vision of strange, thrilling, voluptuous delights. With the sole exception of Schubert's songs, no German music had ever so enchanted me as these melancholy Polish strains.

Hour after hour passed. I played through the whole collection and then some of the pieces over and over again. Tears of joy often dimmed my eyes so that I could not see the printed page. There were some pages far too difficult for me to play at sight; but enthusiasm at a white heat inspired me literally "to the finger tips" till I was amazed at my unprecedented technical feats.

In the history of musical criticism in America, that solitary soirée in University Hall deserves a line. It engendered my ardent propaganda for him whom Schumann called the greatest poet of the pianoforte (though he was almost the only German who realized that) to which I devoted so much of my time in later years, with the result that James Huneker could write to me, on March 8, 1904: "You were not only the first *Chopin* apostle, but also the first *Liszt,* the first *Wagner* in America!"

Professor Paine did not share my enthusiasm for Chopin; he had obtained all his musical education in Germany, where "mere foreigners" like Chopin and Liszt and Grieg were habitually belittled. His music gods were Bach, Mozart, and Beethoven. Of course he played Bach and Beethoven in the German academic way of his time, which, as we now know, was not Bach's own way nor Beethoven's. These masters were emotional, not academic.

I remember one occasion, in New York, when he berated me soundly for approving, in my *Evening Post* criticisms, Paderewski's emotional way of playing Beethoven's sonatas. I could only tell him that I enjoyed them much more the Paderewski way than the traditional German way.

It was in the case of Wagner, however, that my Harvard professor and I disagreed most violently and that I triumphed most brilliantly. When he found I was playing the Wagner scores on the official Harvard piano in University Hall, he was greatly distressed and warned me solemnly that I would corrupt my musical taste. As there were no police regulations on the subject, he could not put a stop to my nefarious conduct, but he and John Fiske put their heads together and concocted for the *North American Review* an article in which my idol was completely demolished, pulverized, annihilated.

THE AUTHOR AS A STUDENT AT HARVARD

Revenge is sweet, particularly when the repentant sinner attends to it himself. I have before me several dozen letters written to me by Paine when I was critic of the New York *Evening Post*. Under date of January 31, 1882, he wrote: "I want to take this opportunity to say that my opinions regarding Wagner and his theories have been modified since you were in College. I consider him a great genius who has had a wonderful influence on the present day. I will reserve my ideas on this subject until we meet."

Four years later he wrote to me: "I have got a splendid subject for a romantic opera in three acts. Scene laid in Provence in 11th century. I am writing my own book—have got about 200 lines done. I will show them to you if you do not object. Please keep it private till I have seen you."

He did come to New York and we talked over the matter minutely over a bottle of Chianti. Later on he kept me informed of his progress with "Azara." March 25, 1900: "I wish I could play you the whole opera. You will find that I have entered upon a new path in all respects—in form, thematic treatment, instrumentation, etc. All dramatic composers must learn from Wagner, yet I have not consciously imitated him in style, etc." May 27, 1900: "I have followed throughout the connected orchestral rhythmical flow, and truth of dramatic expression characteristic of Wagner."

Undoubtedly, Harvard's professor of music had no end of fun composing his opera. But that was all he ever did get out of it—that's about all most composers of music usually get out of their works, the supply of which so deplorably exceeds the demand.

I did all I could to help Paine. I made personal appeals to Emma Eames and Geraldine Farrar to interest themselves in the rôle of Azara, and they were not deaf to my appeals; but nothing came of it. A guarantee fund of $10,000 was discussed. We got up a petition to Conried signed by Carl Schurz and many other eminent men, and that manager seemed favorably inclined, but nothing was done.

After Paine's death his widow had the full score printed by Breitkopf & Härtel in Leipsic—a beautiful piece of work—at a cost of $2,000. No use; "Azara" has never been sung and probably never will be.

My friendship with Paine is one of the most agreeable chapters in the story of my life. He was a most kind and companionable man, and he was so lucky as to have a wife who adored him as a man—his music she did not know from that of any other master! I like to read over his letters. They are full of fun and puns—such puns! "I will meet you at Steinway Hall at 11, unless Tarrytown is so affected by the laziness of its name that the morning trains are slower than the Dead March in Saul," illustrates his playful style.

Student Music and Pranks

If you know anything at all about Harvard you have heard of the Pierian Sodality—a pompously ludicrous name for the students' orchestra which dates back to almost prehistoric times when mastodons, dinosaurs and rhododendrons * roamed the site of Cambridge. But while old in one sense, this orchestra is always new in another; for, every year, its senior members leave college and there are new Freshman members who may or may not be able to take their places satisfactorily.

Naturally, I became solo violoncellist of the Sodality, and at the first concert I played a concerto which made

* Yes, I know!

my Freshman classmates give me an ovation such as Piatti, Popper, Victor Herbert or Casals might have envied.

Our conductor was Jecko—Steven H. Jecko. Poor fellow! He had a time of it getting together a decent ensemble. Most of the youths who presented themselves for admission were flute players, but flutes alone don't quite make an orchestra. John Gorman, an elderly man who worked in a printing office, kindly helped us out with his clarinet.

What we needed particularly was a double-bass player —better known as a bull-fiddler. We had an excellent pianist named Shippen, but pianists are replaceable, so Jecko ordered him to change horses and learn the big fiddle. After a few weeks of hard practise he was admitted to a rehearsal. About twenty bars were played, when Jecko stopped the orchestra and exclaimed with an agonized expression: "For God's sake, Shippen, do you believe in a Redeemer?"

Jecko and I were looked upon as the musical prodigies of the class of '76. Nothing that any musician had ever done was supposed to be beyond us. Banking on this faith we had some fun one day at the expense of a number of students who happened to have a meeting in a hall where there was a piano. Stepping onto the platform I said: "I will now sit down and play a series of chords and discords, and Jecko will in each case name the notes of which they are composed."

He did so, astonishing the natives, who applauded in a bewildered way. Then Jecko took my place and I, looking away from the piano named the notes. Of course it was sheer bluff; we had secretly agreed to say "Correct" to any group of notes the other named as having been sounded.

Eating in Memorial Hall

This morning (January 4, 1925) on reading the preceding day's issue of the Paris-Riviera edition of the *New York Herald,* I came across this item: "The famous Harvard Commons in Memorial Hall, where hundreds [should be tens of thousands] of students have taken their meals at reasonable prices since the Civil War, has been closed on account of the competition of 'one-armed' lunch-rooms in the vicinity of the campus. In issuing the order for the closing of the historic restaurant, President Lowell announced that the deficit of the place had been $25,000 in the past year. The institution was run on almost a cost basis, and scores of students have eked out their tuition by working as waiters, cooks and dish-washers there."

A flood of memories was evoked in my mind by that paragraph. I recall how indignantly Professor Norton talked at a lecture about the hideous new Memorial Building, "an insult to American architecture"; how, for a time, no one could think of what possible use the queer building could be put to, until its availability for a dining hall was suggested; and how we students soon filled it up. We were all hungry, but the food left much to be desired.

At the table to which I was assigned I had the great good luck to sit next to Charles F. Thwing, embryo college president, who has been one of my life-long friends.

Next to President Eliot he has been, as already stated, the greatest of American college educators; his many books are a treasury of information and instruction; and as a man he has a real genius for friendship. I have never known anyone more genial and sympathetic; his smile is like the Riviera sunshine, his laughter contagious. The influence of his personality on thousands of Cleveland students has been as beneficial as that of his scholarship and executive ability.

Jecko also sat at our table, and that provided a chance for one of our pranks. We all agreed that the menu was too monotonous and it was suggested that cheese would make a welcome change. Each student contributed a dime, and Jecko and I, being of Teutonic extraction and therefore necessarily cheese experts, were asked to buy some. We talked the matter over and purchased some very ancient and odoriferous Limburger. Nobody, of course, ate any, and we had it all to ourselves. That ended our career as food purveyors.

One term my neighbor on the other side was a Japanese student who told me a lot of interesting things. Speaking of courtship and marriage he informed me that in his country there was no kissing. He was surprized when I said I would never go to Japan.

Jecko had a good deal of musical talent and might have achieved real distinction in utilizing it, but his conductorship of the Pierian Sodality remained his supreme achievement. It was his elevation to that rank that had made it necessary to get a new bull-fiddler.

When I first arrived in Cambridge it occurred to me that I might add to my scant income by playing in one of the theater orchestras. I called on Mr. Koppel, musical director of the Boston Theater, and he referred me to his first violoncellist, Wulf Fries, the leading Boston 'cellist of his day. He was so able and so prominent that Rubinstein chose him for a joint tour. I came just in time to take his place while he was on this tour. But first I had to be tried. He kindly gave me a few free lessons. After my first piece he exclaimed, "Abscheulich!" (abominable). My bowing left something to be desired; but after a few lessons he considered me up to "concert pitch" and I proudly took his place in the Boston Theater orchestra.

All went well at first, but one evening I was too lazy to count the endless number of bars in which I had to repeat three bass notes, and played a few after the other men had stopped. Koppel looked daggers at me. "Can't even play a simple bass!" he muttered; then he punished me by taking away from me a solo passage in the next piece and giving it to the cornet.

After a few weeks Wulf Fries—who, by the way, was a Norwegian—came back and I lost my job. But the man at the back door of the theater did not know I wasn't playing any more and let me in all the same. So I found my way to the standing room and had a grand time seeing the performances, particularly those given by Lydia Thompson and her company.

Longfellow and Howells

All this fun I owed to my violoncello; but the most wonderful achievement of that instrument was that it opened to me the door to the famous home of the great poet Longfellow, and also to the home of America's foremost novelist, William Dean Howells.

During two terms my college room was No. 13, Hollis Hall. As 13 usually does, it brought me good luck. In the same hall dwelt Thomas Lincoln Talbot, who subsequently became a prominent attorney-at-law in Portland, Maine, and Wadsworth Longfellow, nephew of the poet, later on a famous architect in the same city. Both were about as fine fellows as could be found in the college yard and we soon became warm friends. Talbot also had a 'cello and was a good musician, but he did not try to compete with me. In fact, he and his chum told Longfellow about my playing and the poet promptly expressed a desire to meet me. I was taken to his house for an intro-

ductory meeting and shortly afterward the kind-hearted
poet invited the home-sick boy from Oregon to dinner.

Christmas dinner at that! I sat at his side and he
shared with me all the delicacies (he was an epicure) that
friends from near and far had sent for the occasion. Such
a dinner I had never dreamt of. But I enjoyed his conversation still more. He asked me many questions about
my life in Oregon and you may be sure I was ever so glad
to answer them.

He was particularly interested in what I told him about
the wholesale slaughter of splendid trees. He himself was
giving his time and his powerful influence to saving some
of the beautiful old trees of Cambridge.

His three daughters were of course present, and it was
arranged that I should bring up my 'cello and play duos
with the oldest of them. She was a good pianist and I
enjoyed these evenings, which became more and more frequent. The poet could hear us from his private room;
now and then he came into the parlor for a chat. He was
usually serious in his conversation but once he perpetrated
a joke. He wanted to know all about my 'cello, which was
of the miniature Amati type. When I told him it was over
a hundred years old, he said with a smile: "Rather small
for its age, isn't it?"

I had considerable difficulty in finding time to keep up
the necessary 'cello technique. Playing on a musical instrument was strictly forbidden in the college dormitories during study and sleep hours, which means most hours. Once
I boldly played in the middle of the day. I was then sharing Harold Wheeler's room in Matthews Hall; it was
engaged in his name and he kindly allowed me to occupy
one of the two bedrooms. The day after I had played,
Harold got a note from the Dean intimating that if there
was any more playing in his room out of hours *he* would
have to take the consequences. No—it just comes back

to me—it was even funnier than that: the Dean summoned me to his room and told me to tell Wheeler that if there was any more music in his room *he* would be held responsible!

To come back for a moment to the Longfellow home: I met there, among other prominent or interesting people, members of his brother's family who lived in Portland— not Oregon but Maine. During one summer, while visiting the Talbot family, I saw much of this branch of the Longfellow family, playing duos with the daughter and joining the family on their excursions on their boat.

Howells I got acquainted with through Mrs. McKenzie, wife of the eminent clergyman Dr. Alexander McKenzie, whose church and home were on Garden Street, opposite the famous Washington Elm. Dr. McKenzie was not at all interested in music, but I always enjoyed dining at his table; his talk was stimulating and he was fond of humor. I remember with what zest he told about his meeting Mark Twain the day before, when Mark tried to shock him by telling about having just seen "one of you clergymen performing his Christian orgies over a dead Chinaman."

Mrs. McKenzie was one of the most genuinely musical women it has ever been my good fortune to meet. As a professional, she might have easily become one of the leading pianists of the day. We played together nearly everything that existed for piano and 'cello, including the sonatas and concertos of Rubinstein, Saint Saëns, Schumann, Beethoven and so on; many pages there were which I simplified, but that did not spoil them, for these were the inevitable *bravura* episodes—that is, show music— which did not interest us. We also spent much time playing the Schubert songs, and how we *did* enjoy them! They were at that time entirely neglected by the stupid and incompetent public singers.

Occasionally we called in other musicians and had a trio, quartet or quintet. One time we rehearsed Schumann's piano-quintet. All went well at rehearsals but at the public performance in Dr. McKenzie's church (we gave it for a charitable purpose) I came near extinguishing myself because I trusted too much to luck.

The last movement of the quintet ends with a fugue covering several pages. It is an extremely intricate finale and gets more so from bar to bar. It is the opinion among musicians that if you lose your place you are done for—can't possibly get back into the tonal labyrinth. I *did* lose my place!

Fortunately I did not lose my head. With perfect *sangfroid* I kept my bow passionately fiddling across the strings, without making a sound. I am quite sure there were not six persons in the audience who were "on to me," excepting my fellow players. One of these said to me: "Great bluff! You must be a professional poker player." And I was shameless enough to take this as a compliment.

Mrs. McKenzie and I had a good laugh over it the next evening. My blunder did not diminish her admiration for my playing. This was so great that she often told me that if her own playing ever fell short of what it should be it was because she was so enthralled by my 'cello that she forgot everything else.

What brought about this result was simply the emotional fervor of my playing, a very rare thing among musicians and actually suppressed in music schools patterned after German models. I had a surprizing illustration of this in one of the leading conservatories of Boston.

The director, a famous German musician, wanted to start a quartet, and as there was no 'cellist among the students, I was invited. The first violin was an excellent player, so genuinely musical that he played his part in a Beethoven quartet with a delightful expression. But the famous director soon roared at him, "No expression!" He would have jumped on me too, but refrained because I was not his pupil.

It was at the McKenzie home that I first met Mr. and Mrs. Howells. The great novelist cared no more for the tonal art than the doctor of divinity did. The story was current that when he was asked what he thought of music he answered: "Oh, I see no harm in it."

Perhaps that story slanders him. What I know is that more than once he joined his wife when she came to hear Mrs. McKenzie and me play duos. Mrs. Howells was genuinely musical. She was also a special student of physiognomy. After carefully studying my face one day she made me happy by telling me that my forehead was just like Schiller's. "Perhaps it isn't strange that it should be," I replied. "That poet may be (like the poet Schwab) a distant relative of mine. The village where he was born is not far from the village where my mother was born."

But I have never indulged in genealogical researches, as I believe that every tub should stand on its own bottom. If you are a somebody, the fact that your ancestors were nobodies does not make you less noteworthy. But if you are a nobody and your ancestors were somebodies, that makes it all the worse for you, doesn't it?

To be sure, nobody ever thinks he is a nobody, which makes things pleasant all 'round.

Howells was at that time editor of the *Atlantic Monthly*. I used to find him, in his studio, surrounded by piles of manuscripts which he looked at rather disconsolately, for he had to read them. "It's a sad business," he said; "we can accept so few of them, no matter how good they may be."

One day he showed me two large drawers full of manuscripts. "All these," he said, "have been accepted by myself and predecessors. But I do not see how we can possibly print them."

It was certainly very kind of him, in view of this super-abundance of material, to voluntarily give me a job: that of reviewing some books on musical and philosophical subjects. Thus I began to climb the literary ladder by putting my foot on the top rung, so to speak, and while I was still a student. My usual good luck!

It was Mr. Howells, also, who accepted, and printed in the *Atlantic Monthly,* my first elaborate magazine article. It was on the Wagner Festival at Bayreuth in 1876, which was the occasion of my first trip to Europe, immediately after graduating.

Four years later Mr. Howells found room for an article from my pen on the "Esthetic Value of the Sense of Smell," in which he declared himself much interested. When I mailed the MS., I thought with apprehension of those two drawers full of accepted articles; but I "got there all the same." The article was printed in December, 1880.

EMERSON, HOLMES, AND LOWELL

Cambridge in my college days was a veritable African jungle of literary big game. You could have hardly fired a shotgun in any direction without hitting some celebrity. I do not believe that in any other college town, at any time, so many notables were gathered together. Some of them, to be sure, lived in that suburb of Cambridge casually noted on the map as "Boston," while Ralph Waldo Emerson lived at Concord. He was not connected with Harvard officially, I think, but I often saw him walk across the college yard, or stop at the pump near Matthews Hall for a cup of water. He did this one day when I had just taken a drink. I took off my hat and pumped up a cup for him. He thanked me and asked me what class

I belonged to. That seemed to exhaust his curiosity and he walked on.

In my fragmentary College diary I find this reference to the great essayist: "After a sumptuous breakfast at Memorial Hall, read over Locke's stupid and confused chapter on Power, and Professor Bowen's lecture on Causality. At 11 o'clock went in to recite on these and found, rather to my confusion, that the great Mr. Emerson and two other famous chaps, not known to me, were present. Fortunately, I was not called up to recite, though at the same time I was burning to get off a good argument on Pantheism suggested by Locke's remarks on the origin of our idea of creative power."

Oliver Wendell Holmes lived in the suburb just referred to. He *was* a Harvard professor—of anatomy, if you please! Think of a poet, raconteur, and wit like Holmes lecturing year after year on that bone-dry subject! But his lectures, so medical students told me, were never dry—far from it.

Once I had a chance to meet this "Professor" and "Poet at the Breakfast Table." It was at a literary dinner to which I had somehow been invited. I don't remember, but suspect that I owed this to Professor Norton. At any rate it was he who, with characteristic kindness, took me by the arm to introduce me to Holmes. He mentioned my name and class, and the poet-professor was just opening his lips to say something to me which no doubt would have been either witty or wise or both, when somebody slapped him on the shoulder and turned him around. Thus ended my interview.

James Russell Lowell I never met personally but I attended his lectures to the students. I remember with particular pleasure his impromptu translations of chosen passages from "Don Quixote," which Spanish name he encouraged us to boldly pronounce the English way.

How we did laugh at the amusing sentences delivered
with rare eloquence by the lecturer; such as, "It is no disgrace to be poor, but it's devilish inconvenient."

AGASSIZ, FISKE, AND WILLIAM JAMES

Of course I did not miss the lectures of the famous
French naturalist associated with Harvard: Louis Agassiz. It was certainly instructive as well as entertaining to
hear him explain gallinaceous development from the germ
in the egg to the crowing rooster and the cackling hen.
But alas! The learned professor was behind the times.
He closed his eyes tightly to the flood of light thrown on
natural history by evolution and Darwinism.

When that young and vigorous champion of Darwin
and Spencer, John Fiske, wrote a magazine article aimed
more or less at the belated Agassiz, that eminent scholar
was very angry. "That man Shon Fiske," he exclaimed,
"is one big shackass!"

That "big shackass," I am proud and grateful to say,
became one of my best friends at Harvard.

I have never been able to understand why some persons
resent the doctrine that human beings are descended from
the lower animals. For my part, I feel proud and delighted
at the thought that we humans have, with the faculties
implanted in us by the Creator of the Universe, risen in
intelligence so high above our humble ancestors, from the
primeval protoplasm to our simian relatives.

To my mind, too, it is disrespectful to think of the Creator as having made a world which needed constant tinker-
ing and adding to by "special creations" of higher types.
How infinitely more sublime and devout is the idea of a
Creator who, *by a single act of will power,* launched a
nebula which had latent in its cosmic dust the faculty of
evolving, without further assistance and interference, all

the wonderful plants and animals of this globe of ours, including man himself!

If Oliver Wendell Holmes had lectured on the evolutionary aspect of anatomy he could have pointed out one striking fact which alone proves absolutely that simians are our blood relations. At the end of the human backbone there are found rudiments of the muscles used by monkeys to move their tails. If God had made man in his own image, by a special act of creation, would he have given him those rudimentary tail muscles? Think that over.

The chief trouble with the late William Jennings Bryan and other enemies of evolution appears to be that they lack a sense of humor. And in my opinion they blaspheme the Lord Almighty.

You can imagine what a tremendous stimulus it was to my mind to be in at the start of this big scientific fight; to read the books of Darwin, Wallace, Spencer, Huxley, Haeckel and others as they came fresh from the press; and to be able to enlist in this war under the banner of its American leader, the fiery and aggressive John Fiske. To him I owe eternal debts of gratitude for scientific counsel and guidance. He was always ready to stop in his work and help me solve knotty problems.

Soon I began to write articles of my own on evolutionary topics. The columns of the New York *Nation,* in particular, contain a number of articles I wrote on this subject during my four years abroad. Its editors, Godkin and Garrison, fortunately sympathized with my point of view and never altered my copy.

It was through Professor Paine that I first came into personal contact with John Fiske, who was much interested in music. On August 12, 1875, he wrote me from Petersham, Massachusetts, a letter answering my questions about unconscious activities of mind on which I had to write—we anticipated Freud by half a century! In the closing paragraph he says: "I am very glad to hear that you think of coming to Petersham, with your 'cello. Mrs. McKenzie tells me that Mendelssohn has two sonatas for piano and 'cello. I didn't know it. Please bring them with you if you have them, and do not forget to add a supply of Bach's arias and gavottes. Mr. Paine was here early in July. I thought he was now in Magnolia, but from your letter, he is not there. Mrs. McKenzie and Mrs. Fiske send their regards to you, and we all look forward to some pleasant music when you come."

We did have a splendid time at that summer resort in the Massachusetts mountains. Mr. Fiske always wrote like a philosopher—a most entertainingly wise man, to be sure, and without a trace of pedantry—but personally he was like a big boy—I came near saying a Newfoundland pup, full of animal spirits.

I remember his coming to the breakfast table one morning with a huge sunflower in his buttonhole.

He was quite an expert in piano-playing, which he referred to as "clawing the ivory." Referring to my literary style one day, he declared that I knew "how to sling ink."

It was fortunate for the world that when the director of the Harvard Library died, his job was given to Justin Winsor instead of to John Fiske, who had been assistant librarian. The huge amount of work that job called for would have greatly diminished the output of scientific and historical master works with which he has won a lasting place in American literature. If you have never read the chapters on George Washington in his "American Revolution," you don't know how wonderfully human George was. Fiske had the gift of enthusiasm and knew how to impart it to his readers. His story of Columbus is equally inspiring.

When he began to write these books he did not know how great they were. Mrs. Fiske told me some years ago that when the manuscript sheets came back from the publisher, John used to toss them to the children so they could scribble on the blank sides—it saved paper. Gradually it dawned on her that it might be well to save these pages. A wise decision! After Fiske's death a wealthy Western admirer inquired about these MSS. and paid $12,000 for them.

The children of the Fiske household naturally fell in with his scientific way of talking. One time, he told me, they engaged a new maid, who proved to be surprizingly satisfactory. When the matter was discussed, he muttered something about its being perhaps only a case of a new broom sweeping clean. When this proved to be the case, the five-year-old daughter exclaimed: "Papa, your hypothesis about the new broom was correct." And these children talked about the "nebular theory" and that sort of scientific thing as others do about dolls.

William James, I regret to say, I did not see much of; he might have been as helpful to me as John Fiske had I known him equally well. In my diary I find this: "A new feature of great interest and importance is to be added to our philosophic department the coming year, when an elective will be offered in physiological psychology, the text-book to be used being Herbert Spencer's 'Principles of Psychology.' Dr. James intends to supplement the text-book by a course of lectures and to illustrate the subject by means of experiments on frogs, etc. Some familiarity with Huxley's 'Physiology' will put any one in a condition to get the greatest possible benefit out of this course. It is intended to allow Juniors to elect it in place of the required Metaphysics."

Frogs in the philosophical lecture room to elucidate *human* psychology! Here was an innovation, indeed—

and under the patronage of President Eliot! It was the beginning of the end of the old metaphysical notion that mind is to be found in man alone. The evolutionary Spencerian Psychology finds evidence of a crude mentality in the lowest phases of animal life, wherever there is any nervous substance at all, and then traces it upward till it reaches elephants and dogs and apes; and by this method of what is called comparative psychology a flood of light is thrown on the phenomena of the human mind.

Some readers may wonder what connection all this talk has with the story of my life, which I am supposed to be relating. A very close connection, I assure you. When I applied for a Fellowship which would enable me to study abroad for three years, I chose comparative psychology as my specialty and—rather to my surprize, for this was a bold and unprecedented step—I won.

Professor James's lectures and writings were eye-openers to me and influenced my whole life. They were of literary charm as well as scientifically instructive—remember that he was the brother of the novelist, Henry James, Jr.; and he was glad when he came across style in one of his pupils. When my first book, "Romantic Love and Personal Beauty," was published, Mr. Garrison got Professor James to review it for the *Nation*. You can imagine how proud I was when I read this from his pen: "The style of it is singularly happy. . . . A clean, playful touch which carries one along in the rapidest measures, and often leaves whole sentences sticking in the memory."

PROFESSORS CHILD AND PEABODY

In writing those words, William James was unconsciously paying a tribute also to Professor Child who helped us students to learn to write and to appreciate the true inwardness of English literature, as an authority in which he was second to no scholar of his day. For him we had to write theses, or dissertations, which he corrected and polished till they shone. For these "shines" of my crude style I now feel that I am more indebted than I knew at the time.

In one of my theses I foolishly "went off at a tangent," indulging in a ridiculous tirade about things that had nothing whatever to do with my subject. Professor Child refused to accept this dissertation but kindly allowed me to write another on the same subject. When he got this he was so much pleased that he read from it in the class-room, which naturally delighted me; and then and there I made up my mind to be a good boy and never again to dodge my subject.

Another cause for gratitude: Professor Child was one of the members of the Faculty who made speeches in my favor when I applied for a European Fellowship.

In one of the dissertations which I preserved I find a reference to the absent-mindedness to which I was already addicted while still in my 'teens: "While eating my dessert one day I was hotly discussing some philosophical question with my neighbor (Charlie Thwing) at the table. While engaged in talking I folded up my napkin without looking at it, and then took up what I thought was the napkin ring and tried to put the napkin through it. Meeting with persistent resistance which annoyed me visibly, I had my attention called to what I was doing. To my surprise and the amusement of everybody at the table, I found that I had been trying to put my napkin through the butter-plate."

Talk about absent-mindedness, and every Harvard man of that period will automatically mutter "Dr. Peabody." He certainly was addicted to that habit; so much so that the students invented grotesque exaggerations of it. One evening, so the story ran, the good old Doctor of Divinity walked home in a heavy rain. When he arrived, he carefully put his dripping umbrella into his bed and then stood up himself behind the door all night.

On another occasion he walked along the street for a mile with one foot in the gutter and on arriving in his studio wrote a letter to the mayor protesting vigorously against the uneven sidewalk.

Students will be students. But if we did caricature Dr. Peabody we all loved him dearly, even if we found his sermons in the College Chapel sometimes a little dull. He had an effective way of waking up anyone who might happen to fall asleep, by starting a new division of his discourse with an explosive "But" that would have attracted attention even during a bombardment of Paris by the German "big Berthas."

Moral philosophy and the Evidences of Christianity were the things Dr. Peabody taught us in our Freshman year. I won his heart by being genuinely interested in the problems of moral philosophy and asking him questions. "Most of the students," he once said to me, "want to know only as much as they need to pass the examination."

Among the documents most precious to me which I preserved in my college day I value particularly the following letter he gave me when, after graduating, I was in quest of a position:

Cambridge, Dec. 7, 1877.

"Mr. Henry T. Finck, a graduate of Harvard University, as a student in the Department of Philosophy, has had no superior, few equals, since I have been connected with the department, *i. e.* for a period of seventeen years. At the same time he is possessed of superior native ability, large general culture, and a character of blameless excellence. I regard him as eminently well fitted for a place in the corps of instruction in any college or university.

A. P. PEABODY."

PROFESSORS PALMER AND BOWEN

In almost every department of learning the early years of Dr. Eliot's presidency brought salutary changes and striking improvements. The Macmillan Co. in London just then brought out a new series of text-books on astronomy, physics, and other sciences which in lucidity and up-to-dateness were greatly superior to the books previously used. I again thanked my stars for having led me to Harvard just at this psychological moment in the scientific world.

Nor did the philosophical department lag behind. I have just spoken of William James. Professor George Herbert Palmer also kept up with the procession. He chose Bain's "Mental Science" for one of our text-books and I am mighty glad he did, for Bain was not one of those muddle-headed writers who left their readers groping about in mental darkness; he threw real light on the three divisions of the mind: intellect, emotions, will.

I was hugely pleased, too, with Jevons's new "Logic" and John Stuart Mill's great book on the same subject which followed it in this course. These books with Palmer's elucidations and additions made it easier for us students to avoid flaws in reasoning.

Professor Palmer taught us how to strengthen the memory. "After reading a page or a chapter," he said, "shut your eyes and *force* yourself to recall the contents. Don't peep at the page if a detail resists recalling. *Compel* the memory to bring it back and you will never forget it; otherwise you will."

Palmer made a life study of the first and finest of all romances, Homer's "Odyssey." He made a version of it in English prose which I consider even better than Andrew Lang's. While engaged on this work he used to read to the students what he had done and I am sure we all enjoyed it very much. I also enjoyed the hospitality of his home.

He liked music, but drew the line at opera, which seemed to him unnatural, because "people do not in real life sing recitatives or arias." "True," I admitted, "but neither do they talk in meter or rime. The same objection would condemn many of the greatest spoken dramas."

He could not refute that retort.

We now come to the head of the philosophical department, the unique and intensely interesting Professor Francis Bowen. John Stuart Mill, in a controversial paper, once referred to him as "an obscure North American metaphysician." He lived to rue the day; at least he would have rued it had he been in our class. For Bowen took Mill's examination of Hamilton's "Philosophy" and, in turn, subjected that to the "third degree." When he got through, poor Mill presented the appearance of a mansion that has been smashed, demolished and annihilated by a tornado.

Bowen was as belated and reactionary in philosophy as Agassiz was in science. I shared hardly any of his convictions, yet I revered and adored him and he liked me. He was an enthusiast over the old-fashioned theological metaphysics, which tried to deduce all knowledge out of man's inner consciousness—a presumption that was just then violently assailed by the new doctrine of evolution and the discoveries of experimental psychology.

It was a tremendous intellectual advantage to me to have the older views so powerfully presented by this vigorous champion just at the time when the new doctrines were knocking at the door.

I had come to Harvard believing in metaphysics, enthusiastic in the hope that all problems could be solved offhand in this easy subjective way; but the more I read (under Bowen's guidance) of Kant, Schelling, Fichte, and Hegel, the more I became convinced that the doctrines of these ludicrously famous German metaphysicians (I except Kant) were merely "words, words, words," and I turned from them disappointed and even angry because the study of their works now seemed a sheer waste of time.

One of the things I admired about Bowen was that while he thoroughly believed in the old metaphysics, he was liberal enough to offer us also a course in Schopenhauer.

Yes, Arthur Schopenhauer, who made a business of exposing as humbugs the wordy metaphysicians I have just named (excepting Kant, though him, also, he subjected to merciless, masterful criticism). Bowen, as he often told us, loathed Schopenhauer's pessimism—his efforts to prove that this is the worst of all possible worlds.

What he admired in him was his brilliant style, his power of invective, his amazing ability to throw light on obscure problems, the lucidity of his thought, and his gift for gathering and stringing together pearls of philosophical thought from all countries and ages.

"Whatever you may think of his doctrines, you simply must read Schopenhauer," he said.

Our Schopenhauer class was not a big one, for only those could take it who were able to read German fairly well. To me this class naturally was a picnic; it took me only a few minutes to read over the five or six pages constituting our next lesson.

Less fortunate were my classmates. One morning there was a loud knock at my door. "Come in!" I roared, and in came one of the students in the Schopenhauer class.

"Say, Finck," he remarked, "I thought I could read German, but this page baffles me. Won't you please translate it for me?"

I did so and he left. A little later came another knock with the same request, then another and still another. By that time I could get over that page like greased lightning, as they say out West.

Well, the hour for recital came. We took our seats and the Professor began: "Finck, will you please read Page 432?" I did so, with a glibness that visibly astonished him.

"You translate very well," he commented.

Query: had he, too, found that page too much for him and taken this method of understanding it?

Anyway, it was a big feather in my cap.

When a few weeks later the examination in Schopenhauer was held, I got 100 per cent. "I couldn't have done it better myself," Bowen declared.

Of course, my examination paper showed that I had not only read the pages selected for class purposes, but had eagerly devoured whole volumes of Schopenhauer. How I adored him! His influence on my mental development was greater than that of any other writer and for my early acquaintance with him I feel eternally indebted to Professor Bowen.

Following Schopenhauer, we had a few months when our text-book was Eduard Von Hartmann's "Philosophy of the Unconscious," very fashionable at that time in Germany. Hartmann went Schopenhauer one better. "No!" he shouted, "this is not the worst of all possible worlds. It is on the contrary the best of all possible worlds. And yet it is so bad that it would be far better if there were no world at all."

That was certainly rubbing it in! Pessimism could go no further.

Hartmann ought to be fashionable again. He anticipated most of the doctrines with which the Freudians and psychoanalysts have been strutting about in recent years.

Are they ignorant of his writings, or do they keep them out of sight purposely?

My chief ambition, at this time, was to get highest honors in philosophy, a distinction not often conferred. As Professor Bowen was the chief arbiter in this matter it was important that he should believe in me. I made no secret whatever of the fact that my beliefs were diametrically opposed to his. I made this clear—even when not at all necessary—in my examination papers and the philosophical dissertations written for him.

One day I got a note asking me to come and see him. We had a long heart-to-heart talk. He told me he greatly admired my mental qualities and scholarship but feared for my future because of my lack of religious faith and my sympathy with agnostic and revolutionary doctrines. He wanted to warn me because he felt sure my skepticism would prove detrimental to me.

"Well, Professor," I answered, "you have told us that even the devout and orthodox Descartes went through a period of skepticism. I have no doubt that in the end I shall be found on the right side."

Bowen smiled and was evidently pleased. To be sure "on the right side" might mean either his side or mine; it could be read two ways, like a Delphic oracle. Perhaps he simply admired my tact in delivering such a reply; but he was satisfied. With all his orthodoxy, he was not narrow-minded and he was evidently anxious that I should win highest honors in philosophy.

As the time approached when the decisive examinations would be held I carefully reviewed once more the books we had used—all except Hegel. I had such a ferocious hatred of his pompously empty verbiage that after I had reread about half the pages I shut the book and said to myself: "I shall not memorize another page of this infernal rubbish even if I miss my highest honors for it!"

And I nearly did! The final examination was oral—at the professor's home. We went through Kant and Schopenhauer and the rest of them and my answers were prompt and correct. Hegel, fortunately, came last on the list. I answered the first questions all right but trembled as we approached the place where I had shut the book.

It was one of the great dramatic moments of my life. Two minutes more and all would be lost. Just then the clock struck one. The exam. was over; I was saved—entitled to the words "With highest honors in philosophy" in my diploma.

MORE STUDENT PRANKS

By way of intermezzo, let me relate a few more of the more or less funny episodes in my college life.

In writing about the Pierian Sodality I forgot to refer to a real tragicomedy in my college experiences.

In 1872-73 spelling matches were a craze over all the country. In the college yard someone hatched out the plan of matching the Harvard Freshmen against the same number of young women proof-readers in newspaper and publishing offices of Cambridge and Boston.

I welcomed this plan cordially, as I had always been particularly good at spelling. Indeed, in the public school near Aurora there was no boy who could outspell me and only one girl: the blonde, bright and beautiful Emma Hovenden.

To enliven the match in the Boston Music Hall I went to the trombone player of the Pierian Sodality and said: "Take your instrument and get a seat in the gallery. Then, whenever one of us fellows misses and has to retire to the background let off a blast as if you were trying to overthrow the Walls of Jericho."

On the evening of the contest my classmates all seemed
to have stage fever. N6 one wanted to occupy first place.
I had told some of them that I was a good speller, and as
I had boldly played in public, they argued that I ought
to play first fiddle on this occasion. Accepting the honor I
walked boldly to the first chair on our side nearest the
audience and the man who gave out the words to be
spelled.

The devil must have prompted him to choose for the
first word ACOLYTE. A church word! The curse of
my skepticism began to show itself: I spelled it incor-
rectly: acholyte!

As I walked to the back-ground I dreaded that trombone blast, which would add to my humiliation. But the
trombonist kept silent; he felt sorry for me. He let out
a blast for the next Freshman who missed, and the next
and the next. Then he subsided because the audience,
which had first laughed at the brazen prank, began to hiss.

What annoyed me most of all was that for fully half an
hour not one other word was submitted which I could not
have spelled. I was still one of the best spellers in college;
but my reputation as such was gone forever.

Another occasion when the joke was on me was staged
in the class-room of Mr. Seaver, professor of mathematics.
One day I was one of several students standing before the
huge blackboard chalking out problems in algebra. Mine
was easy and I soon finished it. Then, to while away time,
I absent-mindedly drew a foaming glass of beer on the
blackboard and forgot to rub it out again. When it was
discovered, the class let out a joyous laugh, wondering
what the professor would do. I also wondered.

Professor Seaver was witty as well as good natured.
As if it were part of the regular lesson, he said to me:
"Suppose the diameter of that glass were three inches

and its height six inches, how many cubic inches of beer
would there be in it?" And I had to go back to the blackboard and figure it out, while the other students left.

We used to have enjoyable class dinners, with speeches
and song; nor was the eating a side show. I have before
me a menu of a '76 dinner, dated March 13, 1874, which
includes oysters, on the half-shell and fried, roast venison
and turkey, chicken salad, prairie chicken and blue-bill
widgeon. To-day, only millionaires could command some
of these luxuries. Do the world really move after all?

WRITING FOR COLLEGE PAPERS

The American student seems to be a born journalist.
Every college visible with the naked eyes has its own
paper, and some have more than one. Harvard, in my
time, had three. I found the ancient and honorable *Advocate* already nearly a decade old. Then came the *Crimson,* which had its name changed to *Magenta* because
another college claimed chromatic priority; and soon there
also appeared on deck a comic weekly, *The Lampoon.* All
these were written, edited and illustrated by students for
students. Nobody got any money for his share of the
work; it was all done just for fun.

My San Francisco friend, A. A. Wheeler (who won,
with me, advanced standing in the classics), was one of
the editors of the *Advocate* and I was in regular correspondence with him during vacation. In the autumn of
1874 (our Junior year) he wrote me: "I have just laughed
so over your letter giving an account of your vacation
that I could hardly see to read it." (I wish I had that
letter!) "If an angel," he continues, "should carry me
through the blue heights above and give me a glance at
heaven, I do not think that I would feel a keener thrill

of delight than that which the receipt of your letter and
one from Barrows this evening has given me. The longer
I am away from Harvard, the more the place and all connected with it are endeared to me. I don't know how to
think of separation at graduation."

"Will you write something," he continues, "for my
Advocate Nov. 27th? I should like particularly to have
something from you. Be funny or esthetical. You are
a worthy follower of the laughing philosopher, and yet I
should be satisfied with anything like your article on
'Music'."

It is needless to say that I preserved my articles that
were printed in the college papers; they were the first
things of mine to appear in type. Looking them over I
find that Wheeler had correctly sized me up; most of my
papers were either funny (or attempts to be funny) or
on esthetic subjects; that is, beauty in girls, music, or
nature.

Some of them were not particularly good, even for a
youth of twenty. I remember one, in particular. "Root,
Hog, or Die," which I didn't think much of; I hoped
others might like it better, so I asked Wheeler what he
thought of it. As it had appeared in the other paper and
was not signed, he did not know who had written it. His
answer was "Isn't it silly." I never told him I was the
perpetrator.

My Failure As A Book Agent

Although cordially invited to return to St. Louis the
following summer, I yielded to a horticultural impulse
and went to Rochester, New York. Why Rochester?
Because that was the place where James Vick raised the
flower-seeds which had so delighted me in my Oregon

garden. "What a glorious sight it must be," I said to myself, "to see whole acres of these flowers in full bloom."

It certainly was a glorious sight; I enjoyed it very much. And then I woke up from my pleasure-dream and asked myself what I was going to do for a living. A rather serious matter.

Why not teach music? I had my 'cello with me and I could play the piano; but my ignorance of matters practical was simply scandalous. I went to a music store, thinking I could there find jobs a-plenty waiting for me. One of the clerks asked me to play a piece on the piano and took my address; but of course I never heard from him; summer is the closed season for music lessons, anyway.

Waiting for the answer which never came I found a cheap boarding-house where, by sharing a bed with another man, I could get lodging and meals for $5 a week. The meals were not so bad, but the man I had to room with belonged to the proletariat, just above the tramp level. My aristocratic mind was paralyzed with disgust, but I tried to grin and bear it; I had no money to pay for better surroundings. I even tried to make a good impression on these men by playing for them; but, good gracious! The simple melodies I played were not vulgar enough for their comprehension and enjoyment. They told me plainly that they did not consider such stuff music, and then listened rapturously to an Irish boy playing hornpipes and cheap dances on his fiddle, horribly out of tune.

It was "Wild and Woolly Oregon" all over again!

One of these men, in whom I had confided, advised me to become a book agent and gave me an address. "Glad to have you work for us," said the man I went to, and gave me a set of books—lives of famous men—with directions as to what to do. "Try to get at the mothers and persuade them that if they will buy these books their boys will learn how to become famous, too."

The first day I landed one fish—not a mother but a young college man, recently married. When I told him I was a Harvard student trying to earn my living, he put his name down for a set, although I heard his wife whisper to him pathetically that now they would not be able to get "that set of Dickens."

At another house, after being admitted, I walked down a large hall when an elderly lady came rushing toward me, her arms outstretched ready to embrace me. She was near-sighted and thought I was her son returning unexpectedly. She did not embrace me; nor did she subscribe.

Glimpses of life like these made book-canvassing rather interesting; but my subscription list did not grow fast enough and after a week or ten days I decided to quit. The man who had engaged me was quite angry when I told him. "You have no grit, no perseverance," he declared; "you will never amount to anything in this world. I had intended to send you to Buffalo next week."

Climbing Mount Washington

I have not explained why I was so painfully short of cash when I got to Rochester. It was because I had spent what little money I had saved for this vacation in making my first trip to the White Mountains.

I got off at Gorham which is not far from the foot of Mount Washington. My plan was to climb the 6,300 feet to its summit, and I did.

The fifty pages of my diary describing this exploit are so full of animal spirits and juvenile enjoyment that I wish I could quote them all.

Looking over these diary pages I am pleased to see that the absence of such snowy climaxes as Hood and

Adams and St. Helens, which make the Cascade mountain scenery in Oregon so thrilling, did not prevent me from thoroughly enjoying the sights on my walk of eight miles (including a climb of six thousand feet) up Mount Washington and on top.

For the first time in my life I saw a rain-storm with lightning *below* me. A little later the rain came up and gave the summit a thorough drenching. "How the wind blows and the house shakes," I kept repeating in my diary. It was not safe to go behind the hotel; the wind there was strong enough to blow a man away. I was told that it sometimes blows here at the rate of a hundred miles an hour.

The hotel charged $6 for a room and three meals, a high price for those days. I saved $1.50 by getting up at five and leaving before breakfast, making my meal on wild strawberries later on. When I left the hotel the wind was still blowing furiously. I could hardly walk against it. It blew the heavy mist down my neck, into my nose, eyes, ears—I might as well have been in a drenching rain.

After I reached the second milestone the mist began to shape itself gradually into white clouds, wildly chasing each other in all directions—a sublime scene.

For the first time I was right among the clouds; for the first time I had the thrilling experience—so often repeated in later years in Switzerland—of suddenly seeing, through rifts in the clouds, the mountains and valleys below; for the first time I saw the somber cloud shadows creep or sweep along the mountain sides like huge mountains of queer shapes.

That day I walked seventeen miles, then took train for Montreal and Rochester and that five-dollar-a-week boarding house! If ever there was a drop from the sublime to the ridiculous, here it was!

WOODBERRY AND I

My Mount Washington walk had given me such a glorious impression of New Hampshire that I was glad when an opportunity came to spend the next summer in the same state.

On the third of June 1875, I got a letter saying: "I have just written Harry a long letter detailing a plan for spending our summer together; get him to read it to you and send me *immediate* word about your views about it. The cost I hope will not be above your power—about $60-$75 for the season, I think; that's the highest figure estimated. Affectionately, NED."

Ned stood for George Edward Woodberry, who in later years won international fame as poet, literary critic, and artist in prose, his pages on Taormina and Northern Africa being uniquely interesting.* With Alfred and Harold Wheeler ('77), Charles F. Thwing, John B. Olmsted, Thomas L. Talbot, Wadsworth Longfellow, Charles Henry Barrows, George Miller Cumming, and Stephen H. Jecko, he formed a group of my most intimate college friends of the class of '76.

His plan for the summer was to go to a farm-house near Moosilauke for two months. The Wheelers were to be of the party but they decided to go home to San Francisco, so Woodberry and I went alone.

During our vacation in New Hampshire we spent much time talking about philosophy and playing croquet, in which we soon became so expert that, to make the game more difficult, we chose the most uneven spots we could find and allowed cheating, if it could be done without detection.

Our most interesting experience was a night spent on

---

* His critical and miscellaneous writings have been issued in a six-volume collection. This does not include his biographies of Emerson, Poe, and Hawthorne, in all five vols., or his "North Africa," or his three vols. of poems.

Moosilauke.   The farmer we boarded with drove us to
the foot of the mountain in the afternoon and we
walked up.

The weather had been fine for weeks.   We made no
allowance for the fact that it might change overnight, and
took along no overcoats.   While we were climbing Moosilauke, clouds overspread the sky and as we neared the
summit a fierce gust of wind carried my straw hat out of
sight.   It was bitterly cold when we hurried into the ruins
of what was once a hotel.   Fortunately there was a stove,
but we searched in vain for fuel, till it occurred to us that
we might burn up the floor.

By jumping on the boards we managed to reduce them
to the proper size.   Ned was a smoker, so we had matches.
Soon we had a roaring fire and there we sat all night hug-
ging the stove, looking for all the world like medieval
witches, particularly I, with a red silk handkerchief tied
round my head.

As I jot down this reminiscence I have before me a
pile of letters signed "Ned," more than three dozen in
number, the first dated November 25, 1874, the last
November 27, 1881.   The small script makes them difficult to read.   Woodberry's brother is reported to have
said: "Whenever I get a letter from Ned I take a micro-
scope and a dictionary to read it."   The "dictionary" is a
slander because Woodberry was too great a master of
style ever to use a long word when a short one would serve
as well.

Some of these letters are eight and even twelve pages
long.   They are heart-documents for the most part, revelations of an exceptionally keen mind, strong character,
and warm friend.   They are too *intime* for print and
when I returned them to him he wrote that he had decided
to burn them.

In my letters, which were no less voluminous than his,

I made no secret of my reciprocal affection for him, or my admiration for his rare mental qualities. With characteristic modesty he always parried my compliments. Let me cite an example: "And what can you mean by saying you confess owing much to me for my pointed questionings and clear head? Did I ever ask a question which was not a sneer or a sarcasm or did I ever have a clear head! Poor head of mine; it's been traitorous enough to me, and can it have been true to anyone else? Be sure, Heinrich, you would have found many another as helpful and more faithful than I ever was; it is in you to philosophize, and what is in the plant will blossom under any gardener."

Maybe; but much does depend on the gardener. There is no doubt that my daily discussions with Woodberry were of incalculable value to me because his keen, searching questions curbed my tendency to being swept into premature conclusions by emotional impulses. "I can see what progress you have made this year in accurate and deep thinking," he writes in one of his letters. And in 1881 he paid me a compliment which warmed the cockles of my heart, coming from such a master and judge of style as he was: "You seem to have got the mastery of literary style for all purposes; indeed, I have looked on your success in writing as marvellous and far exceeding anything that would have been anticipated from your Teutonic collegehood in the old days of *Advocate,* theses, and *Crimsons.*"

In return for benefits received from Ned I feel proud to know that I had some influence on him. "I have come very near to your natural views of life," he wrote on January 30, '75. "I suppose you will outstrip me soon in your philosophical studies, you are so admirably equipped with French and German, and have so undivided a love for philosophy. I am going to make the most of your friendship while we still stand on a level and so I beg for full and frequent letters." "Send me your intentions about electives next year as I will try to make some of your courses mine if possible; most of them will correspond with Harry's I suppose, but so far as you can and I can I want to keep up some community of studies with you."

In one respect Ned and I differed widely. He could not be happy unless he had a friend with him; whereas, as he writes, "your walks by the Hudson, and your excursions, are in your manner, the style purely Finckian,— no one else I know could be content with such seclusion in pleasure; but doubtless the other pole of pleasure gets due attention and the Brazilian blood atones for the severe and solitary afternoons. Professor Emerson was surprized to hear you talk of the light in woman's eyes at a certain moment of excitement; he said you spoke 'like a married man'—do you reveal yourself this way at random to every chance-comer?"

OLMSTED'S AMUSING REMINISCENCES

Two of my closest friends in the Harvard years were Charles F. Thwing, one of the great "men from Maine," and the equally big-hearted and always companionable John B. Olmsted of LeRoy and Buffalo, in whose hospitable home I spent so many happy weeks during and after college years. To Olmsted I am indebted for the following vivid reminiscences of our Cambridge experiences:

"You have doubtless written of Jecko, our talented but reckless friend. I do not imagine he ever improved his natural talent. What I remember most vividly was his ability to play the piano, smoke his pipe, sing and swear

at the chorus all at one time. Dawes was not in it with
him as a professor of profanity.

"I suppose that the most remarkable thing that occurred
while we were in college was the meeting of the class of
1876 while they were freshmen and passing a resolution
that hazing ought to be abolished at Harvard! For the
freshman class to take such action as that was so unheard
of that it was telegraphed all over the country and many
paragraphers got a lot out of it.

"Another thing that occurred which I remember was
the painting on University Hall in letters some four or
five feet high daubed on with black paint or tar the words
'This University Is Going To Hell.' You will recall that
after many attempts to scrub it off the granite walls of
the hall, the letters still came out whenever it was a wet
day. A great effort was made to discover the perpetrators
but I do not know if they ever were found.

"Another thing that seems to me worth mentioning is
the fact that when we were in college, there was not a
bathroom in any of the college dormitories—at least none
inside the yard. In Matthews Hall, which was new in
1872, there was some provision made for taking a bath,
but the facilities were located in the cellar in which there
was no heat whatever and you could only get cold water
to run into the tub. You can imagine that not many took
this invitation to go to the Bad. I do not think any other
building had any kind of facilities except possibly Weld
Hall.

"You will recall that our class went into Memorial Hall
as a dining-room in the fall of 1874. It was opened then
for the first time. Were you present at the last supper
in old Thayer Commons in June 1874? If you recall that
occasion, you will remember the terrific bread fight which
took place then and how all the waitresses ran shrieking
out of the room when the boys began to throw teacups

and even plates. I remember closing the eye of an opponent with about two pounds of butter which I picked from a plate in front of me."

THE CENTENNIAL CLASS

College Classes were smaller half a century ago than they are now. The class of 1876, known as the Centennial Class, contained only 143 members besides 58 temporary members, as I gather from the Class Report of 1916 issued by the class secretary Emor Herbert Harding, whom, by the way I got to know more intimately in Berlin in 1879 than I did before in Cambridge. He declares that I introduced him to many quaint dishes in Berlin; so I have not lived in vain.

In spite of the fact that Brother Thwing, when I informed him that I had done 40,000 words of these Memoirs in less than three months, wrote back: "I might call it the *auto*-biography because it is going so fast"—in spite of this, I say, his place in the '76 Hall of Fame is secure. So is that of Woodberry, and that of Barrett Wendell, Harvard professor and literary authority; of Percival Lowell, who earned world-fame by building the great observatory at Flagstaff, Arizona, and becoming the chief explorer of the planet Mars; of Frederick Jessup Stimson, American Minister at Buenos Aires, much-read novelist, legal expert, and author as well as practitioner in the Supreme Court of the United States; and of William Henry Moody, of the Supreme Court.

Less widely known, but important and influential members of their respective communities, were John B. Olmsted, appointed Public Service Commissioner by Governor Hughes in 1908; Charles Henry Barrows, Lafayette Hoyt De Friese, Egbert Henry Grandin, Thomas Lincoln Talbot, E. M. Wheelwright, Theodore Chickering

Williams, Wadsworth Longfellow, Francis Lewis Wellman and a dozen others—not a bad record, I think, for a class of 143 men.

Wellman, by the way, is the most married man of '76; dates of his weddings: 1879, 1891, 1895, 1912, 1920; while John Olmsted probably has beaten all records by sending to Harvard six sons, who graduated in 1902, 1903, 1905, 1908, 1909, 1913.

PART IV

LISTENING, LOAFING AND STUDYING IN EUROPE

LISTENING, LOAFING AND STUDYING IN EUROPE

OFF FOR BAYREUTH

MY FOUR years at Harvard had been a severe drain on my father's purse in spite of the fact that my high examination marks had enabled me to get every year a Scholarship of three or four hundred dollars. Anxious to continue my philosophical studies abroad I had applied for a Parker Fellowship, value $1,000 a year for three years. I failed to get it. To add insult to injury, my father wrote me that now I would have to earn my own living. Can you beat it?

I beat it! There was something of infinitely more importance to me than making vulgar money to pay for my room and board. The first Wagner Festival at Bayreuth beckoned me irresistibly.

Richard Wagner's great life-work, which raised the whole art of music to a higher level, was, in 1876, almost completed. Of all his master-works only "Parsifal" remained to be written. Yet the world had been monstrously slow in waking up to a realization of his colossal achievements. In America, one only of his operas, "Lohengrin," was fairly well known. But I had heard the big orchestras play, in Boston, excerpts from the other works and I had studied the scores. As a result, I was a storage battery of enthusiasm. The impending Bayreuth Festival was to make known the four great dramas of the Nibelung's Ring: "Rheingold," "Walküre," "Siegfried" and "Götterdämmerung," on which Wagner had spent a quarter of a century. It was to be beyond all comparison the most important event in the whole history of music. Could I miss that? Of course not. But how get across the ocean?

Well, there was my kind, adorable uncle Conrad in St. Louis. A line to him, and the return mail brought the $500 I had asked him to lend me. Lend, I say. I would, I felt sure, soon be able to repay it by writing newspaper and magazine articles. John Fiske, who was then writing for the New York *World,* got its editor to engage me for a series of articles on the Bayreuth Festival, and W. D. Howells told me he would welcome one for the *Atlantic Monthly.*

The Centennial Celebration of American Independence was on in Philadelphia. Biggest thing of its kind ever; but to me it was a mere side-show. I was eager to get to Bayreuth as soon as possible. With several other Harvard graduates and students I engaged passage for Havre and Paris on a French steamer. None of us were rolling in wealth. We did not relish the idea of going in the proletarian steerage mingling with the "great unwashed"; but there was something intermediate between that and second cabin, which we chose; and, being Harvard students, we were allowed the freedom of the decks belonging to second-cabin passengers.

Our meals were funny. With some French passengers we sat at a round table, each of us supplied with a chunk of bread and a big spoon. This we plunged into a huge steaming appetizing bowl of meat and vegetable stew in the center of the table. Those who could eat fastest got the most. The stew was excellent, redolent of the French culinary skill, and if we had had any scruples about eating in this communistic way they would have been swept away by the huge appetite the salt air gave us.

Not all of us traveled this primitive way. My class-mate Philip Belknap Marcou, of French descent and wealthy, was in the first cabin. Knowing my epicurean longings, he stuffed his pockets daily with nuts and raisins and other good things from his table and transferred them to me.

It was not the first time he had come to my rescue. There had been a fire in Hollis Hall. A classmate had kicked open my door and rescued my precious violoncello and other things. The hall was not destroyed; but till it was put into order again, which took some months, dear Marcou took me into his room in Matthews Hall. Subse-quently Marcou became professor of Romance Languages at Harvard.

Among the passengers was a girl—an actress—of ravishing beauty, with the flashing black eyes and general brunette type I admired so much. She could not help seeing how I simply devoured her with my eyes. Now, I could read French almost as readily as English but had had absolutely no practise in speaking it. So when she said something to me, I replied that I did not speak French. "Oh no!" she laughed, "vous parlez comme un Parisien." Gaining courage, I had a chat with her every day, she coming over to the second-cabin deck to see me.

How I ever reached that out-of-the-way Bavarian town, Bayreuth buried in the Franconian mountains, I don't remember. But there I was one day, several weeks ahead of the public performances. The rehearsals were in full blast. Why should I not attend those too? Alas, I found that no one was admitted to them. I sneaked round the curved corridors and applied my ears to the key-holes. I heard ravishing new harmonies and tone colors that thrilled me to the marrow. But an attendant discovered me and ordered me out. "Nobody allowed in here," he said.

I replied that I did not see why these precious sounds

should go to waste and added that I had paid 900 marks to hear the performances, so I surely ought to be favored.

He took off his hat, bowed politely and said: "I am extremely sorry, Sir, but I have strict orders to make no exceptions."

Yes, dear reader, I *had* paid nine hundred gold marks, or $225 in American money, for tickets! That was nearly half of what my uncle had lent me and I hadn't the faintest idea what would become of me when the rest was spent. I ought to have been satisfied, surely with hearing two performances each of "Rheingold," "Walküre," "Siegfried" and "Götterdämmerung"; but in my reckless enthusiasm I had bought three "Patronatsscheine", covering all twelve of the performances! Evidence that I had first claim on the Nobel Prize for unmitigated foolishness!

How I Met Wagner

The next morning I was standing in front of the opera house when I saw Wagner himself approaching, arm in arm with Wilhelmj, the Fritz Kreisler of his day, who had consented to be concertmaster in the Nibelung orchestra.

"Why not ask the Meister himself for permission to attend the rehearsals?" I said to myself.

A moment later I was before the two great men, took off my straw hat and told Wagner that I had come all the way from America to write up the festival for the New York *World* and the *Atlantic Monthly,* and that I would be very happy if I could attend the rehearsals.

A cloud passed across his face. "The newspapers have treated me shamefully," he said. "I need no critics here."

"But I am not a critic," I protested, "only a young man of twenty-two who has come simply to describe the new works."

That placated him. "Very well," he said, "have you a Patronatsschein?"

"Three!" I answered proudly.

"I had made up my mind," he said, "to admit no one to the rehearsals, not even Liszt. But he has gone in and I have admitted a few others, so you might as well come too."

He then asked me for my card and told me I would get in if I gave my name to the door-keeper. I did so, and had the time of my life watching the great master superintending every detail of the performance. He had a special little bridge by means of which he could pass from the stage to the auditorium and back any moment. He would sit near us looking and listening, his face expressing a hundred successive emotions. Then he would rush onto the stage to show a singer how to pose or to phrase. The next moment he would look down into the orchestral abyss and beg the players: "Not quite so loud, please. Remember that the singers come first."

It was a wonderful experience for me thus to be in the very workshop of the greatest operatic genius the world has ever known. This Bayreuth Festival was surely the beginning of the Golden Age of Music.

The next morning, as I entered the theatre, Wagner saw me, came and shook hands and asked me if I had got in. I thanked him profusely. How could he thus remember the American youth among all the thousands of persons and things he had to attend to?

A few days later I heard that Liszt, having attended some of the rehearsals, was going away, to return for the performances. I promptly went to the railway station. There was Liszt, inside his compartment, talking through the window to Wagner. I was standing on the platform when Wagner suddenly saw me and walked toward me. For some inexplicable reason I felt as if my presence was an impertinent intrusion,—like eavesdropping. And so I turned and walked away. When I stopped, Wagner had gone back to Liszt.

Now Wagner, with all his temperamental outbursts of wrath (for which there was always a good reason) was an extremely kind-hearted man. There can be no doubt whatever that he wanted to take me and introduce me to Liszt. What a sublime moment that would have been in my life! My idiotic bashfulness thwarted his kind intention. Again I deserved that Nobel Prize! The incident was the more provoking because it was for Wagner and Liszt that I did the most ardent and persistent missionary work during my forty-three years in New York. Could they have foreseen it all—it makes me dizzy to think what they might have done to make me happy at Bayreuth.

Life in Bayreuth was a unique affair during the festival. The town of 20,000 souls was quite unprepared to take care of such an invasion of musicians and listeners. Most of us had to seek rooms in private houses and fight for our meals at the restaurants. Foremost among these was Angermann's. His tables were occupied long before mealtime, while outside were world-famed singers and players and composers sitting on kegs and boxes, glad to get a sandwich and a glass of beer.

With me was my Harvard classmate, A. A. Wheeler, who had secured the job of writing up the festival for the New York *Nation*. He had bought tickets for one cycle only, but became so enthusiastic that he decided to stay for another. I saw my chance. I had had time to think about my folly in spending nearly all I had on tickets, so I sold him mine for the second cycle. While this cycle was going on I rambled in the woods, suffering agonies at the thought of what I was missing.

On the "Siegfried" day—the day I had enjoyed most before—I walked up the hill to the theatre just when the

first act was over. A man was coming down hastily. He
had a return check in his hand. "I will give you this,"
he said, "if you will tell me where I can get the best beer
in town."

"Angermann's!" I shouted, and eagerly grabbed the
ticket.

It must be said in extenuation of this man's conduct
that Angermann served Munich beer. And Munich beer
was as wonderful in its way as Wagner's music.

One of the most remarkable things about this Bayreuth
Festival was that its first two performances were attended
by the old Kaiser Wilhelm. This was certainly a great
triumph for a composer who had been banished for over
a decade from Germany (and would have been shot if
caught) for participating in the revolutionary uprising
of 1848.

After the first act of the "Walküre" I saw the aged
Kaiser on the balcony bowing in response to the cheers
of the populace. The King of Bavaria was there, too,
and Dom Pedro, Emperor of Brazil.

A great magician was Wagner! In England, many
years previously, it was Queen Victoria who came out
ostentatiously in favor of this revolutionist when the
audiences at his concerts were lukewarm and the press
bitterly hostile.

The outrageously virulent and unjust accounts in the
German press of the first Bayreuth Festival aroused my
wrath in the highest degree. I then and there swore
revenge. When subsequently, I wrote my two-volume
works on Wagner's life and operas I got even with these
critics by citing their 1876 verdicts, which most of them
by that time had come to regret bitterly. It is to the second volume of that work that I must refer readers of
these pages who may wish to know what impression the

Nibelung operas made on my juvenile mind at the first Bayreuth Festival.

MUNICH, BEER, AND MUSIC

It was not in vain that I had taken Highest Honors in Philosophy at Harvard. It made me wondrous wise— like the man who jumped into a bramble-bush and scratched out both his eyes. Having recovered $75 of the $225 I had recklessly paid for Bayreuth tickets, I sagely decided to blow that sum in by remaining for a year in Europe.

That is *not*, if you please, *quite* as funny as it looks. Living in Germany half a century ago was absurdly cheap from the American point of view. Not so cheap, to be sure, as in 1923, when, on account of the currency inflation, my friend Humiston went overnight from Dresden to Munich, first class, and paid the equivalent of sixty-five cents in our money!

The cheapest German city to live in was Munich and to Munich I would have gone anyway because it was the headquarters of Wagnerian opera, to me the most important thing in the universe. And I found no special difficulty in making ends meet.

One of my favorite eating places was the Pschorr brewery. There I could feast sumptuously on soup, chicken, potatoes, salad, cheese, and a mug of the best beer, all for about a quarter of a dollar. I wonder if, on these occasions, I ever saw a boy of twelve whose biography I was destined to write forty years later. His name was Richard Strauss, and he was a member of the Pschorr family, living above the restaurant I frequented.

A room could be had in those days in Munich for half-a-dollar a day even in a small hotel, while in a private house—well just read this statement based on personal experience, which I made in one of the newspaper articles on life in Munich that I wrote for New York and Chicago journals: "You can get a nicely furnished room near the center of the city, up one or two flights of stairs, for five to seven dollars a *month* including care of same. For service (brushing your clothes and blacking your boots every morning, with occasional errands) you pay *forty cents a month* extra."

So you see that the $75 I saved in Bayreuth was enough to pay for a whole year's lodging and service in Munich! But I needed even less than that because I happened to get acquainted with a wealthy young American who had intended to remain in Munich but had found the winter climate too damp and chilly and so had decided to go to Italy. He had secured an elegant suite of rooms on the aristocratic Maximiliansstrasse, near the Royal Opera for the tip-top price of $15 a month.

When he decided to leave he found that the landlord stubbornly refused to release him from his contract. As my friend knew hardly any German he asked me to come up in the morning and "argufy" the matter with the owner of the rooms.

When I arrived, an astonishing sight presented itself to my eyes. The room was hot as a furnace and there lay the American,—on his easy chair, between four open windows, violently fanning himself. And well he might, for his six-foot porcelain stove was red hot and gave out heat enough to supply a small inferno.

Seeing my look of astonishment, he laughed and said: "You see, I had just bought eight marks' worth of fuel to last me a few months; but now that I am to lose my sixty marks I don't want to make a present to the landlord of that wood too. So I have decided to keep that stove busy day and night till the wood is all burned up."

After a moment's pause, he suddenly exclaimed. "This

is great! I see a way of getting even with the landlord!
I'll sublet the rooms to you and throw in the wood, all for
one mark, which I'll return to you if you think it's too
much."

And thus I lived in one of the most sumptuous suites
in Munich for forty cents a month—for service. To be
perfectly accurate I made it forty-eight cents (two marks)
allowing for the aristocratic surroundings. *Noblesse ob-
lige.*

There was a reverse side to the agreeable cheapness of
things in Munich, as I discovered when I decided to give
lessons in English. In response to an advertisement I
got a letter from a well-to-do Hebrew who had been in
America. He and his wife spoke English well and he
wanted me to take in hand their three boys.

"What are your terms?" he asked. I replied that I
didn't know what it was customary to pay for lessons.

"There is a young lady who comes here to teach my
boys French. She gets eighty pfennige a lesson. Would
that be satisfactory to you?" he asked.

Now, eighty pfennige was twenty cents in American
money. I had expected at least ten times as much. But
as the young lady was satisfied with twenty cents, could I
be so ungallant as to intimate I considered myself as
worth so much more than she? At any rate, I said "yes."

The Hebrew looked pleased, as well he might, and
gratefully he got me some more pupils on the same terms.

Like most tourists I fancied, when I went to Munich
that it was a sort of German Venice having, in place of
streets, canals filled, not with sea water but with foaming
beer on which the natives steered about on gondolas drawn
by swans with long sausage necks, while the futurist musicians of the Wagner-mad Ludwig II played "Lohengrin"
from the roofs of the tallest houses on both sides of the
canals.

It wasn't quite like that, but almost. Beer certainly did flow in streams and Gambrinus was the god worshipped most fervently. There is a legend, which might be true, about a native of that city to whom a fairy granted three wishes. His first was for "a thousand barrels of beer;" the second, for "all the beer in the world;" the third— after a long pause—"another barrel of beer."

The best beer was brewed at the Hofbräuhaus; it was, as the name indicates, directly connected with the court, under the King's personal supervision. But there were other first class breweries—the Franziskauer, Spaten, Augustiner, Pschorr, etc.; some connoisseurs preferred their product to the royal beer.

As an observer of gastronomic phenomena I was particularly amused to note how suddenly all the beer connoisseurs of the city found it out when one of these breweries had a particularly fine "vintage." Its halls were crowded to suffocation till every drop of the "precious wet" had been consumed, whereupon the worshipers of Gambrinus moved on to the brewery which had the next best vintage. The Hofbräu was always at its best.

The medievalism of German "Kultur" half a century ago (and it was just the same the last time I visited Munich, in 1912), was distressingly exemplified in the beer-halls, large and small. No ventilation was provided for, and the pestiferous air was dense with suffocating smoke (one-cent cigars).

There they sat, emptying one quart mug after another, and now and then it happened that, to emphasize an argument on politics, religion, or Wagner, a mug was hurled at another man's head. I often saw cases of this kind reported in the police-court columns of the local newspapers.

The beer mania reached its mad climax when the Salvator was ripe. The Salvator was even more *süffig* (making one want more and more) than the Hofbräu. It was also much more heady, more intoxicating, owing to the prunes used in brewing it.

For daily use the Hofbräuhaus was good enough for me. Though a royal concern and only a minute's walk from the King's Palace it was a dingy old building, thoroughly medieval in appearance; but for an economical and appetizing supper I knew no better place to go to. On the way to the brewery I stopped to buy a chunk of the deliciously flavorsome all-rye bread (so cheap that it was fed to the horses—lucky beasts!), a little cheese, and a knackwurst, or sausage.

These things I washed down with a mug of the best beer in the world. But being a genuine epicure, I didn't want much, provided it *was* the best. Half a quart of this beer would have satisfied my American thirst, but there were no half measures in the Hofbräuhaus. And you had to find your own mug and wash it at the fountain. Having carefully noted the number on the metal lid, you joined the line and placed your mug on the counter. It was grabbed by the handle with five or six others, by one of the servers, who held each of the mugs under the spigot a second and then slammed them all on the counter where you had to grab yours p.d.q. or run the chance of some one else getting it.

It was great sport and ever so romantic. No wonder the Hofbräuhaus became so overcrowded that, some years later, it had to be rebuilt on a very much larger scale. But the romance and medievalism were gone, the beer being served at your table by waitresses, as in ordinary restaurants.

I often astonished the natives by paying more for my food than for my drink. "You eat an expensive meal!" one of them said to me one evening.

The joke of it was that he had spent just as much as I,

only his money went chiefly for beer. A Bavarian labor-
ing man who had sixty pfennige (15 cents) for his meal
gave 45 of them for beer and the remaining 15 for bread
and a few slices of sausage.

One evening I had enjoyed a lamb kidney, cooked to
perfection—The Munich cuisine was always savory,
though rather bourgeois. Leaving the fat on my plate, I
pushed it away a little and used the edge for my cigarette
ashes.

Opposite me sat a pot-bellied man whose eyes seemed
to be hypnotized by that kidney fat. He looked at it and
at me in turn and finally asked: "Aren't you going to
eat that?"

When I said no "Then may I have it?" he asked eagerly.
I shoved him the plate, ashes and all, and the fat disappeared in a jiffy.

"You don't drink much beer," he then said. "Don't
you like it?"

"Very much, indeed," I replied, "but a half-liter mug
is all I care for."

"I take it you are a foreigner," he ventured.

"An American," I answered.

"Indeed! May I ask if you have any beer in America?"

"We do. Our Milwaukee beer is not bad, nor is that
from St. Louis. But no American beer is half as good
as yours is."

"Nor will it ever be!" he declared categorically.

"How are you going to prove that?"

"Easily," he answered. "Good beer can be brewed only
with water that is sweet, soft and clear, such as we have
here. America lies so near the ocean that you cannot have
any water free from salt."

Next in importance to beer, in Munich, was music.

All the standard operas were given in King Ludwig's
opera house, better, on the whole, than anywhere else. I

never dreamt, in those days, that I would ever be a professional music critic; yet had I plotted and planned to be one, I could not have been more favorably placed for preparing myself for that post. During my winter in Munich I heard most of the great operas, Italian and French as well as German, over and over again, to my great benefit as well as joy.

A happy thought enabled me to do this. With my slender purse I could not have heard all these operas, so I took my *World* articles on the Bayreuth festival, showed them to the manager of the Opera and asked if I could not have a ticket occasionally as correspondent for American papers.

The manager was more than willing. "Just leave your card at the box office the day before you wish to attend, and a seat will be reserved for you," he said.

Thus began my career as an operatic dead-head.

There were also concerts galore, while the King's wonderful military band played in the open every fine day. There was music in all the beer gardens and halls—in short, I was immersed in the musical atmosphere I had so longed for in Oregon. My dreams had come true. I was happy in this atmosphere and I enjoyed the unfettered Bohemian life tremendously.

Before leaving Munich let me call attention to the fact that I owe to it my very existence! When my father had finished his four-years' course of studies as apothecary in Frankfort he went to the Bavarian capital in the hope of opening a shop there. He found there was a law forbidding any but Bavarians from starting business there; so he followed his roving impulse and went to America. Had he remained he would never have met the girl who became my mother. He might have had a son and she might have had a son, but these might have differed as widely from H. T. F. as Lenin differed from Plato.

I Win A Harvard Fellowship

After a year spent at Bayreuth and Munich I began to
pay attention to my father's epistolary exhortations that
it was time for me to look for a life-job. I wouldn't be
likely to find one in Munich, any more than he had; so
I returned to Cambridge, to spend a year there as a resi-
dent graduate, in the hope of winning a Fellowship. The
Harris Fellowship was to be awarded that term. It was
not so big as the Parker which I had applied for in vain
in 1876—barely $600 instead of $1,000; but after my
astonishing experiences in Munich I supposed I could live
on that sum in Berlin, Heidelberg and Vienna "like a
prince," indulging in more pleasure seeking in opera-
houses, concert-halls, restaurants and cafés, and inciden-
tally studying psychology and anthropology.

To be sure I might again fail to get a Fellowship, so
I began to throw out feelers in various directions.

A teachers' agency in New York offered me a chance
to go to Honduras and teach the native boys and girls
English. My love of travel and romance urged me to
take this job; I was particularly eager to renew my in-
fantile (Panama) impression of Central America. I
knew no Spanish, but as most Spanish words are thinly
disguised Latin, I felt sure I could learn all I needed on
the long trip down. But when I found out how unhealthy
the climate of Honduras was for visitors from the North,
I decided to drop this opportunity to die young.

More tempting seemed a call for me as music teacher
in a girls' school in Hillsboro, North Carolina; "salary
$700 and home; nights cool and mosquitoes unknown."

I thought of the pretty girls who would be my pupils.
Though, when I wrote to Ned Woodberry about it, he

sneered back: "'Black-eyed southern girls'—black-skinned ones more likely. You are sure to be disgusted."

No doubt I would have been disgusted to drop from the musical atmosphere of Munich into a village where, as they frankly admitted, there was "a total want of musical culture—the modern school of music is quite unknown."

I don't remember whether I dropped this scheme or whether it dropped me. Their objection was that I was so young and (I had sent my picture) good-looking—dangerous in a girls' school. Heaven knows what might have happened—an elopement, to say the least, in order to get away from the seven hours of daily drudgery.

Among my "feelers" were letters to various universities offering myself as teacher of philosophy. I had splendid testimonials from half-a-dozen leading Harvard professors—but nothing came of these applications. There happened to be no vacancies, and (between ourselves) professors of philosophy are supposed to be more than twenty-two years old.

In Oregon my father was leaving no stone unturned to find a place for me in some college in that State or in California. In the end we might have landed a job, but one day—

Oh! but that was a big day! I went in the afternoon to Dr. McKenzie's church to turn the leaves for Professor Paine who was playing wedding-music on the organ. When the ceremony was over he turned to me and said:

"Well I suppose you are delighted with the news."

"What news?" I asked eagerly.

"Haven't you heard? The Faculty last night awarded you the Harris Fellowship! I made a speech in your behalf; so did Professor Child and Professor Bowen, who predicted you would be an honor to Harvard some day."

This meant three more years of "listening, loafing and studying in Europe!" I was *deee*-lighted.

Everything else was canceled, including college tutoring and lessons in German and on the piano, which had supported me during my resident-graduate year; also an offer to spend the summer playing the bull-fiddle for all-night dancing at one of the big hotels on the Isle of Shoals. How I would have liked that! I was already practising the jumbo fiddle. I haughtily declined, furthermore, the following offer: "Will you go on a trip with an opera troupe, Mr. Carlton's, to St. John for two or three weeks for $25 and pay your board. Your traveling expenses will be paid; board is about six dollars a week. Let me know immediately.

WILL TAYLOR
14 Upton St. Boston."

What impressed me most deeply was the attitude of dear old Professor Bowen. As I have said before, he was extremely orthodox—fanatically so; and he knew that I was a free-thinker, a Darwinist, a believer in exactly the opposite of nearly everything he loved most dearly in philosophy. Yet he stood up for me, pleaded for me, predicted I would be an honor to Harvard. *There* is a *genuine* character for you! Every time I think of Professor Francis Bowen I want to take off my hat and bow reverently.

TWO WINTERS IN BERLIN

Have you ever enjoyed the privilege of browsing in a big library among hundreds of thousands of volumes? To me there is no more delightful thing in the world than thus coming across one precious volume after another—books you had never heard of and never would have, had you not thus met them face to face.

This privilege of browsing in the Harvard Library was

granted to students of scholarly habits, including myself. One day I came across a set of Goethe's works, the first of which contained, in the poet's own writing, a dedication of this set to Harvard, as a gift from the author.

This, I found, was considered one of the greatest honors ever bestowed on the university. I was impressed, too, by the fact that everything German was specially honored in Cambridge. Oregon schoolboys had sometimes called me a "damned Dutchman," but at Harvard my Teutonic descent was quite a feather in my cap; my closest friends began their letters to me with "Dear Heinrich," as the most affectionate thing they could think of. Yet I had deliberately changed my name from Henry Gottlob to Henry Theophilus because I didn't like the German Gottlob.*

On a preceding page I have quoted from a letter written by Professor Norton to me while I was in Munich. He congratulated me on my opportunities for acquiring culture and advised me to study carefully the educational methods in use there.

This exalted opinion of German educational methods was apparently held by all the Harvard professors; modestly they seemed to look on their own teaching as merely a sort of preparation for the exalted knowledge and training to be obtained in Berlin, Leipzig, Jena, Heidelberg, and Munich. And when a Fellowship was bestowed on a student it was assumed that, as a matter of course, he would go to Germany for what music students call "finishing touches."

A Fellowship was good for three years. It would have been interesting to spend one of mine in France, another in Italy or England. But that was not to be thought of. I steered straight for Berlin, where I studied and loafed two winters. The summers I spent, of course, in Heidel-

* Theophilus isn't a correct translation of Gottlob, but it seemed to me near enough.

berg, and the third winter saw me leading a rather wild
life in what Wagner called the "half-Asiatic" city of
Vienna.

To Berlin I went first because it was reputed the foremost university in Germany, as Harvard was in America.
And the Berliners were considered the acme of culture or
at least intelligence, hence it would be a pleasure to associate with them, wouldn't it?

To be sure, I had secret doubts. Heine was my favorite
among German authors and Heine took special delight
in sticking pins and daggers in his delightfully witty way,
into the pretensions and vanities of these Prussians.

Another thing bade me pause. I knew that Schopenhauer, greatest by far of the German philosophers, had
lectured to empty benches at the University of Berlin
while the bombastic word-monger Hegel was so popular
that the students used to climb through the windows into
his hall to make sure of getting seats. Of course these
students did not know what Hegel was talking about,
any more than he himself did. You remember the death-
bed story. "Nobody," lamented Hegel, "has understood
me except X——" After a pause he added sadly, "and
even he didn't."

However, to Berlin I went, in quest of fresh adventures.
I found in order to be accepted as a student at the university one would have to hand in certificates of having passed
the examinations at various and sundry preliminary educational institutions. I wrote a letter to the rector enclosing copies of my Harvard diploma, with reference to
my classical and philosophical honors, and expressing the
hope that this would be satisfactory. And the rector
kindly condescended to accept Harvard as a satisfactory
substitute for German primary schools and gymnasia.

An amusing illustration of the difference between Berlin and Cambridge came to me in the class room of Dr.

Wernicke.   He was a Privatdocent, or candidate for a
professorship, who had announced a course of lectures on
the anatomy of the brain.

The human brain is an amazingly complicated organ—
more so than all the rest of the body put together.   Physiologists were just beginning to study the functions of
different parts of this labyrinthian organ.   Among the
pioneers was Dr. Munck, whose lectures I also attended,
though I felt sorry for the dogs and monkeys he used
for his experiments.   Somebody's Bruno might be among
them.

It was still "darkest Africa" for physiologists.   The
anatomy of the brain, however, could be demonstrated
with cuts and lantern slides by the hundreds.

Nothing happened at Dr. Wernike's first lecture hour.
Only one other student having appeared, he said: "It
is hardly worth while to begin with so small a class.   It
will no doubt be larger next time.   Let us do something
else."

He led the way into a beer hall and ordered a "grosse
Weisse."   That meant a kind of beer (not bad) made of
wheat, I believe, peculiar to Berlin.   It was always served
in huge round glass bowls holding enough for several persons.   We all drank out of the same bowl, each of us carefully keeping his own place on the rim.

This, I supposed, was the professor's treat, but oh no!
When the beer was all gone we threw dice.   I lost, and
paid for the beer.

A huge human brain, fresh from the dissecting table,
was sent for our next lecture.   The doctor patiently explained its structure to us.   But again there were only
two students, and at the next lecture hour I was the only
one.   That ended the course.

Evidently, among all the hundreds of students in the
philosophical department of the University of Berlin I

was the only one who had brains enough to realize the huge importance of studying the brain, the seat of the mind.

Furthermore, I was evidently the only student of philosophy at these headquarters of Teutonic intelligence to whom it had occurred that for a thorough mastery of his subject, nothing could be more helpful and illuminating than the study of psychopathology, or the diseases of the mind. Yet when I asked Professor Zeller, head of the philosophical department, if it were permissible for me to choose this branch as one of the subjects for my degree of Ph. D. he replied under date of October 15, 1880 (in German of course):

"Psychiatry cannot be accepted as a separate department by the side of psychology and philosophy, of which it forms a division. For whatever there is in it that concerns the psychologist—and there can be no doubt that observations on madmen are of great value to him—belongs directly to psychology itself; whereas the rules for the medical treatment of the insane belong in the realm of the medical faculty and cannot be taught in the philosophical faculty."

The venerable professor was dodging. What I wanted was a chance to study mental diseases, and as no opportunity was given for this in the philosophical department, I was anxious to get that opportunity in the medical faculty. But this was denied me, as a help to the doctor's degree. It did not frustrate my plan, however.

"Hang the Ph.D.!" I said to myself. "It is infinitely more important for me to explore the mysteries of the mind than to write 'Doctor of Philosophy' after my name." So I went ahead on my own hook and attended Professor Westphal's lectures at the Charité, or lunatic asylum. They were of particular interest and benefit to me.

Of course, since I had no desire to become a physician

(although that had been my original intention on entering
Harvard), I did not bother about the remedies for mental
maladies; but, on the other hand, I was tremendously
interested in the opportunities to observe the patients, and
in the professor's comments on them.

Every now and then a question of insanity, alleged or
real, comes before the courts. A jury is impaneled, made
up of men who don't know a thing about mental diseases.
They hear the accused man talk quite rationally and con-
clude that he must be sane when in reality he is hope-
lessly insane.

Prof. Westphal showed us a case of this sort. "You
will now meet a man with whom you can talk rationally
as long as you please on any subject. Then see what
happens when I ask him to follow us."

We talked with the man; he seemed as sane as any of
us. Then the professor said to him: "Come down stairs
with us."

"Never!" shrieked the patient. "You know very well,
professor, that I am made of glass and that if I fell on the
stairs I should break into a thousand pieces." Then he
walked away rapidly.

"That fixed idea about his being made of glass," said
the professor, "is the beginning of his mental malady
which will gradually vitiate his whole brain and mind."

On another occasion the dear innocent professor was
seriously embarrassed. Rather unwisely, he asked a
young girl, who had lost her mind through the agony following seduction and abandonment, "Who is the father
of your child?"

"Ah professor!" she answered, winking her left eye and
shaking a finger at him, "you know as well as I do."

To come back to Professor Zeller. I took his course
of lectures on logic but found it so elementary after studying Jevons and John Stuart Mill at Harvard, that I soon

dropped it. The lectures were not up-to-date and were too exclusively Teutonic in their point of view. Not that Zeller was not a scholar. He was—a great one. I had read his wonderfully erudite and yet lucid books on the history of ancient and modern philosophy while I was still at Harvard. I read them again in Berlin—admired them so much that I thought of translating them.

His lectures, however, were, as I have said, too elementary for a Harvard graduate, and the same experience was repeated in the lecture rooms of other professors; so I soon began to "schwänzen" all the lectures, to use the slang of the German students who are much addicted to that practise, knowing that the professors are lenient and do not hesitate to attest to the students' attendance even when aware that the students had not attended.

One of the professors under whom I had hoped to study was Helmholtz. I had read and reread his wonderful, epoch-making books on the sensations of tone and on physiological optics and had hoped to get further light on the senses of hearing and sight at his lectures; unfortunately he had got absorbed in the problems of the higher mathematical physics. I went to one of his lectures and, quoth the raven, "Nevermore." He spent most of his time at the blackboard writing formulas. Some of them he rubbed out and rewrote, so I suppose they were wrong at first. It was a comfort to think that so great a genius and scholar could make mistakes on the blackboard before his big class as I had done at Harvard.

Once I called on him and asked if he was going to bring out a new edition of his book on the eye, the old one being exhausted. He said he would do so as soon as he could find time. In 1925 an English version of the latest edition appeared in three volumes. The Germans are nothing if not thorough.

My attempt to get permission to offer mental pathology

as a branch subject for my promotion as a Doctor of Philosophy having failed, I rashly inquired whether I could choose the English language and literature instead. The answer was that that would be all right.

At first I was pleased, but on thinking the matter over, I got cold feet.   I would be expected, Dr. Zeller wrote me, to know the principal facts in the history of the English language and literature.   Now, while I knew the English language and had read many English books, I had never paid the slightest attention to the *history* of the English language and literature.   Vaguely I realized what that meant.

An American student whose specialty was philology enlightened me on the matter.   When I told him of my "branch subject" he roared with laughter and said:

"My dear young man, do you realize that it would take four or five years of the hardest memory work to pass the Berlin examinations in that subject?   You have no idea of the rigid requirements.   A friend of mine having failed at the examination on English literature to name Richardson's novels in chronological sequence, the professor stopped and said it was no use to go on as he was evidently not sufficiently prepared."

"Look here" my philological friend continued.   "See what I have been doing."

He pointed to the walls of his room, which were plastered with sheets of paper.   On these he had written the changes certain English words had undergone in spelling in the course of several centuries.   "I have to memorize all these," he said.   "From what I know of you I think you would sooner dig stumps or polish boots for a living than thus torture your memory."

I had thought that Harvard had assigned a great deal too much attention to the Memory, the lowest of all mental faculties; but evidently Berlin was infinitely worse.

My plan to try for a Ph.D. was becoming decidedly shaky; but I made one more attempt: Zoology. My Darwinian studies had given me considerable knowledge in that field. So I bought Claus's admirable up-to-date text book and began to "ox." Alas! After a few weeks of this memorizing by the hour, headaches began to torment me day and night. I could not sleep, looked pale as a ghost, lost flesh and appetite, till at last I decided:

"No! The Ph.D. isn't worth that. A mere memory test, anyway. Nor do I need it. If I were to remain in Germany I would of course need a doctor's degree because without it no one can get a position. But in America that is not the case. Nor, if I become an author, will it be of any use to me, since it is not considered in good taste to have a writer's name on the title page followed by an A.B., an A.M., or a Ph.D."

In the meantime, however, I had sent in the required dissertation and was waiting for a verdict on that. I had resolved to withdraw it, when a letter came which made that unnecessary. It asked me to call on the Rector of the University in his home at a certain hour.

He received me very pleasantly and told me he was very sorry but my dissertation had not been accepted as meeting the required conditions.

"Not accepted!" I exclaimed, in such a tone of surprize that the Rector could not help laughing. "But," I added, "articles of mine on philosophical subjects have been printed in leading American periodicals and the great Alfred Russel Wallace accepted one on 'The Development of the Color Sense' which, he wrote me, he found 'excellent' and which was printed in Macmillan's Magazine, London."

"You must not misunderstand me, my American friend," said the Rector, "your dissertation would undoubtedly make an admirable magazine article, but it does not follow the academic lines prescribed. You could re-write it and make it conform to the rules."

He was so polite that I kept my temper, though I felt like exploding and telling him what I thought of his aca-demic red tape. I confess I had paid no attention to the rules, thinking that if I wrote an article presenting an original idea logically and readably, it would be cordially welcomed as proof of a higher mentality than is indicated by mere feats of memorizing. But in so doing I betrayed my igorance of the military rigidity of Prussian academic rules.

After telling the Rector that I had already made up my mind some weeks before to withdraw my application for a Ph.D., partly because of persistent headaches, partly because such a degree was of no special use for an Amer-ican, I carried off my manuscript. In an enlarged form it appeared subsequently in the London *Contemporary Review* under the title of "The Gastronomic Value of Odors," which contains the main thoughts on which I sub-sequently built up two of my books, "Food and Flavor" and "Girth Control."

Among the young Americans I often saw in Berlin, who subsequently became famous, were G. Stanley Hall and Frank Taussig. Hall and I had a common interest in sociological investigations. Taussig had been among my friends at Harvard. In him I record my first case of literary patronage. Knowing that I wrote often for the New York *Nation* he asked permission to refer to me in forwarding for acceptance an article on the Austrian Crisis (1880). The editors were so pleased with this that they printed it as an editorial and Taussig became a regu-lar contributor to what was at that time America's fore-most literary periodical. I had no idea that I would soon be on its editorial staff.

The Berlin Opera was not so good as the Munich Opera,

but there were more good concerts. Among those that
I enjoyed most were those of Bilse and his orchestra.
They were given in a large hall where one could drink and
even eat while listening to the latest symphonies. As a
University student I had to pay only fifteen cents for a
ticket, so I came very often.

Here I first heard and saw the most scholarly of French
composers and one of the most inspired: Saint-Saëns.
"He made," I wrote, "an exceedingly favorable impression on me. He looks just like his compositions, and has
nothing of the long-haired Bohemian air about him. He
is the most graceful conductor I have ever seen. I shall
never forget him standing in the midst of Bilse's enthusiastic players conducting his 'Jeunesse d'Hercule.' He
was very cordially received; his symphonic poems are
great favorites with Bilse's audiences."

Rubinstein was another young genius in his prime
whom I heard at these concerts. He played a piano *concerto* and was applauded tumultuously. But then something happened which made me furious. Half the
audience got up and left, although the second half of the
program was to be a composition by Rubinstein conducted
by himself. It was a gross insult which made me write
a lot of sarcastic remarks about Prussian "Kultur."

Alack and alas! I, too, did a dreadful thing with reference to Rubinstein. On another occasion he was to give
a recital in Berlin. I bought my ticket (and it was expensive) several weeks in advance. At that time I had
a bad habit of studying very late at night—up to one or
two o'clock, making myself a cup of strong tea at ten
to keep myself wide awake. In the morning I slept late
and then went to a café for breakfast and to read the
papers.

One morning the first thing that stared me in the face
was a long and glowing account of the Rubinstein recital!

I had forgotten the date, and my seat had remained un-
occupied! I wanted to tear out every hair on my head.
It was the last chance I ever had to hear this giant of
the keyboard.

In Romantic Heidelberg

German students have a pleasant "progressive" habit of
moving on from university to university. It gives them
a chance to attend the lectures of all the most famous professors in the country. In winter, Berlin, Leipzig and
Munich are specially favored because of the diversions
offered by big cities. In summer the small-town institutions have their innings, particularly Heidelberg with
its romantic surroundings, its magnificent ruined castle,
the rivers Neckar and Rhine, and the many neighboring
haunts of medieval robber barons, always picturesquely
situated.

"Schwänzen," or keeping away from lectures, seemed to
be even more in vogue in semi-rural Heidelberg than in
Berlin. There is a story of a father who came to visit his
son, who had been a Heidelberg student for two months.
They took a cab to see the sights. On passing a large
white building the father asked what it was. The son did
not know, so the cabman was appealed to.

"That?" he replied. "Why, that's the university."

In the summer of 1886 the University of Heidelberg
celebrated its five-hundredth anniversary. At that time I
had been musical critic of the New York *Evening Post*
for five years while Henry Edward Krehbiel was the
Tribune's critic. We had attended the Bayreuth Festival
together, leaving that town the day before Liszt died
there. Having resided at Heidelberg during the summer
of 1879 and 1880 I gave my colleague such a glowing
account of its scenic and other attractions that he was

eager to see it. Not having been a student there, he did not enjoy my privilege of getting a card which admitted the bearer to all the centennial festivities; but the principal one was open to all: the jollification in the old castle. There was music by an excellent band and the best of Rhine wines were served from barrels.

Krehbiel had a happy thought. He ordered a treat of the best wine for the musicians and then another and another. The players were extravagantly grateful. Ignoring their program they asked him what he would like to hear and for an hour he dictated what they were to play. He was radiant; he always liked to boss a job.

My going to Heidelberg in 1879 had been prompted largely by a letter I received from John B. Olmsted. He had, shortly after graduating from Harvard, married one of the loveliest girls in the State of New York and was at Heidelberg that summer with his wife and baby boy. He wanted me to leave Berlin and join them there; gave me a most glowing account of the pension they were living in, just under the old castle, with a large flower garden and a private gate up to the famous ruins. More alluring still was the information that Marie, the landlady's youngest daughter, was "the most beautiful girl in Germany," with large black eyes. In addition to all this, I could have a comfortable room and good table board for 110 marks a month, or about ninety cents a day.

Of course I joined him at once. I spent some weeks that summer and the greater part of the following summer at this pension, studying more or less, mostly from books, for the lectures, so far as they were in my line, were of no special importance. The professor of physiology, in fact, bluntly told me, after I had shown him my Macmillan article on "The Development of the Color Sense," that his talks would be too elementary for me.

Kuno Fischer's lectures, however, I did attend. To be

sure they were on the history of philosophy, with which I was familiar, but he was so wonderfully eloquent a speaker that he made old facts seem new; some of his climaxes were thrilling and made the students applaud as if they were at a theater or a political meeting. I also called on him a few times and got some useful directions for my studies.

Professor Fischer was very much alive to the fact that he was a famous man and, like most Germans, he thought a great deal of the "handles" to his name. One day, in a corridor of the University, a new student, seeing a plainly dressed man with a rather shabby little hat on his head, asked him: "Can you tell me where Kuno lectures?"

The man drew himself up to his full height and answered pompously: "If you mean the Privy Councillor Herr Professor Doctor Kuno Fischer, I lecture in that room."

In the streets of Heidelberg the students played a more conspicuous rôle than they did in Berlin, where the army officers had everything their own way; every day while in that city my indignation had been aroused by their arrogance and their atrocious manners; non-military persons, including ladies, being looked down on and shoved off the sidewalks as if they were yellow dogs. Prussian "Kultur."

The manners of the Heidelberg students, I am sorry to say, were not much better. They, too, monopolized the streets and made night hideous with their yells and the beating of sticks on tables in open-air beer-places. Complaints to officials were without result; the students ruled the town.

When the University of Würzburg had its fourth-centennial celebration I wrote it up for the *Evening Post*. I dwelt on the total lack of manners shown by German students, their coarse faces, made more hideous by their silly dueling slashes and scars; the medievalism in general of their appearance and conduct; and I compared with them the gentlemanly appearance, the aristocratic bearing and the courteous conduct of American students. The Berlin *Boersen-Courier* printed a translation of this pugnacious article, which amazed and angered the Teutons hugely.

The most romantic episode in romantic Heidelberg happened in the pension beneath the castle. Dramatis personæ, black-eyed Marie and the writer of this book.

It wasn't a bit strange that I fell madly in love with her. There were four other young Americans in the pension and every one of them was infatuated; every one of them would have laid down his life for her. She was beautiful, graceful, amiable and always sweetly feminine. And those large black Spanish eyes, with their long, dark dense lashes! She had a habit of modestly lowering those lashes, and then, when they suddenly were raised, the effect was thrilling, maddening. Do you wonder that I addressed her as follows,—in writing, because I could not possibly have told her all this face to face:

"I know that it is customary in Germany in affairs of the heart to communicate with the mother first; but I trust you will pardon me if I follow the American way in this case and appeal to you directly. You have known for a long time from my conduct and the expression of my eyes that I love you. Last summer already this feeling germinated in my heart, but not till this summer, when I saw you again and learned to know you better, did I become aware of its irresistible might. What I have experienced in the last three months in the alternation of feelings of happiness and misery no poet could describe, no musician express in tones. Like a red-hot lava stream this feeling which is called love coursed through my veins. Work was no longer possible; at most, I could give to my books in the morning a few hours of *partial* attention; the rest of the time I was occupied with but *one* subject, *one* thought —your face and the question whether my love was recipro-

cated. Every word, every look you favored me with, was
considered and reconsidered, and often a whole night thus
passed away without a moment of sleep. . . .

"When we had music in the evening I played for you
alone. Sometimes, when I played Chopin's 'My Delights'
with you, I thought you must have noticed plainly that I
meant *you,* and that you would reproach me for confessing
my love so openly in the presence of other persons. I felt,
too, that if my music failed to make an impression in my
favor, all would be lost. . . ."

Did Marie love me? I didn't know and don't know.
John Olmsted, who was back in Leroy, N. Y., wrote me
consolingly (and he was a good observer): "I can't help
thinking she *must have loved you*" (his italics); but I
question his diagnosis. He added: "and what I cannot
decide for myself is whether you were right in not proposing."

Yes, I did not propose! The eight-page letter from
which I have quoted a few paragraphs never left my desk!
I felt sure the girl's mother would not favor the suit; she
did not want Marie to love "or even to marry" me; she was
no fool; she knew that I was a penniless young man of
twenty-five without a position, and living on a fellowship.
That might not influence a girl who loved, but it should and
did the mother, no doubt.

An English lady living in the house told John that the
attitude of Marie's mother was not encouraging. She had
told this English lady that Marie had found me "very
useful"; that she "learned a great deal from me, musically and otherwise," but that apart from this there was
"nothing doing."

In rational moments I, too, began to see straight; to
realize that I was in no position to think of proposing and
marrying. But what could I do? One thing only: *cure
my love!* I had a copy of Ovid's "Remedia amoris." I

read this over and over again. I began to think more
deeply and deeply on the subject, and this was the origin
of my first book, "Romantic Love and Personal Beauty."

It began, as first sketched in my mind, with a chapter
on "How to Cure Love." This, naturally, suggested a
chapter on "How to Win Love." Then I thought how
interesting it would be to trace the evolution of the romantic passion; to show how differently it manifested itself at
different times and in different countries; to dwell on its
connection with personal beauty, and so on. This plan
matured slowly and in 1887 Macmillan and Co. in London
published the book, in two volumes for England, one for
America.

But I am racing ahead too fast. We are still in 1880,
at Heidelberg, in presence of Marie, to whom the world
is indebted—if it is indebted—for the first historico-psy-
chological treatise on Romantic Love.

What I cannot now understand is how I could possibly
muster the courage to sketch out that chapter on "How to
Cure Love," while I was still face to face with Marie; sitting, in fact, next to her at table. But I did it; I have
the nasty thing before me now. It makes me almost shiver
to see how many disagreeable things—true or imaginary—
I could think up about my beloved.

Of course this "Remedia amoris" did not cure me—it
never does, as I admitted in the book. To be sure, I boldly
wrote to John B.: "I don't even feel quite sure now that
I really love her"; but that was sheer bluff. I saw at last
that the only safety lay in flight, cowardly precipitate flight,
and a thorough change in surroundings. My plan was to
cool off my passion amid the glaciers and snow peaks of
Switzerland, then to plunge into the dissipations of life
in Vienna, taking in Venice on the way, and this plan was
carried out.

At Lucerne I had the good fortune to fall in with several young Americans who were also making a Swiss tour for the first time. I wanted to see, particularly, the most sublimely terrifying of all peaks, the Matterhorn. We made that our climax and then crossed over to Italy by the Theodul Pass, 11,000 feet above sea level alongside of the Matterhorn.

It was a hard tramp and I chafed my left foot in a way that made it necessary to rest a few days. I insisted that my companions should go on their way, and so I was left alone, all all alone, in a lonely Italian mountain-inn, the most dismal place I have ever seen. This was most unfortunate, for it made me brood over things I wanted to forget. Nor was I the first man who found himself in the same plight at this melancholy tavern; for in the guest book I found these uncanny lines, which made me shudder:

> "Ye youths who travel to forget a face
> Stay not one night in this accursed place.
> The food is good, the wine is fair
> But the face you would forget is always there."

A few days later I walked down the mountain slopes to the Italian plain. I saw the Milan cathedral, visited Juliet's alleged tomb in Verona and was enchanted with the gondolas, and the Doge's Palace, and St. Mark's in Venice.

Among the loveliest things to be seen at St. Mark's are the mosaics on the floor. One day, as I walked up and down the church studying these and twirling my mustache thoughtfully, a priest in a confessional which I had passed repeatedly took pity on me and said: "You may confess in English if you like."

But how could I tell him, in any language, about a pair of black eyes which continued to haunt me even in this holy temple of art? The priest's sharp eyes had told him that something must be the matter with me. It was not till I had been in Vienna some weeks and plunged into its pleasure maelstrom that those eyes began to fade in my mind. *Similia Similibus.*

A Winter in Gay Vienna

I had found Munich a city of Wagnerian music and superbeer; Berlin, the headquarters of arrogant militarism and academic red tape; Heidelberg, the abode of romance, the home of a black-eyed girl, and the camping-ground of multitudinous students monopolizing the town and wearing microscopic caps, red, white or blue, that always looked as if they were going to fall off their heads.

Vienna I found entirely different from these places or any other cities in which German is spoken.

It is, like New York, a melting pot of many races, European and Asiatic: Teutons, Italians, Magyars, and Slavs. The result, a population which, while it speaks German, is in manners and customs, in courtesy and vivacity, far more like the Parisians than like the Berliners.

Everybody is polite in Vienna. In the restaurants and cafés the waiters always greeted me as "Herr Doctor," or "Herr Baron;" if I ordered caviar and a bottle of choice wine I was even advanced to "Herr Graf" (count).

In the Munich Opera House I had once been rudely accosted by the *portier* (doorkeeper) because I had entered his room without taking off my hat. "Remember, young man," he said, "that I am a royal official."

In Vienna such an asinine affront would have been inconceivable had I worn half a dozen hats on top of each other. Had not the Austrian Emperor himself simply smiled when Beethoven failed to take off his hat as his majesty passed in the street?

Above all things, Vienna was the home of pretty girls, of dancing and light music. When I got there I did not know how to dance though I was twenty-five years old. After a fortnight I saw that I must decidedly "do as the Romans do." To be the only young man in Vienna who did not dance would surely have subjected me to ridicule and contempt, if not ignominious expulsion. So I promptly began to take lessons of the Bohemian maestro, Schwott. He was a first-class teacher but I was anything but a first-class pupil; he had to pick out a girl expert who devoted herself to me exclusively for two hours a day. I was surprized at my stupidity, for was I not exceptionally musical?

When I told Professor Schwott about that he laughed and said: "That has nothing to do with it. It is a fact known all over Vienna that Beethoven never succeeded in learning to dance."

That made me feel better. I made a supreme effort, caught on suddenly, and soon left Beethoven far behind.

When Carnival time came I spent whole nights in the ball-rooms, having a royal time. The difficult art of waltzing now seemed as easy and as natural as reading Homer or Tacitus in the original. Pretty brunettes and blondes were as plentiful as flowers in the Riviera garden and their dancing was as graceful and airy as the flight of gaudy butterflies among these blossoms.

After a night of dancing I found nothing so refreshing as a Turkish bath at four or five A.M. After one of these I often took a bed right in the bath-house and slept till noon. The afternoons, I frankly confess, I devoted to my Fellowship studies.

Not that I attended any lectures regularly at the University; that would have been, for reasons I have referred to repeatedly, a waste of time. But I profited hugely by the books of some of the famous Professors, particularly Brücke, the physiologist, and Krafft-Ebing, whose wonderful treatises on mental diseases and erotic abnormalities I found more illuminating as to the intricate machinery and the subtle processes of the mind than any books on normal psychology I had ever read.

There were many night cafés in Vienna in which there was music from ten o'clock till three. "Damen Capellen" were just then the fashion at these cafés. They consisted of from six to ten young women playing violins, 'cello, bass flute, and piano or organ. These little bands played with remarkable sprightliness and a unique feminine intensity. Like all the Viennese bands, from Strauss's court orchestra to the simplest beer-hall group, they played dance music with a wild abandon and enthusiasm of which those who have never been in the "Kaiserstadt" can form no conception.

It was the most voluptuous and exciting music imaginable, and when Eduard Strauss conducted at a masked ball or at one of his promenade concerts one had only to close one's eyes to feel himself whirling around the hall with his arms encircling the waist of a fair damsel.

What astonished and delighted me most was that whereas elsewhere the waltz was danced with metronomic regularity, in Vienna it had poetic and passionate irregularities, now slowing down a little for a few bars as if to give the dancers a chance to whisper in each other's ears and anon rushing on like a tidal wave.

The great Johann Strauss, known the world over as the "waltz king," did not any longer conduct the court balls regularly; his brother Eduard took his place. He himself was busy day and night composing and conducting his operettas, a new one every year.

Imagine my great good luck in having a chance to spend a winter in Vienna just at this time when not only was Strauss adding regularly to his list of masterworks: "The Bat" (Fledermaus), "The Merry War," "The Queen's Lace Handkerchief," "The Gypsy Baron," and so on, but

two other popular favorites—Suppe and Milloecker—
were shaking from their sleeves their tuneful "Fatinitzas,"
"Beggar Students," and so on. It was the golden age of
the operetta and I, with my usual good luck, was on the
spot when these musical gold coins came fresh from the
mint by wholesale.

All these operettas were full of waltzes, polkas and
other dance-tunes which were promptly issued separately
for the concert and dance-halls and the night cafés. The
whole city was frenzied with joy when a new master-mel-
ody like the "Fledermaus" waltz was thus let loose on the
community. You couldn't get away from it and nobody
wanted to get away, certainly not I, though, strange to
say, I did not at that time, theoretically at any rate, appreciate this light music at its full value.

Of course it was not as high-brow as Wagner's "Tristan" or "Siegfried," but in its way it was no less inspired,
no less a product of genius. Was not Wagner among the
first to pronounce Johann Strauss a genius, and did not
even the austere Johannes Brahms, who had made his
home in Vienna, attend the Strauss first nights regularly?
Johannes and Johann were warm personal friends.

It was not till I got to New York, where one of my
duties was to write up the new operettas as well as the
grand operas, that I fully realized how great had been
my luck in being right in the swim of this light but inspired
dance music when it was first given to the world. At first
I sadly missed the ravishing swing, the half-Asiatic frenzy
of the Viennese performance, which could not be repro-
duced in New York; but fortunately that impression
became dulled after a time. Even without this Viennese
swing, the Strauss operettas and waltzes continued to
enchant me and I became their most persistent and irrepressible champion in America.

The Hungarian gypsy bands, scattered all over Vienna,

LISTENING 157

puzzled me at first when they improvised in their own
fashion; but soon I learned to like them immensely, especially when they struck up one of those captivating tunes
which Liszt has embodied in his exhilarating Hungarian
rhapsodies.

The Imperial Opera in Vienna was, in 1880, in its best
form, under Hans Richter (whom Wagner had chosen to
conduct the first Bayreuth Festival), and with Amalia
Materna as its leading prima donna. There were numerous high-brow concerts, too, in enjoying which, as well
as the operas, I was unconsciously preparing myself for
my New York job as musical critic, of which even then I
had no premonition, though it was to begin so soon.

Pleasure, pleasure everywhere! To a super-epicure
like myself life in Vienna was also most enjoyable gastronomically. Next to Paris, Vienna was the European
paradise for gourmets. If the delicious Vienna rolls,
made of Hungarian flour, were not any better than the
petits pains served in Paris, this was owing to the fact that
the French also used Hungarian flour, the best in the
world. The cost of a meal in Vienna was little higher than
in the cities of Germany but the food was lighter, more
delicate and more digestible.

The Bohemian Pilsener, the favorite beer in Vienna,
was also lighter than the German beers and indulgence in
it less harmful. My poor dear friend James Huneker
always swore by Pilsener. When it was prohibited in
America, his native country fell far below par in his esti-
mation: he would have gone to live abroad but could not
afford it.

The best place to get acquainted with famous Hungarian wines was at a unique resort known as the Esterhazy Keller. In this big cellar there were four huge casks
filled with the red Villanyi, the golden Somlai and two
lighter sorts the names of which I cannot recall. These

wines came from the overstocked vaults of Prince Esterhazy. They could have been sold to dealers at fancy
prices, for better wines never came from the press, but the
Esterhazys preferred to practically give them away. They
wanted everybody in Vienna, however poor, to have a
chance to taste "the nectar of the gods."

All availed themselves of this opportunity. Such a mixture of social ranks was not to be seen anywhere else. To
be able to get for twenty cents, a large tumblerful of Villanyi or Somlai which, in a restaurant, would have cost
ten times as much, was a chance that appealed to tourists,
students, officers and officials no less than to cabmen, cob-
blers, hod-carriers or street porters.

The next curtain will rise on Württemberg, the South
German Kingdom my parents came from.

Uncle Edward and the Prussian Octopus

Among my relatives were two uncles. One of them,
Gottlob Fink, I did not meet. He was my mother's
brother and was a professor at the University at Tübingen. Gottlob Fink was master of fourteen languages.
He translated many books; one of his "stunts" was to
walk up and down the room with, say, a Swedish book in
one hand and a Russian or Arabic in the other, translating
them in alternating sentences to two secretaries.

More remarkable still was his capacity for absorbing
wine. In Stuttgart I heard a good story about him.
There was a nephew who had a lot of money and who once
plotted to have some fun with uncle Gottlob. He went to
Tübingen and invited the uncle to supper at a tavern
noted for its excellent old Rhine wines. While they were
eating he ordered a bottle of the best, then another, and
another, and still another, pouring out most of it into his
uncle's glass. When the tenth bottle was brought, the

Professor suddenly looked at the nephew in an amused way and said: "It seems to me, my dear friend, that you are trying to get your old uncle drunk. Now, I know you are a rich man, but—you haven't enough money to do *that!*"

The other uncle I want to refer to was my father's brother Edward; he was a merchant at Murrhardt, not many miles from Stuttgart, where my father was born in 1822. During my four years in Germany I spent many happy weeks and even months at his hospitable home, getting acquainted with my cousins and their friends, black-eyed and blue-eyed.

While not particularly interested in German politics, I used to enjoy listening to uncle Edward. He was a genuine South German; that is, he hated the Prussians with all his might and main; no Frenchman or Pole ever abhorred them more.

To him the Prussians appeared in the form of a giant octopus trying to get its tentacles around everything in sight and out of sight. The war with France had enabled them to "unite" Bavaria, Saxony, Württemberg, with themselves at the head. But this "union" was simply the encircling and reducing to helplessness, by the octopus, of these other Kingdoms, which now had to dance as Berlin piped.

"Shall I tell you what will happen next?" my uncle continued. "The Prussians are forcing their militarism on us, the gentle and peaceloving South Germans. With our aid they plan next to get their octopus tentacles around France and England and then—don't laugh," he added, "then your turn will come in America."

Often, during the great World War, did I think of uncle Edward's prophesy. That war was the Kaiser's attempt, with the aid of the enslaved German Kingdoms,

to enslave the rest of the world; and we all know that he
came within an inch of succeeding.

Uncle Edward was hugely delighted when I told him
that, as a boy in Oregon, I hated the Prussians and sided
with the French during the Franco-Prussian war. He
was still more delighted when I showed him, in a volume
of Goethe, what the foremost German poet wrote: "The
Prussian is a beast—civilization will make him ferocious."

Before me lies a letter from my brother Edward in
which he sums up a whole volume in one short sentence:
"I am simply disgusted with Germany."

Nevertheless the poor fellow, blinded by love, married
a German girl and took her to Oregon, where a divorce
came in due order. The wedding which I was able to
attend by hurrying down from Berlin, was characteristic
of German life. I quote it from a letter I wrote to a
friend in Cambridge:

"The marriage ceremony having been performed in the
presence of four persons, including myself, we went back
to the house, where the next four hours—from 12 to 4—
were spent at the dinner table. There were mountains of
victuals and oceans of wine; also weak toasts and Teutonic jokes. I soon tired of these and took refuge with
the bride who agreed with me that the carousal was
truly medieval—a regular 'Baerenwirthschaft,' or orgy of
bears."

After the wedding I spent a week with relatives in
Stuttgart. I always enjoyed a short stay in the capital
of Württemberg in spite of certain medievalisms, one of
which was a decided nuisance. I refer to the night-watch-
man who, at that time, still passed along the street each
hour, bawling out the time, just as if people had no clocks.
Wagner showed up the funny side of this custom in his
comic opera, "Die Meistersinger."

On the other hand, one of the most delightful musical

experiences of my life occurred in Stuttgart on the morning of the first night I spent there, and this I found a
decidedly commendable survival of medieval customs. At
six o'clock I was waked up by the sound of four trombones
playing the glorious harmonies of a Bach choral. What
did it mean? The music seemed to come from the clouds:
had I suddenly died and was my soul ascending heaven-
ward?

At the breakfast table I was informed that three times
a day, at 6, 12 and 6, four musicians went up the highest
tower in the city and played a choral, one verse in each
direction of the compass.

Eating and drinking in Germany seemed to be the
alpha and omega of existence. When I first came among
my kind-hearted and hospitable relatives I gave daily
offense by refusing to eat more than three times a day,
or to drink more than one glass of beer or wine. They
felt sure I did not consider the things they placed before
me good enough, though I tried hard to make them understand my epicurism—my art of getting a maximum of
pleasure out of a minimum of food or drink by eating
and drinking slowly and all the time breathing out consciously through the nose.

Throughout Germany I found it customary to have five
or six meals a day: (1) coffee and bread in the early morning; (2) lunch of cold meat or sausage with beer at 10;
(3) dinner at 12; (4) coffee with cake at 4; (5) supper
at 7; (6) beer and sandwiches later in the evening.

What annoyed me particularly was that when I called
on one of my aunts she would shake hands and then disap-
pear in the kitchen to prepare something for me. It made
it seem as if I had come solely to test her skill as a cook.
She was proud of that skill, but, after all——

With the father of my brother's bride I went one day
to the beer-hall where he spent his evenings. There they

sat, five men around a table, eating, drinking and *every one of them talking all the time* at the top of his voice! After about an hour of this the bride's father hit the table hard with his fist and shouted, in the Swabian idiom: "Jetzt lasst aber mi au a bissle schwätza!" ("Do let me have my turn now and get in a word!")

PART V

THE GOLDEN AGE IN MUSICAL
NEW YORK—AND AFTER

THE GOLDEN AGE IN MUSICAL
NEW YORK—AND AFTER

A MARRIAGE OF TWO PAPERS

A SURPRIZE awaited me when I was getting ready
to shake the German academic dust off my shoes
and return to my native country.

Edwin L. Godkin and Wendell Philipps Garrison, who
had, in a few years, made the *Nation* a leading authority throughout the country on politics and literature, had,
during my student years abroad, and previously, accepted
and printed a number of my articles. They now kindly
offered me, when I should be ready to return, a place on
the editorial staff of their paper. Under date of February 23, 1881, Mr. Garrison wrote to me (I was still in
Berlin):

"The earlier you can return the better pleased Mr. Godkin will be. There seems to be a providential fitness for
the *Nation* in your past career and it will be personally a
great gratification to see you frequently."

The surprize referred to came in another letter from
Mr. Garrison dated June 1, 1881. After referring to the
death of Mr. MacMartin, for whose *Musical Review* I had
been writing a series of articles, he went on to say:

"Now I am going to give you some news which will be
quite as startling—perhaps as mournful. Mr. Godkin has
joined Carl Schurz and Horace White in the purchase
and editorial conducting of the *Evening Post,* and will
make a thorough revolution in the staff of that paper. It

is only a question of time when he will leave the *Nation* altogether for his new journalistic connection, and negotiations are even pending which may abruptly close the '*Nation* as it was' with the last number in the present month. If the paper is sold I shall follow Mr. Godkin, and stand by him for one year at least, not knowing what will be my work, nor how I shall like it, and *a priori* detesting the evening paper as a nuisance and a great enemy to book culture.

"After fifteen years of the life I have led, which has not been without its anxious moments, I can only feel sad at the thought of parting with our choice audience, and of leaving the paper in the hands of a conductor who must be inferior to Mr. Godkin, though he may yet make the paper live for a few years. I resign myself as I should if my incomparable chief had been suddenly stricken down and left me no choice but to wind up the *Nation* or to dispose of it to the highest bidder.

"In this feeling you will certainly share, with an outsider's view of the peculiar value of the *Nation* to the country both at home and abroad. Your next thought will be how this change will affect the arrangement we have already entered into. I can answer promptly, that it will convert it into something better. Mr. Godkin will hold you for the musical department of the *Post,* and no doubt give you what scope you desire in the literary and political departments, with a corresponding increase in pay. . . . To be musical critic of an afternoon paper is much less arduous than the same service for a morning daily. I hope on this and other accounts that the prospect will not displease you."

In the Editorial Den

That settled it. The professorship of philosophy could wait till I was older. About the middle of August I entered on my new duties and on September 2 I wrote a letter to my friend Olmsted which gives a bird's-eye view of them:

"It is now just two weeks since I began my work on the *Post* and I feel already as if I had never done anything else in my life. Schurz allowed me two days after arriving in New York to get settled. Garrison invited me to his home in Orange the first night and explained to me just what my work would be. I have of course full charge of the musical department. Godkin wanted me to take the drama, too, but I explained to him that the covering of theatric novelties would too often conflict with my musical duties.

"One of my tasks—and a very pleasant one—is to read all the foreign exchanges, among which, besides such weeklies as the London *Saturday Review, Spectator, Athenaeum,* etc., there are six English, four French and five German dailies. These I look over and clip, summarize, or translate whatever is of special interest. Nothing could suit me better than this work, for most of these papers are just as good as books; you may remember the remark made by Schopenhauer's father that the reading of the London *Times* is an education in itself.

"The only thing I don't like about it is that I have to cut out also the best paragraphs from political leaders, and, as you know, I have never been particularly interested in politics. Sometimes these extracts have to be made in a great hurry, when they happen to elucidate some cablegram just received. All the cablegrams are sent to me at once for this purpose.

"Please don't imagine that I am overworked. Quite the contrary, we editors work only about six hours a day, from nine to four, with an hour's intermission for lunch. In fact, we do pretty much as we darned please; no one spies on us and when my allotted task is done I do not hesitate to leave at three or even earlier, to get some hours outdoors.

"Carl Schurz's room is next to mine; to reach it he has to pass through mine. I find him very pleasant in spite of his aggressively red hair, big feet and revolutionary political antecedents. He tells me the latest news about the president and always speaks to me in German. He has asked me to call his attention to articles that might suggest topics for editorials.

"My room is on the top floor of the *Evening Post* building, eight stories above the street. I have a magnificent view of the Harbor. When there isn't much to do—which is often the case—I sit and twiddle my thumbs and look out of the window watching the big ocean steamers starting for Europe, or returning, wondering when I shall again be on one of them. There is more breeze up here than anywhere else in New York; it gets so strong during the hottest hours of the day that I often have to put weights on my papers to prevent them from being swept on to the floor when the door is open. I didn't know New York is such a breezy summer resort. To be sure, I am exceptionally favored; I always was a lucky dog.

"Garrison helped me find a good boarding-house. I live in a very swell place on Fifth Avenue—yes, Fifth Avenue, if you please, number 287, and I pay the sum of $12 a week for a hall room and good board, which I consider remarkably low for such accommodations—including, among other things, a splendid new Steinway upright in the parlor.

"I often go to Coney Island or Rockaway Beach. Sea bathing (new to me) is delightful now and quite entertaining where such crowds disport themselves in the tumbling breakers. I find swimming much easier in the salt water than in the Pudding River in Oregon."

Carl Schurz

In my editorial den there was nothing I enjoyed more than my daily chats with Carl Schurz. It annoyed me a little that he spoke to me in German, as I have always held that the German language is clumsy and cumbersome compared with English. He had acquired such a wonderful command of English, why not use that? I have never known another foreigner, except Paderewski, who had so thoroughly mastered the idioms of our language.

Schurz was deeply interested in music. Lovers of that art are notoriously inclined to differ in their likes and dislikes; but when my opinions clashed with Schurz's he never made the least attempt to influence me. He did express surprize when I wrote that Lucca, whom I had often heard in Vienna, was an even more fascinating Carmen than Minnie Hauck.

On another occasion, when I had jumped on the violinist Remenyi with needless savagery (young critics will do that sort of thing), he brought in the proof and asked me if I could not tone it down a little, which of course I did. I did not know that he not only admired that Hungarian for musical reasons but for his revolutionary activities.

Fortunately he liked the music of still another revolutionary, Richard Wagner, and allowed me to indulge in as much propagandism as I pleased. He had in 1849 met Wagner personally in Switzerland, that grand refuge of political fugitives, but only casually, and so was unable, to his great regret, to supply any details for the Wagner biography I wrote some years later.

I have already referred to the fact that Mr. Godkin wanted me to be the dramatic editor as well as the musical. If I had been so foolish as to acquiesce I would have ousted—whom do you suppose? No one less than John

Ranken Towse, who subsequently became one of America's two foremost dramatic critics, the other being William Winter.

Carl Schurz wanted me to take the place, also, of the *Evening Post's* art critic! I made it clear to him that while I had spent much time in the art galleries of England, France, Germany and Italy and had heard the lectures of Professor Norton at Harvard I hardly considered myself qualified for such a position. Probably I was foolishly modest. Most of the newspapers had critics, both of art and of music, who had only the most elementary training. I instinctively knew what was best in art, as was amusingly demonstrated one day, some years later, at Jesurum's in Venice, where my wife, a passionate lover of laces, had dragged me. While she picked out what she wanted I looked at the specimens on the walls and finally planted myself firmly before a piece of lace which aroused my enthusiasm. A moment later the proprietor came along with my wife and said: "I admire your taste! This piece which has specially attracted your attention is the choicest and costliest bit we have in stock." So I suppose I might have got along all right as art editor of the *Post*.

Mr. Schurz, unfortunately, remained on the *Evening Post* only a few years. While he was with us, the editorial page, made up of articles by him and Godkin and Horace White, was often a wonderful thing, equaled perhaps only by the London *Times*. But Schurz and Godkin had views which clashed and finally Schurz decided to leave and go into politics.

WANTED ON THE TRIBUNE

Not only did the great triumvirate which had assumed control of the *Post* apparently want me to do most of the work, excepting sports, politics, telegrams, finance and city reporting, but along came Mr. Hassard asking me to do his work on the *Tribune* too! John R. G. Hassard was at that time the leading musical critic of America. I had met him at Bayreuth. He had heard only one cycle and then left for other journalistic feats and this had led me to send to Whitelaw Reid a summary of the second and third cycles, which was printed in the *Tribune*. The letter in which Mr. Hassard made me an offer is dated Tribune Office, November 2, 1882. It reads:

"Is there any probability that the *Tribune* can have the advantage of some musical criticisms from your pen? I am going away for the winter, and it would be very gratifying to me, as well as to my chief, if I could leave the musical department of this paper in your hands. I do not know of course how far your engagements with the *Post* would interfere with such a scheme, or whether you would care in any case to enter into it; but if the proposal is not entirely disagreeable to you I should be glad to talk with you about it. I tried to find you last night at the opera, but was told that you were not there."

Under date of November 7 Mr. Hassard wrote again: "I am sorry that you could not make it convenient to write for the *Tribune* this winter, especially as I hoped that the result of the undertaking would be your permanent transfer to our corps. I am the more concerned since the obstacle is the state of your health. . . . I wish you could have said yes to my former note!"

Had I said yes, Henry Edward Krehbiel would not have become the chief critic of the *Tribune*. Mr. Hassard did not like him because of his unfriendly attitude toward America's foremost orchestral conductor and missionary, Theodore Thomas; an unfriendliness which gradually developed into downright hostility. Mr. Hassard was suffering from lung-trouble; he felt that his days were numbered, and he would have been happy to know that if I had become his successor his policies would be carried out. Had he lived, the *Tribune* and the *Post* would have been musical allies instead of violent opponents—for forty-two years.

NIGHT WORK AND PLEASURES

The real reason why I refused the *Tribune's* offer was that I did not wish to write at night. Schopenhauer had imbued my mind with a full realization of the importance of sleep and I knew from experience that if I worked till or after midnight I would not sleep soundly. The *Evening Post* allowed me till eleven or even twelve o'clock the next day to send my "story" up to the composing room, and I made enthusiastic use of this rare privilege, which no other evening paper allowed its critics.

Other attempts to lure me away from the *Post* failed, for the same reason. Bradford Merrill once appealed to my vanity by telling me I was "too good for the *Post*" and offering me $20 a week more if I would come to the *World*, with a chance of doubling my salary by writing also for the Editorial page. On another occasion, when the *Herald* wanted me, I did not even ask for the rates— which would have been favorable—but declined because of my aversion to night work.

Music is a nocturnal art and few musicians get enough sleep. Not only does their work keep them up late but their favorite song has long been "We won't go home till morning."

When I began my critical duties, Steinway Hall was headquarters for concerts, the Academy of Music for operas. Both were on East Fourteenth Street. Near them was Lienau's, famous for its imported beers, its Bismarck herrings, Astrachan caviar, smoked Kieler Sprotten and other choice "delicatessen." To this place, after the performance, came in droves the singers, players, conductors and critics. There they sat, eating and drinking, talking and chatting and gossiping and slandering till two or three in the morning. At first I tried once more to "do as the Romans do;" but soon I found that I grew dull and stupid, apathetic, uninterested in my work and disagreeable in my comments—none so cross as those who haven't had enough sleep! I soon swore off; the time came when my almost invariable answer to an invitation to an after-theater meeting or supper was a polite intimation that I could not sacrifice my necessary hours of sleep. The result of this self-denial is that now, at the age of seventy, I am as strong mentally as I was thirty years ago, and still enjoy life hugely. Isn't a long life and a happy one better than "a short life and a merry one?"

THEODORE THOMAS

Some men, to be sure, are so robust, so sturdy and rugged, that they can burn the candle at both ends without perceptibly diminishing their vitality.

Theodore Thomas was one of these. At the time when I came to New York he was the outstanding personality and authority in local musical affairs. He was one of the most virile, indomitable and genuine personalities I have ever had the good luck to number among my friends— every inch a man, aye, and a king among musicians.

You will be surprized to hear that high-class musical life in the American Metropolis practically began with Theodore Thomas, and that I was in almost at the start!

Of course there had been famous soloists flitting like comets across the musical horizon and there had been orchestral concerts as well as operas; but it required the Herculean strength, the iron will, the domineering gesture and the stubborn perseverance of a man like Thomas to lay the corner-stone for a real Temple of Music. It is my proud boast that by encouraging him and fighting his enemies I was able to contribute a few stones to this temple.

He once told me that when he began his career in New York he and the eminent pianist William Mason started a small organization for giving chamber music. They knew not how to collect an audience, so they took bundles of their programs and stood at the corners on Fourteenth Street distributing them personally to passers-by!

Could anything give a more vivid idea of the "preliminary" condition of musical affairs at that time? Imagine Franz Kneisel or the members of the Flonzaley Quartet doing anything like that in our day!

Thomas was a born missionary for the divine art. His mind was filled with a holy zeal for it. His wife has related in her absorbing memoirs, how, when he prepared a performance of the Ninth Symphony, he neglected his meals and became inaccessible even to his family for a day or two. The performance then was an event. Never did Beethoven's music sound more gloriously than when he led his great orchestra through its mazes of sound.

But before the community could fully comprehend and enjoy such a masterwork it had to be led to it gradually.

Please don't look annoyed. I am not going to talk about the musical education Thomas gave the American public. The word education has in the musical sense acquired an evil repute. Advertise any musical entertainment (I am not talking about schools) as "educational" and you kill it suddenly, if not sooner.

Thomas's way was to lure the public by including in his programs plenty of pieces that were not above its head. They were the dessert in his menus. To reach the pies and puddings and ice-cream and cake the hearers had to be-

THEODORE THOMAS

come acquainted with the more substantial dishes and soon they learned to like those too.

Johann Strauss was one of Thomas's chief allies. The frequent use of his waltzes was one of the many things that made me admire him so ardently. Pedantry was not one of his traits. It is lamentably prevalent in the musical world. So is the notion that everything in an orchestral program must be dignified and starched like a shirt front. I have a chapter on this subject in my "Musical Progress."

The good that Thomas did was not confined to New York. He was the first to take a first-class orchestra on tour, beginning in 1869, with sixty-four players.

Amusing incidents aplenty occurred on these tours in towns where no real orchestra had ever been heard. Here is a story I have from Thomas himself:

Scene: a barber shop to which he had gone, in the morning following his concert in a new town. While waiting for his turn he heard the barber say to the man in the chair:

"How did you like the show last night?"

"Not much," was the reply. "There were no end-men, no jokes, and them sixty-four fellers were too lazy to blacken their faces."

This man, like millions of others, had never heard anything but the negro minstrels for whom poor Stephen Foster wrote his immortal songs; doing this for the simple reason that there was no other way to publicity in his day.

Fun for newspaper readers was provided at one of the series of spring music festivals in Cincinnati which Thomas conducted for a number of years. Cincinnati was Krehbiel's home town and he never failed to write up these festivals in articles for the New York *Tribune* which did not flatter Thomas. Of course I was always invited to these festivals, but declined because in May my appetite for music had been sated by the bountiful feasts in the metropolis and I preferred to make an early start for my annual vacation on the Pacific Slope or in Europe.

When Joseph Bucklin Bishop (famed in later years for his books on Theodore Roosevelt) became one of the leading editors of the *Evening Post* he persuaded me to go and write up one of the Cincinnati festivals. The festival committee placed at Krehbiel's service and mine bicycled messenger boys to take our articles in batches to the telegraph office. Copies of them we both had promised to one of the local papers. When they appeared the next morning they were a sight to behold. Printed side by side, they reflected Thomas and his doings like two mirrors, one convex, the other concave. It was really most amusing to have these leading doctors from New York disagree so thoroughly. To me the Cincinnati Choir seemed better than any choir we had in New York and I said so frankly.

Among those who enjoyed this critical conflict was the famous tenor Ben Davies, who sat next to me at the breakfast table in the hotel. Ben liked to hear and tell funny stories. He gave us one of his best after a festival performance when we met Thomas for a bite and a bottle of champagne.

Here it is: The impersonator of Don Juan in Mozart's opera was on one occasion a very fat baritone. In the final scene, when a trap-door opens into the infernal regions to swallow up the old sinner who has "ruined one thousand and three girls in Spain alone," the fat baritone got stuck; all his efforts to sink out of sight and let the flames come up from below, were in vain. Whereupon a voice from the gallery shouted:

"Hurrah, boys! Hell's full."

Trouble came into Theodore Thomas's life through the advent of other conductors from abroad; first Dr. Leopold Damrosch, and then the formidable Anton Seidl. There was not really room as yet in New York for another big

orchestra, but Dr. Damrosch and his friends started the
Symphony Society. Much friction and unpleasantness
and financial embarrassment were the result. An advantage of the rivalry was that important novelties were
heard in New York as soon as anywhere in Europe.

Not being an ardent admirer of Dr. Damrosch I stood
by Thomas. But the arrival of Seidl threw a cloud on our
friendship. Not that I praised Thomas less as a Wagner
conductor but I praised Seidl still more.

Following his own instincts, Thomas had, at his concerts, given amazingly fine performances of excerpts from
Wagner's operas. But Seidl, who conducted the whole
operas at the Metropolitan had been with Wagner in his
own home for six years and was finally pronounced by
that master the man who of all conductors had penetrated
most deeply into the spirit of his works. I had been at
Bayreuth; I had heard Hans Richter and others; but
Seidl enraptured me as no other conductor had or has
done; and this rapture overflowed daily into the columns
of the *Evening Post.*

Thomas didn't like it. He was naturally jealous, and
excessively sensitive. One evening, coming across him
accidentally I said: "Hello! Are you still alive?" Quick
as a flash came the answer: "Yes, and more than ever!"

Now, I had simply meant by my question that I had
not seen him for a long time, whereas he, with his abnormal
sensitiveness, twisted it into an intimation that I had
thought him musically dead and buried!

But Thomas, as I have said, was a man. After he had
left New York to found the Chicago Orchestra it happened that the Metropolitan Company of New York borrowed this orchestra for some Wagner performances under
Seidl in Chicago. Overcoming his prejudice, Thomas attended a performance of "Siegfried." He was amazed
and delighted and when it was over he went to Seidl's

room, shook hands cordially and congratulated him on the masterly handling of his orchestra.

It *could not* have been otherwise. To hear Seidl conduct "Siegfried" was the greatest operatic treat I remember in my long career. Seidl told me, concerning this Chicago performance of it that he had been specially inspired by the wonderful acoustics of the Auditorium.

The supreme tragedy of Thomas's life was that he had to leave New York for Chicago because the Western city offered him far better opportunities and guarantees. It was hard luck that he, who had struggled so valiantly to build up audiences caring for real music, should now have to leave them to his rivals. But the Chicago offer was too tempting to be ignored. It made life easier for him, the future more assured; and he was not as young as he had been.

He was greatly missed by his New York friends, prominent among whom was George William Curtis, the eminent editor of *Harper's* and influential political writer and speaker. Our admiration of Thomas often brought us together and I felt proud when he patted me on the back for my articles which, he declared, gave the American public exactly the information it needed about worthwhile music.

It was planned, after Thomas had been in Chicago some years, to have him come back as guest-conductor of a Philharmonic concert. Had he come it would have resulted in an ovation that would have atoned for many early disappointments. But pneumonia carried him off shortly before the date chosen for his concert. His death, unlike his life, was peaceful; the medical watchers could not tell just when it occurred. He had lived in America from 1845 till 1906; he was, therefore, practically an American.

In looking back on my long career as a musical critic

nothing strikes me as so strange as that I should have been so often called upon to act as champion and defender of the greatest musicians against some of my colleagues. To this point I shall recur repeatedly.

Thomas was the first instance. He was often treated with downright ferocity. One of his enemies had critical friends willing to do almost anything to please him—a sad fact on which I prefer not to dwell. It often made me melancholy. The majority seemed to be against me, yet I was right and the public sided with me invariably. "Politics," partizanship and personal animosities did much harm to the cause of music in New York.

When Thomas brought his admirable Chicago Orchestra to New York it proved a tremendous success, financial as well as artistic—a success which I recorded glowingly. But a certain set of critics fell on him like a pack of wolves. When he got back to Chicago he wrote me a letter of thanks, adding that it was the first time in his life he had done such a thing. This was only a few years before the end of a long life spent in *battling* to make the best music known to Americans.

Yes, *battling,* is the word, and I battled with him. He did not wish to be exempt from fault-finding—he knew he was not perfect; but, he once said, "I think that public criticism of an artistic work should be made, at least, in a kindly spirit; then it would not be so discouraging and have such a paralyzing effect on the mind."

The biggest tactical mistake Thomas ever made was his choosing me (because of my unique enthusiasm for Wagner) as editor of the "Handbook of the Wagner Concerts" he gave in 1884, with the three leading Bayreuth artists, Materna, Winkelmann and Scaria as soloists. Why it was a tactical mistake is a point I prefer not to discuss. From other points of view it was apparently not a mistake. It was my first little book (130 pages) and I was proud when I read in the *Transcript* that the whole edition of 3000 copies for Boston was at once exhausted and that copies commanded a dollar premium.

Lest the foregoing pages convey the impression that Thomas's career was mostly a tragedy, let me add that when things went well, as they often did, he enjoyed life hugely. I remember seeing him try to climb a lamppost (Wagner used to stand on his head) long after midnight. It wasn't champagne but the sheer exuberance of animal spirits. And with what zest he used to relate funny incidents! Let me close with one of these.

At a rehearsal the chief trombonist (who was nearsighted) startled Thomas by hurling out a tone horribly out of harmony.

"What on earth are you doing?" yelled Thomas.

"Excuse me!" the player begged. "I didn't have on my spectacles. A fly sat down among my notes *and I played him!*"

Adelina Patti

You have doubtless read about the oratorio rehearsal at which Patti declared she ought to have her own way, as she was the prima donna; whereupon Theodore Thomas, who conducted, exclaimed:

"Excuse me, madam, but here *I* am prima donna."

I don't know the details, but have no doubt that Patti, accustomed to having her own way, was taking liberties with Handel's music, decorating it in her own way in order to show off the beauty and agility of her incomparable voice. She had a way of doing that: Rossini hardly recognized one of his own arias as Patti sang it.

Thomas believed that Handel was greater than Patti; hence the clash.

During my first years in New York, Adelina Patti was

the leading personality in the vocal world, as Thomas was in the instrumental. It is therefore her turn to be put in the limelight.

Though born in Spain of Italian parentage, Patti considered herself practically an American as she came to live in New York as a child. Her first public appearance here was as early as 1859. Then she went to Europe, where she was soon worshiped as the prima donna beyond compare. Not till twenty-two years later did she return to New York, to suffer there a most humiliating failure.

This happened only a few weeks after I had assumed my rôle as critic of the *Evening Post*. My notices of her concerts were shockingly ill-tempered. Let me cite a few sample paragraphs:

"Madame Patti's second concert at Steinway Hall on Saturday afternoon was an admirable illustration of that phenomenal obstinacy which seems so dear to her soul and which she has in common with the *prime donne* of yore. Most persons would have been satisfied after the result of the first concert that the plan of giving, for ten dollars a seat, a series of entertainments in which a handful of wheat was to be served up in a bushel of chaff did not accord with the general notions New Yorkers entertain about concerts. But Madame Patti happens to have an opinion of her own and has expressed it to the effect that ten dollars is not too much for such concerts as she offers. She mentioned among other things that she charged seven dollars even in Berlin when she last appeared there. Now, we happened to be in Berlin at the time, and know that the parquet seats were only five dollars, the others ranging down as low as one dollar; and this was in the Royal Opera House where Patti had the assistance of one of the best orchestras and choruses in the world, and excellent soloists to support her, while here she has absolutely no attraction except her own isolated voice. . . .

"Her concerts are managed on the assumption that they will be listened to by a lot of native Indians and border ruffians. Such, at any rate, was our conclusion when a female violinist, who shall be nameless, struck up Yankee Doodle as an encore for a piece which she had played like a school girl."

As for Nicolini, the tenor, he "seems to appear at these concerts in order to plunge the hearers into an abyss of despair so that they may be raised from it into the regions of pure joy by the charms of Patti's voice."

Slashing as this may seem, it was mild compared with another of my criticisms—a criticism which might have easily nipped my own career in the bud. I don't dare to reprint it here.

At the Fifth Avenue boarding-house which then was my home a young lawyer sat next to me at the table. "I am afraid you are in for trouble," he said at dinner.

"What's the matter?" I asked; and he replied:

"I have just read your article on Patti in the *Post*. It is libelous. In a few days you and your paper may have on your hands a suit for $100,000 damages."

I didn't sleep that night, and in the morning, when I got to the office, there was Godkin, angrily accosting me with the question how I *could* write such objectionable stuff. I humbly apologized. "It's libelous, I now know; but, that being the case, why didn't the managing editor cut it out? That's one of his duties, isn't it?"

The chief forgave me; he knew it wouldn't happen again. No libel suit was brought, and soon I slept as soundly as ever.

One of the funny things about Patti was that each of her visits to America was announced as her farewell. This gave me a welcome chance to indulge in a little sarcasm:

Photograph by Sarony　　　　ADELINA PATTI

"It is not often that the world is blessed with a new thing in music; but the future historian of the divine art will be obliged to record the fact that toward the end of the nineteenth century some genius invented the Patti farewell, which grew so in popular favor that in the course of a few years it came to be a public festival in the temple of Diana in Madison Square, attended by youths and maidens, with choral exclamations and offerings of flowers. And it will also be recorded that old men who had as youths heard Madame Patti sing in the consulship of Mapleson, when her farewell had just been invented, wept with joy on realizing that though she was still 'an exile from home', at $4,000 an evening and had not yet succeeded in coming all the way through the rye, she was as delicious to the senses as the last rose of summer, which had become her special property."

The following also, was "writ sarcastik," as Artemus Ward used to put it: "Patti is becoming more cautious and conservative in her farewell announcements from decade to decade. On the latest occasion she simply made her 'last appearance in Albert Hall.' London has plenty more halls."

My attacks on the prima donna who was idolized by the whole operatic world naturally aroused resentment and unfavorable comment. One of the New York papers said: "The musical critic of the *Evening Post* is scoring Patti unmercifully, and, it is not too much to say, unjustly. Writing of the mad scene in Lucia he declares 'it is in such absurd scenes alone where all dramatic propriety is sacrificed to the prima donna, that Madame Patti commands applause; and this shows her in her true light. She is a great singer but not a great artist. If no one like her should ever again be born, the loss to music—i.e. the art of expressing esthetic emotions in tones—would be slight.' "

After quoting this, the editor adds: "Such vicious and

absurd attacks remove the writing from the province of criticism and weaken even its wholesome stricture."

My critic hit the nail on the head! No doubt, everything I said about Patti's shortcomings was true. She was infinitely more interested in showing off her lovely voice than in the music she sang. The composer was for her a mere peg to hang on her trills and frills. She never attended rehearsals. She asked so much ($5000 cash down) for appearing in an operatic performance that the manager was obliged to economize in all other directions, so that good all-round representations became impossible.

But as a singer she was so glorious, so incomparable, that while under the spell of her vocal art the listeners forgot everything else and simply luxuriated in ecstatic bliss. I myself often wrote glowing paragraphs describing the charm of her voice and the ingratiating spontaneity of her singing. I consider myself fortunate in having been able to listen twice a week to the sweetest and most mellow voice the world has ever heard.

It was like the singing of the nightingales I used to be enchanted with in the Tiergarten in Berlin. Patti was a nightingale; why ask more of her? In her way she was absolutely perfect, and perfection of any kind should be honored and extolled, without any of the buts and ifs on which I dwelt too much.

In plain language, I made an ass of myself. I wanted Patti to be something else. Oddly enough she also was longing to be different! I objected to the flimsy operas she appeared in; so did she! She was dying to score in masterworks like "Carmen" and "Aïda," but they were not in her line. She would have given one of her beautiful black eyes to be able to sing and act Elsa, or Elizabeth or Eva, not to speak of the still more dramatic parts in the Wagner operas. She made no secret of her preferences, and repeatedly attended the Wagner festivals at Bayreuth for the great pleasure they gave her.

My stupid attitude deprived me of the opportunity of meeting Patti personally and hearing her talk—in English, Italian, French, German, Spanish or any other language one pleased—about her varied operatic experiences. When Krehbiel, William Steinway and others proposed to give a dinner in her honor I was of course invited, but naturally declined; she might have snubbed me, and for the best of reasons.

WILLIAM STEINWAY

It would have been strange if William Steinway had not been among the men who planned this dinner to Patti. He was always in the forefront of everything going on in the musical community. In his way he was just as important as were Theodore Thomas or Adelina Patti in their fields.

A whole book might be written on the part the builders of pianos have played in promoting the cause of music in America. The giving of recitals in the United States was a risky thing for any but the most famous pianists. Even these were glad to have their way paved by the manufacturers; and as for the others, they would seldom if ever have ventured to come across the ocean had not these piano-makers insured them against loss.

In return, they had to play the instruments of their guarantors. This was sometimes anything but an advantage. In fact, I could give the names of very good pianists who fell flat in New York because, on the inferior instruments given to them, they could not do themselves justice—could not show that they had command of a beautiful tone. You cannot make a tin pan sound like a silver bell.

It is often said that a Kreisler can get a better tone out of an ordinary fiddle than an ordinary fiddler can get out of a Stradivarius. Maybe; but, all the same, Kreisler never fails to use his Stradivarius, or else his Guarnerius, when he plays in public.

Thanks chiefly to Theodore Steinway, the Edison among piano builders, America achieved first place in at least one department of music. He made innumerable experiments, traveling as far as Africa to get woods and accessories that would insure a rich mellow tone from the keyboard such as had never been heard on sea or land. As a result, the Steinway tone has ranked for more than half a century with such things as the Stradivarius tone and the voice of Patti, as the *ne plus ultra* of tonal beauty.

William Steinway was not, like his uncle Theodore, an inventor. Nor was he a good business man; in fact, he disposed of the big profits of the firm in a way that alarmed the family. He was generous to a fault. Seldom did any one with a plausible musical plan go to him for help without getting it. I was in his office in Steinway Hall one day when he was asked for an advertisement covering the last page of a new musical magazine. "Certainly!" he said; "how much will it be? One hundred dollars? All right." And poor Charles Tretbar, who was a sort of financial chaperon, muttered to himself: "Another $1200 a year!"

When I was ready to get married I went to William Steinway and said I wanted to buy one of his best uprights as a present for my bride. "All right," he said; "make your own price."

"No," I replied, "I don't want you to lose a cent, but it won't hurt you if you'll let me have it at cost price."

He helped me select the instrument; that was in 1890, and until I left New York Mr. Kämmer, the tuner, exclaimed over its beauty of tone every time he came to our house.

Maybe you don't know, but it's a fact that journalistic etiquette forbids—or forbade—the musical critics to name the pianos used by players. Krehbiel once told me he had been offered $100 for merely naming a piano to be played on a certain occasion, without using any adjectives. I mention this to show that William Steinway, in making special terms for my wedding present, did not do so for business reasons, but was simply following out his philanthropic or friendly impulses. Everybody, as I have said, relied on him. Every orchestral or chamber music association was backed by him, nor did he overlook even the opera companies; he once helped Abbey and Grau to the tune of $50,000.

He was a very busy man, William Steinway was; too busy in fact. After an attack of typhoid fever he went back to his desk too soon; there was a breakdown and he died. Doubtless his doctor had advised him to loaf a year, as mine did when I had typhoid. I obeyed and survived; he didn't. Sometimes it is better not to be a millionaire.

While obeying the rules that pianos must not be named in my critical columns, I made two bad breaks in jumping on inferior instruments that prevented the players from doing themselves justice. The day after my first assault an agent came to the managing editor, James E. Learned, pale with rage, and wanted to know what the *Post* meant by maltreating one of its best advertisers.

Mr. Learned replied: "We don't wish our editors to be influenced by the advertising columns. I shouldn't wonder if Mr. Finck never looked at them."

It was not a good way for a newspaper to get rich quick, and the *Evening Post* never did get rich quick, or slowly either.   And because of this lofty policy we all had to content ourselves with modest salaries.

If you don't mind that sort of thing, honesty is the best policy.

The other affair was more serious.   It resulted in a suit for damages—three suits, in fact, two of them being brought by the *Post* against trade papers which had spoken libelously about us.   One of them accused me of being "a hired cut-throat masquerading in the robes of an upright judge."   Dear me!   I had no idea I was poking my finger into such an overflowing hornet's nest.   I had simply expressed my indignation that prominent pianists, whom I named, had indorsed an instrument that did not seem to me a good one.   It was an almost unprecedented thing for a critic to do—hence the row.

When I got a note from the attorney, Lawrence Godkin (son of my chief) saying: "Mr. White told me when the *Evening Post* paid our last bill for these suits, that the *Post* did not care to be responsible for any more expenses in them, so that hereafter I presume that we will look direct to you"—I dropped the matter suddenly.

This was the first and also the last time I ever appeared in the rôle of Don Quixote tilting at tinpanny pianos. Subsequently I followed the much more subtle and deadly plan of simply mentioning the lack of a mellow, luscious tone as one of the player's shortcomings.

That left it to him to place the blame and to reform his business methods.   I learned this neat little trick from my highly esteemed colleague, William James Henderson.

CAMPANINI AND MAPLESON

At the time when I honored New York by accepting a place on the editorial staff of one of its leading newspapers the Academy of Music was the only home of grand opera. I could not but feel flattered when I heard it had been opened in 1854, the year of my birth. How could they know?

The Academy was by no means New York's first opera house. Its immediate predecessor, the Astor Place Opera House, was transformed into the Mercantile Library. There were two others before it, not to speak of diverse theaters temporarily given over to more or less crude performances of plays with music.

As this volume is concerned only with events in which I was "among those present," I have nothing to say about early opera in New York. Krehbiel and Sonneck have ably covered that historic ground. They did not have to go back so very far; as Krehbiel wrote in 1908 of Italian opera in New York, "It seems more than a little strange that its entire history should come within the memories of persons still living"—memories going back to 1825, "when the new form of entertainment effected an entrance in the New World."

Italy had had a primitive form of opera more than two hundred years earlier; some things travel slowly.

Opera-goers who frequented the Academy of Music between the year of its birth, 1854, and 1886 the year of its death as a regular opera house, heard many world-famed artists. Among those who sang there before my day were Grisi, Parepa Rosa, Piccolomini, Mario, and Brignoli; but I had the good luck to hear in this auditorium Adelina Patti, Christine Nilsson, Annie Louise Kellogg, Clara Louise Cary, Sofia Scalchi, Emma Albani, Etelka Gerster (who aroused Patti's jealousy), Minnie Hauck (our first great Carmen), Pauline Lucca, Emma Nevada, Galassi, Del Puente, Ravelli, Maurel, and Italo Campanini, the idolized predecessor of Caruso.

To Campanini, I frankly confess, I was not fair. "He

abuses me like a pickpocket" he once complained to Theodore Thomas in speaking about me.

What aroused my ire was that, like Patti and many other singers of that time, he never lost a chance to show off his voice to best advantage even if, in so doing, he distorted the music as intended by the composer. He did this here and there in "Lohengrin," to my great indignation.

If I hadn't been so young a man I would have thought the matter over and said to myself: "To be sure he does that sort of thing now and then, but on the other hand let us be thankful for the chance to hear Wagner's music sung by this superb voice—a voice that no German tenor, however deeply versed in Wagner lore, can exhibit."

His dramatic fervor in such operas as "Carmen" and "Aïda" indicated that, with due encouragement and opportunity, he might have become an excellent Wagnerian tenor. But I *dis*couraged him.

One of the most praiseworthy things done by this tenor was that he brought his younger brother, Cleofonte, to New York where he was destined, some years later, to win boundless admiration as a conductor of French and Italian works during the Hammerstein seasons at the Manhattan Opera House. Italo brought him over in 1888 to conduct a series of performances of Verdi's new opera, "Otello."

The enterprise proved a pitiable failure. The performances were given too late in the season—the second half of April; they were given in the Academy of Music, which was no longer fashionable among opera-goers; the singers were not of the highest rank; and, above all, "Otello" was not so tuneful as Verdi's earlier operas. It has therefore never become popular in New York. With splendid pluck Campanini threw himself into the cast

ITALO CAMPANINI AS "MANRICO" IN "IL TROVATORE"

when the tenor he had brought from Italy failed to please; but it was too late.

A singer and his money are soon parted when he turns manager. " 'Tis an old story and yet it's always new."

Outstanding among the personalities connected with the Academy of Music in its final years was the irrepressible manager Colonel James H. Mapleson. No matter how often he approached failure he always came up again fresh and smiling. He had the cunning to meet Patti's demands; her $5000 for a performance were always in hand before she stepped on the stage, even if the other singers were not so promptly attended to. Artists told me of checks given them on banks where there was no deposit; but eventually everybody seemed to be satisfied and ready to "come again."

"You are my enemy," Mapleson said to me one evening in the lobby, "but, I assure you, New York has had much worse performances than those I am giving."

He was right, and I did not make sufficient allowance for that fact. My attacks were sometimes unreasonably severe; once he stopped sending me tickets. Before I knew what was going to happen I had invited a young lady of my acquaintance to go with me to hear Patti. The *Post* paid for one of my tickets; I had to buy the other with my own money, which didn't improve my temper. Before the next season began Mapleson came down to the office and asked me to select my own seats!

Instead of giving samples of my ridiculous savagery, let me cite a facetious letter written to me by one of Theodore Thomas's Brooklyn friends and backers, James W. Elwell: "I have written a short sketch of your life and of your cruel taking off, which I shall send to the *Evening Post* to have on hand against the day when you are found dead in the Academy of Music. The sketch incriminates Col. Mapleson to such a degree that I don't see how the police can help arresting him. I think the *Post* should furnish you with a coat of chain armor if it proposes to continue its contrast of North and South in such matters."

The same letter contains some interesting remarks anent Henry E. Abbey, who was soon to be the first manager of the new Metropolitan Opera House. They show what sort of plans were in the air just before the beginning of the great war between New York's two rival opera houses.

"I enclose you a letter of Mr. H. E. Abbey relative to German opera and call your attention to the *Tribune's* notion of Nilsson's remarks about singing in Vienna Elsa to Materna's Ortrud with Hans Richter to conduct. Such a combination with Thomas to conduct, and with Scaria and others from Vienna would be overwhelming and I wish you would come out in favor of it soon. Let us hope the thing can be pushed through. Perhaps Abbey, after all, will be the best man obtainable as manager."

The Great Opera War

Society, not music, furnished the main reason for the building of the Metropolitan Opera House and the resulting abandonment of the Academy of Music after a few years of warfare.

With pardonable vanity, society women like to have others admire their elegant and costly gowns, many of them real works of art. Fashionable gatherings provide opportunities for this, but not on so large a scale as the opera. To sit in an opera box, to have hundreds of glasses leveled at your gorgeous clothes and to have them described in next morning's newspapers—can you imagine anything more likely to make society women favor grand opera?

The plain truth is that, except in Italy and Germany,

opera would be impossible without the patronage and liberal support of fashionable society. No doubt, operatic music makes a wider appeal than concerts, but the expense of a high-class company is so great that nothing could be done without boxes and subscriptions.

The Academy of Music could not have endured long without its boxes and the subscriptions therefor. To be the owner of an opera box became in New York, as it had long been in European cities, a special sign of aristocratic distinction. The best and oldest families in the city vied with one another in their eagerness to own one of these boxes, with the result that soon they were all taken. The supply no longer equaled the demand.

That's what started the trouble. The city was growing rapidly in size and wealth. There was a waiting list for boxes, which grew steadily. Some families on this list got impatient and decided to start an opera house of their own, where they could have first choice.

No time was lost. At a cost exceeding $1,732,000 the Metropolitan Opera House was built in the summer of 1883 in the block enclosed by Broadway and Seventh Avenue, Thirty-Ninth and Fortieth Streets. On October 22 of the same year it was ready for the opening performance!

Among the men prominent in the corporation which built it were William K. Vanderbilt, Robert Goelet, Joseph W. Drexel, Henry S. Marquand, Levi P. Morton, George N. Curtis, Edward Cooper, Adrian Iselin, William H. Tillinghast, Luther Kountze, George Henry Warren, James A. Roosevelt and George Griswold Haven.

In view of the great wealth of this corporation one had reason to expect a building of unusual architectural merit. Paris, Vienna, Buenos Aires, Mexico City and many smaller places have opera houses which it is a pleasure to look at. The Metropolitan, alas! might be mistaken for a warehouse or a state prison.

Nor was its inside what it should have been. The man responsible for it was a builder of distinction, but he had never before planned a theater—an art *sui generis*—the result being that neither were the acoustic qualities satisfactory nor did the stage have some of the necessary structures. Horses, for instance, could not be brought on, and horses are called for in some important operas.

After the opening performance I subjected the new building to a slashing criticism which gladdened the heart of Colonel Mapleson. It aroused the ire of the architect to such a pitch that he wrote a long letter to the *Evening Post* in defense of his work. But the changes made, some at once, others from year to year, justified my comments.

This then, was my home for the next forty years—or almost my home—particularly during my last two decades as one of the critics, when we had to spend most of our evenings and many afternoons, too, in it. Jim Ford, the humorist, reviewing my "Food and Flavor" in the *Herald,* wondered how I could have learned so much about the culinary art since I spent most of my time at the Metropolitan, where cooking was "not allowed in the auditorium, even during the performance of the Wagner operas!"

Henry E. Abbey's operatic ambitions had been realized. He was the head of the firm Abbey, Schoeffel and Grau which ran the first Metropolitan season; it included sixty-one performances of nineteen operas.

A good list of singers had been provided by him, among them Christine Nilsson and two other stars who had been prominent at the Academy of Music: Campanini and Del Puente. He also had Scalchi, Trebelli, Fursch-Madi, Lablache, Kaschmann, and—most important of all—Marcella Sembrich.

Against this brigade Colonel Mapleson, at the Academy, marshaled a company headed by Patti, Gerster, Pappenheim, Nicolini and Galassi. The repertory of both the rival houses was made up of familiar features. There were no novelties and there was too much Italian opera. One house with such a repertory might have prospered, two were one too many.

Startling deficits at both houses did not, however, end the operatic warfare. Mapleson, in the autumn, opened his season as usual; so did the Metropolitan, but with a surprizing change of scenery.

Italian opera having failed dismally at both houses, as well as in London under Mr. Gye, and Mr. Abbey being unwilling to risk losing another quarter of a million dollars the directors of the Metropolitan were in a mood to consider new plans. To everybody's astonishment they adopted one submitted by Dr. Leopold Damrosch to give a season of opera in German. He went abroad, returning two months later with all the arrangements made, and the contracts in his pocket!

Theodore Thomas had been maturing for some years a plan to give German opera—particularly Wagner opera —in New York. His Wagner Festival, for which he brought over Materna, Winckelmann and Scaria, was intended as the first gun in this campaign. He missed the psychological moment and Dr. Damrosch snatched the opportunity. Damrosch had been in New York twelve years as a giver of concerts; no one had ever thought of him as a conductor of operas, but to everybody's agreeable surprize, he acquitted himself very creditably of his new task.

He began with "Tannhäuser," almost unknown in New York two years after Wagner's death! Later in the season he added "Die Walküre," which was its most important achievement by far. Other operas by German composers in the list were "Lohengrin," "Fidelio," "Der

Freischütz," "Don Giovanni" and "Le Prophète," and
"Les Huguenots" by Meyerbeer who, though at the head
of the spectacular school of French opera, was a Prussian
Jew. France contributed Auber's "La Muette de Por-
tici" and Halévy's "La Juive"; Italy "William Tell" and
"Rigoletto."

Among Dr. Damrosch's singers were two women who
belonged to the first rank: Amalia Materna and Marianne
Brandt; with a third, Auguste Krauss, an incomparable
Sieglinde and Eva who, unfortunately, soon forsook the
stage to take care of her husband, Anton Seidl. There
was a good baritone-bass, Josef Staudigl, but the leading
tenor, Anton Schott, had an extraordinarily explosive way
of singing which Wagner would have been the first to
condemn. He was the pet aversion of Hans von Bülow,
who once, at Hanover, conducting "Lohengrin" with
Schott as the Knight, dropped his baton and stopped up
both his ears to shut out the tenor's notes, which strayed
painfully from the pitch, and then exclaimed: "He's a
swine-knight, not a swan-knight."

The financial results of the first season of German
Opera were so encouraging that a second was being
planned as a matter of course. As for the repertory, the
fact that the three Wagner operas in it got twenty-five
performances while the other nine operas together had
only thirty-two between them, pointed the way to the
future.

Just before the end of the season Dr. Damrosch suddenly died of pneumonia. His sudden demise aroused
much public sympathy. Henry Ward Beecher, Horatio
Potter and Felix Adler spoke at the funeral. He left two
sons, Walter and Frank, who for years have played a
prominent part in the musical life of the Metropolis. He
had been a personal friend of Liszt, an ardent admirer of
his compositions; for them he did much missionary work—

a policy in which, I regret to say, his sons did not follow in his footsteps.

What was to be done next? Anton Schott promptly blossomed out with a plan which would make him the artistic director of the company. This feature was turned down by the directors, but his idea of engaging Wagner's favorite, Anton Seidl, as conductor for the coming season, was fortunately accepted. Edmund C. Stanton was appointed manager, with Walter Damrosch as assistant conductor. These two men went abroad and brought back with them, to add to the first season's list, three operatic artists of the very highest rank: Anton Seidl, Emil Fischer and Lilli Lehmann, destined to become, in New York, the greatest of dramatic sopranos, especially in Wagnerian parts—Isolde and Brünnhilde.

SEIDL THE GREAT

The coming of Anton Seidl to New York at this critical moment was a matter of tremendous importance to the cause of opera in America.

We have just seen how Mapleson and Abbey and Grau failed to interest the opera-goers of New York in the stale repertory of the day, though they presented the four leading prima donnas of the time: Patti and Gerster in one house, Nilsson and Sembrich in the other.

Something new was evidently wanted, and that something was the operas of Richard Wagner, as the results of the successful Damrosch season proved.

Wagner had almost reached his seventieth birthday when he died; yet at that moment the only one of his ten great music dramas known to more than a handful of Americans was "Lohengrin"!

The situation called for a great general to conquer the

world for his other masterworks. That general came and his triumphs were phenomenal.

There were other great Wagner conductors in Germany and Vienna at that time, but none of them, not even Hans Richter, the leader chosen by Wagner for the first Bayreuth Festival, could have done what Anton Seidl did.

No other had had his unique opportunities to enter into the innermost spirit of Wagner's music dramas. For seven years (1872-1879) he lived as a member of the great master's household helping him prepare his Nibelung and "Parsifal" scores for public performance and the printer. During the first Nibelung festival he was one of the conductors on the stage. He astonished the master daily by his ingenuity in dovetailing scenic with musical effects; in this important aspect of Wagnerian art he was without an equal, as the master himself declared. He also pronounced him incomparable in his choice of *tempi* (pace) and frequent modifications thereof, on which this music depends so much for its emotional effects.

Seidl's widow showed me once a poem in Wagner's handwriting in which he declared bluntly that Anton was the only one who had "sung himself, from head to sole, into the Ring of the Nibelung." And when Angelo Neumann was getting together a company to carry the Wagner music dramas to German cities that had not yet heard them, as well as to the leading cities of England, Holland and Italy, and asked who should be the conductor, Wagner answered "Anton Seidl."

You can now understand how lucky it was for the Metropolitan directors to secure this same man as leader of their forces during the second season of opera in German.

He was young and vigorous; he was a tremendous worker, and he had enthusiasm to burn. Under his inspiring guidance Lilli Lehmann became, as already intimated,

ANTON SEIDL

the foremost of dramatic sopranos, and Jean de Reszke, greatest of Romeos, later became the prince of Tristans.

I knew all the singers at the Metropolitan personally (most of them intimately) excepting the mediocrities, whom I did not wish to know. These singers held diverse opinions on many subjects, but on one thing I found them cordially agreed: on Anton Seidl's incomparable conductorship. "We feel that things *can not* go wrong when he is in his chair, so we always are at ease, which is half the battle." "If I forget a line," said Jean de Reszke to me, "I look at Seidl and read it on his lips." "He never drowns out our voices with his huge orchestra" was another compliment gratefully proffered. And the public was grateful because he knew how to reduce the duration of "Siegfried," for instance from four hours and a half to three hours and forty minutes without making any damaging cuts. Seidl worked not only with but for the others, with both body and soul. At the end of each act he had to go to his room and change all his linen. He could not have done what Walter Damrosch once did, conducting both "Tristan and Isolde" and "Die Meistersinger" on the same day, yet looking all the time as cool as a cucumber. Personally I never cared much for the cool-as-a-cucumber style of conducting, particularly in Wagner's music dramas.

Under Seidl's baton New Yorkers heard the first American performances of "Tristan," "Meistersinger," "Rheingold," "Siegfried" and "Götterdämmerung." I wish I could add "Parsifal," for which he was peculiarly qualified; but "Parsifal" was not staged in New York till after his death. He did, however, conduct it one summer at Bayreuth and this is what the eminent critic August Spanuth wrote:

"None of the musicians who conducted 'Parsifal' at Bayreuth heretofore—Levy, Richter and Mottl—were so intimately acquainted with the work, or saw it in the process of creation as Anton Seidl did. For it was during the six years that Seidl lived with Wagner that 'Parsifal' was composed. And whenever the Meister had completed a new section of the score, his companion Seidl was the first who had to play it over for him. Such a proceeding makes a more lasting impression on the memory than any subsequent explanations, and for that reason Anton Seidl is indeed in so far a true 'Guardian of the Grail' as he is the real bearer of the Wagnerian traditions. All other 'Parsifal' conductors allowed themselves to be influenced by Frau Wagner. Seidl had made up his mind to go straight ahead according to his lights, and Frau Wagner and her son, who usually assume absolute control of affairs, did not interfere with him or suggest any corrections. . . .

"And when the first performance was over, Frau Wagner, with tears in her eyes, embraced Seidl, and declared that it had been as in the old times, at the last performance given under Wagner's own supervision."

Madame Cosima is also reported to have remarked how much Seidl reminded her of her father, Liszt, by his gestures. I wonder if she suspected, as others have, that her father was also Anton Seidl's father.

What made the public adore Liszt was the thrilling *emotionalism* of his playing.

Czerny wrote concerning Beethoven's playing that "frequently not an eye remained dry, while many would break out into loud sobs; for there was something wonderful in his expression." Anton Seidl had this same gift of expression, this power of evoking tears which usually belongs only to creative geniuses like Liszt and Paderewski; and therein lay the secret of his popularity.

In the concert hall as in the opera house he always laid bare the heart of a work of art and always he reached the heart of the hearers. Only a few months before his death he conducted the Adagio Lamentoso from Tchaikovsky's Pathetic Symphony at the Waldorf Astoria in such a heartrending way that half the audience was in tears, and tears were rolling down his own cheeks, as a member of the orchestra told me.

Richard Arnold, the concert master, told me that the orchestral players were also equally moved. All who were there felt as if Seidl were conducting his own dirge.

Dvořák and Seidl were great friends and often took their afternoon coffee together at Fleischmann's. Seidl was not affable; he shunned society, he was taciturn and shy in the presence of all but his most intimate friends. Sometimes he and the composer of the New World Symphony sat for an hour in silence; then they began to exchange confidences and both grew eloquent.

I shall never forget what Seidl did with that hackneyed piece, Beethoven's third Leonore overture. He made of it what Wagner called it, a drama complete in itself. At the Metropolitan Opera House he conducted it before the second act of "Fidelio" with such fire and dramatic impetuosity that even the fashionable boxholders, most of whom seldom paid any attention to the orchestra, burst out into wild and prolonged applause. *Seidl had made Beethoven as exciting to them as jazz!*

Still another variety of emotionalism in which Anton Seidl excelled was the delicate, dainty style of some of the best French music as exemplified in Massenet's "Manon," which was one of his favorite operas. In Wagner's operas there are many pages of exquisitely tender music, and with this, too, Seidl often moved his hearers to tears. His reading of the "Siegfried Idyl" was inconceivably colorful and ravishing. Too long? When *he* conducted it, I wished it would never end.

Of all the varieties of emotional expression, however,

the one that appealed most to Seidl was the Magyar. He was, like Liszt, a Hungarian, and the passionate impetuosity and lawless irregularity of movement which prevail in Liszt's music were his native element. With him died the greatest of Liszt's interpreters, as well as of Wagner's and Tchaikovsky's and Dvorák's.

It was most fortunate for concert-goers in New York that when Theodore Thomas went to Chicago, his place as conductor of the Philharmonic was given to Seidl. How did the audience like him? Money talks! More eloquent than pages of comment is the fact that before he assumed the conductorship of the Philharmonic that society had never made more than $34,000 in one year. In the sixth year of his conductorship the receipts had risen to $57,000.

It was in the opera, nevertheless, that Seidl was most entrancing and indispensable. Oddly enough, he rose to even greater heights after, than during the seven years of German Opera at the Metropolitan. Hereby hangs one of the most delectable tales in the history of music, which must now be told.

Overthrow of German Opera

On a preceding page I dwelt on the fact that grand opera is impossible without the support of society, and a plutocracy willing to pay lavishly for the most comfortable and conspicuous seats. This applies particularly also to the seven years of German opera given at the Metropolitan. The wonder is that there were as many as seven. For it was no secret that most of the wealthy box-holders did not really care for this kind of opera. They would have much preferred "Lucia" to "Tristan," "Il Trovatore" to "Siegfried." Yet for seven years they patiently paid the piper and allowed themselves to be bored to death by music they did not understand.

Photograph by Mieczkowski

JEAN DE RESZKE AS "ROMEO"

In truth, these society leaders were in a way heroes and heroines—martyrs in the cause of highbrow music. Those of us who reveled in the excellent Wagnerian performances which their long purses made possible had reasons to be extremely grateful to them. But the worm turned at last.

Almost as stealthily and unexpectedly as German opera had been adopted it was cast out of the Metropolitan, to be replaced by opera in Italian and French. The last season of opera in German was that of 1890-91. On January 15, 1891, it was announced officially that Abbey and Grau had been engaged as managers for the next season.

Great excitement was aroused by this statement among opera-goers. It was generally known that, what the box-holders particularly objected to in German opera was the predominance of Wagner; but this predominance was due to the fact that Wagner was just what the *audiences* particularly wanted. Yielding to their clamor, the management wisely devoted to his operas twenty-five out of the last thirty-five performances of the seventh and final season of German opera; and the public used every opportunity of giving tremendous ovations to Seidl and the great singers associated with him, by way of showing its displeasure with the contemplated change.

Abbey and Grau were sufficiently impressed by these demonstrations to take over for their first season Lilli Lehmann, foremost of the German singers, and Anton Seidl, who conducted some performances of Wagner's "Meistersinger," listed in Italian as "I Maestri Cantori."

The principal achievement of the managers who superseded Mr. Stanton was that they brought over to New York at once some great singers who henceforth played a prominent part in the musical life of the Metropolitan. They were Emma Eames, Jean Lassalle and Jean and Edouard de Reszke.

THE DE RESZKE MIRACLE

Jokes are somehow more interesting than serious matters, at any rate to me, and probably to most of my readers. Let me begin therefore by telling about the great Jean de Reszke joke.

This wonderful man—the greatest tenor I have ever known or heard—was brought over to America deliberately for the purpose of helping to break the Wagner spell; but instead of doing so he became the most powerful champion Richard Wagner has ever had anywhere! Not only did he delight the Wagnerites but—now comes the joke—*he made Wagner fashionable!* After he had been at the Metropolitan a few years the special *society nights* were those in which he appeared in one of his Wagner rôles! If that isn't funny I don't know what is.

Imagine what all that meant to me, who had fought so hard and persistently to make Wagner popular in my native country. I wanted to hug Jean for performing this miracle. Of course we soon became warm friends. He was so enchanted with the tributes I paid him in the *Evening Post*—tributes so glowing that Henry Villard intimated I was overdoing the thing (but I wasn't!)—that he expressed a desire to meet me; and thenceforth some of the happiest hours of my life were spent in his company and that of his brother Edouard, also a first-class artist and one of the jolliest souls that ever dwelt on this globe.

The De Reszke brothers had the reputation of being "inaccessible" and very "dignified." Dignified! Whenever they lunched at our home, at 485 Manhattan Avenue, we were in for two or three hours of fast and furious fun. Both of them had an amazing faculty for talking and singing exactly like any one of their colleagues they chose to mimic. It was really sinful to waste all this fun on so small an audience. Extravagantly paid though they were as opera singers, Jean and Edouard de Reszke could have made even more money in vaudeville.

But money was not what they were after primarily. They were born artists, aiming at the highest. When Jean first came to New York his only Wagnerian rôle was Lohengrin and I was not very favorably impressed by that, though I admired his voice very much. Then he came under the magic wand of Anton Seidl and ere long he was singing and acting Wagner rôles more wonderfully than any German tenor, just as he had previously sung and acted French opera parts more delightfully than any French tenor, and at least one Italian rôle better than any Italian tenor.

In this all-round superexcellence Jean was unique. His Romeo, in Gounod's opera, was a real man as well as an ardent lover. The duel scene stands out in my memory as few operatic incidents do. As he stood perfectly motionless, his face alone pictured the full depths of Romeo's despair at losing his love—his wife. Equally wonderful was the lost, groping expression in his eyes, the heart-breaking struggle to remember Brünnhilde after he had drunk the potion Hagen brewed in "Götterdämmerung." He said one day that that was the moment when Siegfried's soul died. And the glory of him as he stood at first revealed on Tristan's ship! Can we ever forget, those who saw and worshiped? His martial yet musical Rhadames, in "Aïda," was another impersonation which made opera seem as real as life itself. His Des Grieux in "Manon," his Werther, his Raoul in "Les Huguenots," and his Faust are among the indelible impressions in this writer's mind.

Edouard de Reszke once confided to me his grief because an operatic basso has so much fewer opportunities

than a tenor for achieving great things. Undoubtedly
the composers have been partial to tenors; yet when
Edouard got hold of a great part like Mephisto, or Hans
Sachs, or Hagen, or Leporello, he made one forget this
fact and pity the tenors.

His Hagen was as terrifying as his Leporello was comic
—except for his dear kind eyes, which couldn't look wicked.
And he never could persuade himself to really plunge the
spear into his beloved Jean's back in the last act. I remember only half-a-dozen things in my operatic experiences so perfect, so delectable, as his singing of Mozart's
air about Don Juan's "mille e tre" victims in Spain alone,
while waving about the huge sheet filled with their names.

In the part of Mephistopheles, Edouard discovered
humorous possibilities that had escaped his predecessors
and that were immensely diverting. A Boston critic took
me to task for approving of these humorous touches; but,
great heavens! They are everywhere, in and between the
lines. In London I once heard Henry Irving improve on
Goethe by interpolating the devil's remark regarding the
tiresome Martha: "I wonder what will become of her
when she dies. *I* don't want her!"

One of the amusing consequences of Jean's popularity
was the eagerness of all the prima donnas to be associated
with him in a cast; they fairly tumbled over each other.
It meant of course, that they would sing to a crowded
audience, but there was another and more important consideration. Time and again I have noticed to how much
greater advantage the famous prima donnas at the Metropolitan appeared when they had the privilege of being
associated with a high-class tenor. Often Geraldine Farrar
poured into my ears her grief because a stick of a tenor
had marred her best efforts. Galli-Curci's best appearance in New York was as Juliette to the Romeo of Lucien

Photograph by Nadar

EDOUARD DE RESZKE

Muratore, whose art seemed to transmute and glorify hers; he was the only Romeo who could hold his own in comparison with Jean de Reszke. And Patti knew not how hugely she blundered when she allowed her beloved Nicolini's tones to mar her exquisite singing. There was a naughty story that she charged $1000 less for singing with Nicolini (including his fee) than for singing alone! *Ben trovato* if not true.

I have written elsewhere* of Jean's marvelous impersonations of Tristan, Siegfried, Lohengrin, and Walter. He fully realized how much he owed to Seidl in his efforts to get "under the skin" of the Wagnerian characters. Among the tributes cabled from abroad when Seidl died was one from Jean referring to him as "the greatest of all Wagner conductors"—a tribute doubly significant because he had just been singing under Hans Richter in St. Petersburg. He used to say "Seidl carries us in the hollow of his hand."

The casting out of German opera from the Metropolitan naturally put Seidl for a time in the background. It was through Jean de Reszke that he was restored to his proper place. Jean made this restoration a condition of his appearing in certain rôles. As there seemed some danger of the Wagner operas being put in the hands of an Italian (Mancinelli, a good conductor, *but*. . . . !) my wife and I went to see Jean during an intermission. He did not share our fears. When we wondered whether Grau could be persuaded to do the right thing, he drew himself up and with the imperious mien of a king exclaimed: "Si je le veux je le veux!" And his will was law.

Jean (he preferred to be called just Jean) made Wagner opera fashionable in Paris as well as in London. One season he sang "Siegfried" no fewer than eleven times in the French Metropolis. There will never be another like this Polish tenor.

* "Success In Music and How It Is Won."

Emma Eames and De Gogorza

The years of all-star opera which constitute the Golden Age in the annals of New York began with the engagement of the De Reszke brothers and several great prima donnas. Outstanding among these was Emma Eames. She was the Marguerite in a cast including the two De Reszkes and Lassalle, the result being that "Faust" was sung eight times in rapid succession to overflowing audiences.

It was as Juliette that Miss Eames made her début at the Metropolitan, where her rare personal beauty, her exquisitely pure and lovely voice and her refined musical instincts won an immediate triumph for her, as they had previously in Covent Garden, London, and at the Grand Opéra in Paris.

What made her art in these two operas the more alluring was that Gounod himself had coached her in them. He was so enthusiastic over her rare combination of gifts, which made her an ideal prima donna, that he simply forced her on the manager of the Opéra, who was amazed and delighted at the lovely American's immediate success.

To Madame Marchesi belongs the honor of having "discovered" Emma Eames, it is usually said, but I am not so sure of that. One time, when I happened to be in Cambridge, Professor Paine told me he had found a young girl who, he believed, would become a great prima donna. He wanted me to come with him and call on her, and as he added that she was remarkably beautiful I was more than willing.

She was living with her mother (who became a famous teacher of singing) in a modest apartment on Temple Street, Boston. I was delighted with her voice and personality—it was a case of love at first sight for both (I mean both voice and personality), as I frankly confessed to her when she had become famous.

Before she became famous I met her once more. At the railway station in Lucerne, Switzerland, I saw two ladies, evidently Americans, trying in vain to explain in German what they wanted to have done with their trunks. Lifting my hat I said: "I know German; is there anything I can do to help you?"

"Why, here is Mr. Finck!" exclaimed Emma. It was the budding prima donna from Boston and her mother. They were on their way to the usual summer festival at Bayreuth. So was I, with my handsome friend Edgar J. Levy, for a time musical critic of the *Globe* and subsequently Comptroller of New York City for years, regardless of party changes. Of course we all took seats in the same car going direct to Munich and became well-acquainted. I was horribly jealous of Edgar because, somehow, he managed to more or less monopolize the conversation with Emma. From Bayreuth she went to Paris, where her career began soon thereafter.

Emma Eames was an extremely aristocratic young lady. She never made the slightest attempt to win the personal friendship of critics. Once, when I commented on my good fortune in having got on such friendly terms that we called each other by our first names, she said it was lucky we had met before she came to New York else we might never have become friends, as she hadn't much use for critics, however friendly, and avoided them purposely.

Once a friend always a friend with her, rather an unusual quality in a prima donna as they are often as changeable in the matter of intimacies as they are in their rôles.

In most of the operas in which this American prima donna appeared, her aristocratic mien and bearing were a distinct advantage, the only exception being Marguerite in the first scene, where she was not sufficiently the simple village maiden; but that was gradually mended.

Among her Italian and French parts that I recall with particular pleasure are her pathetic Micaela in "Carmen" and Desdemona in "Otello," her Ero in Mancinelli's opera, her Iris in Mascagni's best work after "Cavalleria Rusticana," her Elvira and Donna Anna in "Don Giovanni," her refined yet thrilling Tosca, her Pamina in the "Magic Flute," her Aïda, and above all the Countess in "The Marriage of Figaro." When she and Sembrich sang the letter duo in this tuneful comic opera it was almost impossible, with eyes closed, to tell which of the two happened to sing, so amazingly alike in timbre and golden purity were their voices.

In assuming such parts as Donna Anna, Tosca and Aïda, Mme. Eames entered the dramatic field so persuasively that it became obvious that she, too, would find her place among the great Wagner singers. Had Seidl lived to guide her—as she herself said to me—she might have become an Isolde or even a Brünnhilde; but as it was, she enriched her repertory with Elsa, Elizabeth, Eva and Sieglinde, each of which had a unique poetic charm.

Speaking of Sieglinde reminds me of an incident wherein I got a sample of Emma's "pep." There was to be an operatic benefit for Seidl's widow; all the singers were eager to co-operate, but it was extremely difficult to make up a program doing justice to all of them. With misgivings I wrote to Emma and asked if she would be willing to appear in the second act of "Die Walküre." Now, in this act there is little for Sieglinde to sing—too little, Miss Eames thought. She gave me a piece of her mind in a letter which, on second thought, she destroyed. Then she wrote another, declining to take part in the benefit, but enclosing a check for $500.

On the subject of benefit concerts she once told me

Photograph by Falk

EMMA EAMES

an amusing incident which occurred in London.. Several
ladies of the highest aristocratic circle called on her to
ask if she would kindly sing for their pet charity. After
a moment's thought she answered sweetly: "I will, on one
condition. You are all wealthy ladies, far wealthier than
I. Now my usual *cachet* is £300.. I will contribute that
by singing, on condition that each of you will sign for the
same amount."

The visitors said they would consider the offer and left.
She never heard from them again, it is needless to say.
The charity of society women too often resembles Mark
Twain's climbing of the Swiss snow mountains—by proxy.

Miss Eames disliked that kind of women, and some
other kinds too. To my wife she said one day: "I love to
give parties for the pleasure of leaving out certain persons
who want to come."

She had a sharp tongue, and wit to burn. If I recorded
here everything she told us on various occasions about
certain operatic managers, conductors and singers it
would increase the sale of these Memoirs mightily.

Emma Eames was born in China—her parents happened to be at Hong Kong. Their home was Bath, Maine.
When she retired from the stage she bravely tried to make
that city her home but finally went back to gayer Paris.

Among the many interesting memories I have associated with that city none is more vivid than a dinner
at La Pérouse's, one of the famous restaurants *de luxe*.
Emma and her husband, Emilio de Gogorza, were the
hosts, my wife and I and Pol Plançon the guests. Plançon was not only the greatest French basso of his time
but one of the most famous epicures in the world's most
epicurean city. No doubt the head-waiter had that in
mind when he made a special trip to a suburb to get a
melon for us. It was a great melon! And when the same
head-waiter carved the duck, with a dexterity that made

us exclaim in astonishment, he said, proudly, that he had received second prize for carving at a contest of waiters. Delightfully Parisian, wasn't it?

One of the unique lunches at our home in New York was given to Emma Eames and her first husband, Julian Story and to Mr. and Mrs. Julian Hawthorne. The father of Julian Story, the famous sculptor, and Nathaniel Hawthorne, still considered by many America's foremost fiction writer, were very intimate friends at Rome, but their sons had never chanced to meet.

Emma Eames was less happy with this, her first husband, than with her second, Emilio de Gogorza. Among concert baritones he has been unrivaled. He uses his glorious voice in a temperamental way that always arouses tremendous enthusiasm. No one has ever sung Spanish songs in such a thoroughly Spanish way except perhaps Marguerite D'Alvarez, but she lacks his wonderfully pure voice.

Edison insists that no critic equals the phonograph as a voice-tester. Judged by this method Emilio de Gogorza stands supreme. No other "records" are quite as satisfactory as his. For eight years he was at the head of the artistic department of the Victrola Company, showing famous singers how to do it.

MATERNA, BRANDT AND LEHMANN

Before I continue my gossip about the great prima donnas who, in the Grau years made possible the epoch-making all-star casts, I must turn back to say a few words about some of the singers and the star casts of the seven years of German opera. Thanks to these singers, and to Seidl, not a few of these performances belong in the golden age of musical New York. There is no room here for details about the operas; I shall write only about the singers.

Amalie Materna, Marianne Brandt, Schroeder-Hanfstängl, Auguste Krauss (Seidl) and Anton Schott were the leading singers in the first German season. Of the last two of these I have already written. Materna and Brandt were the first representatives heard in New York of the new style of dramatic vocalism. Both had enjoyed the coaching of Wagner himself who—though it is not generally known—was the foremost of voice teachers and without an equal also in the art of making real actors out of the singing puppets so numerous in his day.*

In Brandt, Wagner had found a born artist who could do great things of her own accord yet derived tremendous benefit from his teaching. Her Ortrud in "Lohengrin" was easily the most thrilling of all the impersonations of that hateful character the world has seen and heard. Unequaled also was her Fides in Meyerbeer's "Le Prophète"; I can name no actress on the purely theatrical stage that could have surpassed her in emotional grandeur in that part, or as the loving wife in Beethoven's "Fidelio."

Not even Schumann-Heink gave so gruesome a picture of Erda,—Erda, rising unwilling and remote, at Wotan's command and finally swathing her head with her dun veils and sinking back into the earth's depths, a very part and personification of them.

Beauty is, no doubt, a great asset in the winning of success on the stage, but it is by no means an essential. The triumphant careers of Materna and Brandt, neither of whom had beauty of either face or form, should encourage to perseverance any young woman who, with real talent for singing and acting, may hesitate to go ahead for lack of personal charm. To be sure it is very much easier sailing for beautiful women like Lilli Lehmann, Emma

---

* See the chapter on Wagner as a teacher in my "Musical Progress."

Eames, Emma Calvé, Geraldine Farrar, or Lillian Nordica.

Lilli Lehmann was very beautiful in face and form when I first saw her in 1876, singing and swimming the subaqueous part of the first Rhine maiden at the Bayreuth festival. Wagner had been simply bowled over by her personal beauty as well as her lovely voice; he was eager to adopt the girl when she was sixteen, but her mother wisely refused; she couldn't feel quite sure that his intentions were solely musico-dramatic.

In 1882 Wagner elected Lilli queen of the flower maidens in "Parsifal." When he died, the following year, he had no idea that she was destined to become the greatest of all Isoldes and Brünnhildes—the foremost dramatic soprano, in fact, of her time, if not of all time. To him she had been simply a lyric and colorature soprano with an exquisite voice. That was what she was on the operatic stage at large and might have remained had she not been summoned to New York and come under the influence of Anton Seidl. It's an interesting story.

For fifteen years she had won applause at the Royal Opera in Berlin as the first colorature singer. Owing to Prussian red tape in such matters, she would have found it practically impossible to ever take up another side of the art operatic than the florid or ornamental. She was not excluded from the more emotional parts, like Marguerite and Carmen; but it was in London that she first had a chance to show that her real sphere was in a Wagnerian part like Isolde.

That was in 1884; she then came to the Metropolitan in New York, where she was allowed to follow her natural dramatic impulses. This freedom she liked so much that she broke her Berlin contract, preferring to pay a fine of 13,000 marks rather than return to her former colorature field.

LILLI LEHMANN AS "BRÜNNHILDE"

Not that she despised that side of her art. To the end of her stage career she had a hankering, in particular, for the part of Bellini's Norma, which makes the highest demands on both the colorature agility and the emotional dramatic powers of a singer. This Italian opera, in fact, might have been cut to order for her, like a tailor-made garment. Probably no other German prima donna ever had so much of the Italian in her art as this adorable artiste.

Niemann, Alvary, Fischer

Jean de Reszke's euphonious way of singing Tristan and Walter and Siegfried was the ideal way Wagner had in his mind. Scaria was a German basso who lived up to his ideal of singing beautifully and enunciating distinctly at the same time; his Gurnemanz at the Bayreuth "Parsifal" festival is among the treasures most cherished in my memory, and I did not wonder at seeing Wagner so often walking about with him arm in arm. Of the German tenors Heinrich Vogel, the idol of Munich and also favorably known in New York, came nearest to Scaria. But as a rule Wagner had to content himself with cruder vocal material.

Albert Niemann was one of the Wagnerian singers who triumphantly overcame the disadvantage of having a voice not conspicuous for natural beauty. His fame as Tristan, in particular, became so great, in New York as it had been abroad, that at his farewell in this opera $4 parquet seats were sold for $10 and $15.

His artistic sincerity is attested by the fact that when he came to the Metropolitan he promptly began to restudy the Wagner parts with Seidl. He had had a much longer experience with these parts than this young conductor, but he felt that Seidl had a knowledge of these scores which he could have obtained only at first hand from Wagner himself. As soon as Niemann returned to Berlin he induced the intendant to offer the conductorship of the Royal Opera to Seidl. This offer was twice repeated in later years, but luckily the great Anton remained loyal to his adopted country. No one else would have been worthy of conducting that memorable all-star cast of "Tristan and Isolde" which included Lehmann, Brandt, Niemann, Fischer and Alvary. Grau, in his palmiest days, never improved on that.

In this performance Max Alvary had a small part— that of the Seaman, but the way he did it made it easy to foretell that he would soon take his place in the Metropolitan's list of foremost artists. He not only had a fine voice and a natural gift for acting but he was a remarkably good-looking and well-proportioned young man. His aspect and the cast of his voice made him an ideal Siegfried. So wonderful was he in this part that if America had been an operatic country as it was a theatrical one, he might have spent his life touring in this part, as Joseph Jefferson did, practically, as Rip and Bob Acres.

In the all-star performance of "Tristan" just referred to, Fischer was, of course, the King Marke. This was one of his most impressive parts; but his specialty was Hans Sachs in "Die Meistersinger." This part was so amazingly suited to his natural aspect and personality, his mellow voice and his capacity for gently humorous action that, in an operatic country, he (like Alvary as Siegfried) might have given up all his operatic years to touring as (may I say it?) a Sachsophone.

When Fischer reached the end of his twenty-one years in New York, a benefit performance was arranged for him in which once more he appeared as Sachs. The receipts were nearly $10,000; it was one of the biggest ovations stored up in my memory.

There was one thing about this superb basso that puzzled me. One afternoon, when he was making a call at our house, I spoke of the evident joy it gave him to impersonate Hans Sachs, the jovial cobbler-poet.

"It gives me no particular pleasure to impersonate that part or any other," he answered. "I cannot remember more than three performances in my life that I enjoyed."

I could hardly believe this, as I had always held that nobody can do anything well unless he enjoys doing it. But he held on to his assertion.

Let us now return to my reminiscences of the prima donnas, American, French, German and Australian, who enabled Maurice Grau to make his régime at the Metropolitan, the Golden Age of musical New York.

EMMA CALVÉ

The Metropolitan Opera House enjoyed unusual prosperity during the season which began on November 27, 1893.

It had rarely happened that any opera was sung more than five or six times in one season. But during that operatic year Bizet's "Carmen" had the unprecedented number of fifteen performances.

Emma Calvé had come across the big pond to display her witchery of voice and action before New York operagoers, the result being, in the words of the historian Krehbiel, "the most sensational triumph ever achieved by any opera or singer."

Excellent and truly fascinating Carmens had been heard before, among them Pauline Lucca and Minnie Hauck; but, compared with the vivacious Calvé, from the South of France, they were like champagne without sparkle.

She had everything in her favor that a fairy could possibly bestow on an operatic artist: a beautiful and amazingly expressive face; a voluptuous figure, with a rare grace of movement; a voice which, at its best—and it usually was at its best—was as lovely, sensuously, as Patti's and infinitely more soulful; a skill for acting realistically which amounted to genius, often making one forget the superlative beauty of her voice; and the supreme gift of magnetism.

What is magnetism? A hundred times I have asked myself that question, and have concluded finally that its essence lies in not being afraid of the public—in being as natural on the stage as off.

If Calvé had been afraid she would never have been called upon to sing Carmen fifteen times in one season, though her personal, vocal and histrionic gifts had been even more preeminent than they were. She was no more afraid of her hearers than the Seville gypsy girl, whom she impersonated, was afraid of the officers and the bull-fighter with whom she flirted.

She was not even afraid of the critics. Some of them objected to the bold improvisations with which she often surprized the audience; but that did not prevent her from indulging in wild pranks, like throwing herself suddenly into Jean de Reszke's lap, whenever the whim came over her. Jean, I know for he told me, did not like this (funny man!), but the audience did, and Emma did and I did, and it was this childlike impulsiveness and unafraidness that constituted a large share of her magnetism.

In following her Carmen from scene to scene I always felt as if I was not witnessing a theatrical representation but seeing the actual events, as taken down by a movie camera, just as they were supposed to have happened in front of the cigar factory, in the smugglers' den, the camp in the mountains and outside the Seville bull-ring.

A music critic is like a traveler on an express train.

EMMA CALVÉ

Operatic impressions, night after night, month after month, flit past him in such rapid succession that few of them are retained in his memory. But of Calvé's Carmen I have lost few details; to recall them I merely have to shut my eyes and let my fancy drift back. An agreeable pastime, I assure you.

Among all these remembered details the most vivid is the picture of her face in the scene when she reads her fate in the cards. The surprize, the horror of this girl, bubbling over with the voluptuous joy of life, when she sees her death so near, were depicted in Calvé's features with thrilling fidelity to nature. No other Carmen has ever come within a mile of her in this tragic episode; nor has any other matched the harrowing scene of her assassination in front of the bull-ring, or the coquettish charm of the opening scene.

Her Marguerite in "Faust" stands out in the same way from other Marguerites by its intense emotionalism. The woful agony of despair in the church scene wrings my heart even at this day.

Philip Hale once printed in his *Musical World* a talk with Calvé which was a surprizing revelation showing how brain work supplemented her natural dramatic instincts. She had evidently pondered deeply over Goethe's unhappy character before portraying her on the stage.

Once she improvised a detail which was certainly most effective. After her brother Valentine, slain in duel with her seducer, has cursed her and died, the men and women in the chorus sink on their knees and sing the brief death chant with which the intensely emotional Gounod knew how to thrill his audience to the spinal marrow. At this moment Calvé got up and walked across the stage, showing a face in which the beginning of her insanity was marvelously portrayed.

It was, as I have just said, a striking, as well as appropriate detail, yet I begged her—though afterwards I was sorry I had done so—to omit it because it distracted the attention of the audience from that sublime dirge. She never repeated it. Too bad! Critics are such fools. And yet I was right.

To most opera-goers of her time Calvé was Carmen and Carmen meant Calvé. This, also, was too bad, for some of her other impersonations were not in any way inferior to her Carmen. Of her Marguerite I have spoken. As Santuzza in "Cavalleria Rusticana," she was the heavy-footed operatic counterpart of the great Duse herself; abject despair can go no further. In that delirious military opera, "La Navarraise," which Massenet wrote for her, she held the audience breathless with feverish excitement from start to finish. In "Mefistofele" she displayed her versatility by assuming the part of Helen as well as that of Marguerite.

The overwhelming demand for her Carmen kept her from developing her repertory as much as was desirable. It was, naturally, for the most part French—Calvé was the foremost French prima donna of all time. She could transmute silver into gold. Ambroise Thomas's "Hamlet," which I had looked on as a feeble opera, thrilled me when Calvé appeared as Ophelia. The vocal embroideries in the mad scene, which had seemed to me trivial and absurdly out of place, were, as sung by her, so saturated with emotion that they moved me to tears.

If Richard Wagner could have seen and heard Emma Calvé in any of the operas I have named he would have been breathless with excitement and overwhelmed with joy—and grief. "Why," he would have asked in despair, "was this wonderful artist, my very ideal of a singing actress, not born with a voice such as my heroines call for?"

Calvé herself bitterly regretted this. She longed passionately to sing and act Isolde, in particular, but for such a part her glorious voice was not sufficiently voluminous and robust. I often longed, though to see her as Senta in the "Flying Dutchman." That would have been a rare treat.

In the last years of her operatic career Calvé indulged in capricious rhythmic irregularities which aroused the ire of the critics. But to the end she remained the idol of opera-goers. I have spoken of the fifteen repetitions of "Carmen" at the Metropolitan Opera House that were called for in the season of 1893-94. But even that record was exceeded at Hammerstein's Manhattan Opera House where, during the 1906-07 season "Carmen" was sung nineteen times, under the inspired direction of Cleofonte Campanini. These were probably, in perfection of detail and ensemble, the most perfect performances ever given anywhere of Bizet's masterwork which is, in my opinion, the most inspired of all operas excepting those of Wagner. I recall those performances with the same shivers of delight as the first Bayreuth festival.

Calvé often sent me notes thanking me for my enthusiastic articles on her artistic achievements. Long after she left the opera house and went on the concert stage, my wife and I became acquainted with her. One thing we particularly desired to know was why her voice instead of deteriorating, was actually as lovely as in the days of her greatest popularity. In vivid French, illustrated as of old by her graceful and speaking hands, and eyes full of alluring charm, she said: "I have been studying, studying Mozart, Grétry, for hours each day. Pupils came to me and for them I have worked, studied, to regain ma voix de jeune fille"; and this miracle she had accomplished.

With the loss of her juvenile figure had gone, as a matter of course, the endurance necessary for operatic work. Yet she was very anxious in 1923, to appear in New York once more as Carmen. It would have been the sensation

of the season and it was to be done for charity. But the
rulers of the Metropolitan were obdurate. She appealed
to me for aid and I pleaded eagerly for her plan in the
Evening Post. The semi-official answer was that it could
not be done because "Carmen" was now Farrar's opera
and she would not consent to the appearance of so formidable a rival.

I wrote to Geraldine about this and she promptly and
indignantly denied the accusation. She had not heard
her great predecessor since she was a child and was more
eager than anybody else in the world to witness her impersonation. She added her pleas to Calvé's but in vain.
Calvé had to content herself with recitals. Farrar went
to hear her, was overwhelmed with joy, and this is what
she wrote to me about it:

"I have had *such* a wonderful afternoon at Calvé's concert and such a *leçon de chant!* Oh, how lovely, luscious,
and happily young her voice is! What *délice* to bask in
the phrasing and ease of really fine singing! I couldn't
resist; I sent a real 'flapper' splashy card of thanks with
some American beauties, and I wanted to go to her afterwards, but there was such a crowd I feared to add to her
fatigue. *Quelle femme!*"

NELLIE MELBA

Another bright star in the operatic firmament, in this
golden age of musical New York was Nellie Melba, Australia's great contribution to the realm of vocal music.

The first time I met this brilliant singer was at a dinner
given by the eminent London critic and biographer of
Patti, Herman Klein. When I found I was to sit at her
right, I was somewhat embarrassed, for I had been rash
and reckless, like the man who "spoke disrespectfully of
the equator."

MELBA AS "MARGUERITE" IN "FAUST"

I decided to have it out at once. "I was afraid you might snub me," I began.

"Why?" she asked.

"Because, when you came to New York, I alluded to you as the kangaroo prima donna."

She burst into a merry musical laugh which still rings in my ears.

"Oh, that was nothing! My husband was known everywhere as kangaroo Charlie!"

Melba was one of the singers specially brought to the Metropolitan to help drive out Wagner. I did not want Wagner driven out, hence my somewhat disrespectful reference to the prima donna from Kangarooland. What annoyed me particularly was that she was such a delightful singer. I would have been happier if she had been inferior and had failed dismally.

Melba was a songbird of the canary family. After hearing her sing a dozen notes one felt sure that, like Patti, she did not have to endure the usual years of toilsome training. To be sure she did study with a certain fashionable teacher, but, as Jean de Reszke once sarcastically said to me, her voice was naturally so beautiful and so well placed that no teacher could mar it.

No one could help enjoying her limpid voice and its spontaneous utterance. She found it a little difficult to gain a foothold in New York because Eames, coached by Gounod himself, was just then monopolizing attention with her delightful impersonations of Marguerite and Juliette. Melba's art was not conspicuously emotional; she excelled in the brilliant fioriture of the Italian *bel canto* style. Among her best parts were Gilda and Violetta. In the all-star casts of the Golden Age her name counted for much. To perfect a cast she did not hesitate to sing Micaela in "Carmen," the gipsy girl being on this occasion the vocally and personally alluring Zélie de Lussan, whose glorious large black eyes were as full of music as a whole opera. The first time I met her she sat opposite me at dinner. Presently she said to me pleasantly: "You are a good observer"—which made me realize that I had been staring at her outrageously, actually neglecting my food for the feast of eyes.

A humorous and also somewhat tragic incident in Melba's career in New York was her attempt to sing Brünnhilde in "Siegfried." She had been brought to the Metropolitan, as I have said, to help atone for the intended neglect of Wagner's operas, just as Jean de Reszke had been. But Jean had become the very prophet of Wagnerism; and here was Melba, colorature soprano, insisting in her contract for the year 1896-97, that she, and she alone, was to be permitted to sing Brünnhilde! Could anything be funnier?

Apparently this bargain with Melba had prevented the manager from engaging for that season Lillian Nordica, the ideal Brünnhilde in "Siegfried." Nordica, an extremely temperamental artist, was naturally wroth thereat and looked at the whole thing as a personal insult on the part of Jean de Reszke, who had advised Melba to try this part. But as Jean himself explained the matter to me, this advice had been simply the outcome of his great enthusiasm for Wagner's art, which had made him eager to enlist all the greatest artists in its service.

Nordica refused to be appeased, and for a time there was a break in her friendship with the great tenor. The reconciliation, the following season, resulted in the most passionately, personal performance of "Tristan and Isolde" imaginable, the plot of this opera lending itself admirably to this purpose. I shall never forget that performance, especially the first act, which rose to such dramatic heights that the other two were, funnily enough, almost an anticlimax.

As for Melba, she suffered cruelly for her attempt to invade a branch of the art operatic for which her voice was not built. In the effort to attain the resonance called for in the final act of "Siegfried" she damaged her organ so badly that she had to retire from the stage temporarily. This gave much pleasure to certain persons who saw confirmation in this of the old myth that Wagner's music injures the voice. But Lehmann and Nordica sang Brünnhilde year after year, and the more they sang it the more gloriously their voices exulted and triumphed in this wonderful music. You can not use a rose bush for the same purposes as an oak. As Madame Sembrich once said to me in speaking of Farrar: "She couldn't sing the Queen of Night as I sing it any more than I could impersonate Madame Butterfly as she does."

MARCELLA SEMBRICH

Conspicuous among the millionaires in New York who helped along music and cultivated the friendship of great musicians was the banker Elkan Naumburg. He had a habit of inviting them to dinner; I was usually "among those present," and I assure you I enjoyed those dinners, for gastronomic reasons as well as others. The wealthy Hebrews know more about good food and good music than most other New Yorkers and I must not forget to mention Mr. Naumburg's choice collection of Rhine wines.

One of the first guests I met in this home was Theodore Thomas. Naumburg wanted to start a quartet, with Thomas as first violin and myself as 'cellist, to rehearse at his house; but how could we have found time for such orgies?

At one of these Naumburg dinners, given in honor of Marcella Sembrich, my friendly foe or hostile friend Krehbiel said to me: "I thought you would be here to-night. Sembrich is about the only thing in music we two cordially agree on."

This was an absurd exaggeration; there were hundreds of things in the musical world we agreed upon, many more indeed than we disagreed on; but Madame Sembrich certainly led the procession of the things we both adored to the limit.

It has often been said, and with truth, that singers are not so musical as pianists and violinists. Sembrich is one of the exceptions. She was not a mere warbler, she was musical to the finger tips. Paderewski called her "the most musical singer" he had ever heard. She had plenty of musical intelligence to become a famous pianist or violinist. At a benefit performance for Mr. Abbey, which netted $16,000, she sang airs by Mozart and Verdi, played a Chopin mazurka on the piano, and also the violin obbligato to Christine Nilsson's singing of the enchanting Bach-Gounod "Ave Maria." Can you name another singer who could have done these three things?

As a girl, Marcella had earned her living going about with her father officiating at dances in the homes of wealthy Poles, playing both violin and piano. She had the ambition to become a pupil of Liszt, but fortunately the rare charm of her voice was discovered in Vienna; and in Athens she started her world career as prima donna.

She made her début in New York, which was to remain her home for so many years, on October 24, 1883, in "Lucia," the same opera which had, some months previously, brought her an ovation in London. The ovation was more than duplicated at the Metropolitan and Maurice Grau had reason to rub his hands gleefully. Another artist was his who could fill the vast auditorium alone by the magic of her art and name, and who gave also wonderful strength to those all-star casts to which he owed the fact

To my dear friends
Mr. and Mrs. Henry Finck
"Merry Christmas"
and a "Happy New Year!"
1910-11   Marcella Sembrich

Photograph by Aimé Dupont

MARCELLA SEMBRICH

that he could retire some years later with a fortune honestly earned by his managerial wisdom.

They were expensive, those all-star casts, but Grau's motto: "Throw money out of the window and it will come back through the door," was found a strikingly profitable way to success.

In listening to Sembrich I often wished Mozart might have lived to hear her in his operas. Her singing was like his music: perfect in euphony, style, and taste. She was probably the most perfect Mozart singer of all time. Her tones were like a string of pearls of the kind that cost a million a necklace, all exactly alike, not a flaw to be detected even by an expert.

I must have heard her over a hundred times, yet only once (in "Lakmé") do I remember hearing her sing out of tune—a matter of tremendous importance in a coloratura soprano. One may pardon an intensely dramatic singer like Geraldine Farrar or Rosa Raisa an occasional deviation from the pitch, but a singer of florid music should be impeccable. For every faulty tone her emoluments should be docked $10.

Krehbiel, special champion of Patti, admitted that Sembrich's voice had "warmer life-blood in it," while sharing the other's velvety softness and brilliancy. She did not emotionize the florid measures in "Hamlet," as Calvé did, but she touched all hearts with the pathos of her Violetta in "La Traviata"; and as the heroine of Paderewski's "Manru" she deeply moved the audience.

I was just going to write that this was her best part, when I remembered her Susanna in "Figaro," her Queen in the "Magic Flute," her Gilda in "Rigoletto," and her comic impersonations, Rosina in the "Barber of Seville," Zerlina in "Don Giovanni," the "Daughter of the Regiment" and Norina in "L'Elisir d'Amore." Each of these seemed her best part—while you were under its spell.

A surprizing, nay, amazing circumstance relating to her impersonations of comic characters like Zerlina and Rosina was that she achieved the illusion of reality notwithstanding her defective eyesight. "You have no idea how very shortsighted I am," she said to me. "I cannot see ten feet ahead on the stage. Before the performance I go on the stage and have the distances I must cover measured off; my colleagues also whisper directions to me."

She had been brought up in the belief that a colorature soprano can get along without acting, all she needed to do being to stretch out her arms at frequent intervals. She soon got rid of that idea, with the gratifying results just referred to.

Yet, unlike most opera singers she did not need acting and costume to reveal her art at its best. Her song recitals—which invariably crowded Carnegie Hall with exceptionally high-class audiences—were to some even more enjoyable than her operatic impersonations. She sang her songs in half-a-dozen languages. Her recitals exerted a wide influence as examples throughout the country. Conservatory misses followed her example even as to the six languages, usually with dire results.

When Sembrich went on the stage she adopted her mother's name, her own name, Kochanska, not being one the public would have been quick to remember. I always liked to hear her speak Polish, though I understood not a word. One evening I went in to see her in the artist's room after a recital. As soon as she saw me she left her other friends, hastening across the room to meet me. With an anxious expression on her face she eagerly asked: "Tell me frankly, my dear Henry, did I sing very badly this evening? You see I am just back from a long concert tour and I fear I have not done myself justice."

Assuming a grave air I replied: "Why no, Marcella,

you sang as well as usual, with one very serious exception."

"What was it?" she asked anxiously.

"Your Polish accent," I replied, "was simply abominable."

Tapping me on the shoulder with her fan, she exclaimed:
"You naughty man, to tease me so"; and smiles
returned to her face.

Once, indeed, I did address her in good Polish. My wife
and I were spending a fortnight with the Paderewskis at
their château at Morges, on the Swiss side of Lake Geneva.
Madame Sembrich and her lovable husband and former
teacher, Guillaume Stengel, were spending the summer
near Lausanne, about ten miles away. One evening they
came over for dinner. Knowing of this coming event
some days in advance I persuaded Paderewski's sister to
teach me a few sentences in Polish with which to welcome
Madame Sembrich and dear Guillaume. I succeeded in
making them open their eyes in surprize, but after I had
exhausted my stock of sentences I had to add: *"Je parle
polonais comme un perroquet."*

At this dinner Paderewski played me a naughty trick.
I had told him what had happened in New York a few
months previously. Professor Stengel had been indulging
in the bad habit of sending me for Christmas (as Antonio
Scotti did) a box or two of very choice cigars. Not being
a smoker, I always sold the cigars and gave the proceeds to
some charity.

One day my wife and I were lunching with Marcella
and Guillaume at the Savoy Hotel, which was their winter
home. When the dessert was disposed of, Guillaume told
the waiter to bring me a couple of cigars. Here was a
dilemma! In all my life I had smoked only two cigars
and both of them made me "seasick." My wife watched
anxiously to see what I would do. Of course—after hav-

ing silently accepted those boxes of cigars—I could not say "I don't smoke." Foxily I put the two cigars into my vest pocket, but Guillaume protested: "No, no, smoke them right here! Marcella doesn't object."

What could I do? Lighting a match I took a few puffs, then put the cigar on my plate and pretended to have forgotten it.

Well, at Morges, what do you suppose Paderewski did? He told the whole story right at the table, like a naughty boy, and everybody had a good laugh.

While Sembrich's concert audiences were of a much higher grade than those Patti audiences to whom "Home Sweet Home" was the climax of all music, she did not disdain the music of the people. Once she gave an entire recital of folk-songs in Carnegie Hall. When I received an advance copy of the program I sat down and wrote an editorial in which I deplored the fact that Stephen Foster had been overlooked. I knew of course what had happened. Krehbiel had written the program notes and advised the singer on her selections.

Now, Krehbiel adhered to the foolish opinion that no song can be a folk-song if its composer is known. That definition, of course, excluded "Old Folks at Home" and all the other Foster songs.

The absurdity of that definition can be made obvious by a simple question.

Suppose a book worm took a collection of songs universally sung as folk-songs and, after years of hard work, succeeded in discovering the composer of every one of them—would they suddenly cease to be folk-songs and become art-songs?

Foster could not have written an art-song to save his life. All his music was folk-music—written for the dear common people by one of them. The most typical of all

German folk-songs is the "Loreley," though everybody knows it was composed by Silcher to Heine's poem.

Sembrich could not change her printed program, but she compromised by including a Foster song among her encores. So I buried the tomahawk.

Interesting things happened when Sembrich retired from the operatic stage. The date was February 6, 1909, the operas from which selections were sung were "Don Pasquale," "Il Barbiere," and "La Traviata" and among the singers who appeared with her were Farrar, Caruso, Scotti, Bonci, Campanari, Didur, Amato. Precious gifts were made to the departing favorite and the ovations were continued throughout the performance. Sembrich made a speech and afterwards had a reception and supper in the Hotel Savoy.

The following night a dinner was given in her honor at the Hotel Astor by a committee of musicians; there were over a hundred and fifty persons, mostly celebrities. Speeches were made by Paderewski and others and an amusing detail was the singing of the "Merry Widow" waltz, which was then all the rage; first by Krehbiel (who was toast master of the occasion), then by ten other musicians in succession—Madame Homer, Mrs. Krehbiel, Mrs. Toedt, Farrar, Gogorza, Dippel, Scotti, Frank and Walter Damrosch and Caruso. The text consisted of the names of the operas in which Sembrich had sung and which were printed on the menu. Though this had been rehearsed in a few hurried moments, as Krehbiel confessed in his "Chapters of Opera," it seemed to the audience an improvisation. When Caruso, only a few feet away from me, opened his lips to utter his share of this simple and rather vapid tune I was thrilled by the mellow quality of his voice and the ease with which the tones come out of his mouth, as I seldom had been even in the opera house.

Earlier in the evening I was talking with Paderewski

when Caruso came to introduce himself to the great pianist. He said something in Italian, but Paderewski shook
his head and said: *"Non parlo italiano."* So they con-
versed in French, which both of them spoke fluently.

Lillian Nordica

If America is the land of big things, Lillian Nordica
must be put down as the most American of all singers.
Her voice was huge; the biggest orchestra could not sub-
merge it in its tidal waves of sound.

Mere bigness, to be sure, is nothing to be proud of; I
could name some singers of the past whose voices were
huge, stentorian, like the roar of an active volcano. The
audiences applauded them; *I* wanted to cut their throats
with a non-safety razor.

Nordica's voice was big, yes; but it was not, like those
voices, raucous, vociferous, bleating, roaring. At its best
it was as beautiful, as smooth, mellow, velvety and luscious
as the voice of any prima donna I have ever heard. Think
what an advantage this combined power and beauty gave
her!

Patti, Gerster, Tetrazzini, Calvé, Sembrich, Melba had
to keep strictly in their field if they wished to escape trouble, as we saw in the case of Melba a moment ago. Nordica could roam and rove wherever she pleased. Like
Lehmann, she began her operatic career singing light
rôles with coloratura trimmings and at the same time she
excelled in the oratorio style, which often calls for skill in
florid (ornamental) vocalizing. And like Lehmann, she
gradually rose to the Alpine heights of Wagner's most
dramatic parts, the heroic heights of Isolde and Brünnhilde.

Eames might have reached those heights had she not
retired from the stage prematurely, and had not Seidl

died. Under his guidance she had become, as we have seen, an ideal Elsa, Elizabeth, Eva and Sieglinde. There she stopped, partly because of ill health.

Nordica was free from this handicap. She was as beautiful in face and form as Eames and at the same time she enjoyed superb health and endurance. Owing to that, she could sing the "Love-Death" at the end of "Tristan and Isolde" with a voice as fresh and pure and mellow and mighty as it was at the beginning of the opera. The *Allgemeine Zeitung,* the leading newspaper of Munich (the headquarters since 1872 of Wagnerism) wrote after she had been heard there: "It was a pleasure to hear Isolde for once actually *sung.*" Score one for America!

At a rehearsal I once heard Seidl apologize to the Isolde for having to drown her voice for a moment. "Wagner taught us," he said, "that in his music dramas the voice is more important than the orchestra, but in this place the full strength of the orchestra is so necessary to the overwhelming climax that the voice must for a few bars be disregarded."

He need not have said this had Nordica been the Isolde. Her voice easily rose above the mighty surges of sound produced by a hundred fortissimo players. In the soaring melodies of the last scene in "Siegfried" the superbly complicated and sonorous orchestra was as a mere guitar accompaniment to her voluminous emotion-laden voice. And when she came to that thrilling high C she rose to it as easily as if her voice had had wings—unlike some other Brünnhildes who always filled me with dire apprehensions of disaster when that climax drew near.

Nordica's gloriously spontaneous high C in "Siegfried," and her high C in Rossini's "Stabat Mater," would have sufficed to raise her to the first rank among dramatic sopranos. Of historic importance also was her Brünnhilde in "Götterdämmerung." Here again, as in "Tristan," her

superb health and natural vocal strength enabled her to
rise above the orchestra, in the last scene as in the first,
with magnificent eloquence. It is with her—and her acting was equal to her singing—that the Immolation scene
is inseparably associated in my mind. And I can recall no
singer who could make Elsa more interesting than she did;
not a moment of boredom. Nor—to mention a non-Wag-
nerian opera which Wagner admired though it was by Meyerbeer—can I recall a soprano and a tenor who could raise
my enthusiasm to the boiling point as Nordica and Jean
de Reszke did in the superb love duo of "Les Huguenots."
Ah, those were golden nights! A point worth noting is
that the greatest impersonators of Aïda ever heard in New
York were the two Americans, Nordica and Eames.

Nordica was not, like Patti and Melba, a singer born
with a perfect vocal equipment. She had to work, work,
work. On this she dwelt frequently and emphatically in
our talks; and I knew, from what I saw and heard in her
home, how necessary to her as a coach was the amazingly
clever Romaine Simmons, who knew the Wagner scores
as thoroughly as the great conductors did, and who kept
at her everlastingly till she was perfect. Genius, says
Edison, is one per cent inspiration and ninety-nine per
cent perspiration.

Anton Seidl, of course, supplied the finishing touches,
and shared his inspiration with this American pupil who,
to his great joy, made it unnecessary for him to curb his
orchestra in the exciting climaxes.

No detail was too trifling for him. One day the great
soprano and her conductor created much astonishment in
one of the big department stores on Broadway by grasping a few yards of one filmy material after another and
waving it to and fro. Were they crazy? No! They were
simply trying to find the best material for the scarf which

To Abbie — from Lillian
1901 —
Isolde =

Photograph by Histed

LILLIAN NORDICA

Isolde waves in the nocturnal garden as a signal to Tristan that he may come, as the King has gone hunting.

You can understand, after reading the foregoing, why Nordica was so offended when Grau gave the "Siegfried" Brünnhilde to Melba. He soon found out his mistake, which ruined a whole season.

I might fill pages with pictures of Nordica's acting and appearance on the stage. Among the unforgettable scenes is that of her coming down the Rhine as the captive of the drugged Siegfried, looking, in her rare personal beauty, like a living Titian.

It was natural that one of such a fascinating personality should be married—thrice married. Her first husband, who was supposed to have gone up in a balloon and never returned, my wife and I never saw; but we saw much of her second and third husbands.

The second was Zoltan Doeme, a Hungarian of strikingly handsome aspect. He had a superb tenor voice but was not sure of his highest tones and was too lazy to train them. His epicurean and varied inclinations in the matter of feminine beauty made her divorce him. My wife and I tried to intercede for him, but this led to a temperamental outburst compared with which the first act of "Tristan" seemed a placid idyl.

George Washington Young was the name of her third husband. We frequently spent our week-ends visiting the happy couple in their large and splendid bungalow on the Jersey Coast at Deal. He happened to be a millionaire, and there was no lack of good things to eat and drink.

Nordica was decidedly a gourmet, even a gourmand. When she lunched with us she always requested maple-syrup cake, delectable, but oh! so rich! At one Thanksgiving dinner which we shared with her, there were six kinds of pie and none was neglected. The dinner followed five hours of "Parsifal" and after it she wanted us to share her box at the Winter Garden. "Caruso will be there too," she said. So we went, though I loathed vaudeville. After enduring the tortures of boredom for an hour we excused ourselves to our hostess, and on the way out I said to my wife emphatically: *"That's my idea of hell!"*

Mr. Young was generous to a fault. He happened to be agent for a new British ale intended to beat Bass. As I like it, he said, "I'll send you some to your summer home in Maine." When we got to Bethel I expected to find a case of a dozen or two bottles. What I did find was two huge cases each containing *twenty-four dozen* bottles! Most of them quenched the Gargantuan thirst of a farm hand who, after we returned to New York, found his way into the cellar daily—or nightly.

In sad contrast to her triumphant career on the stage were the last months of Nordica's life. There had been unwise speculations and heavy losses. Instead of retiring on her laurels, the famous prima donna went on a world tour, including Australia and the adjacent wild and woolly islands. To the great indignation of Melba the Australians did not acclaim her great colleague and friend; to be sure there was an excuse in the fact that her health was broken down and she did not sing well.

Then came a harrowing tragedy, a tragedy in which Romaine Simmons showed that a friend in need is a friend indeed. He took constant care of her, when, on a lonely island, she was tormented to death by millions of pestilential flying insects, and the noise of countless frogs. When she died she had wasted away till she weighed but a hundred pounds and looked like a little girl.

SCHUMANN-HEINK, HOMER, FREMSTAD

A good deal of mischief has been done in the operatic world by the notion that a contralto cannot rise to the same dizzy heights of fame as a soprano. At the Metropolitan Opera House it happened repeatedly that a contralto or a mezzo-soprano damaged her voice and shortened her career by insisting on singing soprano parts.

It cannot be denied that there are fewer great characters to impersonate by singers with low voices than by singers with high voices. Yet Brandt was as highly honored and as much admired in her years at the Metropolitan as Lehmann, though she entirely lacked Lilli's personal charms.

Ernestine Schumann-Heink also lacked the beauty of Venus. Except in her early stage years, when she was a sort of maid of all work in the Hamburg Opera House, she did not aspire to soprano parts but lavished her whole voice and soul on the rôles suited to her, with the result that she became as widely known and admired and loved throughout the United States as any soprano or tenor, excepting Farrar and Caruso who alone commanded more attention and higher emoluments.

The first time I met Schumann-Heink personally was when I went behind the scenes to congratulate her on something she had done particularly well. She greeted me with open arms—I thought she was going to hug me—and thanked me effusively for the nice things I had written about her in the *Evening Post*. Then she said: "I am afraid you will be disappointed in me personally for I am nichts als eine gewöhnliche deutsche Hausfrau (nothing but an ordinary German housewife)."

I laughed and said that the main thing was that she was a big artist, with a big heart. "That heart pulses through everything you do, and that's why I adore you."

Big hearts are lamentably rare among singers. To Schumann-Heink her rôles were as dear as her beloved children, and that was perhaps the chief secret of her huge success.

Her voice, too, was big; as big as Nordica's, if not bigger, with a ground swell in it coming from the slower vibrations of a low voice; a tidal surge that fairly swept her hearers off their feet, though they were sitting.

When I gave up my career as critic after forty-three years of service, I felt as if I never wanted to hear any more music. But there were a few exceptions. I would gladly have walked down from Harlem and paid for my own seat to hear Schumann-Heink once more sing that glorious religious song of Schubert, "The Almighty," in the version for orchestra made by Liszt.

Can you recall thrills and feel them again years afterwards? I can, when I recall that song as sung by this "Hausfrau." I have heard many famous preachers, but none whose eloquence overshadowed that of Schumann-Heink pouring out "Die Allmacht," in mammoth tones direct from her mammoth heart.

Among her operatic climaxes (she was the greatest of all Ortruds, Erdas, Brangaenes) I recall, with always renewed emotion, the warning scene in the second act of "Tristan": how those big, glorious, rotund, luscious tones of hers floated down from the parapet into the auditorium after mingling with the mellifluous orchestral tones—I shiver deliciously as I write this. No, I am not tired of music after all; *that* is one of the things I want to hear again. To me, it has always seemed the climax of the most emotional of all operas.

Everybody knows how grateful Schumann-Heink has been to Americans for taking her to their hearts. In Hamburg she was getting a mere pittance. Grau, with his keen eye for stars, brought her to New York, on a contract based in part on her German earnings. When she made a sensation at her Metropolitan début, he tore up that contract and gave her a much better one. Grau was a gentleman.

ERNESTINA SCHUMANN-HEINK

To be sure he had his peculiarities. Jean de Reszke once said to me: "Grau will give you a cigar—but he won't give you a match."

One day the newspapers brought the agreeable news that Schumann-Heink had become an American citizen. She did not lament this step during the war when she had to let her sons go and fight the Germans. America is her real, her permanent home. Like Paderewski, she has a ranch in California, where she raises extremely high-brow oranges, judging by a sample box she once sent me.

After one of her recitals in New York I introduced to her a girl who was among my pupils in the Brooklyn Master School of Music. She promptly saw a chance to do something nice for an American. "Come to see me at my hotel to-morrow morning," she said. The girl went, but found the great contralto depressed over a newspaper notice. "Come to my place in New Jersey on Friday and remain till Monday," said the singer. The girl did so and what she learned in those three days was worth more than a whole year's course in the best conservatory.

Full-blooded contraltos seem to have a natural inclination toward big families. Madame Schumann-Heink's family is numerous. A big family also is owned by the "American-born Schumann-Heink," Louise Homer, also a member of the Metropolitan Opera Company for years. In the absence of the greatest of contraltos I was always glad to see Madame Homer in her place; glad to hear her as Brangaene and in the other big Wagnerian parts for low voice.

She made her Metropolitan début as Amneris; I can not recall any singer, native or foreign, unless it be Edyth Walker, who made a deeper impression by her impersonation of this unhappy princess, jilted by the general who prefers her slave Aïda. She was not too proud, on occasion, to content herself with a small part like the Voice in "Parsifal;" not too lazy to learn conscientiously a part in a new opera which was likely, as W. J. Henderson would say, to have only one consecutive performance.

In Puccini's best opera, Madame Homer showed, as Suzuki that Cio-Cio-San is not the only character for whom the audience is expected to feel sympathy; usually, Madama Butterfly monopolizes the interest. As the Witch in another one of Farrar's great operas, Humperdinck's "Königskinder," she was different again—an amusingly gruesome personage. Utterly diverse still was her lovely impersonation of Gluck's Orfeo, when the all-star cast, under Toscanini, included Johanna Gadski, Bella Alten, and the sweet-voiced Alma Gluck. Nor have I forgotten her La Haine in "Armide," or her Marina in "Boris Godounoff."

Olive Fremstad was not a true contralto, like Homer and Schumann-Heink, but rather a mezzo-soprano; and this may partly excuse her ambition for high soprano parts which shortened her stage career. As I look back at her impersonations—there were not many—I find I like best her Venus in "Tannhäuser," which vies in perfection with Lilli Lehmann's. What a splendid voice! What a superb figure! Fremstad was so marvelously sculptured that she had but to pose and lift her arms to make the audience feel that they were beholding great acting. Her Sieglinde was as delightful as her Venus. Her Isolde had a legion of admirers, marshaled by Huneker and Krehbiel; so did her Brünnhilde. In these high parts, however, my ear missed the tone quality called for: it was viola timbre where the violin was wanted. More serious was the strain to which the highest tones subjected her voice.

Fremstad was a pupil of the venerable Frederick E. Bristol, now in his eighties but still teaching; Myrna Sharlow, Marie Sundelius and Ericsson Bushnell are other

prominent pupils of his. He disapproved of Olive's ambition for high C's and this led to a temporary break.

Before this occurred, Mr. Bristol had invited me to a
dinner in honor of Fremstad. I sat at her right. Now,
I am not a ready after-dinner speaker, like my colleagues,
Henderson and Krehbiel. As for Fremstad, she turned
pale with fright when she found she was expected to get
up and say something. "Oh, Mr. Finck!" she cried. "I
cannot make a speech to save my life. You must do it
for me!"

It was my turn to be scared. The summons came at
once. I got on my feet without the faintest idea what I
was going to say. As my eyes rolled about wildly, they
alighted on a plate of olives. Quick as lightning came
the rescue.

"Ladies and gentlemen," I began, "everybody says that
olives are an acquired taste, but here at my side is an Olive
everybody likes at once!"

Great applause; the battle was won. Having made a
good start, I got along all right with the rest of my speech.

Olive was delighted and ever so grateful, as she had
been for the numerous eulogies I had bestowed on her.
Yet when, some time later, I began to criticize and im-
plore her not to risk damaging her beautiful voice by singing too high, she said: "Mr. Finck is no longer my friend."
But I was her friend; her best friend; had she listened
to my warnings she would not have left the stage at an
age when she should have been at her best.

It was too bad about those top tones, for otherwise her
voice was strong enough to stand any strain—even that
of Strauss's "Salome." When I asked her about that she
said: "I had no end of trouble learning my part but after
I had once mastered it, it stuck in my memory for good."

Or bad. Poor Fremstad had been to all this terrific
trouble for one solitary performance!

As to Fremstad's change from mezzo to soprano, it must be said that she had the encouragement of both Lehmann and Jean de Reszke. Jean was doubtless influenced by the fact that he had been originally trained and launched as a baritone but soon found he was a true tenor, of an unusually virile type.

Grau's All-star Casts

One of the most astonishing "breath-away-taking" events in the history of the Metropolitan took place on February 20, 1899. On that date Maurice Grau gave a performance of Meyerbeer's "Les Huguenots" which enlisted six of the world's foremost operatic artists: Sembrich, Nordica, Maurel, Plançon, Jean and Edouard de Reszke. With some misgivings he raised the price for this performance from the usual $5 for an orchestra seat to $7. The result was such that he was more convinced than ever that it pays to give Americans the best that can be found. So, all-star casts became the rule during his reign as absolute ruler of the world's foremost opera house.

Was it really that? Undoubtedly. Europe had no city that could present anything like the wonderful casts habitual with Grau during the years of his incumbency, 1896-1903. Nor, in looking back, do we find anything equal to his casts except perhaps in Paris in the days of Rossini and Meyerbeer. But in Grau's day Paris was quite out of the race.

It was extremely fortunate for the music lovers of New York that Maurice Grau was sole ruler of its opera house for seven years. His career before he assumed this position showed that he believed in speculating in the best of its kind. As manager of Rubinstein he cleared $60,-000. The clever French comic-opera singer Aimée added to his income mightily. Offenbach, Salvini and Ristori

were under his care during their American tours; and then
came the Metropolitan apotheosis of this man from Austria. Born in that country Grau had come to America
at the age of five and in later boyhood had sold librettos
at the operatic performances given by his uncle Jacob
Grau. How we Americans dote on this kind of a career
—from a libretto seller to the most brilliant operatic manager known to musical history!

In the preceding pages I have dwelt with emphasis on
the special merits of some of Grau's chief singers, thus
making the strength of his casts obvious even to those who
never heard these artists. It remained for his successor
Heinrich Conried (for whose appointment I was responsible, as we shall see later on) to introduce Geraldine Farrar and Enrico Caruso; but Grau with his keen eye for
rising stars had already engaged these also. Moreover,
he had secured the greatest of French baritones (I do
not forget Maurel) Maurice Renaud, and Conried
stupidly canceled this engagement, though it involved the
payment of a fine!

There had been occasional all-star casts before Grau,
as for example, at the first American performance of Wagner's "Tristan and Isolde," on December 1, 1888, when
Lehmann was the Isolde and Niemann the Tristan, with
Brandt as Brangäne, Fischer as King Marke, Alvary as
the Seaman and Seidl the conductor.

Memorable also was the "Faust" of 1893-94, which
combined in one dazzling cast Calvé, Jean and Edouard
de Reszke and Lassalle. This, in fact, may have suggested his policy to Grau when he became sole manager, a
few years later; for the opera, with this cast, drew such
vast audiences and so many of them that my witty friend,
W. J. Henderson, who had been attending performances
at the "Festspielhaus" in Bayreuth, called the Metropoli-

tan a "Faustspielhaus"—a characteristic *bon mot* much relished in professional circles.

What Grau did was to make such casts habitual. Sometimes he started with two stars, adding others from performance to performance, thus keeping up the excitement over his princely offerings, and compelling even the blasé critics to attend repeatedly.

The day after an all-star performance in honor of Prince Henry, I found myself sharing public interest with the Kaiser's brother. I always hated the farcical evening dress to which men are condemned, and refused to wear one even though I might be the only man in the Metropolitan parquet not thus attired. With the ticket for this gala occasion, however, came a note from Grau informing me that positively no one not in dress suit would be admitted. So I put one on, with the result that several morning papers called attention to this startling innovation, while the wits of the *Evening Post* concocted a special edition in which my appearance in evening dress was set out in huge headlines as completely overshadowing the princely visitor.

Jim Huneker had the time of his life telling, in a whole column in the *Recorder,* how I had refused to take orders in this matter on another occasion. A wholesale dealer in sweetbreads had made so much money, and was such a warm admirer of my idol, Anton Seidl, that he undertook to finance a series of Seidl concerts at the Waldorf Astoria. They were very high-brow affairs, those concerts, at $5 a seat, and evening clothes were *de rigeur*. I came without mine. As it was not a regular concert hall, the man at the door did not know me and said I could not go in. "Very well," I replied, "then I shall go home and get a good night's sleep. But I tell you one thing: Mr. Löwenstein will be mightily disappointed when he hears I was not admitted."

Just then an assistant of the manager who knew me came to the rescue and I entered triumphantly.

You can imagine what a chance this incident gave Jim for constructing one of his thrilling prose poems. I wish I had room to quote it.

Let me add a few more details explaining, why, as a rule, I was Grau's ardent champion. He had such a huge company of high-class artists of all nationalities that he could perform every opera in the language it was composed in. No other opera house in the world could do that because none had a sufficient number of singers versed in one or the other of the several styles called for. French and Italian artists *can* sing a German opera, just as German artists *can* sing Italian or French operas; but the results are usually not altogether delectable. Grau accustomed New York audiences to performances that were idiomatic and had style.

Though an Austrian by birth, he was an out-and-out Parisian in his predilections. French opera therefore received more attention in his days than it ever had before him or ever again got at the Metropolitan. Meyerbeer was particularly favored, which was fortunate for him; for Grau's successor, Conried, dropped him from his list.

Everybody was struck by this difference. When the Lotos Club gave a dinner in honor of Conried I was asked to be the principal speaker. Of course I was expected to use the lash more or less, so I conceived the idea of having in my hands a number of letters from defunct opera composers (received, of course, from the dead letter office)—letters praising or censuring the new manager according to the amount of attention the alleged writers had received. Meyerbeer's letter began: "Who is this man Conried? Has he never heard of me?"—which, of course, brought down the house.

Grau tried to give the New York audiences just what

they wanted. When he found that the Wagner operas were not desired in Italian, with an Italian conductor and Italian singers, he promptly restored the Wagner repertory in German, under Seidl, who, though a Hungarian, surpassed all Germans as an interpreter of their greatest master's music dramas.

Grau even had the audacity to open one season with "Tristan and Isolde"—an astonishing innovation, for the opening night had always been looked on as largely a society affair. Well, his great singers and Seidl had made Wagner fashionable!

A great manager was Grau. I had often criticized him rather sharply in matters of detail (when he "gave the cigar but withheld the match"), but I also lauded him as he deserved to be, and when his impending retirement was announced I wrote a regretful editorial which pleased him so much that he came in the evening to seat T 2 to shake my hand warmly and to thank me. It was the last time I ever saw him.

SEIDL'S DEATH AND FUNERAL

On March 28, 1898, when I went downstairs for my breakfast, I was horrified to see in the morning papers, columns on the death of Anton Seidl. It could not be true! I had seen him only a few days before, looking tolerably well—but here it was, black on white, with all the details.

I hurried upstairs to tell the sad news to my wife. We sat on the bed and cried like babies. Not only had he been one of my most intimate friends but to him we owed more thrilling moments of musical ecstasy than to anybody else. It seemed as if without him our musical life would not be worth living any longer.

On the afternoon of the fatal day Seidl lunched on

shad roe and sausages, and then went to Fleischmann's, as usual, for his coffee. Nahan Franko saw him there and he seemed well. From the café Seidl walked to the house of his manager S. Bernstein; on the way he felt ill and shortly after reaching Bernstein's he had a violent attack of nausea. He complained of something hard in his stomach and said he wished he had not eaten that sausage. The symptoms increased in violence and at ten o'clock he expired, despite the efforts of several physicians who had been summoned. They and the coroner's physician agreed that the immediate cause of death was some irritant poison, probably ptomain, but they also found cirrhosis of the liver and other degenerative changes which indicated that the acute attack had simply accelerated the advent of death which could not have been long delayed.

Mrs. Seidl, who had given up a promising operatic career in order to devote herself entirely to the care of her beloved husband, was entertaining some friends at dinner when news was brought to her of her dying spouse. Her stony grief when she realized he was dead was terribly distressing to those who strove to comfort her. It was a long time before the relief of tears came.

On the day of the funeral I was in the room where the coffin had been placed when she rushed in, frantically exclaiming: "Have they closed the coffin already?" They had. She was to see him no more.

Among the many messages of condolence received was one from the Metropolitan Company offering the use of the opera house for the funeral, and this was accepted.

Twenty thousand persons, it is said, attended the funeral of Beethoven. Wagner, Brahms and other modern masters had great honors paid them when they lay in their coffins; but it is doubtful if any musician who was not a creator of new works but simply an interpreter, ever was so imposingly honored in his death as was Anton

Seidl. For nearly a week every Metropolitan journal devoted a column a day, and on the Sunday following his
death a whole page, to the great conductor and his sudden
death.   Nearly twelve thousand applications were made
for tickets to the memorial services at the Metropolitan
Opera House, though only four thousand had room in it;
and while the services were in progress, and before, when
one hundred and fifty members of the Musical Union
played Chopin's funeral march outside, Broadway, for
seven blocks was one surging mass of people blocking
traffic.

No statesman or general could have been more lamented,
no poet or philanthropist more mourned than was Anton
Seidl. "His funeral was more impressive than any music
drama I ever saw or heard at Bayreuth," wrote Huneker;
and that was my feeling too. I have never seen so many
people weep in public as in the Metropolitan on this
occasion, when Tchaikovsky's Adagio Lamentoso and the
Siegfried Dead March were played and all eyes were
riveted on the coffin.

The orchestra pit had been floored over, and here was
placed the catafalque. The pall-bearers were Richard
Watson Gilder, Eugene Ysaye, Rafael Joseffy, Edward
MacDowell, E. Francis Hyde, Charles T. Barney, Rich-
ard Arnold, James Speyer, Oscar B. Weber, Louis
Josephthal, Walston H. Brown, Xavier Scharwenka,
William H. Draper, E. M. Burghard, George G. Haven,
Zoltan Doeme, Carlos Hasselbrink, Paul Goepel, Julian
Rix, Albert Stettheimer, A. Schueler, Henry Schmitt, and
Carl Schurz, besides five of the New York musical critics:
H. E. Krehbiel, August Spanuth, Albert Steinberg,
Edgar J. Levey and Henry T. Finck.

The funeral address was by the Reverend Merle St.
Croix Wright, while Mr. Krehbiel read an eloquent tele-

gram from Robert G. Ingersoll, who was absent on a lecture tour.

In Seidl's day, operatic and orchestral conductors were not paid lavishly, like prima donnas and tenors, as they were later in the days of Toscanini, Mengelberg and Stransky. He worked very hard but all his income from the Metropolitan, the Philharmonic, the Brooklyn Seidl Society and Coney Island concerts was needed for his daily expenses. He died at the early age of forty-eight and left little for his widow except an unsaleable cottage in the Catskills.

Something had to be done for her. The Metropolitan artists gave a benefit performance which netted a handsome sum. Another five thousand came to her from the sale of a sumptuous Seidl Memorial volume which I planned and edited. I asked all the eminent artists who had sung under him to contribute a few pages of reminiscences; also other prominent musicians, as well as critics. All responded cordially and the result was a volume quite worth the five dollars asked for it. Among the contents were Seidl's own writings, and his letters from Wagner. There are many entertaining details about his personal habits and his love of dogs—he had half-a-dozen of these. But the most important section of the book is the story of his life as written by his widow.

When I asked her to contribute these biographic pages she was dumbfounded. "I have never written a word for print," she said. "Never mind!" I answered. "Simply write me a series of chatty letters telling me all you remember about him. Everything at random just as it comes back to you. I will translate what you write and put it into literary shape."

She did what I asked and the result was a most interesting story, for it was written *con amore*.

One reason why Seidl did not prosper in a worldly way

was that he was extremely shy and reticent. He knew not the art, so well understood by some others, of enlisting the generous interest of wealthy patrons. The San Francisco millionairess, Phoebe Hearst, contrived some unique entertainments for him one year; but when she said to him: "We must do something more next season," he, instead of grasping the golden opportunity, held out his hand and said "Yes, thank you. Good night."

Colonel Ingersoll

It was owing to Seidl that I have had the great good fortune of numbering Robert G. Ingersoll and his family among my best friends for many years. Ingersoll was not a trained musician. As he repeatedly told me, he could not follow all the intricacies of a Wagnerian score, yet he never missed a chance to hear a Wagner opera under Seidl, whose dynamic eloquence and art of climaxing stirred every fiber of his soul. Seidl never made a real speech in his life, yet he had the oratorical faculty of Robert Ingersoll. "His enthusiasm and his emotionalism," Ingersoll said to me, "make me understand and hugely enjoy scores that otherwise would be entirely beyond my comprehension."

Seidl, though a devout Catholic reciprocated the affection of the "great infidel." Though a very busy man he found time now and then to come to the Ingersoll home and play by the hour from the Wagner operas. This was an entirely different thing from the playing of a printed opera score arranged for piano. Seidl had the *orchestral* scores in mind when he played, introducing a multitude of details overlooked in the ordinary arrangements; one seemed to hear the actual violin tones and the 'cellos and flutes and horns and trombones.

Robert Ingersoll had a sense of humor and laughed

heartily at the jokes told on him. His friend Henry Ward Beecher is alleged to have asked him one day playfully: "When you die, what poet's name will your fate suggest?" Answer "Robert Burns."

On another occasion Ingersoll is supposed to have called on Beecher. While waiting for his appearance he admired a splendid globe in the great preacher's library. When the preacher entered, the Colonel said: "Who made this globe?" With ready wit and a mischievous smile Beecher answered: "Nobody."

Let me say here that if Ingersoll did not believe in quite the same Creator that most Christians believe in, he was in his actions much more of a follower of Christ than most alleged Christians are. A friend of mine happened to be one day in a butcher's shop where a starved old woman was trying to buy a soup bone. She hadn't quite enough money, and the butcher, a regular church-goer, refused to let her have it. Just then Ingersoll came in. After hearing the poor woman's plea he ordered the butcher to pack up a porterhouse steak, give it to her and charge it on his bill.

After the death of the Colonel and his wife, we still spent happy hours in the Ingersoll family circle, now presided over by their fascinating daughter, Mrs. Walston Brown.

GODKIN AND WALTER DAMROSCH

Once I nearly lost my job on the *Evening Post*. Coming to my room at the usual hour, I missed the smiling countenance of my genial roommate, John Ranken Towse (the printer will please get that second name right; it always threw the famous dramatic critic into a towering rage to have anyone spell it Rankin). On my desk I found this alarming note from him.

"My Dear Finck. You must curb your fiendish desire to bludgeon young W. D. with your satire. Personally I should be delighted to get the pair of you in a sixteen-foot ring and see you fight it out, with skin-tight gloves or bull fiddles, but I must deny myself the pleasure. The fact is that Linn has positive instructions, which he has passed on to me, not to permit anything of the sort to be printed in the *E. P.* In view of this you had better keep your ammunition in reserve. Yours paternally J. Ranken Towse."

Linn was the managing editor. He had never interfered with my work except once when I spoke disrespectfully of the tune of "Home Sweet Home," a cheap Sicilian ditty which he liked, though he was otherwise an estimable and pious gentleman. In this Damrosch case he interfered because Godkin had ordered him to do so.

Poor Mr. Godkin! He was sorely besieged by the friends of Walter Damrosch, who were distressed because I did not write about him as enthusiastically as I did about Seidl and seemed to think they could make me do so by bothering my chief. Godkin was gouty and temperamental and hated to be pestered, all the more as he did not care a straw for music and musicians, their rank, their squabbles and their rivalries. It was therefore rather hard that he should be the target of the adorers of W. D.

One day I was summoned to his office. He looked incensed, with a proof of my latest criticism before him. "Can't you let up a little on Damrosch?" he asked, adding: "Not that I care personally what you say, but the women are tormenting the life out of me."

To my surprize the criticism before him went in just as I had written it, but the city editor sent me a confidential warning that the chief was really angry and that if I wanted to keep my job, I had better drop my part as roaring lion and coo as gently as a sucking dove.

In a spirit of mischief I adopted that advice literally. My remarks on that night's performance were as inoffensive as bread pudding; they were merely a commonplace record of events, without a touch of sarcasm or comment.

It so happened—to my malicious joy—that that performance (it was "Götterdämmerung") was exceptionally unsatisfactory so that nearly all the critics jumped on it with both feet. It made my chief evidently feel ill at ease at having interfered with me, and he never did it again.

After all, therefore, he liked me better as a lion than as a dove! There is a pertinent story about Horace Greeley who, when a deputation of ladies called on him to complain of his dramatic critic said to them: "I gather from what you say that everybody is talking about the *Tribune* critic's articles." "Just so," was the response. "Well," exclaimed the great editor, "that's just the kind of a critic I want on my paper. Good-day."

Nevertheless I confess that Godkin did me a lot of good by curbing my fierceness. In a note dated February 8, 1892, he wrote: "I have just as high an opinion as Mr. Garrison of your musical judgment and of your work generally. I have never found fault with anything but your failure to write about these musicians in a critical mood; you treat them sometimes as criminals for not coming up to your standards, although they are probably doing as well as they can and at all events are 'God's creatures' as the Oxford Don said about people who had not graduated there."

I wonder if my boss had ever heard of the notice to cowboys printed in large letters and exhibited on the stage of a wild-western concert hall: *"Please don't shoot the pianist, he's doing his durndest."* Oh, how much I suffered during forty-three years from pianists and fiddlers doing their durndest!

One day Godkin said to me with reference to a severe

criticism I had penned of a famous opera singer. "You should never write anything about an artist, especially a woman, that you would not be willing to say to her face."

At first I was quite staggered by that eleventh commandment; but gradually I learned to live up to it until I became known as the most amiable of the New York critics.

With one of Godkin's maxims, contained in another letter to me, I never agreed: "A critic should have no more passion or prejudice than a bronze statue."

Dear me, what a dreary Saharan thing such passionless criticism would be! Godkin himself was never guilty of it. As a critic of politicians he was so passionate that his copy sometimes had to be edited. One year he dared not, for weeks, go about town except in a cab because his violent attacks on Tammany had endangered his life.

My idea of the "compleat" musical critic was that he should don his armor and fight fiercely for what he thinks the best and most important things in art. This accounts for my hostile attitude toward Walter Damrosch in the early days of his busy and successful career, during which he has done so much to make the masses, all over the country, familiar with the best music: In those juvenile days of his he seldom if ever, in my opinion, did justice to the great masterworks he undertook to conduct, and I exposed his shortcomings mercilessly.

Let me add right here that in my fiercest comments on Walter Damrosch I never said anything so wicked as what Ernest Newman wrote about him in London, at the time when the generosity of the multimillionaire Harry Flagler enabled him to take his New York Symphony Orchestra on a European tour: "His performance of Elgar's First Symphony on Saturday was unspeakably, irredeemably bad—coarse, clumsy, tasteless, soulless. I am told Mr. Damrosch is a great admirer and lover of this work.

Photograph by Alman & Co.

HENRY T. FINCK AT FIFTY

I do not doubt it, but I am irresistibly reminded of the boy who became a butcher because he was so fond of animals."

When you bear in mind that Wagner's music dramas, properly interpreted, were to me the climax of mundane pleasure, you will understand, if not pardon, my hostile comments on Walter Damrosch. For two seasons he stood in the way of my hearing those music dramas as Seidl, and Seidl alone, could conduct them. Seidl had been side-tracked; had it not been for my continuous pleas and scoldings he might have remained so.

Not only Damrosch but Mancinelli had their whack at these operas while Seidl was idle—Seidl, whom the singers and the public adored because he could make the operatic orchestra sing and sigh and whisper, exult, plead and threaten, storm, rage and overwhelm, as no other conductor could.

When I found out that systematic efforts were being made in certain quarters to eliminate this wonderful man altogether; when a friend of mine heard the remark: "we shall get rid of Seidl within a year," I set aside all rules of "judicial criticism" and devoted my energies mainly to passionate pleadings for Anton Seidl. I might have failed, so powerful were the forces working against him; but at the critical moment Jean de Reszke came to the rescue, as I have already related, by insisting that the Wagner operas he appeared in must be conducted by Seidl.

These two men succeeded amazingly in shaking Grau's determination never to have any Wagner opera in his repertory except "Lohengrin." Walter Damrosch profited by that foolishness to the tune of $53,000 when he appeased the public clamor for Wagner operas by a series of performances. These, to be sure, were so far from perfect that when he repeated the series the following year, he came out with a deficit of $43,000. He should have listened to his friend Andrew Carnegie who advised him, after the first season, to rest on his laurels.

I feel a thrill of enthusiasm for Walter Damrosch every time I think of his supreme achievement, which was the bringing over to America of Anton Seidl. I also admire him immensely for his skill, amounting to positive genius, in enlisting the services of millionaires on behalf of his orchestra.

For years the pocketbooks of Carnegie and others were open to him to help himself almost *ad libitum*. Then came the climax: the offer of Harry Harkness Flagler to make up the inevitable deficits of the New York Symphony Orchestra to the tune of $100,000 a year. And Flagler also financed this orchestra's vastly expensive trip to Europe.

I fancy—though this is merely a wild guess—that this generous Maecenas spent something like a quarter of a million in one year on his musical friend. Was ever a babe born with such a big golden—nay, platinum—spoon in his mouth?

Walter Damrosch is one of the wittiest and most eloquent after-dinner speakers I have ever heard. He even reconciled me to speeches at concerts. His remarks on his programs were sometimes the best things about them; he talked so entertainingly (sly dog) about certain dull novelties that they received ten times as much applause as would have been bestowed on them had he said nothing. Some of the "futurist" composers are under great obligations to him for not only playing their preposterous works but giving them the advantage of his wit and eloquence.

Romantic Adventures, Narrow Escapes

Those who are doing me the honor of reading these pages will doubtless be glad to leave the opera house and concert halls for a while and let me talk about travel and conservatory girls and bosses and marriage "and sich."

Have you ever tried to recall the moments in your life when you were in danger of losing it?

My first narrow escape came when I was a schoolboy, five or six years old. Somebody had given me a wheelbarrow, rather large for my size, of which I was the obedient servant when we went down hill. One day it took me down to the river. We were heading straight for a precipice. Had it not been for a factory girl who rushed out and caught me, my earthly career might have ended then and there.

Many years later my wife and I were stopping at a hotel in Naples which had a dangerous elevator. The car —a mere platform— was not enclosed, but simply rose from the center of the hall, and at every floor it just managed to squeeze through. One day, after starting, I suddenly remembered I had forgotten the key to our room. I put out my head and shouted to the concierge to send it up. A second later, had not my horrified wife pulled me back, my head would have been crushed to pulp or cut off altogether.

In Bethel, Maine, one summer there came to the farmhouse where we were boarding a big boy whose inseparable companion was a rifle. All day long he was shooting at one thing or another in the most reckless fashion. I was hidden in a cornfield one day when suddenly I heard a bullet whistle past my left ear and strike a nearby tree.

I made a bee-line for that boy and gave him such a tongue lashing as he had never had. "If you ever again fire that rifle within a mile of this house I'll take it and drop it into the Androscoggin river," I threatened.

He didn't; his rifle was too dear to him. As for me, this is what he said to my wife: "Everybody has got to kill his man some day or other."

Afterwards I discovered he had a pleasant habit of hiding sticks of dynamite under his bed! His room was next to ours.

One of the most romantic episodes in my life occurred in Spain, during my first visit to that fascinating country. After a week at Granada, spent mostly in admiring the artistic details of the Alhambra I started out across the Sierra Nevada mountains on a trip which, for a lone un-protected male with a gold watch and some loose cash, was not without its risks, especially in the region of the gipsy cave-dwellers who have, as I was afterwards told, a pleasant habit of murdering lone travelers for the sake of what they can find in their pockets.

For a time I had traveled by what might be called a stage. When that reached its terminus I hired a wagon without springs, drawn by a pair of mules. The driver entertained me by the hour prattling about his private affairs. Presently we reached a wide plain and there a thunderstorm burst upon us the like of which I had never seen before.

I like thunderstorms; in fact, I adore them, but this one was a little too much of a good thing. We were the only outstanding object in the whole plain. Every two minutes a huge flash of lightning crashed down near us and I feared that every next one would pass through our bodies. They were followed by roars of thunder so loud that the terrified mules stood stark still trembling all over and then began to run as fast as they could.

The third narrow escape on this romantic trip came later in the afternoon. Saying that he must rest his mules for a couple of hours, the driver took me to a wayside inn which had all the appearance of a robber's den. Around the kitchen stove a dozen men, wrapped in blankets, were lying asleep. In the adjoining room I sat on a bench. There was nothing wrong in that, but I should not have looked at my gold watch. It was seen by two evil-looking men sitting on another bench and drinking wine. Presently I saw them whispering together. A moment later one of them came over and sat down next to me in an insulting way. He had his right hand under his cloak. I had been told that when such a thing happened, "look out for a dagger." No doubt the ruffian expected me to resent his action, which would give him occasion to stab and rob me.

I was weaponless, so I tried strategy. Knowing that the English were hated in that region I told him I was an American; that I was simply seeing the country, which I found very beautiful. That seemed to halt his plan of immediate aggression. "Where are you going?" he asked.

"We start for Baza shortly," I responded.

That was a lie. We had just come from Baza. He made a few more remarks, pleasantly, then asked again: "So you are on your way to Baza?"

Then the two left. There can be no doubt that they went a mile or so toward Baza, selecting a spot where I could be comfortably murdered and plundered.

This danger I escaped by traveling in the opposite direction. But the Spanish danger wasn't past yet. At another inn I stopped for a glass of wine. There were seven others to be served in what was a sort of a cave. We stood up in a line. The hostess gave each of us a cup and filled it up. I, being the aristocrat, or plutocrat, of the occasion paid for all the wine, according to local custom. It was my treat.

A Typhoid Episode

Query: had the hostess baptized that wine with unclean water containing typhoid germs? I don't know; I may have imbibed them elsewhere, but I have always suspected that wine of being the cause of the typhoid fever which laid me low and very nearly finished me. Fortunately when the incubation period of these germs was over, I was in Switzerland, at Mürren.

Mürren is one of those magic words which give me a little thrill every time I see them. More than half a mile above Interlaken, it is situated where one has a glorious view of the Bernese Alps, especially the Jungfrau, queen of them all; a view equaled in all Switzerland only by that of the Matterhorn and Monte Rosa from the Gorner Grat, above Zermatt.

It so happens that I am writing these words at Interlaken, with the snowy, spotless Jungfrau before me; last evening there was a thrilling Alpine after-glow which suffused the whole mountain with a wonderful pink hue; and in a few days we shall be once more in Mürren.

It was lucky that on that previous visit in 1889, when I came to the Hôtel des Alpes, the doctor sat next to me at table. He noticed my lack of appetite, my husky voice and other suspicious symptoms. So, after dinner, he gave me a thorough examination. "It is undoubtedly typhoid fever" he said and shook his head when I told him that I had spent the whole morning climbing frantically to get up an appetite, when I ought to have been in bed. That climb made my case much more serious than it would have been otherwise.

I had myself carried in a chair down to Interlaken. The hospital there happened to be full; there was no private room and the ward was not to be thought of. So I took my valise and the next train for Berne.

There, at the Insel Spital, I was so lucky as to secure a room. It was large and scrupulously clean; the young nurse who took care of me mopped it up every day. Her room was next to mine; a little bell summoned her to my bedside any time I wanted her, day or night. She gave me liquid food—eggnog or bouillon—several times a day. I was urged to drink aerated water (syphons) by the gallon. This was provided, together with good Italian wine and French brandy. The hospital doctor came to see me twice a day, the university professor once. And for all this, what do you suppose I paid? One dollar a day! I was in the hospital just one hundred days and my bill amounted to five hundred francs.

In those days the proportion of fatal cases of typhoid was, I believe, twenty in a hundred. I came within a quarter of an inch of being one of the twenty. One day I found myself nervously plucking at the bedclothes, and I complained to the nurse that I was constantly sliding down from my pillow. She looked grave but said nothing. Afterwards, when I was out of danger, she told me that those two things almost always meant impending death. The professor came near killing me. Phenacetin had just been born; it was the latest medical wonder. I was one of the unfortunates on whom it was tried out. Once an hour I got a dose; it made me perspire madly, which was advantageous; but it was not known then that this drug is extremely injurious in its action on the heart. I pulled through in spite of it; several doctors have since told me that if I hadn't had the strength and the heart of an ox I would have died a victim of scientific experiment. A noble death, no doubt, but I wasn't hankerin' for it.

My own ignorance provided another narrow escape from death. When the actual fever was over I got up one day and walked briskly across the room to get something in my coat. On the way back I fell down in a heap; when I recovered consciousness I crawled back to bed, my heart beating like furiation. I rang the bell. The nurse came, looked at me (I was red as a lobster) and ran for the professor and the doctor. They hurried in, followed by a dozen students, to whom the professor said that it was "a case of relapse." When the students were gone I heard him whisper to the doctor: *"Da ist nichts mehr zu machen"* (It's all over with him).

Imagine my feelings! To have escaped typhoid and then committed suicide by walking across the room! I did not know that after this debilitating malady a man has to learn to walk again, just like a baby. The nurse taught me. This implies that I didn't die then and there, in spite of the professor's prediction. Of course he didn't know I had walked across the room and attributed my flushed face to the microbes getting busy again in my intestines. I was too scared to tell him what had happened. The next day he looked surprized and said: "Well, we shall see."

While I was convalescing, a man called one day to speak to me. He had heard at his hotel that "an American student" was ill at the hospital and thinking I might be short of funds he took from his pocket a handful of gold and silver coins which he begged me to accept. I told him, with thanks, that while I wasn't rich I had all I needed.

Other instances of kindness move me deeply when I recall them. Dear Garrison, when I sent him a postal saying I was in the Berne hospital, looked in his list for the name of a subscriber in that city to *The Nation*. He found one, Simon Gerber, and sent him a letter suggesting that he might be interested in calling on an editor of *The Nation* ill in his city.

Mr. Gerber was a wholesale exporter of Swiss cheese, a highly-educated man (his being a subscriber to *The Nation* would alone have proved that) who had married a lady from one of the old patrician families. He not only came to see me, but insisted on sending me choice French wines from his cellar. And when I was able to leave the hospital he invited me to spend a few weeks in his home, where his wife had special dishes cooked for me daily. I have never met kinder souls in my life.

They wanted me to stay longer, but the Swiss October fogs and storms had set in so I followed the invitation of the chief forester of Switzerland to come to Locarno, on Lago Maggiore. He, too, had had a narrow escape from typhoid and during convalescence we had chatted together many hours. Most interesting was the transition from the Swiss skies to the Italian. As my train entered the St. Gotthard tunnel a snow-storm was raging. Emerging from the nine-mile tunnel I saw a blue sky and the sun was warming the air voluptuously.

A Winter In California

I don't know any one who has throughout his life skipped about more constantly than I have; a couple of months after I passed through the St. Gotthard tunnel I turned up in Southern California! A doctor had told me that, yes, I *might* return to my journalistic work at once; but that if I did so I would probably be more or less of an invalid all my life, whereas if I loafed a year I would regain my full health and strength.

I decided to loaf—not in European Italy with which I was familiar, but in the south of "our Italy," new to me. On the way I stopped in New York a week or two, to get Albert Steinberg, the "living *bon mot,*" started as my temporary successor.

At Anaheim, near Los Angeles, my youngest sister, Josephine, was living, with her husband, Max Nebelung, one of the "oldest inhabitants," familiar with all the manners and customs of Californians and Mexicans. Under their roof I spent one of the happiest winters of my life; a winter in name only.

From my brother-in-law I got an amount of accurate

information which enabled me to make the chapters on Southern California in my "Pacific Coast Scenic Tour" (which was the result of my one-year loaf) far more interesting than they would have been otherwise.   An abundance of romantic material was at hand.   In those days every California town of the Southwest still had its Chinatown and its Mexican colony for local color.   Quail and wild pigeons were as plentiful as blackberries in Oregon.   The cactus wilderness was peopled with cottontails and jack-rabbits; mocking-birds sustained their reputation as being dangerous rivals of European nightingales. Orange groves were already in full swing, and Catalina Island was not yet a Coney Island.   Once more I thank my stars for letting me live in those semi-wild days, with just enough civilization to point the contrast.

THE VILLARD FAMILY

My passion for travel grew apace as I was hugely enjoying the Yosemite, the Grand Canyon, Alaska, and other regions described in my book on the Pacific Slope. In October I returned to my journalistic duties in New York, but my heart was set on going west still further till I reached the Far East in Japan.

One evening, at a concert in Chickering Hall, Henry Villard and Mrs. Villard sat behind me.   When the entertainment was over Mr. Villard said: "If you are going uptown come along in our carriage."

On the way he asked casually where I was going to spend the coming vacation.   "I am planning a trip to Japan," I answered.   He said nothing more, but a few days later I got a letter enclosing a pass for a free trip from San Francisco to Yokohama and back; it was signed by George Gould!

Henry Villard was a big-hearted man and he had a

wife to encourage his generous impulses, the sister of Wendell Philipps Garrison and daughter of William Lloyd Garrison. That pass to Japan was a characteristic deed. All sorts and conditions of men and women came to them for help, and few failed to get it.

As the *Evening Post* had been bought by Mr. Villard, he was my real boss, but he let me go my own way. A few times he intimated that I was overdoing my enthusiasm for Seidl and Jean de Reszke, but I kept right on enthusing, as that seemed to me by far the most important function of a critic.

Dobbs Ferry on the Hudson was the Villard home and there I often spent my week-ends. Mrs. Villard was a good pianist and ensemble player; her daughter Helen played the violin well. I brought my 'cello along and we played trios by the hour.

One day there was a grand reception at this place, of the German men of letters and financiers whom Mr. Villard had invited for a free trip across the continent on the Northern Pacific Railroad of which he was the president. It was an expensive undertaking, no doubt, but it was good business, for the region traversed was thus made familiar to the readers of German newspapers. Paul Lindau wrote a book on the trip. He was always amusing. He had never seen an artesian well and was comically surprized on coming across Villard's.

During the first Wagner Festival, Lindau had written a series of "Sober Letters from Bayreuth" which had aroused the wrath of the Wagnerites. When I casually referred to these, he adroitly changed the subject. He had, as I knew, entirely changed his mind on that matter and did not like to be reminded of his former folly. At a performance of "Die Walküre" at the Metropolitan I sat next to him in a box. To my intense amusement he

kept on calling my attention to beauty-spots in the music!
I had seen those beauty-spots in 1876; he hadn't.

In the city home of the Villards, there were many
notable gatherings of the town's intellectual aristocracy.
Often, too, I was invited to dinners when celebrities were
present. I enjoyed particularly, one evening when the
Australian explorer, Carl Lumholtz, was the guest of
honor and told us some of his adventures among the canni-
bals. One of these man-eaters begged Lumholtz to let
him walk ahead of him because, when behind, he could
hardly repress his desire to stick his spear through him.

One of the dishes at this dinner was that super-delicacy,
terrapin liver. Answering my question, Lumholtz said:
"Yes, I like terrapin liver very much, but I think I find
python liver still more delectable."

Mrs. Villard was not only a perfect hostess but she
found time and means to further various enterprises. Her
pet charity was the Diet Kitchen, which supplied poor
babies with pure milk. Additions to the fund were made
by an annual concert. I never hesitated to help her secure
big artists for these concerts. To be sure, it was not
strictly "according to Hoyle" that a critic should thus use
his influence, but charity covers a multitude of sins.

We remained good friends though I never shared her
enthusiastic interest in negroes and in woman suffrage.
I have held, in particular, that negro influence in American music has been absurdly exaggerated. The pages on
this subject in my "Musical Progress" were fiercely bom-
barded by the negro journals published in New York.

As for woman suffrage, I used to lecture on the subject, besides writing many articles on it, mostly for the
New York *Independent,* edited by my good friend, Hamilton Holt. A copy of the best of these, "Evolution of Sex
in Mind," I sent to President Roosevelt and got a reply
promising that he would read and digest it. For a time

he seemed to lean to my side, but afterwards he yielded to the terrific suffragette pressure.

My contention was, not that women were not good enough for politics, but that they were too good for the rough game of political football. After all, I argued, politics isn't the only important thing in the world. It is well enough for men to be absorbed in it, but if women follow their example what is to become of literature, art, music, of which they are the chief supporters?

When Henry Villard died, his son Oswald became my boss. Before that happened we had worked several years in the same room and were known as "the twins," though I was many years the older; we looked somewhat alike. He was fond of music, cultivated his voice and played the 'cello. One of the ways we differed was that he was intensely interested in politics. This interest was fostered by Carl Schurz, who had great faith in his pupil. Although Schurz was a radical and revolutionary, he would have been surprized had he lived to see how far his pet Oswald was destined to outstrip him in radicalism.

Destined, I say; for Oswald Garrison Villard is the grandson of William Lloyd Garrison and blood will tell. When he sold the *Evening Post,* partly because of differences with the Government, he took up the *Nation* and changed it into an organ that would have made his conservative uncle, Wendell Phillips Garrison, howl with dismay. All the old subscribers were alienated, but the new crop of readers was several times as large. My views being diametrically opposed to those of Oswald, I ceased to write regularly for the *Nation,* yet we remained good friends otherwise, and continued to call each other by our first names.

While holding different views, I could not help admiring his courage and audacity, as well as his rare journalistic ability, incisiveness, wit and vivacity. No one, it is safe to say, has ever yawned over one of his editorials, and the new *Nation* became as a whole, a decidedly readable periodical. I don't suppose it ever paid expenses any more than the *Evening Post* did, but Oswald Villard could afford this journalistic "steam yacht," as he had inherited plenty of cash.

When I resigned from the *Evening Post,* I was pleased to read in the *Nation* the following tribute from Oswald's eloquent pen, even though it does refer to one of the many occasions when I made a fool of myself:

"Now that he is on the subject of personalities, the Drifter cannot forego the opportunity to express his regret that Henry T. Finck, for more than forty years the music critic of the New York *Evening Post,* has voluntarily left that once brilliant daily. Finck calls himself seventy years of age, but it is a transparent lie, for his heart of youth can never have grown so old. A joyous child he always has been and always will be, always with passionate loves and passionate hates, now championing Wagner in the days when to do so was to write oneself down a conceited, affected jackanapes, now abusing Brahms and living to repent that in considerable degree. Strange how few of us are capable of championing more than one radical departure from the beaten paths! Of course, Finck loved too dearly both his Paderewskis and his Geraldine Farrars to be an ideal critic—but them he loved so ardently and so faithfully! His learning has been prodigious, and not only in the musical field. For many, many years the sole reviewer of musical books for *The Nation,* Finck has served it well in numerous other fields. Seventeen books stand to his credit of which one, 'Romantic Love and Personal Beauty,' had a sale to make one dizzy. His book on gardening is real *vade mecum* for the gardener, and as for his latest 'Girth Control,' it is a scientific blow at the Fat-men's Club—a body blow in fact and—we must confess it—aimed beneath the belt.

"Yes, Henry T. Finck, too, has personality, individuality, character—whatever you choose to call it. He is a living example of what absolutely full self-development does for a person, for he has been 'Expressing Henry' all his life (except when he has palmed off some of his able wife's music criticism as his own). Which reminds the Drifter how once the second edition of the *Evening Post* nearly failed to appear. Accustomed always to absolute freedom from the copy-desk blue pencil, or any control by business office, or managing editor, or owner, Finck naturally was bitterly outraged one day when he came back from lunch to find in the first edition in utterly garbled form a musical criticism he had sent up in the morning. His shrieks of pain, his outburst of rage that after thirty-five years his virtue should thus be outraged by this mishandling of his copy brought a half-dozen editors to his side. A posse *comitatus* started with Finck for the composing-room to find the guilty man, since no editor had even glanced at the copy. The composing-room protested its innocence and to prove it produced Finck's unaltered manuscript. Comparing it with the printed page Finck made the startling discovery that the newspaper in his hand was not the *Evening Post* but its rival the *Globe* and the guilty criticism not his but a rival critic's! The Drifter has the authority of six eye-witnesses that alcohol played no part in this transaction, and that Henry Finck never in his life went downstairs so fast as on this occasion or amid such shrieks of laughter. In fact, if Henry Finck had turned professor instead of critic he would undoubtedly have been the Fliegende Blätter kind, he would at times absentmindedly have put his umbrella to bed and himself in the hall clothes-closet.

"So the Drifter wishes Henry Finck years of joy and happiness and as much of the red wine of his new home on the Riviera as is good and proper for him. Some day the Drifter may be ready to give up wandering the world o'er and writing for his special corner in *The Nation.* When the day comes he hopes he'll take with him as much love and affection as does Finck."

Not A Mary After All

I have been made dizzier climbing the sides of the Matterhorn than by contemplating the huge sales of my "Romantic Love and Personal Beauty" to which Villard refers. Rockefeller and Carnegie were still, I regretfully confess, ahead of me financially. But the sales of that work did encourage me to look the problem of marriage squarely in the face.

As it was my first book, I was naturally very proud of it and took along a copy in my valise when I made my first trip to Spain. My dear college friend, Edward Strobel (who subsequently became Professor of International Law at Harvard and then principal legal adviser to the King of Siam) was at that time secretary to Mr. Curry, American Minister at the Court of Spain. He showed me the sights of Madrid, diurnal and nocturnal, with collegiate thoroughness. Through him I met Mr. Curry and his niece, a Virginia girl of dazzling beauty who made such an impression on me that I decided to make her a present of the cherished copy of that book in my valise.

A moment's reflection convinced me that I could not do this. The Virginia beauty was a decided blonde and my book had a chapter: "Brunettes versus Blondes" which would be sure to displease her. Presently—happy thought —this is what I did: I gave her the book after writing

Photograph by Davis & Sanford

ABBIE HELEN CUSHMAN FINCK

in it, following her name: "Please remember that the chapter on 'brunettes versus blondes' was written before I had seen you."

That was, I rather think, the cleverest thing I ever did in my life. All the same, I did not marry that girl; nor did I marry one of half-a-dozen other beauties who had temporarily dazed me. Most of these, as it happened, were Marys. John Olmsted knew all about them, from my letters. One day he sent me a post card with the initials of four Marys and Maries, followed by the query: "Why in Hades don't you get Married, you much Maried man?"

Seven years later I did marry, but not a Marie. Her name was Abbie—Abbie Helen Cushman, a descendant of the Thomas Cushman who was a supervisor of the pilgrims that gathered in Leyden before sailing for America. I first saw her at a rehearsal in the Academy of Music of Mrs. Thurber's American Opera Company. Her mother and her sister had gone to France to be with her father, who was ill. She herself was left in care of relatives—the family of James E. Learned, managing editor, for several years, of the *Evening Post*.

Mr. Learned was an intimate friend of Theodore Thomas, who conducted these performances, and through him he had tickets for the rehearsals. His daughter Nellie, whom I knew, sat next to Abbie. One glance and I hastened to sit right behind them, casually as it were. I was introduced to Abbie and the first glance of her dark, merry eyes stabbed my heart as even Heidelberg Marie's eyes had not done. I was lost then and there. The girl was only seventeen and we were not married till four and a half years later, but married we were inevitably. I tried several times, like a big salmon trout hooked at last, to escape, with the aid of minor flirtations, but in vain. The ceremony took place in October 1890, and we took the usual wedding journey to Niagara Falls and down the St. Lawrence river to Quebec.

She had no figure worth talking about at that time, being slight as a school girl, which makes it the more remarkable that I, a born sensualist if ever there was one, should have fallen so madly in love with her. It was genuine romantic love: eye love, face love, soul love. And she had a mind as well as a soul. Music was her passion, and her preferences usually were the same as mine. Soon she began to help me with my critical work and after a few years she could write so cleverly in my style that few could detect the author.

Villard referred to my palming off her articles as my own. I couldn't help that because, at that time, the *Post's* critics did not sign their names. My own articles, too, often reflected her influence. A woman's eyes see things a man's don't see. I got the benefit of her subtle observations. Sometimes she jotted them down for me to use. At other times, particularly in the case of new operas, we divided the task, she writing about the costumes and scenery, I about the music and the performance.

When her enthusiasm was fully aroused, as in the case of the incomparable French baritone Renaud, I was only too glad to let her do it all—I could not begin to write so subtly and interestingly as she did. When Farrar sang we sometimes amused ourselves writing a joint article— a few of my sentences being followed by a few of hers and so on. These mosaics, Geraldine knew were written by "the twins" but she, unlike Renaud, never could tell which "twin" was responsible for this or that sentence.

Abbie also wrote magazine articles. One on "Renaud" and another on "Paderewski at Home" appeared in the *Century*. When we visited Grieg at his villa near Bergen she wrote a letter home which I included in my biography of that uniquely original melodist and harmonist. It got more praise from reviewers than any of my pages.

Her supreme achievement came when I had broncho-pneumonia—a case of lung poisoning from tainted air in a concert hall. The Chicago Opera Company was in town. She took care of it, including the new operas, as well as of the Metropolitan and the concerts. She did it so well that people said: "Why no! Finck is not sick—I see his articles in the *Post* every day."

But the marvel of it was that while taking care of my work she also took care of me.*

This case of pneumonia had an amusing sequel in Paris. When we went on the steamer I was still so weak that I could not carry a small valise. During the trip I regained some of my strength. Unfortunately we arrived at Cherbourg too late in the evening to land: the steamer lay in the harbor, and there was so much noise that I did not sleep a wink all night. I resolved to go to bed that evening with the birds.

From our Paris hotel we telephoned at once to our friend Renaud, as we had promised. "You must come and dine with us tonight," he said. We explained that I was ill and had not slept, but he insisted on that date as he was going to London in the morning to sing and might not be back till after we had left Paris. So we accepted.

All went well at first, but M. Renaud unfortunately prepared a cocktail. Madame Renaud refused to drink hers and insisted on my doing it for her. One has to be polite in Paris; I drank it. Dinner did not begin for half an hour. I drank, with the delicious food, several glasses of choice wines, including *tisane de Champagne*. I began

---

* I wanted to add more about my wife but she has firmly edited out most of my references to her.

to feel queer, but I had never been intoxicated in my life any more than my uncle in Tübingen. Presently I heard my wife say: "Henry, you are drunk!"

I remember the savory lamb. What followed that is a blank in my mind, to this day. My wife, who allowed me to eat to the end but not to drink any more, says that after dinner I walked upstairs with my arm around Madame Renaud's waist, then sat in a corner and slept two hours, when a cab was called to take us back to our hotel. On arriving—I am just repeating what my wife said—I got out, paid the driver, gave him a tip, and we went up to our room. There I put away my spectacles as usual, undressed and went to bed. And when I awoke in the morning, I remembered, as I have said, the dinner up to the lamb, and nothing beyond.

Was that the usual thing, I wondered. How about you?

One thing is sure: my uncle would have been ashamed of his degenerate nephew. But had it not been for the exhausting pneumonia, the sleepless night and the two premature cocktails on an empty stomach I would be able to boast to this day that I have never been drunk.

Mrs. Thurber's National Conservatory

It was at a rehearsal of the American Opera Company that I met, as just mentioned, the girl who became my wife. This opera company had been planned and was financed by Mrs. Jeanette M. Thurber; to her, therefore, I am indebted for my happy married life.

The performances of this company were only an episode in the busy life of this ambitious woman. Her pet achievement was the National Conservatory of Music of New York. On that she spent, in the course of years, about a million dollars, giving a free education to hundreds of young Americans.

It was actually a National Conservatory after the first decade of its existence. In 1891, on the same day that the U. S. Senate passed the International Copyright Bill, there was also signed another bill incorporating the National Conservatory of Music, with Mrs. Thurber, W. G. Choate, Chauncey M. Depew, Abram S. Hewitt, F. R. Lawrence, John Hay, S. P. Langley among the incorporators.

This was the first instance of anything done by the National Legislature in behalf of music.

No American Conservatory has ever had one half as many famous musicians on its staff of instructors as Mrs. Thurber's has had. One of the foremost pianists of his day, Rafael Joseffy, was at the head of the piano classes for nearly twenty years. One of the leading European composers, Anton Dvorák, was for several years its Director. Among the other eminent musicians associated at various times with this school were Anton Seidl, Victor Herbert, Wassili Safonoff, James G. Huneker, Oscar Saenger, Emil Paur, Camilla Urso, Adele Margulies, Samuel P. Warren, John Cheshire, Frank Van der Stucken, Bruno Oscar Klein, Victor Capoul, Horatio Parker, Emil Fischer, Emy Fursch-Madi, Jacques Bouhy, Romualdo Sapio, Leopold B. Lichtenberg and Ilma di Murska.

My own connection with the Conservatory began in 1882. It started with four lectures which Mrs. Thurber asked me to prepare and deliver at Chickering Hall. An amusing incident occurred at one of these. To make it easier to read the lectures I had had them typed. Having faith in the girl who did this I did not look over the copy before going on the stage. As I was reading it aloud before an audience of several hundred I came across my

reference to Schubert's Serenade, "Hark, Hark the Lark."
The typist had put this down as "Schubert's Sleighride,
Hark, Bark the Lark." The audience shrieked with joy
when I called attention to the change.

Thenceforth, for nearly four decades, I delivered every
season twenty-four lectures on the history of music to a
class of students—mostly girls—varying from less than
a dozen to more than fifty. These lectures helped me a
great deal by teaching me gradually how to present facts
in a way to interest the youthful mind. I noted a fact
which educators too often overlook: that the more entertaining I made my talks the more readily the students
remembered them.

Musical history can be made dry as dust, and generally
is made so. I tried to make my chapters as exciting as
stories of adventure. I have been asked to publish these
lectures, but may not do so because of the foolish prejudice
among educators against textbooks that are entertaining.

Mrs. Thurber always aimed at big game. After Dvorák
returned to his native Bohemia she engaged as Director
of her Conservatory Safonoff who was also for a few
years, conductor of the New York Philharmonic. He was
as fiery, as temperamental, as daring as you would expect
of one who, as a Cossack, used to amuse himself throwing
a spear into the air and then riding forward furiously to
catch it as it came down. His supreme achievement was
the Cossack march in Tchaikovsky's "Pathetic Symphony." This he built up into a wild climax that was of
overwhelming grandeur.

When Safonoff came to New York he did not know a
word of English. He soon learned, however, because he
wasn't afraid of blundering, which is the secret of learning
a language rapidly. I helped him quite a little. He was
particularly pleased with this current limerick I taught
him:

There was a monk in Siberia
Whose life got drearier and drearier
Till he burst from his cell
With a hell of a yell
And eloped with the mother superior.

He repeated this at receptions to all the ladies he met to prove that he was getting on swimmingly with his English.

When he had returned to Russia Mrs. Thurber tried to get Humperdinck, the composer of the two delightful operas, "Hänsel and Gretel" and "Königskinder." The second of these had just had its première at the Metropolitan, (the first performance anywhere) in his presence; and, thanks largely to Farrar's delectable Goose Girl and her live geese on the stage, had made a tremendous sensation.

Mrs. Thurber asked me to offer him the Conservatory Directorship. So, during a performance of his opera, I searched for him behind the scenes and finally found him sitting on a property stump. He was at once interested in the offer, which meant $25,000 a year for him, in advance. He accepted provisionally, but said he had to get permission from the Prussian Government, which might refuse to release him from his duties as professor at the Royal Academy of Music in Berlin. That was precisely what the Government did, so Humperdinck was lost to New York.

DVORÁK AND THE "NEW WORLD" SYMPHONY

I was sorry at this failure of my negotiations in behalf of Mrs. Thurber because I had hoped the National Conservatory might under him become again what it had been in the Dvorák years, a gathering place of the most promising young American composers. In the matter of handling an orchestra, in particular, Humperdinck was almost the equal of Wagner himself, whose pupil and assistant he had been for years at Bayreuth.

Among the American composers who studied with Dvorák were Rubin Goldmark, Harvey Worthington Loomis, William Arms Fisher, Henry Waller, Harry Rowe Shelley and two colored musicians, Harry T. Burleigh and Will Marion Cook, all of whom soon achieved national distinction.

Rubin Goldmark is a nephew of Carl Goldmark, composer of the sensationally successful opera "The Queen of Sheba." After reading the manuscript of a trio which the nephew had written for his class, Dvorák exclaimed delightedly: "Now there are two Goldmarks." And so there were. Rubin's creative genius developed gradually and in later years the première of a new tone poem from his pen was always pleasurably looked forward to by Philharmonic audiences. Unlike most novelties, they were always played more than once.

Rubin Goldmark has also been a leading spirit at clubs and social gatherings of musicians. As an after-dinner speaker he has had few equals; his supply of anecdotes and jokes seems inexhaustible.

Henry Waller wrote a charming operetta, "The Ogallallahs," and then disappeared mysteriously from my ken. Harvey Worthington Loomis has written mastersongs that will some day be better known; there is nothing ephemeral about them. As for Harry Rowe Shelley, I am waiting to see if his "Romeo and Juliet" will mark as great an advance over Gounod's as that does over Bellini's.

William Arms Fisher developed into a first-class writer of songs some of which are far better than most of the new German and French songs imported. As editor-in-chief of the Oliver Ditson Company he did useful work in separating chaff from wheat. One day he came from Boston to discuss with me his plan for the Musicians' Library—a series of volumes embodying the mastersongs and piano pieces of all the musical nations, edited and commented on by prominent musical writers. I thoroughly approved of this scheme, which turned out one of the things American music-publishers have most reason to be proud of; and I personally contributed several volumes concerned with Schubert, Grieg, and miscellaneous mastersongs.

One of the advantages resulting from this Music Lovers' Library was that it led to an acquaintance with its New York publisher, Charles H. Ditson and his witty and vivacious wife, Alice, who soon were included in the circle of our most intimate friends. The last time I met Charlie (in May 1926) he told me that the best-seller among all the collections in that Library had been my "Mastersongs by 20 Composers," twice as many, he said, had been sold of it as of any other volume. Alice I should have liked to engage as my assistant, for she knows all the news and gossip of the musical world. She has a real salon on Wednesdays at which one meets everyone worth meeting.

All the young composers in Dvořák's class became good friends of mine although only one of them attended my lectures on musical history. This one was the baritone Henry T. Burleigh, who is undoubtedly the leader among America's colored composers. There is more white than black in his excellent songs—intentionally, no doubt—yet they reflect great credit on his race. I never had a more intelligent listener and he took down my talks complete in shorthand. When Dvořák was gathering material for his "New World Symphony" Burleigh aided him with hints about Southern Plantation songs. It may be as well, however, to state at once that there are but very faint if any traces of *real* negro characteristics in this composition.

Mrs. Thurber was responsible for this masterwork and she is therefore to be thanked for the most inspired orchestral score ever composed in America. Dvořák did not wish to leave Bohemia, (where he was teaching to support his family); but the offer of $15,000 a year from Mrs. Thurber was not to be resisted. He was not happy, however, away from home; that seemed clear to me every time I saw him in his home or with his classes at the Conservatory. One day Mrs. Thurber, in view of his obvious and constant longing for his homeland, suggested that he should write a symphony embodying his experiences and feelings in America. He promised to do so, and in the slow movement he pathetically embodied his homesickness.

Nothing could be more ridiculous than the attempts that have been made to find anything black (negroid) or red (Indian) in the glorious, soulful melody which opens this movement. In melody, rhythm, harmony, instrumentation nothing could be more white than these inspired pages. Only a genius could have written them.

The first performance of this masterwork was the most memorable event in the long history of the New York Philharmonic Orchestra. When Seidl first looked over the manuscript he was overwhelmed with emotion. He rehearsed the score with eager enthusiasm and at the final rehearsal an incident occurred which showed how deeply he had penetrated into its spirit.

Dvořák was present. By some strange momentary aberration, or whatever you choose to call it, he had marked the slow movement "andante." Seidl, led by a correct instinct for its intense pathos, played it much slower. When he got through Dvořák went to the conductor's desk and marked the movement *adagio*. It is worth while adding that the admirable Boston Orchestra, which stuck to the "andante," never created such wild enthusiasm with this work as did the New York Philharmonic at this première and subsequently. In the season of 1914-1915 this orchestra played it eighteen times, and some years later, on the road, it surpassed this record on tour under Josef Stransky, whose interpretation was second only to Seidl's. Stransky is a Bohemian, and when all is said and done, the "New World Symphony" is more Bohemian than anything else, except in the slow movement, which is cosmic and eternal.

Dvořák's idol was Schubert. Whenever I visited him I found a volume of Schubert's piano pieces (which Rubinstein thought even more marvelous than the songs) lying on his Steinway. "I have my children play them every day," he said. He called my attention specially to some beauty spots in the sonatas which had escaped me.

Richard Watson Gilder, reading what I had written about Dvořák's enthusiasm for Schubert, asked him to write an article about that composer for the *Century Magazine*. Dvořák refused point blank on the ground that he was no writer. Gilder then appealed to me for help, but Dvořák shook his head. Afterwards I filled a few pages with questions about Schubert which I gave him to read and think over for a few weeks. I then called on him and jotted down his answers. With this material I composed an article, quite properly signed by Dvořák, which the great Schubert specialist, Sir George Grove, pronounced the best ever written on that prince of melodists. Needless to say that Mr. Gilder was pleased, too. Dvořák refused to accept any payment. It had been, for him, a labor of love.

Joseffy was another genius whom, like Dvořák, I pitied for having to teach. Sometimes he had pupils worthy of a pianist of his rank but often he didn't; yet he always gave of his best. My wife was for several years a member of his class; she did not play for him but she jotted down his wise and witty remarks. Steinberg dubbed her "Mrs. Boswell."

At these lessons she became familiar with hundreds of piano pieces some of which even I did not know. When one of these was played at a recital as an "encore" she could tell me what it was. And when, during the intermission, minor critics or out-of-town correspondents came down the aisle, as they were wont to, to ask me what that second or third encore was, I had the answer all ready.

While usually conscientious, Joseffy had his days when he "played hooky." Mrs. MacDowell, secretary of the Conservatory, told me of a telegram she once got in which he said he could not give a lesson that day as he had missed the Tarrytown train. The telegram was in his own handwriting! He had left it at an office near the Conservatory and it had been simply put into an envelope and delivered by a messenger boy. It began: "Dear Mrs. MacDowell."

Edwin Hughes found among Joseffy's manuscripts an autograph letter in which Liszt named Joseffy as his successor and heir. Rosenthal is the most brilliant of the Joseffy pupils. Joseffy's own dazzling feats on the keyboard were the more remarkable in view of his short, thick hands. When asked if large hands were not an advantage in piano playing he answered: "Oh, a man may have big hands and still be a big fool."

EDWARD MACDOWELL

At the time when I became professor of musical history at the National Conservatory it had a most efficient secretary in the person of Mrs. MacDowell, mother of the young man who was destined to become America's foremost composer. She was extremely bright and amusing and I often stopped for a chat with her. On one of these occasions I saw lying on her desk a collection entitled "Eight Songs."

"What's this?" I said, picking it up.

"My son's latest compositions," she replied. "Take them home if you like."

I did so, and when I played them over on our Steinway I felt like shouting "Hats off, a genius!" as Schumann did when he first came across a piece by Chopin.

From that day I became the champion, the panegyrist, the high priest of Edward MacDowell. I needed no one to confirm my opinion that America at last had a musical creator ranking with the great ones in Europe. The music told me that; and from year to year, as his genius matured, I grew more enthusiastic. I am not so foolish as to think I made MacDowell famous; his music did that; but my glowing comments and my bold claims for him greatly accelerated the growth of that fame. Nothing is so contagious as genuine enthusiasm, especially on the part of one who has shown by his writings that he knows what he is talking about. I once asked Mrs. MacDowell how many Mac-Dowell Clubs there were throughout the country. "About one hundred and fifty" she replied. I am vain enough to believe that my glowing comments accounted for the existence of some of those clubs.

Anton Seidl made a sensation when he declared, in a magazine article, that MacDowell was a greater composer than Brahms. But he spoke the plain truth up to a certain point. I find more original melody in MacDowell's songs as a whole than in the more numerous ones of Brahms; and in his piano pieces the American leaves the German so far behind that you can hardly see him.

It is significant that in Germany itself one of the leading publishers, Schott's Söhne, announced a few years ago that MacDowell's were getting to be "most in demand of all piano pieces." There is in them a wealth of genius and a depth of feeling that will dazzle the world more and more from year to year. Don't fail to read the admirable remarks on these pieces in Lawrence Gilman's book on MacDowell.

Orchestrally, on the other hand, Brahms is far, far ahead of MacDowell. In part, this is due to the fact that the American's works for orchestra all belong to his earlier, immature period. In one of the intimate talks I had with him in his log cabin at Peterboro, New Hampshire, he told me of plans for new and larger orchestral works which, no doubt, would have exhibited his genius at its ripest.

It must not be forgotten, at the same time, that there are many inspired pages in his early suites, particularly the "Indian." The Dirge in that has not, for poignancy, for musical beauty and pathos, and for depth of grief, its equal in Europe except in the works of Beethoven, Chopin and Wagner.

MacDowell's music is more difficult to fathom and project than Brahms's. Many a time have I heard the symphonies of this profound German master done to perfection. But of the Dirge from the "Indian Suite" I have heard only one performance that revealed all its miraculous wealth of musical beauty and melancholy. I simply gasped on this occasion. Leopold Stokowsky was the conductor. To him I take off my hat. He had taken the same pains with the American's piece that he had with Brahms, and the result was thrilling. Lucy Gates, the delectable Mormon soprano, once told me that after she had studied MacDowell's songs with the same devotion as those of the great German masters, she found American audiences quite as enthusiastic over them, sometimes more so. In their simple tunefulness these songs seem as easy and obvious as folk-tunes, but gaze steadily into their crystalline depths and you behold a harmonic sea change into something rich and strange—gold fishes and corals and gracefully interlaced seaweeds of many kinds and colors.

Teresa Carreño, the brilliant Venezuelan pianist, who was one of MacDowell's teachers (I once met her at Mrs. MacDowell's and wondered no more why she had captured so many husbands—a handsomer woman the Lord has never created) astonished the natives in Germany by showing them that a mere American had done big things in music. She specialized in the concertos and she usually repeated one of the movements—simply *had* to.

I can not dwell here on all the pianists who have distinguished themselves making the sonatas and the shorter and more tender and poetic pieces of MacDowell known to the American public. Conspicuous among them is Augusta Cottlow, a true missionary who preached MacDowell from her girlhood and with ever-increasing eloquence and popular success. Unlike Carreño, whom Huneker aptly called the Valkyrie (or war maiden) of the piano, she emphasized the tender, feminine side of this music.

Foremost among the MacDowell missionaries is the composer's widow. Year in and out, in good health and bad (she has been a great sufferer) she has talked about his music at women's clubs and in concert halls all over the country and played it as only she could play it. She alone knows all the subtle changes in expression marks which he introduced in his printed pieces during the last years of his life. These changes are now, fortunately, being made public in new editions. I was glad to hear from her not long ago that the sales of her husband's music are still growing from year to year.

In 1925 *The Pictorial Review* gave Mrs. MacDowell its annual prize of $5,000, as to the woman who had done the most useful work in behalf of American progress. She

devoted this, as she had devoted the proceeds of her recitals, to the Peterboro Colony which carries out Edward
MacDowell's dream of a place where representatives of
all the arts can dwell together in summer and act and react
on one another.

Marian MacDowell's ill health is a result of the devotion she showed to her husband during the years when
his mind gradually failed so inexplicably. It was not real
insanity, but a sort of mental decay, as in a very old man.
I remember the first symptoms.

"I don't like Edward any more," I said to my wife one
day. "He talks and acts so queerly." Alas, he could not
help it, as became obvious before long.

He was naturally a very strong, virile man, but he had
been overdoing, composing and teaching at the same time
and not resting in summer. He might have been saved
had he accepted the invitation, to rough it among the
Indians for a year, made to him by his devoted friend
Hamlin Garland, the masterful delineator of western life,
whom I am proud to number among my own friends, too.

When Columbia University offered MacDowell a professorship in music he hesitated to accept it. His mother
also was in doubt. She talked the matter over with me
and I strongly advised that he should say yes, because it
would be rated a great honor and would give him a prominence that would also help him as a composer. I was a
fool.

It did give him the prominence. There were days when
he and Marian had a hundred letters to answer. He had
to prepare his lectures (they have since been printed) as
well as deliver them and tend personally to dozens of students in college as well as private students. To do all this
and compose too was too much. His brain weakened and
the saddest of tragedies followed.

One day when I called at the Westminster Hotel I

Photograph by Oscar Maurer

EDWARD MACDOWELL

found Edward sitting at a small table amusing himself, just like a young child, by playing with a pile of twenty-dollar gold pieces. His mind was almost gone; yet, strange to say, his sense of humor remained. He laughed with that pleasant chuckle of his when I said cheerfully: "Aha! I know what you are going to do with that gold. Bribe the critics!"

More strikingly still was this survival of the sense of humor (which was so strongly developed in him) manifested at Peterboro. He had been worrying for days over a photograph of myself hanging on the wall in his bedroom. "It must be fatiguing for Henry to be hung up that way all the time" he kept on saying.

I went outside where he was sitting. "You mustn't worry, Edward," I said, "at my being stuck up on the wall, for you know I always have been stuck up."

At this wretched pun he laughed heartily. He himself had been an incorrigible punster. Sometimes, at dinner or supper, we vied with one another in committing atrocities on words till our wives fled in dismay. If we are to be punished for these sins in another world we shall be in good company, including Beethoven and Shakespeare.

PADEREWSKI

MacDowell's two chief idols were Grieg and Paderewski. To Grieg he dedicated two of his four sonatas; these, as well as others of his works bear testimony to the potent influence on his own genius of the great Norwegian's stupendous melodic and harmonic originality, which made him one of my idols too.

"Some call it hair, I call it piano playing" was one of Edward's quaint ways of expressing his admiration for Paderewski.

On another occasion he said to me: "Some of the critics,

I see, accuse him of pounding. But if Paderewski wants
to pound why shouldn't he?"

Rubinstein was accused of pounding the piano; so was
Liszt; so was Beethoven. In each of these four cases it
was due to the player's frantic attempt to convert the piano
into a huge orchestra which alone could express his feelings in an adequate manner. Rubinstein's biographer,
Alexander MacArthur, tells us that when that Russian
giant was in one of his leonine, orchestral moods he would
fret and fume and wish he had twenty pianos to play on
at once. Of course he "pounded."

I never heard Beethoven (he died a quarter of a century
before I was born) but I heard Rubinstein and Liszt and
Paderewski and how I adored them when they "pounded"
in moments of surging passion and violent emotion! At
such moments Rubinstein also dropped notes or played
wrong ones, but no one cared—except unmusical pedants.

During his first three American tours Paderewski was
the victim of many fleabites by such unmusical pedants.
He had no "walk over" by any means. The Steinways
brought him over in 1891 for a series of five concerts with
orchestra. Walter Damrosch, who conducted these concerts, reveals in his Memoirs that the first of these brought
in only $500, gross receipts. During the intermission at
his first appearance one of the critics passed me, shaking
his head, which aroused my ire. "Look here, old fellow,"
I said, "don't you make a fool of yourself. This is the
greatest pianist since Rubinstein."

But the next morning this critic did make a fool of himself. If, said another critic, Paderewski could play this
like Pachmann and that like D'Albert and that like some
other pianist, and so on, six times, "he too would be a great
pianist." It was to laugh.

I cracked him up to the sky from the start and the public was with me most emphatically. The Madison Square

Garden Concert Hall was soon found too small, wherefore Carnegie Hall was, for the first time, used for piano
recitals. Soon that was jammed as recital followed recital. Then and there the enthusiasts who could not get
seats started the habit of rushing down to the footlights
at the end of the program and compelling Paderewski to
add six or eight or more pieces to his list. I have known
him to add a whole hour of extras to his two-hour recital.
And once, after all this, he played an hour in the evening
for the French statesman, Clemenceau!

Time and again Paderewski came to America, each time
taking home with him a larger check. As his manager,
Hugo Görlitz informed me, by request, his check for the
first American tour was $95,000; for the second, $160,-
000; the third, $248,000. And it continued to climb stead-
ily. His first tour after he had been Prime Minister of
Poland brought him nearly half a million dollars in
five months. Sixty-six recitals brought in an average of
$7,000. San Francisco, having a mammoth hall, exceeded
that average by contributing the record sum of $24,590
for a single recital. And the audience paid him the highest of all tributes—tears. One hearer wrote to the *Exam-
iner* that no fewer than twenty-seven listeners near him,
including several men, used their handkerchiefs freely.

Why could Paderewski ask twice as much for tickets
as other pianists and yet fill the hall weeks in advance?
What was the mystery, the secret, of his success?

Even a reader not versed in music will understand that
it was the same secret that enables a great orator to draw
big audiences and sway their feelings. Take one of Mark
Twain's speeches, now gathered in a volume, and let any
Tom, Dick or Harry read or speak it. There may not be
even a snicker or a smile in the audience. But when Mark
spoke these speeches they evoked roars of laughter.

Deems Taylor, the brilliant critic of the New York

World, writing about one of the Paderewski recitals in New York, tells of the surprize he noted on the face of a conservatory miss, who perused the printed page of a Chopin mazurka while the great pianist performed it. He played all the notes as printed, just as she had done, yet the thing sounded so different that she hardly knew it.

What had he done? While respecting the printed notes, he had introduced a multitude of shades of expression that changed the face of the music as the face of a beautiful woman is made still more so by smiles or other expressions of mind and emotion. We have the testimony of Berlioz that Chopin himself, in playing these pieces, introduced innumerable, unbelievable nuances in the expression. Paderewski's secret is that his playing, too, was "veined with a thousand nuances."

In the storm scene of Verdi's "Rigoletto" while the jester's daughter is being murdered in place of the Duke, there are heard from the mouths of invisible chorus singers dismal sounds like the moaning of the wind. These same sounds are suggested in Chopin's Etude No. 5, opus 10 by a *crescendo* mark and a *decrescendo* (second line on page 18, Schlesinger Edition); yet of all the pianists I have heard Paderewski alone saw the thrilling possibilities of that little climax, on which he lingers a little.

I have just written on a slip of paper "1891" and above it "1925." Subtracting (oh, I know *some* arithmetic!) I get 34. That is the number of years I have known Ignace Jan Paderewski. It was in 1891 that I first shook hands with him, at a dinner given by his manager to make the New York critics acquainted with him. We were all young and (don't smile) bashful. None of us had the courage to take the seat at his right or left till De Koven broke the ice. *He* wasn't *very* bashful. I was—honor bright— but I got bravely over it. After a few years I wasn't afraid to call him and his wife Ignace and Hélène—him, the future Premier of Poland and the successor of Liszt in everything, including the faculty of hobnobbing with Kings and Popes. Just before I sat down to write this, I read in the London *Times* how the King of England had received the great pianist and bestowed on him one of the highest honors at his command; and a few weeks ago I read of how, during his last stay in Brussels, he was the personal guest of the King of Belgium—Why not? He has been for three decades the King of pianists, and he will be famous long after most monarchs of his time áre forgotten.

Paderewski did not attend my wedding, as I was married the year before he came to America. He did, however, come to the wedding of my wife's sister Bessie to a young lawyer, Carl A. Hansman. He had asked to name the date so he could be present. When that date approached he was in Montreal and his next concert was to be in Boston, but he came all the way to New York to keep his engagement.

One of the scenes at this wedding would have made a unique snapshot: Paderewski on his knees fondling our large gray cat. This same cat once had the honor of a dinner invitation from Paderewski.

I had in Sarah E. Cushman an exceptionally amiable and well-behaved mother-in-law, but once when Paderewski called at our house I wished my wife had never had a mother. He had been compelled to play his first minuet at every recital throughout the country and was of course ever so tired of it. Imagine my feelings when she asked him if he wouldn't play his minuet for us. He acceded, with a smile, but it was the feeblest smile I have ever seen on his face.

Personally, I never asked the great artists who visited us to play or sing. Once, though, I did ask Paderewski to play for me several new songs he had finished in his head but not yet written down. They were enchanting. Subsequently, when they were printed, he drove up to 485 Manhattan Avenue one afternoon to deliver us copies personally. Some of them were too difficult for my fingers—and most fingers. That's one reason why these songs are not so widely known as they should be.

One of the lunches the Paderewskis took at our house nearly ended in a dietetic tragedy. We knew that he always drank Apollinaris water with meals, but somehow we had forgotten it this time till the lunch was on. The waitress was hurriedly sent to the nearest drugstore for a few bottles. She brought Apenta—also put up by the Apollinaris Co. and marked "elegant and efficacious." Many a time in later years we laughed at that "elegant and efficacious," and once, at Morges, had a frolic at which a bottle of Apenta had a prominent part. I hope the Apollinaris Company will send me a nice check for this free advertisement.

The friendship of Paderewski has been one of the things that have helped to atone for the awful boredom to which a musical critic is frequently subjected. The oftener I met him the more my admiration of his mind—quite apart from his music—increased. Talk with him on any subject you please and he knows more about it than you do—or at least than I do. About American politics he knows more in a day than I do in a year and the same with European politics. Ask him about Argentinian agriculture or Chinese ethnology, and again you will be surprized to find he knows all about it.

Once I had the pleasure of entertaining him at lunch in my home shortly after the Russian Revolution had been started. He knew all about the men who first took up the reins so promisingly and talked fascinatingly about them for an hour. Then he shook his head and predicted what would happen because Russia wasn't ripe for a republic.

IGNACE J. PADEREWSKI

He could not, however, foresee the impending horrors of Leninism and Bolshevism.

So far as I know I was the first journalist to call attention to the fact that Paderewski was infinitely more than a musician and to suggest that "he may become King or President of Poland—who knows?—and no one is more worthy of such a place." On January 11, 1919, I cited the comments of Alfred Ottenheimer on my assertion:

"Probably a year ago Mr. Finck wrote the same silly, inane nonsense, and how a serious newspaper like the *Evening Post* can permit such stuff to be printed is quite beyond the comprehension of your average reader. I should think Mr. Finck's closest friends would, without delay, call in a first-class alienist. . . . If one thinks of the complicated political and social questions that will confront the future ruler of Poland and then imagine Mr. Paderewski deciding them just because he is a superb piano player it is simply ludicrous."

And Mr. Ottenheimer knew how to kill two birds with one stone for he added:

"For over twenty-five years I have read your paper and never burdened you with a letter, but such stuff as proposing Mr. Paderewski time and again for a position about which he knows as much as Mr. Finck does about music—which is enough said—is more than I can stomach without a protest."

When Clemenceau met Paderewski at the Versailles Peace Conference he said: "So you have left music and become a politician! What a fall!"

The great Frenchman hit the nail on the head.

Premiers have their uses but they are sure to lose their jobs long before they have ceased to be at their best, as we see in the cases of Clemenceau himself, Poincaré and many others. Paderewski was the best man and patriot Poland could have found for the premiership; he had all the qualities needed for making a political leader: exceptional intelligence, astuteness, a deep insight into human nature, an unequaled comprehension of the fearfully complicated political conditions of Eastern Europe, authority, manliness, knowledge, eloquence; but he was helpless in the odds that opposed him. We have two political parties, which is just two too many, but Poland had thirteen.

Paderewski was too good, too great a man to waste his brains on such partisan football tussles. He had a grand plan for a Greater Poland of nearly 40,000,000 souls, which alone could insure the future peace of Europe. But he was thwarted, so he returned to music, where he was master of all he surveyed, High Priest of the Divine Art.

Let me ask: is any king of Poland known to all the world and beloved as is Chopin? and is any Polish politician so well known as Paderewski the pianist? Clemenceau's pleasantry, I say it again, hit the nail on the head exactly. A great musician is above a politician.

For nearly six years, during his political adventures, Paderewski, as his wife told me, did not touch his piano. He was now sixty-three years old. "Would his fingers regain their pliancy?" was asked anxiously. It is a remarkable fact that no company was willing to insure the financial success of his first American tour after he had been Premier of Poland—the tour which yielded nearly half a million dollars!

And *had* he regained all his powers? By way of a comprehensive answer to this question let me repeat what another of the superpianists of our time, Ossip Gabrilowitsch, said to me: "We had better all become Premiers and then come back to music!"

I am asked sometimes what—quite apart from the music itself—was the most thrilling moment I can recall in my long professional career. I answer, the moment when

Paderewski, returning to music, came on the stage at Carnegie Hall, which was packed as it never had been, boxes intended for four having eight in them. And this vast audience, from parquet to roof, got on its feet by a unanimous impulse to show the respect due to the world's foremost musician.

The most anxious moment in my career also was in Carnegie Hall, some years before this. American Jews had hatched out a most ludicrous and outrageous story to the effect that Paderewski had contributed $20,000 toward the support of a newspaper which "had no other purpose than the agitation of killing the Jews of Russia"; a story as atrociously idiotic as the tales told about Jews killing Christian children; yet a surprizingly large number of otherwise sane and intelligent American Jews believed this slander against one of the most complete gentlemen and most kind-hearted personages that ever lived; a man as incapable of such a crime as Cardinal Gibbons or John Burroughs would have been.

Repeatedly, threats had been made against Paderewski's life if he gave another recital. This had been done, as my wife and I knew, on the occasion of the Carnegie Hall recital I am speaking of. Yet the great pianist paid no heed to these threats. Our hearts stopped beating twice when in the midst of a piece, a whistle sounded from the gallery. Again they stopped beating when we noticed an opening in the ceiling right over the pianist, growing larger and larger till two heads were visible. But apparently it was simply a couple of stagehands eager to hear and see the famous player.

On the day when the President of Poland was murdered Paderewski was to give a recital in New York. The house had been sold out weeks in advance. It was decided to keep the news from him, as he would have been too agitated to play, and it seemed too bad to disappoint his thousands of admirers. It so happened that he played as even he had never before played. The music was a succession of emotional waves that sent thrill after thrill down our backbones.

During the second intermission his stepson, Mr. Gorski, came to see us. We told him how we felt about this recital, and he replied that Paderewski had just said: "I feel to-day as if I had been communing with God."

We knew it instinctively. Paderewski had made us feel the meaning of the word genius as no one else ever had.

This refers to reproductive genius; but as a creator, also he knew how to make the pulse beat faster; he ranks far higher as a composer than is generally known. As in the case of Liszt and Rubinstein, his sensational success as a pianist has stood in his way; the public is disinclined to believe that a man can be supreme in more ways than one. But of his piano pieces some are equal to Chopin at his best; his symphony is a masterpiece; and his "Manru" gave me more pleasure than any other new opera produced at the Metropolitan in a quarter of a century except "Parsifal" and "Königskinder."

I wish I had jotted down some of the pithy remarks Paderewski made to me during the rehearsals of "Manru." On the whole he was satisfied. Three performances near the season's end were given at the Metropolitan, to jammed houses, even though, on the afternoon of the third, he was playing in Carnegie Hall to three thousand more enthusiasts. Then the opera was dropped, mysteriously, incomprehensibly.

Again and again I pleaded for a restaging, but in vain; which surely showed a lamentable lack of business sense on the part of Otto H. Kahn and Giulio Gatti-Casazza; for any opera not even half as good as "Manru" could have been made a huge success with the cooperation of its composer during one of his sensational visits to this country.

The Metropolitan's manager was reported to have said that he would promptly accept a new opera by Paderewski, without even looking at it. The way to encourage him to write a second opera would have been to do justice to his first. One of the happiest and proudest moments in my life was when Madame Paderewska told me confidentially, after I had written a glowing article on his works, that he had, after a long interval of silence, begun to compose again. "Friend of Manru" she called me, with a tender smile.

It is a strange thing that one so adept with the composer's pen, so eloquent in his speeches, and so entertaining in his table talk should have done so little in a literary or epistolary way.

"We have three letters from you," my wife once said to him. "Impossible!" he replied.

It certainly is hard to get a letter out of him; and as for magazine articles, let me tell you a story.

One of Paderewski's most intimate friends in New York was Richard Watson Gilder, but Gilder, with all his gentle and subtle persuasiveness, was unable to get an article out of him on Chopin, which he was dying to print in the *Century*.

Remembering my success with the coy Dvorák, Gilder then implored me to help. I adopted the same method as with Dvorák, filling a few sheets with questions concerning which all music lovers would have been eager to read Paderewski's views. I gave these to him. The next time I saw him he complimented me on my questions—and that was the end of this little scheme.

Fortunately I had better success when I asked him to contribute to my book on "Success in Music and How It Is Won" a chapter on so-called Tempo Rubato, a subject of tremendous importance on which most musicians display the exalted intelligence of oxen.* I told him it was his artistic duty to enlighten the musical world on this matter and he—well, "he seen his duty and done it." It's a wonderful chapter and it makes one weep to think he has not written more things like it."

A volume could be filled with the anecdotes he tells about his experiences. Here is one. It occurred at the Windsor Hotel. He was playing billiards, a game to which he is passionately devoted, one afternoon when a stranger said to him: "You look surprizingly like Paddierooskee."

"That isn't strange," was the reply, "for I am Paderewski."

"*You* Paddierooskee?" exclaimed the other; then beckoning a friend on the other side of the room he shouted: "Jim, come over and let me introduce you to my very particular friend, Mr. Paddierooskee."

One day my wife and I arrived in London from Paris, not knowing what was going on in the musical world. Presently we saw an announcement, in huge letters, of a recital to be given that afternoon by Paderewski. We drove to the music store where the tickets were sold; I told them who I was and promptly received a present of two guinea-seats. They were in the front row. Of course we went to his room when the recital was over.

"I have invited some friends to dinner to-night," he exclaimed "Come and join us."

We promised to do so, but forgot to ask where to go. Returning to the music store, we inquired where the pianist was staying.

"Yes," a man told us when we had rung the bell at the place we were told to go to, "Mr. Paderewski engaged a

* See the chapter on "The disgraceful Tempo Rubato Muddle" in my "Musical Progress."

suite of rooms here and paid for it in advance several days ago, but when he found the number of the house was 13 he left and never came back."

In despair we once more drove to the music store and told them about the invitation to dinner. "Try the Hanover," they said. "He generally takes his guests there."

"Is Mr. Paderewski dining here?" we asked at the Hanover.

The man at the door looked us over suspiciously and said: "No, he is not here."

Fortunately, he went up-stairs to tell Paderewski that he had sent away "the Spinxes," as he "suspected we were newspaper reporters."

A moment later the pianist's manager and two other guests were hurrying along the streets in several directions to overtake us. We were rounded up and brought back triumphantly.

It was a wonderful feast of edibles and wits, as Paderewski's dinners always were. While we were eating, a barrel-organ man planted himself right in front of the restaurant. After he had been grinding out a simple tune monotonously for a while, I said:

"Hello! he has changed his key."

With a mischievous twinkle in his eyes Paderewski looked at my wife and said:

"He is very musical,—for a critic."

Then and there I made up my mind to get even with him some day. The occasion presented itself at Morges, on Lake Geneva, during the fortnight we spent with him in the summer of 1912.

Every Thursday afternoon visitors were allowed to enter the grounds, to see the flowers, the vegetable and fruit gardens, the hothouse full of grapes, and the fancy poultry on which Madame Paderewska spent thousands every year. On our first Thursday our hosts had gone away, leaving us alone. Noticing some ladies in the garden, I said to my wife: "I'll sit down and improvise. They will think it's Paderewski and tell all their friends about their good luck."

When our host came back I told him about these ladies, adding that they would now go back home and say to their friends: "You think you know how Paderewski plays because you have heard him in a concert hall; but you have no idea how much more inspired he is when he improvises in his studio, as we heard him."

Friends of ours who had been guests at Morges had told us about various pranks played on them. I was not spared. In the bedroom assigned to me there were articles and utensils which, when touched or lifted, played a tune. In the morning Paderewski asked me innocently if I had heard anything during the night. Quick as a lightning flash the answer came to my tongue: "Oh yes, I heard some chamber music."

There were seven pianos—mostly Steinways—in this Chateau Riond Bosson. The pianist's studio was under my room and there I heard him practise by the hour, largely mere exercises to keep the fingers limber.

"Don't you find that an intolerable bore?" I asked.

"It takes all the strength of my will to keep at it," he replied.

To my great joy he was preparing for a recital the stupendous sonata of Liszt, whose chief apostle he has been for many years. No musician knows Liszt's works as thoroughly as he does, which is the reason why no one admires them more enthusiastically. I am fond of my old friend Philip G. Hubert, one of the best critics the New York *Herald* has ever had, but when I heard him beg the great pianist not to play the Liszt rhapsodies any more I was glad that Paderewski simply smiled—and played *two* of them at his next recital.

The dinner hour at Morges was variable—any time between eight and nine, or later. On our first evening it was later. Our fault; we were waiting to see if they would appear in full dress—and they were waiting to see what we would do! Finally we all came down in evening dress; there was much laughter over the affair and after that we didn't bother about attire and Paderewski wore his becoming white flannels, of which he was seemingly as fond as were Mark Twain and Doctor J. H. Kellogg.

During this visit we learned to know Madame Paderewska better than before, and to know her was to love her. It was really touching to see how devotedly she took care of her famous husband. She had her pets: two dogs that were furiously jealous of each other, and parrots, and her prize poultry, but these, after all, were a mere side-show.

Our hosts were almost offended when we left after a fortnight, fearing that we hadn't been having a good time. We had to promise we would stay longer next time we crossed the Atlantic. Then came the World War; the prize chickens were served to Polish refugees and Paderewski lost nearly all of his first great fortune.

The last time we lunched with Paderewski at his chateau was in September, 1925. He had just returned from Chamonix, where he had made two speeches, one in English and the other in French, in honor of John Ruskin. He had on his piano a photograph of Mussolini whom he had met on a recent Italian tour and learned to admire immensely; also photographs of the Belgian sovereigns whose guests his wife and he had been.

Among the guests was Miss Lawrence Alma-Tadema, daughter of the famous painter. She had spent most of the fortune she had inherited helping along the Polish cause during the war. Paderewski's adorable sister, Madame Wilkonska, who was already a friend from our previous visit, was also there. Paderewski seemed in splendid health and was blazing with animation and charm. The tender warmth of his welcome was all his own. In spite of his preparations for an American tour—we heard those strong and patient fingers working at his task—he gave us not only the luncheon time, but a long half hour afterward, before we all went out with Madame Paderewska to visit the aristocrats of the chicken farm, especially the new red and white, Polish-colors breed of chickens which she and her poultryman had created. She seemed far from well. Paderewski had, with an anguished face, told us of her severe illness in London in the spring.

Before we knew it train-time came. For the first time in many years, Paderewski embraced me and kissed me on both cheeks. Again and again he hugged my nephew Carl, kissing him tenderly. "He has real emotion that child. He is wonderful. I saw tears in his eyes when I kissed him goodbye." Indeed we all had, for we felt it might be the last time we should ever see Paderewski.

I was greatly interested in his view of the Scopes trial which had just taken place. He felt that Bryan had been a sort of anchor for tradition, holding against the overwhelming wave of the new, the iconoclastic, the destructive forces of to-day. I was also interested to hear him, a devout Catholic, speak of the Old Testament as the history of a primitive people, rather than as an integral part of Christian belief.

ERNEST SCHELLING AND GRANADOS

Liszt loved teaching; to it he devoted most of his time during the last four decades of his life after he had given up playing in public. In this respect Paderewski differs widely from his idol. He has really had only one private pupil, the American composer Ernest Schelling, who married the fascinating New York society girl, Lucy Draper.

They, too, had a chateau, not far from Paderewski's, and to it we all went one evening for dinner, Lucy being an ideal hostess. Ernest showed me some compositions he was at work on. They were juvenile, but already betrayed the evidences of genius which have since placed him in the front rank of American composers as well as pianists.

He, and seemingly he alone, has written great tone-poems inspired by the war, in which he himself played a dangerous and heroic part. It can not be said of any other American composer, so far as I know, that the Boston Symphony Orchestra accepted and began to rehearse one of his works before it was finished.

Among the pianists of to-day Schelling is one of the most brilliant and poetic. I shall never forget his superb playing of the Paderewski concerto. But apart from his own creative work, his most important deed has been the featuring, in his programs, of the pieces of Granados, Spain's leading composer, and the resulting "boom" of these works.

Poor neglected Granados! I met him one day at lunch. There was something pathetic about him; and how much more we would have pitied him could we have known that he would lose his life a few weeks later, a victim of German submarine frightfulness.

Poor Granados, I say again. He was delighted to come to New York to see his opera "Goyescas," at the Metropolitan, but it was done so badly that it gave him more pain than pleasure.

For his children's sake he was glad of the money he got. On account of the war he was afraid to accept checks or banknotes and took all his gains in the form of gold which he wore in a belt under his clothes. When his ship went down in the English Channel some of the passengers were saved, but Granados was pulled to the bottom of the sea by the weight of the gold.

Had he been as strong as Paderewski I verily believe he could have saved himself. Much has been written about the Herculean strength of the great pianist's muscles. I almost dread his hand-shake. He can crack a pane of French plate glass a half-inch in thickness by simply placing one hand upon it as in playing the piano, and striking suddenly and vigorously with his middle finger. At Morges, Schelling told me how he, a full grown man, used to stand on the calf of Paderewski's bent leg.*

JOSEF HOFMANN

One afternoon, in the year 1887, Krehbiel and I went to the Windsor Hotel to see the young prodigy Josef Hofmann who had come with his father to New York after making a sensation in Europe. He was a friendly boy, only eleven years old. I took him on my lap and showed him *Harper's Weekly,* which had a two-page picture of Siegfried's fight with the dragon, Wagner's opera having just had its première at the Metropolitan.

Looking first at the picture and then at me, with big wondering eyes, the boy asked:

"Are there any dragons in America?"

Usually I have frowned on infant prodigies. They seldom bear out their early promise. Little Josef proved an exception; he played as well at forty as he did at eleven— or nearly so. I say this seriously. There were some delectable details in his juvenile playing of Chopin's concertos, which I missed in the performances of later years, as well as in those of other pianists.

He had his hobbies, automobiles (he made some important inventions) and other things. His soul was not

*For the great pianist's third American tour (1895) Whitingham and Atherton got me to write a little book of 48 pages, "Paderewski and His Art," of which 25,-000 copies were sold. It contains a sketch of his career, full accounts of his first two tours and comments on his playing. (Out of print)

always in the music when he gave a recital; but when in the mood, he was second only to Paderewski. I never enjoyed that other great Pole more than I did Hofmann the last time I heard him, in a Schumann program, for the benefit of the starving sisters of Schumann.

I met Hofmann chiefly at dinners and I noted with pleasure how free he was from jealousy of his great rival and how he shared my enthusiasm for him. Joseffy once said to my wife: "Paderewski is a genius; the rest of us are just pianists." But Hofmann is more than just a pianist. So was Joseffy.

When he made his first American tour he was, as I have said, only eleven years old. I soon noticed alarming indications that he was being overworked, so I started an agitation for saving his genius to the world. A wealthy music lover offered the funds for enabling him to retire a few years for the sake of his health. He became a pupil of Rubinstein, and when he returned to the stage he was a robust young man as well as a great artist.

FRITZ KREISLER

Some years ago I defined Russia as "a country with one hundred and eighty million inhabitants, mostly professional violinists and pupils of Professor Auer."

Every other week, year after year, another one of these young violinists made his début in New York; all of them were good players and not a few—Kubelik, Elman, Heifetz, Zimbalist among them—won brilliant successes. Concerning these players I have no personal reminiscences, as I met them only casually or not at all.

Nor have I met the great Ysaye, I regret to say, although once, so the famous Brussels prima donna Yvonne de Treville told me, he hunted for me all over New York to prove to me that he undoubtedly was, as

I had said he was, the best interpreter of César Franck's symphony; for he had with him a copy of the score into which Franck himself had written the same words of praise.

Fritz Kreisler, fortunately, I have not only known, but known intimately for a number of years; he has long been just "Fritz" to us, his wife "Harriet." I have a vague recollection that I did not enthuse particularly over him when he first came to New York as a very young fellow. But subsequently I "boomed him for all he was worth." As usual on the arrival of a new genius, I was the first to hail him as such, the first to courageously proclaim him the King of violinists. Nay, as his genius matured, I came to the conclusion that he must be the greatest master of the violin that had ever lived, and I wasn't afraid to say this in print over and over again.

There was never anything purely sensational about Kreisler's playing; he never stooped to "fiddlers' tricks" to astonish the natives. For that reason his hearers were few at first and increased in numbers slowly; but when once he had won big audiences they were his for good, whereas the sensational fiddlers start big and gradually fizzle out. It would be easy to give names.

In recent years there has been actually a comic aspect about Fritz's popularity. His manager, my old friend Charlie Ellis, just sat comfortably in his easy chair and let the recitals take care of themselves. There were no advertisements, no advance notices sent to the critics. The enthusiasts found out the dates for themselves and when they were due Carnegie was crowded to the ceiling though one year he appeared in more than twenty recitals in New York City alone, with 105 more in other places.

What started Kreisler as a "best-seller" was his version of Dvorák's "Humoreske." This, for several seasons, he

FRITZ KREISLER

simply had to play at every recital; the audience refused to budge till he had performed this rite.

I have related how Dvořák erred in marking the slow movement of the "New World" symphony "andante" while it was really an *adagio* or *largo,* as which Seidl played it. The inspired Bohemian peasant composer (he was the son of a butcher) made a similar mistake when he wrote this "Humoreske" which Kreisler made famous and which returned the compliment by making him famous. It was published by Dvořák as a piano piece and while its opening bars partly justify its title, the piece as a whole, with its unspeakably touching melody in the sentimental part, should have been named Reverie, to say the least; its sweet melancholy has brought tears to my eyes oftener than any piece I can think of at this moment.

Kreisler's violinistic instinct told him that this piece was better suited for his instrument than for the piano and that it called for sentimental, not humorous treatment. Without him this now universally admired gem would have remained unknown to the world.

He performed the same rescuing service for dozens of other melodic gems buried mostly among the forgotten sonatas of the seventeenth and eighteenth centuries. All these short pieces enthused his hearers and helped to account for his overflowing audiences.

Would you believe it? I had to wage a fierce war against some of the other critics by defending Kreisler for displaying these treasures to his audiences! They wanted him to plant only mammoth hollyhock sonatas and sunflower suites in his garden, while I tried to justify his preference for fragrant pansies and sweet peas and Burbank poppies.

Yes, these short Kreisler pieces (which everybody now plays) are like those old garden flowers which Burbank,

Eckford, and other gardeners of genius have changed into new creations of dazzling beauty.

Quite as beautiful, if not more so, are Kreisler's own compositions, the Tambourin Chinois, the Caprice Viennois, the Introduction and Scherzo, and so on. They are as delightfully Viennese as the Musical Moments of Schubert or the waltzes of Strauss. Oh that there were more of these soulful melodies, more violinists who could play them as soulfully as Kreisler does! Often have I begged him to devote less time to recital giving, more to composing. But Fritz is a stubborn man. Once I felt called on to write him a ferocious letter calling his attention to the duty a man of genius owes to the world. He had typhoid fever—a mild case; but this disease calls above all things for absolute rest; yet he was giving his daily recital because he did not wish to disappoint the audiences.

He was playing with Death.

The creative side of Kreisler's genius has not been dwelt on sufficiently by the musical critics, and it isn't their fault; he once told me he didn't dare tell how much of himself there is in the pieces he has exhumed, edited and published. He is too modest to attach his name to all of them in hyphenated fashion. But I never failed to point out his share when I felt sure of it.

One day he brought forward at a recital the admirable viola player Lionel Tertis in a version of a Sinfonia Concertante by Mozart. Of this I wrote: "The climax of the three movements was the cadenza. In these unaccompanied episodes the players rose to thrilling heights of tonal splendor and harmonic richness. It seemed as if four men were playing instead of two; nay, here and there a sextet was suggested. Kreisler looked very modest while playing these cadenzas, but I bet my bottom dollar that these glorious episodes were only one-third Mozart, two-thirds Kreisler."

Could Kreisler have written the violin concertos of
Beethoven and Brahms? He could not. Neither could Beethoven and Brahms have written the wonderful cadenzas
which Kreisler has introduced in their concertos: they
didn't know enough about violinistic possibilities for that.
Every time I heard Fritz improvise (he varies them) these
cadenzas I was overwhelmed with delight. How did he
dare take the themes of these masters and develop and
combine them in a way which made their own treatment of
them seem elementary and almost commonplace?

In Boston there was considerable indignation at his
audacity in making the audience admire his cadenzas more
than the rest of these concertos. It was naughty, to say
the least, wasn't it? And yet, isn't there something to be
said in favor of a fiddler who can condense the fragrance
of an acre of flowers into a few drops of attar of rose?

Wherever Kreisler is known he is as much esteemed for
his character as he is admired as a musician. During the
war I received one day a special delivery letter from my
friend Ruth Sawyer, the eminent novelist. She wanted
me to come to the rescue. Kreisler was booked for a recital
in Ithaca; all the seats were sold and everybody on tiptoe
of expectation when a certain patriotic league tried to
stop the recital on the ground that Kreisler, while an Austrian officer, had helped, on a certain date and place, to
"crucify American soldiers."

It was easy for me to expose this falsehood. Kreisler
was in America on the date of those barbarities. He had,
as an Austrian officer, served in the war only six weeks,
fighting Russians, not Americans. He received a wound,
was pronounced an invalid, was honorably discharged and
came to America. Over here he was under observation
for months by the Secret Service, but since not a shadow
of suspicion arose as to his actions, he was allowed to go
his way and delight music lovers as before.

Ruth Sawyer had this elucidation printed in the Ithaca papers and the opposition to the Kreisler recital was dropped instantly.

In Pittsburgh, too, there was a row. Kreisler was accused of sending the money he earned in America to our enemies in Austria. He had sent some money to his aged father, but, he testified, "the bulk of my earnings has gone to the Brotherhood of Artists, founded by me for the purpose of extending help to stranded artists and their dependents regardless of their nationality. For fully three years my contributions were the sole and unique support of seventeen British, Russian, French and Italian artists and their entire families who found themselves stranded and utterly destitute in Austria at the outbreak of the war."

It was some years before the war, on a steamer crossing the Atlantic, that I first met Fritz. One day I heard some marvelous improvising on the piano. I went in and saw it was the great violinist. He could have easily become a formidable rival of Paderewski. At social gatherings and lunches in New York we and his other friends, among them Ruth and Grace Martin, always begged him to play the piano for us; his manner of intertwining his own melodies with those of other Austrian masters was in the highest degree delectable.

Fritz has a way of attributing all his successes to his wife. She admitted to us that she could not have written his book "Six Weeks in the Trenches" better herself. I confess that she has sometimes talked when I would have preferred to listen to Fritz, who could discourse as eloquently on Schopenhauer as on Brahms, but I never failed to enjoy her anecdotes. Here is one:

When she was crossing the Atlantic on one occasion, the great Russian conductor Safonoff was also on board. She wasn't seasick while he lay pale and limp in a steamer chair. To cheer him up she began to whistle the Russian national hymn, but he lifted up his hands imploringly. "Please don't do that," he exclaimed, "or I shall have to get on my feet."

MAUD POWELL

I have personally met a dozen women composers who frankly admitted that their pieces or songs were equal to any now written by men. Nay, Rupert Hughes, who wrote on music before he became a famous novelist and movie millionaire, once said something not unlike the above. My answer was condensed into one word "Whew!"

But when we come to the performance of music, skepticism ceases. Rubinstein said that there are a dozen women who have musical talent of a kind to every man; that talent, however, he added, seldom seems to survive the sight of a handsome young man. Is man then, after all, to blame for the fact that there are no great female composers?

In my long experience as a critic I have heard a dozen operatic sopranos and contraltos not a whit inferior to the dozen foremost tenors, baritones and basses. Can I name women violinists and pianists quite the equals of Paderewski and Kreisler? I can not, but I can name Maud Powell who was second *only* to Kreisler and Guiomar Novaes, who is surpassed *only* by Paderewski. Concerning them I want to say a few words before we return to the Metropolitan Opera House.

Maud Powell lived only fifty-one years. Her activity covered little more than three decades, yet she was one of the pioneers of women musicians in America. When she was a girl there was still a strong prejudice against women in instrumental music. Pianists of the fair sex were beginning to be tolerated, but the violin—surely the line must be drawn there!

No doubt it did seem odd to see a slender girl of twenty stand on the stage conspicuously, playing a violin concerto, with Theodore Thomas and the eighty highly-trained men of his orchestra serving as her accompanists; but it was a spectacle to which music lovers soon became accustomed, thanks to Maud Powell more perhaps than to any one else. To-day there is a growing feeling that Berlioz was right when he called the violin the woman's voice in the orchestra.

When Huneker accused Maud Powell of not sufficiently emphasizing the feminine traits of the music she was playing, she explained that she did this purposely because of the existing prejudice against women violinists. Subsequently she became the very incarnation of femininity in violin playing although she never forgot how to emphasize the masculine side too. Like Chicago's foremost pianist, Fannie Bloomfield Zeisler, she showed that a woman player can be forceful and impetuous without being mannish.

Maud Powell was a niece of Major Powell, who so courageously explored the terrifying mile-deep Grand Canyon of the Colorado River She inherited some of her uncle's daring, as shown in her courageous playing of novelties that other violinists had been afraid to put on their programs; as shown also by her exploring of new fields for musical missionary work. Many a remote and secluded place, east and west, north and south, owed to her its first acquaintance with high-brow music as interpreted by an artist of the first rank. I say high-brow music; she played for these remote audiences the same high-class programs she offered in New York or Boston.

When I asked her if that wasn't a mistake, she said not at all; she had found that these out-of-the way hearers insisted on having the best and showed resentment if the player "stooped to conquer."

Among the many stories she told me of her adventures in remote regions there was one which impressed me particularly as revealing the esteem which is inspired by a famous name. She had arrived with her accompanist and his instrument at a station where no conveyance could be found for taking the piano to the concert hall. There was no time to lose. To her great relief four men working near the station offered to carry it; but when she took out her purse to pay them they seemed hurt and explained that the honor of doing a favor for so great an artist was more than sufficient payment.

After her marriage she adopted a new fashion of traveling which made it particularly easy to reach out-of-the-way towns. Her husband, H. Godfrey Turner, was the son of a famous English journalist; what is of greater importance, he knew more about running a car than any chauffeur that ever lived. He became her manager, devoting all his time to this job, and together they traveled in their Franklin from town to town, gipsy fashion. I have often urged Sunny to write a little book about their adventures.

We call him Sunny because he looks a good deal like Sunny Jim, formerly so conspicuously pictured in the huge placards of a breakfast cereal company. Sunny Jim wasn't pretty; neither is our Sunny; he accepts his nickname placidly, uses it in his own letters, which bubble over with humorous sallies. He is the funniest Englishman I have ever met—I should say, he was that before Maud died.

In "Musical Progress" I related how she stopped at a large hotel in Texas where the food was so bad that she could not eat a bite. On the way to her room she said indignantly to the elevator boy: "This is positively the worst hotel I have ever been in;" to which the boy retorted: "Yes, madam, that's what everybody says."

Experiences like this broke down her health—I have often wondered how traveling artists *could* survive the assaults on their digestive system made by the average American hotel food. She had, also, a doctor who advised her to drink two quarts of milk a day. When she told him this disagreed with her violently, his answer was: "Drink *three* quarts a day." She did, and one day she collapsed during a recital. With her died the greatest violinist of either sex America has ever produced.

A world tour as soloist of the Sousa band—thirty weeks with two concerts a day—was one of Maud's proudest achievements. She wrote me a letter about it from which I quote a few lines: "At our last concert, at Blackpool, just before sailing for home, the boys gave me an ovation. When I finished my number—the Saint-Saëns Rondo, which they accompanied beautifully—they applauded, shouted and the drummer clanged his cymbals. The audience caught the meaning of it all and joined in vigorously.

"Afterwards, when the band bade me good-bye, they made speeches: 'enjoyed every note of my playing,' 'honor to be associated,' 'privilege to know' etc. Two men said simply 'God bless you' and one man broke down altogether. It all touched me deeply. Sousa kissed my hand and said: 'You have held your own right up to the last note.' "

Maud told me once how Sousa (like Theodore Thomas) never failed to pay his men in full no matter what his losses. Soon, to be sure, there were no losses; on the contrary, what with his world-famed band, his hugely popular marches, his operettas and his novels, all of them tremendously successful, the "March King" prospered so that he lost all count of his income. At any rate, when I wrote to ask him what was the biggest sum he had ever earned in a year, he couldn't tell me. Neither could Vic-

MAUD POWELL

tor Herbert. They may have suspected I was officially connected with the collector of income taxes. But I was simply collecting material for an article on the earnings of musicians.

If I may be allowed a guess, it is that both Sousa and Herbert had their $100,000 years.

Guiomar Novaes of Brazil

In my early days in New York one of my best friends was a Brazilian named J. C. Rodrigues. He was greatly interested in music and asked me to contribute to a musical periodical he had helped to start. Afterwards he went back to Rio de Janeiro where he became owner of the leading daily paper. Once the Government was after him and he had to hide for a year. Gradually he evoluted into a millionaire and lived in a palace near the President's.

Occasionally we ran across him—in London, at the Grand Canyon, and other places. One day I got a note from him saying he was in New York and would I come to the Hotel Astor and lunch with him. When I arrived he introduced me to a very small and thin elderly lady, Madame Novaes, mother of eighteen children, and her youngest daughter, Guiomar, a very good-looking brunette of the darkest Portuguese type.

Novaes's mother spoke nothing but Portuguese; she herself, fortunately, spoke also French. She had been studying in Paris, she told me, and was anxious to make a success in America as a pianist. Outwardly I smiled when she said this, inwardly I groaned. I told her how many, how *very* many pianists were in the field, competing and spoiling each other's business. "However," I added, "you have an advantage; you could easily make a name for yourself and prosper if you played Brazilian tunes at social gatherings."

This didn't seem to appeal to her, and soon I found out why. A few days later Percy Grainger and his mother invited me to come and hear a wonder-pianist from Brazil. I accepted eagerly. She played a Chopin scherzo and I was simply stunned. Good heavens! If Paderewski, or Chopin himself, had played it I couldn't have been more overwhelmed with delight. A pianistic genius, if ever there was one! Was I destined to be her discoverer?

Alas, no! I can not claim that honor. She had been discovered in Paris, and in London, too, as I found on looking into her career. Her first discoverer was the Brazilian Government which sent her, when sixteen, at its own expense, to study at the Paris Conservatory. There she won the first prize—a grand piano—coveted by 380 rivals.

An unprecedented thing happened at the examination for this prize. Among the judges were some of the most eminent musicians of the period. These poor men had to listen critically to all these scores of candidates, hearing the same pieces over and over and over again. Yet when Guiomar Novaes had played Schumann's Etudes Symphoniques they asked her to repeat it—*for their own pleasure!* Has ever a music student had such a compliment paid her?

When she played in London the *Daily Telegraph* wrote that "at times one almost laughed in sympathy with her dear delight in her own interpretations, and every now and then one actually gasped at the depth of feeling she could put into her playing."

When she appeared in New York, four years later, she had become one of the greatest pianists of her time, or of all time. The critics were simply bowled over. For once they were unanimous. Huneker remained to the very end of the recital, including all the encores, and next morning he wrote in the *Times* about "the sheer rainbow versatility of the astonishing young woman," whom he called "the Paderewski of the Pampas." And Henderson, whom debutantes dreaded as a leopard ready to tear them to pieces, completely changed his spots writing about this "little girl from Brazil" nearly a column of panegyrics in his most poetic vein, and ending with a reference to her playing of Chopin's G minor Ballade as a reading which "in its range of tonal beauties and its immense virility only Paderewski or Hofmann could have equalled."

I have a special reason for citing these encomiums. An impression was created that I exaggerated the merits of this Brazilian and that I was responsible for her vogue. Her genius was responsible. I admit that I harped more on her genius than any one else. In my usual fashion I held on with the tenacity of a bulldog and wrote like a super-press-agent. I simply couldn't help it. My happiness when I heard her play was so great that it oozed from my pen. A specimen or two must suffice: "When a young girl from Brazil can make a veteran critic, blasé after a season of interminable music, as happy as a boy who has been taken to the circus for the first time, she must be something very extraordinary indeed. The joy, the rapture of listening to such playing are beyond description. To talk about beautiful touch and tone, about phrasing and shading, seems mere technical twaddle in face of such a revelation of the very soul of music."

Again: "What makes her playing so entrancing is that she seems to do it as if in a trance. She reminds one of what Sir George Grove said about Schubert: that it seems 'as if in his pieces the stream from the great heavenly reservoir were dashing over us, or flowing through us, more directly, with less admixture of any medium or channel, than it does in those of any other writer.' In the same way Miss Novaes seems to get her inspiration direct from heaven. One has a feeling, when she plays Beethoven, as if she were in long-distance telepathic com-

munication with him—as if, indeed, he himself were at
the piano. And when her piece is by Chopin or Schumann
or some other master, it is they who apparently are personally guiding her hands and brain. This is no hyperbole;
it is an impression which makes this girl one of the seven
wonders of the musical world."

One more snapshot: "She belongs to the rare species
of musicians who love their art more than themselves.
After one of her pieces, when the applause was particularly
persistent she ended it abruptly by beginning to play, with
an air of saying: 'Please stop and let me show you how
beautiful the next piece is!'"

You will now understand how Grainger could say to
me he would rather hear Novaes than any other pianist
of the day.

More than once, at lunch, she has joined me in laughing
at the advice I gave her at our first meeting: that she
should specialize in Brazilian dance tunes. But it is time
to go back to the opera, still in its golden age.

How I Made Conried Manager

"Good morning, Mr. Conried, would you like to be
manager of the Metropolitan Opera House?"

"Why—I have never thought of such a thing. What
makes you ask?"

"Would you accept the position if it were offered to
you?"

"I certainly would," he replied, after a brief pause.

"Very well," I continued, "read the *Evening Post* to-
night and see what will happen within a few days."

With these words I left Conried's office at the Irving
Place Theatre, hurried down to the *Evening Post* and
dashed off an editorial in which I pleaded with all my

Photograph by Mishkin

GUIOMAR NOVAES

might and main for Heinrich Conried as manager of the Metropolitan.

Grau's death had left a vacancy to be filled. There were several candidates, among whom Walter Damrosch seemed most likely to be the winner. Now I hadn't the slightest doubt that Mr. Damrosch would make an excellent manager; he had the requisite knowledge, experience and business ability; he spoke several languages and was a "good mixer." But—he was a composer and a conductor! The idea that he might produce a new work of his own most every season and personally conduct all the most important performances, did not fill my soul with unmitigated joy. So I came out for Conried.

He, like Abbey, had never managed a grand opera company, but he had had experience with operetta companies and was famed as a stage manager. He had brought over to America some of the foremost German actors and actresses, among them Helene Odilion, Kathi Schratt, Possart, Sonnenthal, Barnay. He had repeatedly, at his own expense, given model performances of classical dramas for the students of American universities and been rewarded for his disinterested services with honorary degrees. Into the hands of such a man, I argued in the *Post,* it would be safe to place the interests of our famous Opera.

One of the morning papers—I think it was the *Times*— seconded my motion. The Directors of the Metropolitan met that day (February 14, 1903) and the next morning I got this note:

"My dear Mr. Finck:—

"It gives me great pleasure to inform you that I will be the successor to Mr. Grau, and I sincerely hope that you will lend me, at all times, your most valuable assistance.

"Yours faithfully,
"HEINRICH CONRIED."

For five years Conried remained ruler of the Metropolitan forces. These years may be included, as I have said, in the Golden Age of Opera in New York, the age of great singers and conductors. The new manager was so lucky as to inherit from his eminently successful predecessor a bunch of the great singers to whom he had owed his successes. Conspicuous among these were Sembrich, Eames, Calvé, Melba, Nordica, Schumann-Heink and Homer; Scotti, Van Rooy, Dippel, Burgstaller, Mühlmann, Reiss and Plançon. To these Conried added, from year to year Caruso, Ternina, Fremstad, Edyth Walker, Goritz, Bella Alten, Geraldine Farrar, Lina Cavalieri, Bessie Abott, Burrian, Morena, Bonci, Riccardo Martin, and Chaliapin, to mention only those most prominent.

With such a galaxy of singers it was easy for Conried to provide the public with the all-star casts it adored, and he often took advantage of his opportunities.

Outstanding among his achievements were the first production outside of Bayreuth of Wagner's swan-song "Parsifal"; the American première of Humperdinck's charming fairy opera "Hansel and Gretel," and of Puccini's masterwork "Madama Butterfly," with Farrar and Caruso, in presence of the composers; the production of Johann Strauss' enchanting "Die Fledermaus" with an all-star grand opera cast; and of Richard Strauss' hideous musical nightmare "Salome."

My Fight for "Parsifal"

"You lucky man!" said a theatrical manager to Conried when that bold bad manager was preparing to stage "Parsifal" and was attacked therefor in hundreds of newspaper articles and public letters of protest written by Cosima-Wagnerites, clergymen and others: "You lucky man! Your show advertises itself!"

And Conried, charging $10 a seat, made about $200,-000 out of this "Rape of 'Parsifal' " (as his enemies called it), of which fully one-half was clear profit.

The alleged crime for which he was pilloried was that he had stolen from Wagner's widow the monopoly of this sacred opera which she had held for twenty years at Bayreuth. So valuable was this monopoly that when Conried, although not obliged to do so (for there was no protection by copyright) generously made her an offer of $20,-000 for the American performing rights, she scornfully waved it aside and continued to fill the air with her angry ululations. Suit was actually brought in America but the court decided in favor of Conried on November 24, 1903.

Cosima Wagner's stock argument was that Wagner himself had declared that "Parsifal" should never be sung anywhere except in Bayreuth. But he had said the same foolish thing about the four Nibelung operas, yet shortly afterwards they were taken on tour all over Europe, with his special permission and blessing, by Neumann and Seidl. Had Wagner lived in 1903, and Seidl too, he would have undoubtedly been eager to place "Parsifal" also in that great leader's and Conried's hands; for he was too rational to cling forever to the plan of withholding his most sublime work from all of his admirers the world over except the handful who were rich enough to make the trip to Bayreuth.

Many readers of the *Evening Post* wrote to the editor complaining of my apostasy from Wagnerism but I am proud to say that Edvard Grieg was right when he wrote to me: "You are, like myself, one of the greatest admirers of the incomparable master, but not one of the Wagnerites. In my opinion this rabble constitutes his worst enemies."

One subscriber wrote to the editor: "The talk of the town is that your musical critic is so happy in defeating Damrosch for manager of the opera that he would side with anybody and therefore is so biased in favor of Conried!"

Not the least amusing and amazing side of this controversy was the contention that "Parsifal" is, as one writer put it, "an immoral, irreligious, quite nearly blasphemous work." Committees representing clergymen called on the Mayor, asking him to intervene on this ground, and wagers were made up to the very day of its first performance, on December 24, that it would be forbidden.

The Reverend Heber Newton delivered a lecture which may have kept the Mayor of New York from doing a foolish thing. In this lecture, which was entitled "Parsifal: Its Moral and Religious Significance," the eminent divine said: "There is the Holy Supper scene; but you should have no religious scruples regarding that scene, for it is no communion in the sense of the church; there is no minister present. It is simply a representation of the early Christian love feast out of which ultimately the communion grew. I am glad that some of our clergy have been quick to discover this."

Possibly, too, the Mayor was influenced by a criticism I printed in the *Evening Post,* made by Doctor Hanslick, Wagner's most ferocious enemy, who would have been glad if the religious aspect of "Parsifal," had helped him to new weapons. But he wrote as follows: "The actions we see are of a religious character, but with all their dignified solemnity they are nevertheless not in the style of the Church, but entirely in the operatic style. 'Parsifal' is and remains an opera, even though it be called a festival play for the consecration of the stage."

On the whole, I think I never fought harder for a thing than I did for the emancipation of "Parsifal." I always dearly loved a fight—with the pen. My wife often said to me: "If you had lived in the days of swords, you would have had a duel on your hands about once a fortnight."

Well, this battle was won, and what a glorious time we had in consequence! Conried provided an all-star cast including Ternina, Homer, Burgstaller, Van Rooy, Blass, Mühlmann and Goritz. The scenery was superior to that at Bayreuth, especially in the magic garden; I shall never forget the "ohs" and "ahs" of delight that rose from the large invited audience at the final rehearsal when the curtain went up on this dazzling scene. And under the direction of Alfred Hertz the performance was simply thrilling.

Hertz, by the way, had been brought over by Grau. When he made his début with "Tristan," the critics fell on him like a pack of wolves. I, almost alone, stood up for him, proclaiming him a conductor of the first rank. He soon became generally recognized as such. I have a framed photograph of him on which he wrote some time after his début:

"It was *your* words that gave me the courage and strength for new deeds. To you I owe what success I have won in New York."

Conried wrote me a word of thanks when the "Parsifal" battle was over and the smoke had cleared away. It was dated December 26, 1903, and read:

"My dear Mr. Finck:—
Let me thank you from the bottom of my heart for your kindness. I know what was at stake. Thank God, I have won.
Believe in my sincerity and gratefulness.

Yours,
HEINRICH CONRIED."

When, in 1903-04, the enterprising and always praiseworthy Henry W. Savage made up a good company for performing "Parsifal" throughout the country I was able to do him, also, a good turn. He had started out by giving the score uncut, being afraid to anger the rabid Wagnerites by leaving out anything. I pitched into him for this foolish timidity, pointing out that a five-hour opera had no chance for success on the road, and adding flippantly that "Parsifal" needed to have its hair cut anyway. He wrote me a letter in which he thanked me profusely for giving him the courage to carry out his original intentions. In its trimmed form the opera was a big success everywhere.

With my friend Hertz I had many a tiff about cuts. He stubbornly refused to make any. One day I said to him: "At last night's performance of 'Die Meistersinger' I kept wondering during the ninth half-hour: 'Will this d—d thing never end? Do you think it wise to subject one's enthusiasm to such a strain?" But he refused to budge. Seidl was much more sensible on this point.

The "Parsifal" performances in New York became known as "the Metropolitan prayer meetings." Not everybody enjoyed the slow pace and the ecclesiastic solemnities of the first and third acts, while all revelled in the voluptuous, caressing music of act 2 and the graceful, seductive dances of the flower girls. I heard a true story of a father who was reluctantly dragged to "Parsifal" by his daughters. After nearly two hours of insufferable boredom while the first act was on, he escaped, telling the girls where he was to be found at the end of the opera. But they hurried to him after the second act. "It was entirely different after you left!" they exclaimed, and told him about the flower girls. And he went back with them for the third act. . . . His comments are not on record.

Strauss Versus Strauss

Encouraged by his success with "Parsifal" Conried got ready for another sensation. Having secured the American rights to Richard Strauss' noisy setting of Oscar Wilde's noisome "Salome," he got Hertz to rehearse his orchestra and his star cast (including Fremstad, Weed, Burrian, Van Rooy, Dippel, Reiss, Mühlmann, Blass) and on January 22, 1907, the first performance took place. It was also the last. Nearly everybody seemed shocked and disgusted. Before it could be repeated Conried received this notice: "The directors of the Metropolitan Opera and Real Estate Company consider that the performance of 'Salome' is objectionable and detrimental to the best interests of the Metropolitan Opera House. They therefore protest against any repetition of this opera."

Conried had to yield. He fumed and raged, but there was no redress, although some of the expenses incurred were made good. This time he had no occasion to write me a letter of thanks, for I had been one of the most violent assailants of this operatic monstrosity.*

I was with Conried, on the other hand, when he produced the ever delightful "Fledermaus" of Johann Strauss, a masterwork of melody which Richard S. could no more have achieved than Johann S. could have perpetrated "Salome," or "Elektra." In another one of his operas ("Rosen Kavalier") Richard paid Johann the flattery of imitation by including in it some waltzes of great charm; still, he could never have penned "Die Fledermaus," the entrancing melodies of which took the whole world by storm.

In Vienna and the cities of Germany it was customary to produce this operetta annually at the grand-opera

* My reasons for condemning "Salome" may be found in full in my Strauss biography.

houses with grand-opera singers, who looked on this event as a picnic. In staging it at the Metropolitan, Conried was, therefore, merely following a good foreign example. He provided a fine cast including Sembrich, Dippel and Goritz and everybody had a good time.

Conried himself took part in this performance. He could not sing, but he created much merriment as the jailer who repeatedly hangs up his silk hat on an imaginary peg.

That Conried was an expert stage manager, I have just stated. He spent much time in reforming this department of the Metropolitan. One day he told me of an extraordinary thing that had happened. In Wagner's "Walküre" the clouds are of great importance and difficult to handle. He had taken some of his best stage hands and rehearsed the cloud movements for three hours. At last he exclaimed:

"Very good! If you do it as well as that to-night I shall be much pleased."

"But Mr. Conried," exclaimed one of the men, "we shall not be here to-night. Our eight-hour day expires at five o'clock."

Among Conried's principal achievements I have named the first performances in New York of two operas which won tremendous popularity—Humperdinck's musical fairy tale of the lost babes in the woods, "Hänsel and Gretel" and Puccini's best work "Madama Butterfly." The fairy tale, emotional, melodious and comic became a great favorite of children of all ages; it was sung eleven times the first season and kept its vogue year after year. "Madama Butterfly" was given with an all-star cast such as even Grau seldom equaled: Geraldine Farrar, Louise Homer, Enrico Caruso, Antonio Scotti and Albert Reiss. And this brings me to a consideration of the two stars to whom Conried was indebted for many of his triumphs.

For two decades, Farrar and Caruso remained the most popular and profitable artists connected with the Metropolitan Opera House.

GERALDINE FARRAR

A great-grandson of Nathaniel Hawthorne, Julian Smyth (whose father used to be literary editor of the New York *Times* and then became the creator of the *International Book Review*) was at my home with his parents one afternoon when Geraldine Farrar happened to call for a chat. The boy watched her with big eyes, fascinated by her beauty, her gestures, her talk, her musical voice. When there was a moment's lull in the conversation he went over to her and said: "I am coming to see you!"

Love at first sight! Julian was five years old.

Many thousands have thus fallen in love at sight with this American singing-actress, off the stage as well as on —I could never quite make up my mind whether she was the more fascinating as an operatic heroine or at table entertaining guests with her brilliant talk.

In my library there is a large album which shows at a glance wherein lies her power over boys and girls, women and men. It was given to me by her as a Christmas present and contains some seventy photographs of herself in the attire and facial make-up of a score of operatic characters. It is hard to believe that the same girl can have sat for all these pictures, so varied is the style of beauty, so chameleonic the changes of expression.

Geraldine once told me how she came to cultivate facial expression. Her great teacher, Lilli Lehmann, tied her hands behind her back to prevent her from indulging in the customary ludicrous gesticulations which most prima donnas seem to think the equivalent of acting, and then said: "Now express your feelings."

No doubt this helped. But a dozen Lillis could not have enabled Geraldine to give her facial expression and beauty such infinite variety had she not been born with a special gift for such expression, just as others are born with a special talent for various other things. It made her beauty irresistible.

She knew this, too. The Berliners, among whom she made her operatic début, simply lost their heads over this "American beauty." So great was their enthusiasm that they allowed her to do anything she liked, even to singing her part in Italian when all the other parts were sung in German. Dr. Muck, the strict disciplinarian, protested, but the royal family approved and that settled it.

The furore of the Berliners over this young American girl did not by any means make certain her success in New York when Conried brought her over. There is a familiar saying that the Metropolitan Opera House has been the grave of many a European favorite. Geraldine could not know but that it might be hers. Yet she did a thing for which I have always admired her particularly.

Zoltan Doeme, Nordica's second husband, had written us several enthusiastic letters about this wonderful American prima donna. "You will have a new sensation when you see and hear her," he declared. He also gave her a letter of introduction to me. It gave her a chance to see me before her début, to dazzle me as she subsequently dazzled Julian Smyth and thousands of others, and thus bias me in her favor. But she did not present that letter till after her début and after I had written a rapturous column of praise about her Juliette.

That column—I marvel as I write this—was almost the only cordial praise she got after her Metropolitan début. The public was delighted but the critics were cross—so hostile, cold, or reserved that had not Conried sided with me, the directors would have probably taken advantage of the clause in Geraldine's contract enabling them to call it off after her fourth appearance.

That calamity (the Berliners were hoping and praying it would happen) was averted, and in a short time Geraldine enjoyed a popularity second only to Caruso's. Some of the critics, to be sure, kept up their hostile attitude— W. J. Henderson, in particular, loved to ruffle or pull out her beautiful feathers—and my wife and I had a number of indignation meetings with the young prima donna and her mother. Geraldine made not the slightest attempt to conciliate the critics but treated them in the sauciest manner imaginable. If censured for doing this or that thing in too Farraresque a fashion she responded by making it more so.

There were times, I confess, when she was a little too Farrarish for me too, especially in the "Carmen" period and when she first went into the movies. I have an amusing letter from her on this subject, dated August 9, 1922, from which I quote a paragraph:

" 'Carmen' was the first public offering of my 'flicker' repertoire. It caused a riot and greatly upset apprehensive Metropolitan subscribers. Fantastic stories were spread abroad that I assaulted chorus girls in the opera, due to the malignant violence prescribed in the movie. That I chewed the ears of timid supers and slapped King Enrico such a resounding smack that the audience gasped as it caused him to falter in his song and sputter maledictions. All pretty reading perhaps, but none of these charming inventions occurred. The same chorus girl yearly continued to be a zealous foil in the first act, chosen principally for a wealth of lovely hair which she could release at will for spectacular purposes. A substantial check at the end of each season whetted her enthusiasm and was never to my knowledge employed to defray hospital charges. The supers were not battered by fan, heel, or palm, though some professed a 'sentimental slaughter,' in real flapper-like letters, unashamed of their feelings, too. As for my good comrade Caruso, it was never possible to quarrel with him nor was there ever reason for me to do so. However, one may religiously remain within four walls silent and unseen yet be a vivid spectacular figure for the 'news hound' and the 'dull season' publicity scout."

Opera singers do not usually abhor publicity or *réclame,* but there were times in Miss Farrar's career, especially during the Tellegen trial, when reporters were rigidly excluded. Once when we went to lunch we found her residence besieged by them. Some waited several hours till I came out again and then implored me for information. I explained that, having come as a guest and not as a journalist, I had "no news." The reporters felt relieved when I added: "Not even for the *Evening Post.*"

Asked for a list of the movies in which she had appeared, Geraldine gave me the following: " 'Carmen,' 'Maria Rosa,' woven about some incidents of my own life; 'The woman God forgot'—a fine production of Montezuma's land and Cortez's conquest of it; 'The Devil's Stone'—a modern story with reincarnation as background; 'The Turn of the Wheel'—Monte Carlo intrigues; 'The Hell Cat'—a Wyoming narrative of primitive emotions; 'Shadows'—a big material theme; 'The Stronger Vow'— an Italian vendetta story; and the peer of them all and my favorite, Joan of Arc, called 'Joan the Woman.' This latter took over three months' solid work and was an event for all concerned. Then came the moment to depart from shadowland, which I did, after making a photo-play, 'The Riddle Woman,' in the East during the summer of 1920."

"Jerry-Joan" was the name given to Miss Farrar by her soldiers in the making of her favorite film. Some of them afterwards went as real soldiers to France whence they sent her medals of Joan.

GERALDINE FARRAR

When I reproached her for having deserted music for the movies, even temporarily, she replied:

"I can truly say I was as inspired in playing Joan as I had been years before when you were so enthusiastic over my Elizabeth in 'Tannhäuser.' Both offered such opportunities for appeal of the highest kind. I enjoyed every bit of my life in the studio, and the work and varied interests never failed to intensely occupy my time and attention. Its worries and preoccupations were amusingly different from the opera routine, but none the less, they were there, a scratch on the nose, a fever blister, a stye on the eye—quite as fearsome as any vocal disability. The camera is a harsh and unflattering judge of the smallest imperfection."

Maybe I flatter myself, but I have a haunting suspicion that I was responsible for Geraldine's taking up "Carmen" (not in the movies but, previously, at the Metropolitan). Bizet's masterwork had been neglected for some years to my distress. I begged her again and again, almost on my knees, to appear in it, pointing out its suitability to her style of singing and acting; but she refused stubbornly on the ground that no one could succeed in this part after Calvé.

After thinking the matter over, I applied a little psychology. "Very well," I said, "if *you* don't want to revive Carmen I am going to suggest in the *Post* that the fascinating Lucrezia Bori, who resembles you so strikingly in many ways, should do it."

Perhaps it was a mere coincidence, but shortly afterwards it was announced that Geraldine Farrar would appear as Carmen the following season.

In one of her letters to me Geraldine refers in her amusing fashion to the doleful predictions as to the loss of artistic prestige she would suffer if she went into the movies. "My motion-picture plans have been followed,

as you probably know, by frantic attempts on the part
of other vocal luminaries to hasten towards the concentrated vicinity of the lens. When Caruso was approached
later he consulted Mr. Gatti-Casazza upon this important
side-step. Being an authority on matters operatic, this
latter's statement to me, anent their joint affirmative decision is amusing, to say the least. I quote Mr. Gatti when
he replied to me in discussing this matter: 'Bene, I told
Caruso if Signorina Geraldine had ventured it, I thought
he could risk it too.'

"Weren't they brave? I for one am glad Caruso will
live on the screen even though the dramatic importance
of his offering has made no wide appeal."

In her own case the acting was quite as important as
the singing, sometimes even more so. Her strength lay
in the combination of the two; she sang with her face, she
acted with her voice. When life at the Metropolitan was
made disagreeable to her (I shall return to this in a later
chapter) she went on tour as a concert singer, which
was all right—Nordica, Sembrich, Schumann-Heink and
other great opera stars had done the same thing, giving up acting. But how about giving up singing and
becoming an actress? When I asked Geraldine she
answered: "I might be tempted by Belasco's offers. But
one doesn't become Sarah of the Celestial Voice overnight
because one gets weary of the Metropolitan and its cacoph-
ony. Twenty-odd years of slavish prostration to the
lyric art is by no means a recommendation to evolve a
dramatic genius. One would be more apt to evoke the
caustic comment from singers: 'she's better in the movies,'
and from actresses: 'she's better in the opera.' Personally,
I think *I* am better away from it all."

After a few seasons of recitals (the programs of which
included an unusual number of mastersongs) she nevertheless returned to the operatic twin arts of acting and

singing, giving "Carmen" in tabloid form all over the country. I feared for her voice, as she had to sing nearly every night, but she knew how not to overdo. In a letter dated December 5, 1924, she told us of her "heavenly trip to the coast," although she had been "baked in Texas, sunburned in California, drenched in Seattle mists, snowed under in Oregon, blown to bits in Montana and swathed in Wisconsin fogs"—"I am slender as a sapling and have a dance that keeps me so, too, combined with daily promenades. Life in the car never is dull, the days fly and I accomplish all 'too little'," although, as she adds, "no army mule ever worked harder. I feel well repaid, especially in a vocal way."

She had taken along her new teacher who rejuvenated her voice by a new method of "tonal massage" of the vocal cords.

There are many "secrets" of Miss Farrar's success and among the most important of these is this thorough enjoyment of her work and her art as exemplified in the preceding citations. And as with her singing and her acting and filming so in the matter of costuming: it has been a matter of genuine artistic passion to her. As a child she coveted artistic gowns and when her coffers were full of money she went to Madame Paquin in Paris who took special pride in collaborating with her in evolving new creations, as she wrote in her all-too brief autobiography, adding: "She combined me such lovely things as *made my heart thrill* to appear in them." And speaking of the costume worn at her New York début as Juliette she says: "It was not the usual conventional robe of stiff white satin but *a heavenly concoction* that my clever wizard of a dressmaker had faithfully and beautifully modeled after a Botticelli painting." The italics are mine.

Readers of the *Evening Post* used to wonder how I, a

mere man, could write so expertly about Miss Farrar's wonderful costumes. I didn't! My wife did.

I need not dwell here on my reactions to Miss Farrar's original impersonations of Marguerite, Juliette, Mignon, Elizabeth, Violetta, Manon, Butterfly, Zerlina, Cherubino, Tosca, and the rest of them, as I have done so in detail in my book "Success in Music and How it is Won." Outstanding among her later successes are her Louise, her Navarraise, Zaza (which she raised from a dismal failure to a sensational success) and her Ariane, the most difficult of her impersonations and one which harmed her voice. I can see her now in her studio puzzling over its vocal problems and the double flats and sharps which she eliminated and replaced in her scores by the notes actually to be sung. But her crowning achievement—not even excepting her Butterfly—was the Goose Girl in "Königskinder." How marvelous this was is best shown by the fact that even Krehbiel quite lost his head over it: "With what exquisite charm Miss Farrar was likely to invest so romantic a heroine the artist's admirers might easily have guessed; but it is doubtful if any imagination ever reached the figure which she bodied forth. She was a vision of tender loveliness, as perfect in poetical conception as in execution. Memories of the picture which she presented walking through the massive town-gates followed and surrounded by her white flock will die only with the generation that witnessed it."

This live white flock, let me add, was Geraldine's own audacious conception. The composer had not dared to demand anything but stuffed birds. She told me all about her difficulty in convincing him and the stage manager that live geese were a possibility on the operatic stage.

They *did* create trouble occasionally—particularly once when they all started to cackle noisily at the moment when the King's son kissed the goose girl.

ENRICO CARUSO

While I often chatted with Caruso, usually in French, although he spoke English fairly well in the last years of his life, the most striking glimpses I ever enjoyed of his personality were had at the farewell supper given at the Hotel Astor to Madame Sembrich by a number of her admirers, to which I referred briefly in the pages devoted to her.

It was arranged that Caruso should take my wife to his table. I sat opposite and enjoyed his naive, boyish conduct every moment. He did not seem to care much for the speeches but busied himself while they were being delivered by making cartoons of the speakers and other notabilities present, on menus or any scraps of paper he could beg, borrow or steal. I noticed presently that he began a caricature of my wife. It did not seem to satisfy him, for he kept shaking his head and muttering "elle me tuera, elle me tuera" (she will kill me).

When he could find no more paper, he made an elaborate sketch of the pianist Ernest Schelling on the table-cloth. I wondered afterwards if the waiters realized the value of that table-cloth. It might have been framed and sold at auction.

He was very proud of his knack at caricaturing—more so, in fact, than of his fame as a singer. One of the books lying on a table in our home is a volume of cartoons published by Marziale Sisca. I often open it, sure to get a laugh at one of the great tenor's clever distortions of celebrities in the musical world and out. When my book, "Musical Laughs," was in preparation the publishers had the happy thought of asking Caruso's publisher's permission to use two of the best of his cartoons to illustrate my volume and the request was kindly granted.

What made his voice so wonderful that it converted the huge Metropolitan into what I once ventured to call a "Carusel" for happy audiences to enjoy themselves in? His exceptional vocal cords? No. My friend Doctor Mario Marafioti, the famous laryngologist, who took care of Caruso's throat for years, told me that there are many singers who have better vocal cords than this tenor, yet they are no Carusos. Wherein, then, lay his secret? *In the resonance of his body cavities.*

Doctor Marafioti, in his epoch-making book "Caruso's Method of Voice Production," dwelt on the exceptional resonance of the great tenor's chest, pharynx, lips, mouth and other head cavities, particularly the nose. He also had a most ingenious way of securing special resonance and tonal color by curling his tongue, shaping it into a triangular cup. The doctor often saw him pull his tongue repeatedly before a performance to make it more relaxed.

Caruso was far from being, like so many other singers, a voice and nothing more. He was an artist, and his art developed from year to year. A friend once told me he had a whole set of Victor records which showed strikingly how Caruso's way of singing his favorite arias—his phrasing, breathing, shading and emotional expression—improved from year to year. I have not those records: but I heard Caruso year after year at the Metropolitan and my memory provides many of these details and improvements, which caused me to write more and more enthusiastically about the great Enrico.

As an actor, too, I saw him improve rapidly from season to season. When he first came to New York he was capable of so ludicrous a blunder as appearing in "Faust," even in the dismal prison cell of the last act *wearing white gloves.* Between that brainless performance and his later achievements as an operatic actor lies a world of artistic effort and improvement.

The comic vein revealed in his volume of caricatures was also manifested on the stage in some of his parts, notably Nemorino in "The Elixir of Love." Did any one in this part ever think of so many ways to get the last drop out of that elixir bottle? He tried to reach its depths with his tongue, he squeezed it as if it had been a lemon, he shook it and he peered into it with anxious eye, rejoicing that it still held some of the precious stuff. Nor was he less amusing in his clumsy love-making and in his fear of the conquering officer, who carries off his sweetheart from under his very eyes; and it was never twice the same.

His glorious voice, to be sure, had even more to do than his droll acting with making this ancient opera a modern best-seller. When he sang the great aria "Una furtiva lagrima" the audience became positively rude, clapping hands, yelling, stamping and refusing to let the opera go on. But Caruso did not wish to repeat the aria. On one occasion, when the tumult persisted though he had shaken his head over and over again and shouted "hush" several times, he carried a chair on the stage and sat on it solemnly with folded arms till the applause subsided.

It was in the French operas of his repertory that he won his greatest triumphs as an actor, as well as some of his chief vocal achievements. There were moments in his Faust, Samson, DesGrieux ("Manon"), Don Jose ("Carmen") and Eleazar ("LaJuive") when he rose to the exalted heights of such supreme masters of French operatic acting as the baritones Victor Maurel and Maurice Renaud and the great French tenor with the Italian name, Lucien Muratore. His Eleazar, in particular, was a marvel of histrionic Jewish portraiture.

It was in this part that he made his final appearance. He was a sick man and should have been in bed. My physician was in my seat that evening and told me afterwards how Caruso frequently put his hand on his side as one suffering great pain. The doctor was surprized that the great tenor should be allowed to sacrifice himself to his sense of duty to the management and the audience.

With Caruso there disappeared from the world the most luscious voice that ever came from a man's throat.

His successor might have been an American. One evening when I was standing just inside one of the entrances to the auditorium, Madame Nordica came in. Listening a moment she asked: "Is that Caruso singing?" "No," I answered, "it is Riccardo Martin." But Martin was not a *persona grata* with the rulers of the Metropolitan. It's a painful subject, on which I prefer not to dwell. He was a greater tenor than Gigli or Martinelli or Chamlee or any of the others who have tried to walk in Caruso's shoes, and who, let me add, have earned much applause and well-deserved praise.

An unpleasant episode in Caruso's career in New York was the monkey-house scandal. I have the inside facts of the case from a *Tribune* reporter who studied it carefully. The man who brought the accusation of improper conduct was a discredited policeman, whose word was taken against the great tenor's indignant denials. Not knowing what the public verdict would be Caruso felt very nervous at his next appearance on the stage. Would he be hissed? He was applauded furiously. To give him courage, the kind-hearted Madame Sembrich, whose high moral standards were known to all, arranged to appear with him. When the verdict came from the audience he almost fell on her neck and wept.

Everybody connected with the Metropolitan adored Caruso. He was on terms of intimacy with all, yet there had never been a breath of scandal. He was always ready to give his autographed photograph to any chorus girl or stage hand that wanted it, and during the holidays he distributed presents by wholesale on the stage and off. His

CARUSO AS "DON JOSE" IN "CARMEN"

generosity was well known, and huge sums were squeezed out of him by his countrymen on one pretext or another.

He had too much money, that was the trouble. Not only did he earn $2,000 or $2,500 every time he sang, but the phonograph brought him fabulous sums. On this subject I have an interesting anecdote.

One day a representative called on Caruso to persuade him to become one of the Victrola singers. The tenor was willing enough. He offered to make a new record whenever desired if he were paid 200,000 francs in advance, relinquishing all claims to later compensations.

The Victor man explained that the company preferred to pay him royalties on the records sold, as it did all the other singers. Caruso demurred and finally, in an access of temperament, seized the contract, which his visitor had made out on the royalty basis, and threw it into the fire; whereupon the representative took his hat and left.

A few weeks later he accidentally came across Caruso who reproached him for not calling on him again.

"But you tore up the contract."

"Yes, but I have changed my mind. Bring back the royalty contract and I'll sign it."

He did sign it—and the difference to him! Instead of $40,000 once and for all time, the royalties on his records have in years brought him and his heirs (these are official figures) the huge fortune of "several hundred thousand dollars a year."

An Evening Post Happy Family

When Oswald Villard sold the *Evening Post,* Thomas Lamont became its financial sponsor while its director was borrowed from Harvard: Professor Edwin F. Gay. At a dinner given in honor of the occasion, the managing editor, Mr. Puckette, made a witty speech in which he referred to the town talk that "The *Evening Post* is getting Gay."

But neither the efforts of Gay nor the millions of Lamont could make the *Evening Post* what it had never been: a financial success; and so, a few years later, it was sold again, this time to "The Man from Maine." Cyrus H. K. Curtis had made fortunes in Philadelphia with the *Saturday Evening Post, Ladies' Home Journal* and *Country Gentleman* by giving subscribers tremendous value for an absurdly small sum. Could he, I wondered, make the New York *Post* a success charging five cents for sixteen or twenty pages? If he does succeed, Edward Bok ought to write another book about him.*

Under Professor Gay the staff of the *Evening Post* had remained what it had been under Villard and before: a happy family. Alfred McCann, the great food-reformer (whom I christened the "dietetic Sherlock Holmes"), once told me that the writers for the *Globe* seldom met and hardly knew each other, usually sending in their copy, without having a room in the office; and this was and is, I believe, the case in most of the New York newspapers. The *Evening Post,* on the contrary, was a sort of club house, where every editor spent the whole day in his own den and made daily calls on everybody else.

Yes, we were a happy family, and most of the brothers and sisters in it were decidedly worth knowing. Boss Gay was a genial man, always glad to see his officers and men and chat with us. He called me to order once after I had printed a rather flippant joke on the prohibition question, which he himself took very seriously.

The editor-in-chief, Rollo Ogden, had been a friend of mine ever since he had joined the staff as assistant to Garrison in the literary department. His occasional editorial

---

*When the *Evening Post*, in the last week of August, 1926, moved into its magnificent new building nearer the river, its price was reduced to three cents.

articles were of such outstanding merit that it was only
a question of time when he would become the chief. Some
of his stirring appeals during the war still tingle in my
memory. They were equal to Godkin at his best fighting
for New York against Tammany.

When Mr. Ochs, the multimillionaire owner of the
Times, won Ogden away, we were glad for his own sake
for he got a salary more adequate to his merits and a
very much larger audience; but we sadly missed him at
the head of our table. He is now the Premier of American
journalists and long may he wave. Let me add that my
wife and I spent many pleasant week-ends with the Ogden
family in Summit, New Jersey, and summer months in
Maine.

Alexander Dana Noyes was another one of our leading writers whom Mr. Ochs spirited away and put at the
head of his own financial department. I *know* that Noyes
was the foremost authority on money matters in America;
I know it because everybody said so and because the all-
knowing Robert Bridges got him to write a monthly
article for *Scribner's Magazine.*

Bridges, by the way, also was for some years on the
Evening Post staff. He, too, is a poet, and a better one,
I think, than his English namesake. He helped to make
Life a success; he has occasionally asked me to write an
article; and he shares with his predecessor, Edward Bur-
lingame, the honor of having made the genius and the
works of Stevenson so familiar that everybody now knows
whom R. L. S. stands for.

Noyes occasionally gave me free advice (in return for
free opera tickets) on advantageous investments, and
while he always read my columns, he forgave me for never
reading his. I wouldn't have understood them. In money
matters I am as hopeless a dunce as in mathematics. To
be sure, when my cousin, Frank E. Aiken, once com-

plained to me that while he had a knack for making money he didn't know how to spend it, I asked "Don't you think every man ought to do what he can do most successfully?" and he said, "Certainly;" but when I added: "*I* know best how to *spend* money—let's go into partnership: you earn and I spend," he balked.

Two of the foremost editors were Simeon Strunsky and Royal Davis. Both of them are among the wittiest writers —and speakers—of the period, and both can turn out an editorial, long or short, on any subject at a moment's notice. Davis stuck to his *Post* when Curtis bought it, adapting himself to altered conditions, while Strunsky joined the Ochs forces. To him I am specially indebted because he suggested my writing for the *Evening Post* editorial page a series of articles on my garden in Maine. These were reprinted in a book, "Gardening with Brains," which became a best-seller.

Other prominent members of our happy family were the three writers who had in a few years made the *Evening Post* literary supplement a power in the land: Henry Seidel Canby, one of the two Yale professors (the other is William Lyon Phelps) whose command of English is only equalled by their amazing knowledge of it in all its phases and periods; the poetic and versatile Wm. Rose Benet; and Amy Loveman, who has the astonishing fund of information expected in a member of the Heilprin family. When the new management wanted to popularize the literary supplement, the three editors rebelled, resigned, and started the *Saturday Review of Literature* which continues their policy in a most alluring fashion to high-brow readers. With them flocked also the popular author of *Where the Blue Begins,* Christopher Morley, whose "Bowling Green" was a unique feature of the *Post's* editorial page for years.

Concerning our dramatic editor I might write a whole

volume, for John Ranken Towse and I occupied the same room for several decades; let me say right away that in all this time we never fought, or even quarreled. To be sure we often "argufied" and sometimes quite warmly, especially on the subject of sports. Towse, now in his eighties, has remained an Englishman though he has been in New York more than half a century; he thinks the English form of government far superior to the American, and I agree with him cordially. He is an Oxford man; every year the Oxford-Cambridge race keeps him in a ferment of excitement for a week, and he follows other sport events with keen interest.

"How can a man of your intelligence get so wrought up about whether one boat or the other beats by a few lengths?" I used to ask, and that started the discussion. Of course it was very stupid of me to ask such questions. As a professional pleasure-seeker I ought to rejoice in anything and everything that provides harmless amusement to men and women. I have often regretted that I was born without a sporting sense; I might as well have been born color-blind or tone-deaf.

Once I went to a horse-race. It was in Munich. Just as the race was nearing its end I saw near me a beauteous gipsy girl, whereupon the horses existed for me no more; which shows what a hopeless subject I was from a sporting point of view.

The Germans shout "Deutschland über alles." My motto has always been "Beauty above all things—be it in music, women, dogs, scenery, flowers, forests or anything else." There is little or no beauty I can see in sporting contests—not even in football! Don't you feel sorry for me? Towse did.

He had been a member of the Oxford crew and he persevered in the habit of daily exercise (especially walking) throughout his seventies; which accounts for the fact that in his eighties he was still able to do a full day's work, sit up till one or two, writing his comments on the night's new play and be ready for another one at 8 o'clock in the evening. I never saw or heard of a more conscientious man.

When William Winter died, there could be no more debate as to who was America's foremost dramatic critic. Towse's experiences are told in his book "Sixty Years of the Stage" in which nearly all the prominent actors, actresses and playwrights of half a century are embedded as in amber for all time.

If you will read that book you will wonder how the saying could arise that "the *Evening Post* was founded for Mr. Towse to dislike things in." To be sure he did not always praise; but when he didn't there was usually abundant reason.

A standing joke in the office was: "Towse says the new play isn't worth a paragraph, but he is giving it a whole column all the same."

This column-habit was one which was difficult to break when the Philadelphians stormed the *Evening Post* office; but Mr. Bond, the new managing editor, was inexorable and Towse had to yield. "Why growl," I said to him, "if you get just as much money for half a column as for a whole?" I had been giving the same advice for years to composers, urging the modern need for brevity.

One of the things that gave Towse's critical comments value was that they covered the whole play, whereas the morning-paper critics habitually left in haste about the middle of it to get their copy ready for the night editor. Towse and I had twelve hours more in which to write our stuff, if we desired them. The critics of other evening papers were no better off than those of the morning papers; they *had* to write at night, for their copy was due before nine in the morning. We were allowed till eleven or even twelve—which, to be sure, kept us out of the first edition —not a big one. We didn't worry.

I can not but laugh when I recall how indulgent Villard and my other bosses used to be. I breakfasted at eight, then took my collie out for half an hour's walk, then jumped on what used to be the last elevated express downtown—it was known as the "millionaires' express"—then sat down and wrote my stuff, sending it up sheet by sheet. All this nonsense would have been stopped by the Curtis crowd; I gave them, however, no chance to discipline me, but hied myself off to the leisurely French Riviera for a perpetual vacation.

Towse had the advantage over me of variety and novelty. I was lucky (to use an optimistic word) if I heard three or four new operas in a year while he frequently had three or four new plays in one week. You have no idea how hard it is to write a readable "story," year after year for decades, about the same operas. However, one can repeat, and nobody knows. I have heard of a Hamburg critic who calmly reprinted his articles once in five years. Nobody found him out.

Towse was on friendly terms with the other great critics, but for the rabble of scribblers in his field he had such contempt that he always refused to appear in group photographs with them.

Unlike—very much unlike—myself, he refused to meet celebrities of the stage. Had I followed his policy, these memoirs would have been curtailed of their best pages!

Towse had many funny stories to tell but he never featured his sense of humor. It was exhibited at its best one evening when he put on his overcoat and headed for the door. The manager, seeing his preparations for departure, said: "You are not going Mr. Towse? There is another act coming." And the critic retorted:

"Yes, I know. That's why I am going."

I now come to Charles Pike Sawyer, who for decades collaborated with Towse and me in the musical and dramatic departments. We simply could not have got along without him.

Charles Pike Sawyer was known to everybody, from boss to office boy and printer's devil, as Charlie. As a gatherer of theatrical and musical news he came in contact with all the managers and actors and actresses and chorus girls, all of whom hailed him joyously as Charlie. The typists and other girls in the office loved Charlie (as they did me). The "cupboard" may have figured in this love, *quien sabe,* for you see we often had tickets for them. All the same we used to look back shudderingly at the bad old times when there were no girls in newspaper offices.

What would I have done, for instance, without Hettie Harris? She was the secretary of John Gavit, probably the best managing editor the *Post* has ever had. She helped me with my musical work; once she got out a musical supplement all by herself. She has a lovely and well-trained voice and she spent two years on the stage, but returned to her pen work as more congenial. She told me she didn't love me, so it must have been the opera tickets that persuaded her to condescend to do all my typewriting; and such neat and perfect typewriting was never seen before on land or sea.

To say that I am extremely fastidious about my manuscripts is to put it mildly. Every comma is in its place; Brownell, the famous art critic, who used to be MS. reader for the Scribners, once told me my copy was the most flawless they saw in his office. But the time came when book MSS. had to be typewritten. Then the typist became of supreme importance. I have told of one girl who nearly blasted one of my lectures by making me read about "Schubert's Sleighride, Hark, Bark the Lark." When I had written my book on Richard Strauss (to order) for Little, Brown & Co. and forwarded my flawless MS. to Boston it came back by return mail because the printers refused to handle it unless it was typed. I had it done by a girl who made a specialty of typing. She made so many blunders that I got a bill of $100 for corrections in excess of what an author is allowed! So you can guess why I value Miss Harris's work when I write a book; I know there will not be a single blunder in it when it goes to the publisher.

For many years Sawyer was the *Post's* sporting editor. As such he performed what was then a novel feat: he stood on a bridge and telephoned a boat race direct to the office with the result that the *Post* was out in the street an hour ahead of its rivals and the other sporting editors nearly committed suicide.

So highly was Charlie esteemed as sporting editor that he was always engaged to manage the annual dog-show and horse-show. I once accepted tickets from him for the dog-show, but was so enraged over the way in which all beauty, intelligence and affection had been bred out of collies by the sportsmen in their insane rivalry for long noses that I never went again.

The horse-show tickets I refused—I hate horses, except to feed lumps of sugar to. But the horse-show dinner— that was quite another affair. I always attended that (thanks to Charlie) although I didn't belong there any more than the man in the moon. There were funny speeches and, what was infinitely more important, there was genuine razor-back ham and the waiters had strict orders to keep the champagne glasses filled to the brim.

The time came when Charlie tired of sporting tasks. He did press-agent work for Columbia University, but, apart from that, he gradually concentrated on amusements in theaters and concert-halls. His "The Mirror," made up of gossip of the stage, was one of the most popular features of the *Post* for years. More and more, too, I needed him in my department. In addition to grand opera and concerts I had light operas to cover. In the days of Gilbert and Sullivan, and Lecocq and Audran, and Strauss and Suppé and Milloecker and De Koven and Victor Herbert there was still time for me to write about their delightful novelties and I enjoyed the work of such favorites as Lillian Russell and Marie Jansen, Alice Nielsen and Marie Tempest, and other operetta queens and such clever comedians as De Wolf Hopper, De Angelis, Francis Wilson, Raymond Hitchcock, Sam Bernard, Frank Daniels, Jimmie Powers (why have they no successors?). But as grand opera performances and concerts multiplied I unloaded all these lighter things on Charlie who rejoiced in them and wrote about them entertainingly.

When the movies came Charlie attended to them too. Yes, Charles P. Sawyer was a busy man. Everybody came to him for advice on all sorts of things. What he didn't know wasn't worth knowing. In summer he kindly took care of my department and letters; and when I resigned and quit journalism the Curtis people wisely made him musical editor, with Ernest Newman as musical critic for the first year. Newman proved rather obstreperous. He refused to cover more than one event a day (my wife and I had often covered three or more) but Charlie had the privilege of telling him what he must cover.

Among those who are now helping Sawyer is Chas. H. Davis, who also often wrote for me on the opera. Famed as a photographer, he saw the stage from his professional point of view, which gave a unique interest to his articles.

THE ASTONISHING OSCAR HAMMERSTEIN

One morning a good many years before this, Sawyer came into my den and said: "I have a message for you from Oscar." "Wilde?" I asked.

"No—Oscar Hammerstein. He wants me to tell you that if you ever come into one of his theaters again he'll break every bone in your body."

As I had no particular desire to go to one of his theaters, I felt that the 206 bones in my body were safe for the time being.

How had I aroused Hammerstein's wrath?

He had given a grand opera performance with only one good singer (and she was not good enough to die young) and I had spoken of it disrespectfully. I had refused to print his flattering press notices and committed other crimes of which a bill of particulars was given by him in a five-page letter addressed "To the Proprietor of the *Evening Post*." On the last page he says amiably "Should this imp dare and enter my theaters I shall certainly eject him . . . even if such infamous literary leeches as this Finck is in the employ of the great *Evening Post*." (He was too excited to bother about grammar, even as Rubinstein used to play wrong notes.)

Some years passed and once more Charlie Sawyer came to my room to tell me about Hammerstein. "I came across Oscar just after he had read your comments on last night's opera at the Manhattan. 'I didn't know Finck was such a friend of mine!' he exclaimed, all aglow with enthusiasm and gratitude.

"'You fool!' I replied. 'Finck is neither your friend nor your enemy. He pats you on the back when you do something well and jumps on you when you don't, that's all.'"

If Oscar Hammerstein had broken all my bones every time I entered his Manhattan Opera House he would hardly have had time to attend to his managerial duties. I spent a great deal of my time in one of the best seats in the auditorium and, during intermissions, on the stage, at his urgent invitation, so I could chat with the great singers he had engaged.

Yes, he had great singers and plenty of them, some of them unheard by the audiences at the Metropolitan; and he had the wonderful Italian conductor Cleofonte Campanini. Between them they gave performances which decidedly belong in the Golden Age of Music in New York.

Oscar Hammerstein had pluck—lots of it; and pluck is a quality which Americans admire above all things. Single-handed, without one millionaire to back him up, he entered the operatic arena, like a medieval knight, to fight the management of the Metropolitan which was backed up by the famous horseshoe of multimillionaires. And he fought so valiantly and dealt such heavy blows that the rival house more than once sent out its S.O.S. distress signals and finally decided it must get rid of him one way or another. The New York press and public applauded the lonely knight vigorously. His fight to give opera-goers treats which the Metropolitan had inexcusably withheld from them is the most interesting story in the musical annals of New York. It made Oscar Hammerstein an immortal. Not for anything in the world would I have this episode sponged out of my memory.

His great deed, his unforgettable achievement was that he gave New York for the first time a real French opera season. Grau had featured the masterworks of Gounod, Bizet and Meyerbeer, but Hammerstein went much further; he brought musical Paris bodily across the ocean; he gave New Yorkers a chance to hear practically the whole personnel of the Opéra-Comique, including several eminent artists who had helped to create famous operas by Massenet, Debussy and Charpentier, under the personal supervision of their respective composers.

These three composers had been particularly neglected at the Metropolitan. To be sure, four of Massenet's two dozen operas ("Manon," "Werther," "Le Cid" and "La Navarraise") had been sung at the Broadway house, but they were not done, usually, in the genuine Gallic spirit. To these four works by Massenet, Hammerstein added five others that had never been sung in New York: "Thaïs," "Le Jongleur de Notre Dame," "Hérodiade," "Grisélidis" and "Sapho." As interpreted by Maurice Renaud, Mary Garden, Dalmores, Gilibert and other artists of the genuine French school, these operas, together with "Louise," "Pelléas et Mélisande," "The Tales of Hoffman," and others, made a deeper impression than similar works had done at the other house.

Luck had favored Hammerstein in providing him with an auditorium peculiarly suited to these operas. It was not one of those vast expanses in which subtle shades of vocalization and facial expression were—together with orchestral delicacy—dissipated. Berlioz was right when he said that for the most thorough enjoyment of music our nerves must vibrate with the not too-distant tones. In the Manhattan they did vibrate.

While extolling the admirable acoustic qualities of the Manhattan Opera House I censured Oscar for not providing adequate ventilation. The following day, when I came to a rehearsal, he button-holed me and told me all about it.

"I have made a most interesting discovery, quite accidentally," he said. "It is that stagnant air is a better conductor of sound-waves than moving air. The excellent acoustics of my theater are therefore due largely to the fact that there is no ventilation."

"Do you see anything green in my eyes?" I asked. He laughed and never tried any more of his bluff on me.

A CHAMPION OF FRENCH MUSIC

To me the triumph of French opera at the Manhattan was a matter of special gratification. I had, to be sure, made my début as a fervent champion of Wagner operas. Questions of nationality, however, had nothing whatever to do with this. I was just as passionate a press-agent for good Italian or French operas when they needed a champion. "Aïda," for instance, was not popular for several seasons after its première. I scolded the public time and again for neglecting it. I needed to hear it but once to know that it was the best, most stirring opera ever composed in Italy and I used all the eloquence at my command to convince the skeptical public that I was right in advancing an opinion which is now held universally.

Similarly with French masterworks. While no one could have been a more ardent lover of German music than I, nothing aroused my ire more frequently than the supercilious attitude of Germanophiles toward French music. The historian of the Boston Symphony Orchestra, for example, records the fact that the first encore demanded of it was for the "Danse Macabre" of Saint-Saëns. Then he adds loftily that "in spite of occasional offerings like the 'Danse Macabre' Gericke was putting into practise his belief that these concerts should be put on a classical basis."

Upon which my comment was: "Stuff and nonsense! That symphonic poem by France's foremost orchestral writer is just as 'classical' in its way as a Beethoven symphony." I would not hesitate to say the same thing of Rossini's "William Tell" overture. Have you ever heard

Toscanini conduct it? It is as full of juice—the juice of genius—as a ripe Spanish orange.

When Saint-Saëns, "ce jeune maître," came to New York at the age of seventy to play the piano and exhibit some of his orchestral works, the enthusiasm of the audiences was reflected in my glowing comments. I dwelt on the abundant translucent melody, the polish and elegance, the sparkling rhythms, the use of dissonance as a means and not as an end which proclaimed him a representative of the true French spirit in music. He played the piano with amazing nimbleness, but was not quite satisfied with himself; for, when I called on him after the recital, he sat down and repeated one of the pieces on the program. Then he exclaimed: "That's the way I *should* have played it."

Saint-Saëns was the first great composer to follow Liszt's lead in writing those short and coherent symphonic poems which are, formally, so great an improvement on the interminable German symphonies with their four incoherent movements. When I asked him why he had never composed any more of these pieces besides the four which had become so popular he replied: "Because I had no more ideas." That, too, was thoroughly French.

The performances of Massenet's operas given at the Manhattan aroused my enthusiasm to such a degree that I gladly acceded to the request of the London publisher, John Lane, to write a book on Massenet and his operas. To this I must refer the reader as regards my correspondence with Massenet. If you read that book you will understand why he would have received me with open arms when next I visited Paris. Unfortunately, that was just after pneumonia had nearly ended my career. I knew he would send me "boxes" to hear his operas, and as nothing could have persuaded me to enter one of the unventilated Paris theaters just then, I thought it wise not to call on him. This was shortly before he died; so I never had a chance to meet the man who has been for decades France's most popular composer.

Some years later I received a letter from a prominent French journalist in New York who had been reading my articles lauding French music. "If any critic ever deserved the ribbon of the Legion of Honor you do," he said, and he asked if I approved of his taking steps to secure it for me. I thanked him cordially but declined. I felt like Grieg who said that the Legion of Honor was an honor one shared with a legion; and I recalled the Parisian joke about a man who had disappeared but whom the police promptly found after being told that he did not wear the ribbon of the Legion of Honor.

CAMPANINI'S TRIUMPHS

Oscar Hammerstein was not a born protagonist for French operas. It was not till his second season at the Manhattan that he specialized in them and produced the novelties which made such a sensation. The greatest of all French artists, Maurice Renaud, was, to be sure, with him from the start but Renaud's chief triumphs the first season were in an Italian opera, "Rigoletto," the jester's part which was enacted by him no fewer than eleven times.

"Carmen," to be sure, beat that figure. It had the record number of nineteen performances; in fifteen of these the heroine was Bressler-Gianoli, while Calvé added the other four, near the close of the season. Yet, incredible as it may seem, the real "prima donna" (as Theodore Thomas would have said) at these nineteen performances of "Carmen" was the conductor, an Italian, Cleofonte Campanini.

If I had been churlish in acknowledging the merits of the splendid tenor, Italo Campanini, I atoned for that by my enthusiasm for his younger brother. He simply swept me off my feet as he did everybody else. He proved, to my utter amazement, that a perfect ensemble *can* be quite as important as an all-star cast. The way he made all the parts dovetail, removed every weak spot, and imparted an entrancing swing to the whole, was one of the seven wonders of operatic history. To this day I shiver delightedly when I recall the successions of thrills he provided with the sublime quintet and other details that are usually bungled.

Please don't tell anybody, but this Italian's conductorial genius almost made me agree with the opinion of Nietzsche (expressed after his quarrel with the prophet of Bayreuth) that "Carmen" is the opera of operas and Bizet even greater than Wagner.

Twenty-two operas were staged during this first season at the Manhattan and most of the 113 performances of them were conducted by Campanini himself. His capacity for hard work was almost unbelievable. Rehearsals every morning and again in the afternoon. A performance in the evening and after it—to bed? Oh no! More rehearsing of this or that detail. The conductor's zeal and enthusiasm were contagious, so that all did their best, including the chorus of fresh young American voices which fell most agreeably on my ears.

Campanini gradually learned some English, but to his friends he insisted on speaking French. I must say I have never heard bad French spoken so fluently. It quite took my breath away.

He was an admirer of female beauty, and Hammerstein more than once complained to me bitterly of the extra expense he had to incur paying for singers engaged by the conductor more for their good looks than their fine voices.

While Hammerstein was a shrewd manager, he could hardly have foreseen how much his engagement of Cleo-

fonte Campanini would mean for him, or guess that
it would scare the Metropolitan's management into securing a worthy rival in the person of Arturo Toscanini,
another maestro of the first rank. When, not long afterwards, still another conductor of the highest rank, Giorgio
Polacco, was enticed across the Big Pond, the Italians
tore out their hair. "Is there no limit to the greed of these
Americans?" they exclaimed. "Not satisfied with kidnap-
ing our best singers, they are now buying our great conductors."

Besides making himself indispensable in the ways I
have described, Campanini helped Hammerstein to bring
together a bunch of high-class vocalists. Here are some
of the names: Maurice Renaud, Mary Garden, Luisa Tetrazzini, Nellie Melba, Emma Calvé, Alessandro Bonci
(to offset Caruso), Charles Dalmores, Schumann-Heink,
Charles Gilibert, Gerville-Réache, Bressler-Gianoli, Regina Pinkert, Mario Ancona, Lillian Nordica, Emma
Trentini, Mario Sammarco, Hector Dufranne, Eleonore
de Cisneros, Amadeo Bassi, Jean Perier, Giovanni Zena-
tello, Lina Cavalieri, and John McCormack. With such
names Oscar was able to do some conjuring.

MAURICE RENAUD

Among these artists, the two who contributed most to
Hammerstein's success were Maurice Renaud and Mary
Garden—Maurice even more than Mary. One of the best
things Krehbiel ever wrote was that "where Renaud sits
there is the head of the table." He also spoke the plain
truth when he said that "the chief triumph" in the performance of "Thaïs," in which Mary Garden made her
American début, "was won by M. Renaud." I will therefore talk about him first:

Indelibly impressed on my memory is the day when I

took Winifred Ogden to hear Renaud in "Don Giovanni":
she saw me, a veteran critic, trembling like an aspen leaf
from excitement over his enactment of this part. No one
who saw him can ever forget the extraordinary manly
beauty of this Don Giovanni. Nor can one forget the
ardor of his eyes when he wooed Donna Anna, the emotional depth of his use of her name—he had the same
emotional intensity in pronouncing a name as that of Jean
de Reszke in the way he breathed the final "Isolde" of
Wagner's work. On the other hand, Zerlina was pursued
somewhat as if she had been a very pretty, very gentle,
very soft kitten. His superb looks and lordly insolence
in the ballroom scene; his amused indifference to Masetto's
grief over Zerlina are unforgettable. But the supreme
moment of the rôle was after the supper in the last
act. When the ghostly statue appeared, Renaud's face
expressed the whole horror of the situation. I can remember no gesture, excepting the unavailing effort to tear his
hand from the statue's stony grasp. But his eyes! They
were stricken yet unafraid. Death had come and he met
it unflinching, but not with resignation. Life had been
too full of fascination, and unlike Lenau's Don Juan, it
had not turned to ashes on this Don Juan's lips. Still full
of pride of body and joy of living he went to his doom.
Théophile Gautier once wrote that Don Juan was a character impossible to portray owing to all its exigencies of
fascination and physical splendor. Would that he could
have found that Don Juan had lived, once at least, on the
actual stage. Maurel was superb in the part, by far the
greatest, until Renaud eclipsed him, not only by superior
qualities, but by a different mental attitude, for he made
of Don Juan a man overflowing with youthful spirits,
beauty and health rather than a determined seducer. From
that moment I became Renaud's unofficial press-agent—
my, what volleys of enthusiasm my wife and I fired off.

They were heard throughout the city and the Renaud audiences soon reached high-water mark.

As Renaud was always an artist who received very high prices, Hammerstein began, economically as he thought, by engaging him for a half-year each of his first two seasons, but, like Maurice Grau, he found that the best economy was to engage him for the whole season and, each time Renaud sang, to have a full house. During the last memorable Manhattan Opera House season, he even found it advisable to add five or more extra performances to the forty guaranteed.

On November 25, 1907, "Thaïs" was sung for the first time in America. Renaud's Athanaël, heard many times before he left in mid-season for Europe, was in its main lines always the same, but what infinite variety he brought to the smaller details. Sometimes the outstanding recollection was of his tenderness; sometimes it was the hard fanaticism of the ascetic which was the dash of intensest light on his canvas. In the first mood the scene in the desert with Thaïs, his contrition for her suffering, his tender solicitude for her bleeding feet, were the high lights. In the second mood he towered above her like an avenging deity, as she cried out to be spared; his eyes burned with an almost insane fire. Then came the fall, and what a fall! From Heaven to hell! His hands, yearning, demanding, terrible, told the story as nothing else could, of those endless centuries of unutterable torture, the soul damned before it had left the body, the face hideous with its unrewarded sufferings, its unquenched desire.

Almost an operatic miracle was his triple performance in "The Tales of Hoffmann," three impersonations of the spirit of evil so different that one could hardly believe they were taken by the same person. Renaud is a tall man, very nearly six feet, and he is of generous build. I shall never understand how he screwed himself into the

figure of the fearful little Alsatian Jew whom he portrayed in the first act of the "Tales." He was greatly
interested in that form of French operatic art, the "mélo-
drame" which includes both singing and speaking, and he
and Gilibert often indulged in impromptu and witty additions to the spoken dialogue with great enjoyment both to
themselves and to their audience. This was especially the
case in the first act. How indescribably funny they were
when, each distrusting the other, they bargained for the
doll.

In the second act, Renaud's beauty was second only to
that of his Don Giovanni. A Venetian gallant, in powdered hair, as indifferent to the certain death of his opponent as a graven image, he almost took one's breath away.
Again in the third act he became grotesquely ugly, a sort
of exaggerated Paganini figure with a huge and evil head,
and hands which suggested claws.

His Rigoletto would take pages to describe with his
strange mixture of passionate paternal love, his twisted
body and soul, and the birth of his hatred toward the
Duke, with the desolateness of his revenge. The intense
suffering in his face in the scene with his betrayed daughter and the change to evil joy seemed too real to be
assumed. His Valentin, seen but twice in New York,
was a young and vivid man, not the usual puppet; then
there were Hérode; and a most evil and satiated Mefisto
in Berlioz's "Faust"; Wolfram, the greatest I have ever
seen and many more. In some ways, the most exquisite
of his rôles was that of Boniface in the "Jongleur de Notre
Dame." He was so tenderly interested in the poor little
waif, so inspired with the miracle of the sage-brush and
the Infant Christ, so enthusiastic about his vegetable peel-
ings, so comprehending when Jean performed his poor
little tricks before the Virgin, to the horror of the other
monks. We often went to his room between the acts

and I shall never forget that it was only by his delightful smile that one could recognize the slightest resemblance to Renaud in this corpulent, partially bald, red-haired, bearded, convent cook. He did not always wear the beard. I remember he was having rather a difficult time to make it stick that first night and constantly feared that it might come off. Sometimes, if his voice was not in prime condition, he was too nervous to fight the obstinacy of that beard.

One interesting feature of Renaud's make-up was that, like a Rembrandt portrait, it was as fine nearby as at a distance. There were no smears and blotches to mar the picture he painted on his flesh in place of canvas. Except when he had to change his costumes, we were always welcome in his dressing-room and we often sat and watched him change his make-up, asking questions as to the why and wherefore of the different colors and shadows he used. It was most interesting to verify results from the auditorium. We were sure to be welcomed cordially by Madame Renaud and their winsome adopted daughter, Zaza, who made us think of Titian's splendid young girls. (During the war the Germans would have been less eager to capture Paris had they known that Mademoiselle Zaza had been, in the moment of danger, hastily sent away.)

I wish I could show you the costume pictures we have of Renaud as Hérode, Mephistopheles, Don Juan, Rigoletto and himself—so unlike that some of our visitors refuse to believe it can be the same man.

He often came to see us of afternoons. My wife's easy French was an attraction for him and his own was so clear and perfect in enunciation that no one could fail to understand him. Even in ordinary clothes, I have seen him suddenly transform himself into a Parisian *voyou* as an illustration about some former rôle. A thrust forward of the chin, the sinking of his head between his shoulders and Renaud had vanished, leaving a strange being from the streets in his place.

When we met him again he was in his winter home at Nice where he has lived the better part of the year since he was invalided in the war. I told him an anecdote I had read about him during the war: that in the trenches he had sung Wolfram's song to the Evening Star and that he was applauded furiously by the Germans in a nearby trench. "Is there any truth in this story?" I asked, and he answered: "Not a word."

He was caught in a trench with four other men when a projectile crashed down on them. He was accidentally protected by a couple of iron bars which kept enough of the weight off his body so that he wasn't killed outright, like two of the other four, or quite so seriously injured as the other two; but he was fearfully hurt and it took him a full year to regain his health.

Now he is mainly occupied in enjoying life, smoking, remaining indifferent to draughts and to somewhat increasing weight. His career is behind him completely, irrevocably, and he has no regrets for those days. Never a self-advertiser—possibly more people would have come to know his greatness if he had been more in the public eye in America—he has completely vanished now from print. He has taken up oblivion as a fine art, says he is dead to the public artistically, and that they can have no possible interest in him in any other capacity. He loves the movies, and dotes on his two adopted grandchildren, Madame Zaza's two babies. In the old days he always said that when the time came for him to retire, he would bury himself in his home and books with good grace; and he has performed another miracle in the changing of rôles to a perfectly contented man, who remembers with no regrets

that he was once a great operatic artist—he is too modest
to say one of the greatest, if not the greatest, opera singer.

MARY GARDEN

I met Mary Garden but once, and that was owing to
Richard Watson Gilder, who, as I have before said, kept
the readers of the *Century Magazine* well informed on
musical events (a policy pursued also by his famous successor, Robert Underwood Johnson).

After Miss Garden's great successes in three of her best
rôles, Gilder asked me to write an article about her. It
was to be mainly critical, but in order to introduce a personal touch I decided to call on her. She told me about
her early career and how she, though Scotch, came to be
regarded, even in Paris, as a Parisian artist to the finger
tips, leading prima donna of the Opéra-Comique.

There was not a word in this article that could have
offended the vainest of vain prima donnas. In my *Evening Post* comments, also, I had usually spoken of her art
in a more laudatory style than most of my colleagues.
And yet at a later date I was ignominiously snubbed and
ignored.

When I was writing my book, "Massenet and His
Operas," I wrote to Miss Garden asking her if she could
help me to make my portrait of the great Frenchman more
lifelike by telling me an anecdote or two about him; for
I knew he had at one time coached her. (Here let me
digress a moment. About this time Victor Maurel, greatest of French baritones before Renaud, came to our house
one afternoon, as I wanted to get something about Massenet out of him, too—it's the way of biographers. Well,
he remained three hours, talking away in his amusing, dis-
jointed manner, about everything under the sun except
Massenet. Again and again I tried to bring him to the

© *Mishkin*

MARY GARDEN IN "THAÏS"

point and finally all I got was the confession that while
he knew a number of stories about that composer they
would hardly look well in print.)

Possibly, Miss Garden felt that way too. But she might
at least have answered my letters. There were two of
them, sent *registered* to the address in Paris given me by
Hammerstein himself. Not a word in reply! Yet I did
not resent this snub, as you may see if you will read what
I said in my book about her impersonations of Massenet's
heroines.

Why did she snub me? I think I know. She hated the
New York critics fiercely. At one time she threatened
to write a book about us, exposing us in all our hideous,
loathsome worthlessness. You see, we were unanimous in
our conviction that while she was one of the greatest
operatic actresses of all time she was not a great singer—
and she herself thought it was just the other way. *Hinc
illae lachrymae!* Willie Henderson, bold bad man as he
always was, actually made fun of her singing.

Willie went too far. While her organ was the strangest
voice I ever heard, and hardly to be called beautiful, she
yet succeeded now and then in doing vocal stunts that were
amazingly effective. Her high A in "Thaïs" was always
lovely, and there were plenty of beauty spots in all her
operas. In the matter of temperament and emotionalism
she sometimes almost—if not quite—equalled Geraldine
Farrar, notably in "Louise" and the ineffably touching
"Juggler of Notre Dame," which Massenet himself was
said to have changed so that a soprano could sing the tenor
part. Will those who saw her in that part ever forget her
gentle luminous eyes, her resemblance to the stainless Gal-
ahad, her tender awe-struck voice in the last—spoken—
words of the second act? It was one of the loveliest pieces
of acting ever seen on any stage.

I never liked her first act in "Louise." Already her

future had cast too pronounced a shadow on the girl's character. She was not sufficiently innocent, in look, dress, or demeanor, but the following acts left little to be desired in their perfection, and the final act, especially when Gilibert appeared as the father, was superlative acting.

Mélisande, in its strange remoteness, was one of the finest things she did. No one could have conveyed better than she did the peculiar shadowiness, the dreamy look, the thrills of pale-blooded terror which constitute this real-unreal creation of Maeterlinck. She built unerringly from the first moment to the last. It was curious that, on the other hand, with Monna Vanna, the picture of chaste and perfect medieval wifehood, she should so have mistaken a make-up as to make the lady look like a most undesirable person, Monna Vanna with the eyes of a Messaline! She did these things sometimes. Her Cleopatra in Massenet's opera was singularly fascinating, both imperial and debased. Fiora in Montemezzi's "Love of Three Kings" was a living flame, an embodiment of passion, and even Miss Garden's costume partook of the flame-like portrayal.

Probably no mortal could make Mary Garden acknowledge that she has limitations, but, deep in her keen mind, she recognizes them. I've often admired her and been amused by her bluff. She has almost no gift of facial expression—the exact opposite of Renaud—but she always has some clever gesture with which to divert your attention and make you forget that her face has said nothing.

VICTOR HERBERT

One of Mary Garden's supreme achievements was the impersonation of the heroine in Victor Herbert's "Natoma." This, the best opera ever composed in America, had been, of course, rejected at the Metropolitan, where they were developing a brilliant virtuosity in doing the wrong thing. It had its première in Philadelphia, on February 25, 1911, by the Chicago Opera Company under Andreas Dippel, who, by the way, before he became a manager, had been for a time one of the most serviceable of tenors at the Metropolitan (*Life* once had a picture of him sitting at home in his undergarments, ready, at the call of the telephone, to jump into any one of a score of costumes grouped about him and hurry to replace some colleague disabled during a performance).

The Philadelphia audience was so tremendously enthusiastic over "Natoma," a grand opera, at last, by the most popular of our operetta writers, and over its interpreters (among whom were, besides Miss Garden, John McCormack, Gustav Huberdeau, Hector Dufranne and the admirable Italian baritone Mario Sammarco), that the novelty was promptly brought to New York, where it had another triumphant reception.

Joseph Redding, who wrote the libretto, placed the scene in Southern California. The heroine is an Indian girl who, among other things, dances a sword dance; there are abalone shells, and other details of local color aplenty. As a whole the libretto seemed to me exceptionally well-done, but some of my colleagues assailed it violently and this gave me a chance to make a good speech—the only good speech I ever made in all my life, with the exception of one at the Lotos Club to which I have already referred. It was at a dinner given by Herbert's friends in honor of his triumph.

Critics, I began, have a way of assailing librettos, but never had I seen so violent an onslaught as was made on a certain opera book I had in mind.

As I said this the dinner guests—including about a hundred persons prominent in musical and literary circles—

began to look embarrassed or indignant. Is this speaker, they wondered, going to be so awkward and ill-mannered as to cast slurs on the "Natoma" libretto, with Mr. Redding sitting near him at the same table?

Regardless of the dismay and depression I had caused, I went on to read the scathing, crushing verdict of seven critics on said libretto. Then I continued: "Now gentlemen, I know that Mr. Redding is right here. I have not yet had the pleasure of meeting him. But what's the difference anyway? The criticisms I have just read were not written about 'Natoma'; they were written about Richard Wagner's greatest music drama, 'Tristan and Isolde.'"

Such a howl of joy as went up after these unexpected words I had rarely heard. The applause was deafening and lasted several minutes, till I became quite embarrassed. It was certainly agreeable to be thus acclaimed; yet I continued to refuse invitations to all dinners at which I was likely to be called upon to make a speech.

I remember several occasions when I had mentally composed what I considered a good "impromptu" speech; yet, when the toastmaster came to ask if I would be willing to say a few words I always said "No."

Victor Herbert and I had been good friends ever since he had come to New York in 1886. Though born in Dublin (his grandfather was the famous Irish novelist Samuel Lover) he had been musically educated in Stuttgart, where his skill as a violoncellist won him a place in the court orchestra. The engagement of his wife (Miss Foerster) by the Metropolitan brought him to New York where he became solo violoncellist of the Philharmonic under Theodore Thomas. He also conducted for a time the Twenty-Second (now the One Hundred and Second) Regiment Band as successor to Gilmore, and the Pittsburgh Symphony Orchestra.

As soon, however, as he felt sure of his daily bread he began to specialize in composing. He once explained to me how, since there is no demand in America for serious home-made compositions, he chose the field of comic operettas. Some forty of these works came from his astonishingly facile pen. I wish I had room to dwell on the pleasure the best of these gave me.

Everybody liked Herbert. There was a boyish enthusiasm about him which captured all hearts, and when, now and then, he personally conducted one of his works, the joy was unbounded. He had a happy faculty of composing music which, like that of Johann Strauss or Edvard Grieg, was popular and yet thoroughly artistic, abounding not only in catchy tunes, but in happy details which might escape the attention of the average theater-goer but were there for those who have ears to hear and relish them.

Speaking of Grieg recalls an occasion when Herbert and I nearly came to blows. He shared the outrageously unjust notion (industriously fostered by Germans) that Grieg borrowed all his melodies from national sources. When I protested violently he said:

"It's no disgrace to borrow folk-melodies. The greatest composers have done it."

"It is not a disgrace," I answered hotly, "to borrow tunes; but it *is* disgraceful to accuse one of the five or six most original creators of melodies of all time of borrowing them. *All* of Grieg's melodies are his own except a few collections which are issued separately and plainly marked as arrangements of folk-tunes."

Some of Herbert's own melodies are as fresh and almost as unique as Grieg's. They abound in his operettas. It makes me melancholy and pessimistic to think that these delightful operettas, like those of Sullivan and Johann Strauss, are now neglected. Fortunately, the best of Herbert's tunes are available as records on the Victor talking-

machine. Which of them would I recommend particularly?
I prefer to give a list which Herbert himself gave me for
illustrating a lecture on his stage works which I was to
deliver at Wanamaker's:

1. "Babes in Toyland." Vocal selection.
2. "Badinage."
3. Entrance of the Sultana, from "Rose of Algeria."
4. "Because You're You." From "Red Mill."
5. "Yesterthoughts."
6. Italian Street Song. From "Naughty Marietta."
7. "Mlle. Modiste." Vocal selection.
8. "Land of My Own Romance." From "The Enchantress."
9. Organ: "Natoma." Page 325 to end of opera.

He ought to have added his adorable "Kiss Me Again,"
which I consider equal to the best of Strauss's waltzes.
Try it by all means. It is one of the most enchanting mel-
odies that have ever come from a man born in Ireland, and
Ireland is a very musical country. On the whole, I con-
sider Victor Herbert the greatest musician of all time with
Irish blood in his veins; greater not only than Balfe and
Wallace, but than John Field, Sullivan and Stanford.
Irishmen everywhere should consider it a point of honor,
as well as patriotism and pleasure, to keep alive the
stage works of Stanford (especially "Shamus O'Brien"),
Arthur Sullivan and Victor Herbert.

ROSA RAISA AND POLACCO

Before Hammerstein ceased to harass the directors of
the Metropolitan (who were reported to have paid him a
cool million of "hush money") he had revived Richard
Strauss's "Salome" successfully with Mary Garden, and,
in his last season, had staged the still more harrowing
"Elektra." London was at that time having a Strauss

craze; it wanted to know all about Hammerstein's production of "Elektra." The London *Times* asked me to cable an article about it but I had to refuse because of home work. The Glasgow *Herald* cabled for a letter about it, and this I wrote because there was plenty of time before the departure of the next steamer. I hated to do it, however, because this opera inspired me with disgust.

Let me pass on to an infinitely more interesting event, when the Chicago Opera Company (which largely carried on "The Hammerstein policies") revived Puccini's "Girl of the Golden West." When this opera was first produced at the Metropolitan, on December 10, 1910, with a star cast including Caruso, Destinn, Amato, Reiss and Andrea de Segurola, in presence of the composer and with Toscanini as conductor, it seemed to me, as it did to all the critics, far inferior to its predecessor, "Madama Butterfly." I still think this so, as far as the first act and the third are concerned; but the second act, as sung by Rosa Raisa and conducted by Polacco, now loomed up as the biggest thing by far that Puccini had ever done. Rosa Raisa had previously convinced me that Bellini's "Norma" is a far more dramatic and stirring opera than I had supposed. Of her Minnie in the "Girl" I said: "The passionate vehemence of her acting and singing were thrilling. I have seldom in forty years heard dramatic singing so emotional. Great is Rosa Raisa."

Concerning Polacco I wrote: "How he found all that superb music in the second act is a mystery to me; but he found it. Puccini put it there; his score is as wonderful as the best of Wagner's—amazingly complicated, yet clear when there is a Polacco to unravel it. It was the finest operatic conducting heard in New York since the death of Anton Seidl."

In Chicago as in New York Giorgio Polacco was adored by opera-goers. When Mary Garden became manager as well as prima donna of the Chicago Opera Company, the first thing she did was to cable to him. He came and took off her shoulders the burdens she could not have borne alone. He told me afterwards he had never worked so hard in his life; and Miss Garden, thanks to him, was able to act and sing better than she ever had done before, in New York.

More than once I invoked a blessing on Harold McCormick, whose generosity enabled the opera-goers of New York as well as Chicago to enjoy, year after year, the art of Rosa Raisa, Mary Garden, Galli-Curci, Bonci, Marshall, Riccardo Martin, the incomparable French tenor and actor Lucien Muratore, Baklanoff, Titta Ruffo, and others.

GATTI-CASAZZA AND TOSCANINI

Victor Herbert once confided to me that while his pet "Natoma" held its own in the Chicago repertory, it made no progress elsewhere, and he seemed inclined to believe this was due largely to its being in part an Indian opera. "No more Indians for me!" he exclaimed vehemently.

The prejudice against such operas seems the stranger in view of the fact that there is no social prejudice against Indians as there is against negroes. Tsianina, who has sung for years on tour with Cadman, is petted everywhere in the best society, as much as if she were a Pocahontas. She has been a welcome guest at our house.

One of the most praiseworthy things ever done by Otto H. Kahn, chairman of the board of directors, and manager Giulio Gatti-Casazza was that for some years they pursued a policy of giving a chance to American opera composers. Thus it was that Horatio Parker's "Mona" came to be heard, and Henry Hadley's "Cleopatra's Night."

GIULIO GATTI-CASAZZA

The latter was miscast, while "Mona" was, as a wag suggested, "too Mona-tonously like an oratorio."

Its cast included a bear which, for reasons known only to itself, made a vicious lunge at Hertz, the conductor, whenever he came near.

"Perhaps he thinks Hertz is the composer," Halperson of the *Staatszeitung* suggested wickedly.

Among other American operas produced at the Metropolitan was Reginald De Koven's "Canterbury Tales." Concerning this, which its composer, so I was told, considered the best opera since "Carmen," I wrote a criticism which so displeased him that he sent a long telegram to the Editor of the *Post* in which he said I didn't even know the difference between major and minor! Poor Reggie! Maybe that was the reason why he applied for my place. He didn't get it; but he got the job held on the *World* by the witty "Ned," alias Edward, Ziegler. Ned, however, did not worry, for Kahn promptly appointed him associate manager of the Metropolitan.

On the whole, the American-Opera experiment at the Metropolitan had so little success that I don't blame Kahn and Gatti for giving it up as a bad job. I wish, though they had waited for the opera in preparation by John Powell, the Virginian super-pianist, so well-known for his negroid compositions. There is, fortunately, no color prejudice along the musical line.

Victor Herbert also had a chance at the Metropolitan with his "Madeleine," but it was a dead failure. In giving up Indians Herbert had made the fatal mistake of adopting as a model "Le Donne Curiose" and similar works by Wolf-Ferrari into which Toscanini had infused a brief span of life in New York.

In 1908, Arturo Toscanini had been brought over from Milan with Giulio Gatti-Casazza—or was it Arturo who brought over with him Giulio? I could never quite make out. All that I know for sure is that when Conried failed in health and became unable to attend to his duties, the Metropolitan directors who favored Italian opera imported these two men. Mr. Gatti gave so much satisfaction that he has held the fort ever since.

Fears that these two gentlemen from Milano would completely Italianize the Metropolitan were freely expressed. Conried had surely been sufficiently conciliatory when he devoted 272 of the operas given under him in five years to the Italian tongue, 217 to the German and only 60 to the French; would his successors reduce the German repertory also to the dimensions of the French?

These dismal forebodings were promptly and emphatically downed. Toscanini loved Wagner's operas beyond all others; he had done more than any one else to acclimate them among his countrymen; and as for Gatti-Casazza, he had, as manager of the Milan Scala, Italy's leading opera house, shown such partiality for these same operas that some of the chauvinistic newspapers fell upon him fiercely.

While the majority of the Metropolitan's directors undoubtedly favored Italian operas, the public had shown a noticeable partiality for Wagner's works. In order to conciliate this faction, Andreas Dippel was appointed comanager with Gatti-Casazza, to preside over the operas in German. For these he had his own orchestra and chorus with plenty of rehearsals. The result was that (to give a sample instance) "Lohengrin" was produced with a completeness of detail and perfection of ensemble surpassing even the Bayreuth performances. I was stirred particularly by certain choruses which are usually omitted because of their difficulty; as done under Dippel they were simply overwhelming in their grandeur.

For practical reasons this dual arrangement could not last; Dippel was dropped after the second season and the undivided authority passed on to Gatti-Casazza, with no detriment, as I have already intimated, to the cause of German opera. Let me add that to Dippel belongs the honor of having made us acquainted with Bohemia's best opera, Smetana's "The Bartered Bride," which revealed the glorious voice and rare dramatic art of Emmy Destinn to perfection.

Destinn, by the way, was usually listed among the German singers, but she is a Bohemian, which is quite another thing. One of the charms of her impersonation in the "Bartered Bride" was that she gave life-like pictures of Czech manners and customs. I never met her personally but I have letters of gratitude from her, as I have from nearly all the singers I heard in four decades that I could praise cordially. They all appreciated my policy of dwelling on the best things they did instead of the worst. The best things are the rare ones that call for mention.

Gatti-Casazza inherited from Conried a choice group of singers, including Sembrich, Eames, Farrar, Fremstad, Gadski, Morena, Homer, Bonci, Burgstaller, Burrian, Riccardo Martin, Reiss, Campanari, Mühlmann, Goritz, Blass, Scotti and Caruso. In his early years he also specialized in great conductors—giants like Toscanini, Polacco, Hertz, Mahler; the first three of these were actually for a few seasons busy at the Metropolitan at the same time! Those were golden days, but they did not last. When all three of these had departed I ceased to be voluntary and unpaid press-agent for the Metropolitan Opera House, except on special occasions.

May I reveal an office secret? Perhaps the fact that I was much more apt to praise than censure made my occasional censure the more stinging. At any rate, it happened over and over again that when I had made a disagreeable remark about a Metropolitan performance, an official deputation consisting of two or three High-

Muck-a-Mucks was sent to 20 Vesey St. to protest to the editor or the proprietor against my manifest wickedness and total depravity. It was not a very dignified thing to do, was it? And if I had had a speck of vanity in my make-up, it would have made me insufferably conceited to find so much importance attached to a line or a paragraph of mine. But the *Post* was a power in the land.

In the case under consideration *a single word* had sufficed to bring down the official deputation! I had accused the rulers of "eliminating" the Metropolitan's three great conductors. *Eliminating!* Red rag to a bull! I was asked to retract that word. I surely must have known that they had "resigned voluntarily?" But I didn't; in fact I knew that Hertz was heart-broken because Artur Bodanzky, alleged to be a protégé and importation of Otto H. Kahn, was taking his place. I knew, too, that Polacco's engagement ran another year—he brought suit to get the salary therefor.

So I refused to retract the word "eliminate" as far as it referred to these two men; but I did retract it as regards Toscanini. To this day I don't know why he left the Metropolitan, no doubt voluntarily. Did he have ambitions to become artistic director and dictator? Was he dissatisfied because he could not always get all the rehearsals he wanted? Was he huffy because while his conducting of "Tristan and Isolde" was universally acclaimed as marvelous, his "Meistersinger" was considered too rigid for a comic opera—too unyielding toward the singers? Did he want *all* the Wagner operas, loth to share them with a Hertz, a Mahler, a Bodanzky? I don't know.

I don't believe that even Max Smith knows just why Toscanini left the Metropolitan—Max, formerly the able critic of the New York *American,* who had been for years in constant communication with him, orally, by letter and

From Sculpture by Onorio Ruotolo

ARTURO TOSCANINI

telegraphically, telephonically, telescopically and tele-
pathically. I asked him about it the other day (July,
1925) in Milan, his idol's home town. He thought Toscanini left New York primarily because he did not find the
conditions favorable for carrying out his artistic ideals.

Max then took us around by the stage entrance into
the Scala Theater to see and hear the great conductor
rehearsing his orchestra for a Swiss concert tour. It was
astonishing to see how quickly he made his men grasp his
intentions. When things went badly he shook his fists at
them; when particularly well, he applauded. I heard
that Hertz was coming in a few days to attend these
rehearsals; was sorry to miss him.

During the intermission Toscanini came down for a
chat with us. To my surprize he spoke English, and
fluently. When I met him the first time, in New York,
he spoke only Italian and French. On that occasion I
told him that it was his illuminating interpretations which
had first opened my ears to the manifold beauties of Puccini's scores. He even made me like "Cavalleria Rusticana." Evidently the age of miracles is not gone by.

END OF THE GOLDEN AGE

The golden age of opera lasted well into the first years
of the new régime; then it turned into silver—sometimes
even brass and tin. The disappearance of giant conductors was followed gradually by the disappearance of giant
singers. We were told there were no more giants; but
did not Hammerstein and the Chicago Company discover
them aplenty? Sembrich, Eames and Nordica were still
almost at their best when they left—left because the atmosphere for prima donnas was not the same it had been
in the days of Grau.

Grau worshiped his prima donnas; at any rate, he

acted as if he did, which amounted to the same thing. He let them dictate their own terms, make their own conditions, and practically run the show to suit themselves. He paid them big sums cheerfully, knowing that they more than earned them, for the house was always full and he was amassing a fortune. But not all mortals are as complacent as Grau was; some like to run their own show, to make it clear that they are boss in their own house. Apparently that was what happened at the Metropolitan. Here is what the historian of Opera in New York says:*

"About the middle of the season Mr. Gatti made it known that the war had brought with it what seemed to him the psychological moment for a reform which would look toward the emancipation of the institution from the exorbitant demands of singers. . . . A great deal of gossip was created by the fact that Signor Caruso would cut his season short in order to sing at Monte Carlo." The directors promptly declared that the "reform" was not aimed at him, and he did not go to Monte Carlo. Had they heard from the subscribers?

Next to Caruso in popularity was Geraldine Farrar. Beside him, she alone could be counted on to fill the house no matter what was the opera or the rest of the cast. She was the last representative of the Grau prima-donna-rule, which was doomed. But she was obliging; she had complacently limited herself for several seasons to seven or eight of her most profitable rôles. She hoped to return the following season to two of her very best parts, Elizabeth in "Tannhäuser" and the Goose-Girl in "Königskinder"; for this she had won, almost unaided, the biggest of all successes of the season 1910-11.

This dream of a revival remained a dream, and as for Elizabeth, that was given to Maria Jeritza. Friends of Farrar began to suspect that she was to be disciplined and

* "More Chapters of Opera in New York," by H. E. Krehbiel. P. 333.

humiliated when she was not chosen to open the following season, although her seniority, her rank, and her profitableness to the management entitled her to that privilege. It was given to Amelita Galli-Curci, who told me herself that she accepted it unwillingly because she felt it belonged to Farrar, the Metropolitan's foremost artist since Caruso's death.

One day when my wife and I were lunching with Geraldine, she told us about other ominous things. Her contract was expiring. Theretofore, when that was the case, she had always been approached many months in advance for a renewal, but this time nothing had been done so far. Evidently her wings were to be clipped, but her employers did not realize what they were up against. Without waiting for their offer she flew to Boston with unclipped wings and told Charlie Ellis that she was at last ready to accept his oft-repeated offer for a concert tour. The contract was signed on the spot—a contract assuring her larger emoluments than even the Opera had paid; and when Gatti came with his contract she quietly told him it was too late.

Thus New York lost its favorite prima donna in the height of her popularity and glory. The scenes of frenzied enthusiasm at her farewell performances are indescribable. Used as she was to ovations, she was simply dazed and overwhelmed—breathless, as she afterwards told us, and almost unable to stand on her feet.

Maria Jeritza

Being business men—though not particularly astute ones—the Metropolitan's rulers of course had had no desire to lose their most profitable artist. They knew Farrar's high spirits. Doubtless they would not have played so risky a game had they not felt sure that their latest acquisition would make amends for whatever might happen.

This new artist was Jeritza, the operatic idol of Vienna. Like other opera-goers, Otto H. Kahn became enthusiastic when he saw and heard her at the Opera there, and promptly engaged her for New York. Here she won instant and huge success although the opera in which she made her début ("The Dead City"), while it enabled her to display her wonderful hair to advantage (the plot might have been suggested by a hair-dresser) did not give her opportunity to display her voice to best advantage. It impressed me as a voice of agreeable quality which had been damaged by neglect of the higher education such as Sembrich, for instance, might have given, and I said so. In her acting too, there were exaggerations which suggested the vaudeville stage. My criticisms were rather severe—more severe, perhaps, than they would have been had I not felt that this Austrian had been imported as a cudgel to beat and discipline America's favorite opera singer.

A war of prima donnas is one of the things opera-goers dote on. Wild rumors soon were set industriously afloat. One of them asserted that Geraldine, after witnessing Maria's triumph as Tosca, had promptly modified her conception of that part radically. The only objection to this tale was that Geraldine had not seen Maria's Tosca and that her own version of it (Sarah Bernhardt was her coach) had been just as vehemently applauded many a time.

In the meantime, quick to take a hint, Jeritza had become a pupil of Sembrich. In her entertaining Memoirs there is a long chapter about these lessons. Soon I had other proof that the new prima donna had the instincts and aspirations of a true artist. Her Thaïs did not please my wife or me and we wrote together a whole column to explain why. (My wife had attended nearly all the truly

JERITZA AS "TOSCA"

Parisian performances given with Mary Garden and Renaud at the Manhattan.)

The morning after this appeared I was called up on the telephone by Josef Stransky, conductor of the Philharmonic Orchestra. "I was visiting Jeritza yesterday when the *Evening Post* was brought in," he said. "After reading your article on her Thaïs she threw herself on the sofa and sobbed half an hour. Suddenly she got up and exclaimed: 'He is right! I had no one to tell me those things in advance. I want to know that man! I can learn from him.'"

"Would you come to my house some day and meet her?" Stransky continued.

"I should be glad to meet her," I said, "but wouldn't it be rather awkward after what I have written?"

"Oh no! She doesn't bear you the least ill will. She feels grateful."

After this revelation of a noble artistic character I did not hesitate to go. We met Jeritza at Stransky's and soon became good friends. Her singing, under Sembrich's guidance, improved by leaps and bounds, so that she could safely undertake a concert tour, which would have been impossible before those "finishing lessons"; and soon I was able to write about her in a different tone altogether. She had worked to conquer, although there was no need of her doing so, for the public was hers from the start. But how much better the rough diamond looked after its polishing!

I shall never forget the delightful way she sang, at a New York concert, Grieg's "The Swan," in an orchestral arrangement made by Stransky. Grieg himself would have been enchanted, and Sembrich herself could not have improved on it. Jeritza had been "saved from her friends," who had acclaimed her with all her faults. I acclaimed her after her faults had been eliminated. I was particularly pleased, too, with her improvement in facial expression. At the climax of the second act of "Tannhäuser," when Elizabeth intercedes for the sinful Knight, the play of her features was as subtle as Farrar's.

For this American, Jeritza had unbounded admiration, especially her Butterfly. The first time I chatted with her she told me she had already seen it three times and talked longer about this than anything else. She regretted the foolish newspaper stories about rôles taken from Farrar and given to her. As a matter of fact the only Farrar part which Jeritza sang was Tosca, and Farrar continued to sing it too. Who was responsible for all the idiotic newspaper tales about these two singers?

BORI, EASTON AND GALLI-CURCI

Among the artists who, during the consulship of Giulio Gatti-Casazza, most frequently gladdened my soul were Lucrezia Bori and Florence Easton, one Spanish the other English. I have related how I once made a special trip to Spain to study the beauty and grace of her women and wrote an article about it for *Scribner's*. Had I known of Señorita Bori and her coming to New York I might have saved myself all that trouble and expense. To see her fascinating poses and graceful gestures in the rôle which made her famous, Fiora in Montemezzi's "Love of Three Kings," was to witness an epitome of all the most alluring attributes of Spanish womanhood. Add to this her uniquely refined artistic personality and the impression was overwhelming.

"What do you do to make Mr. Finck write so rapturously about you?" Mr. Gatti more than once said to Miss Bori. That was before I knew her personally; unfortunately I did not meet her till two seasons before I gave up newspaper work. We then dined with her and found her as attractive off the stage as on. She spoke French like a *Parisienne,* and Italian fluently. But her Spanish! I thought I knew that language *un poquito,* but when I heard her rattle it off at the rate of fifty-seven miles a minute I took refuge in French and English—yes, she speaks English too.

Her triumphant career in New York was most unfortunately interrupted a few years by an operation on her throat which for a time made her admirers fear it had ended her career altogether. There was great joy when she returned with her voice actually improved. I remember how, when she first came to the Metropolitan, Miss Farrar was reported to have been somewhat disturbed by rumors that the Spanish soprano was a duplicate of herself and even "more so." There was something in these rumors; often, in enjoying the art of Bori with eyes and ears I was reminded of Geraldine in her less intense moods. She was the American Farrar translated into Barcelonese. You can imagine how she is adored in Spain; but Spain could not have added $100,000 a year to her bank account. In such cases patriotism must be modest in its claims.

Bori's Juliette was a treat to remember; so was her Snow Maiden. In Mozart's "Cosi Fan Tutte" she revealed a rare vein for comedy. She is in her best years and seems destined to become *the* favorite at the Metropolitan.

Florence Easton had to struggle for a foothold at this institution but after a thorough trying out she was found almost indispensable because of her versatility; in Italian opera, in French, in Wagner, she was always at home. I enjoyed particularly her impersonation in Liszt's "Legend of Saint Elizabeth," for producing which masterwork I take off my hat to Mr. Gatti-Casazza.

Her resonant, agreeable voice at its best reminded me often of Nordica's—there can be no higher praise.

The most remarkable thing about Easton is not her versatility or her voice but the fact that she is an English woman who recklessly displays an ardent temperament. She sings emotionally, thrillingly. In England, you know, the display of emotion has always been considered bad form; that's why great opera singers in that country are scarce. Easton's "bad form" has changed her from a mere singer to a great artist.

A genuine artist, furthermore, is Amelita Galli-Curci, but she is not always a good singer. She is actually, what many singers are not, a *musician;* she might have made a reputation as a violinist or pianist. That, however, is not what made her famous. Her popularity is due to the fact that she is that *rara avis,* a florid soprano. While composers no longer write colorature arias with runs and trills and roulades and dainty staccati up in the air, the public still loves them; and when a singer comes along who can do them it "says it" with crowded houses and frantic applause. Flaws are disregarded. Galli-Curci often sings distressingly out of tune but her Eiffel tower staccati are true to pitch; they are the business end of her voice and they have given her an income rivaling Caruso's.

Nothing annoys me so much as exaggeration. I fulminated against those who placed this new singer on a level with Patti—Patti, the model of pure intonation. I pointed out that an American girl, Lucy Gates, granddaughter of Brigham Young, has a lovelier voice than Galli-Curci and as great a facility of execution, *besides* the gift of singing in tune always; but the craze over Galli-Curci continued.

She is, as I have said, an artist; her lovely Juliette alone would prove that. She is also a lady, and she is kind-hearted—and forgiving! When I met her, first at one of Mrs. Frederick Steinway's famous dinners, and afterwards, on the steamer *Paris,* she showed not the slightest

GALLI-CURCI AS "GILDA" IN "RIGOLETTO"

resentment at my rather violent criticisms; so we became quite chummy; our common interest in gardening supplied an inexhaustible topic of conversation. She specializes in cauliflower and promised to send me, from her home in the Catskills, a crate of her choicest when I get back to Bethel, Maine. No bribe here, if you please! She was aware that I am no longer a professional critic! (Schumann-Heink once sent me a box of oranges from her California ranch. I think I deserved more than one.)

Galli-Curci knows of course that she often sings out of tune and wishes she didn't. But she doesn't know why her intonation is at fault any more than you do, or I, or her husband, with whom I talked the matter over on the steamer for a whole hour. The thing is a complete mystery; all theories fail to explain it, most of all the one he seems to favor.

A BUNCH OF SINGERS

Bori, Easton and Galli-Curci have been among Gatti's worth-while singers. Among the others heard under him during twelve seasons are Maria Barrientos, whose small but exquisite Spanish voice gave much delight, particularly in Rimsky-Korsakoff's adorable opera "The Golden Cock," in which she sang the highly ornamental part of the Princess far better than did Galli-Curci or any other vocalist; Frieda Hempel, Berlin's favorite colorature singer but preferred in New York in lyric parts, in which, for vocal beauty and refined style, she had few equals; the golden-voiced Roumanian beauty, Alma Gluck; Marie Delna, the famous French prima donna; Claudia Muzio; the Australian, Frances Alda; the great Olive Fremstad; the Hungarian giant, Margaret Matzenauer; the Americans, Edith Mason, Mabel Garrison, Marie Rappold, Marie Sundelius, Sophie Braslau, Anna Case, Anna Fitziu and Louise Homer; the Germans, Melanie Kurt, Elizabeth Rethberg, Margarete Ober, Berta Morena, Barbara Kemp and Johanna Gadski, whose pure and genuine soprano voice was a rare treat after the attempts of diverse contraltos to sing the Wagnerian heroines—to play them, so to speak, with viola instead of violin.

Conspicuous among Gatti's singers of the male persuasion were Burrian, Slezak, Gigli, Martinelli, Dinh Gilly, Chamlee, Riccardo Martin, Edward Johnson, Witherspoon, Whitehill, Carl Braun, Mühlmann, Sembach, Griswold, Ananian, Amato, Rothier, Bada, De Luca, Bonci, Bender, Bohnen and the incomparable Chaliapin, who, however, never was a regular member of the company and appeared only occasionally in his unforgettable impersonations in "Boris Godounoff," "Mefistofele," "Faust" and the "Barber of Seville."

A goodly list of singers as it stands, but they were not all of the same time, and at no time were there enough of the big ones to keep up the Grau standard of all-star casts which made his age the Golden Age.

It almost makes me shudder to recall the names of the new operas staged during the consulship of Gatti-Casazza; most of them bring back memories of cruel boredom. To name a few of them, at random: "La Wally," "Le Villi," "Lodoletta," "Cyrano de Bergerac," "Canterbury Pilgrims," "Julien," "Le Donne Curiose," "Il Segreto di Susanna," "L'Amore Medico," "Mona," "Madeleine," "Pipe of Desire," "Germania," "Francesca da Rimini," "Mme. Sans-Gêne," "Marouf," etc.,—none of these were worth staging, in my humble opinion; but I don't much blame the manager. Operas worth staging are scarce.

On the other hand there were operas like "The Golden Cock," "Snow Maiden," "Girl of the Golden West," "Koenigskinder," "Goyescas," "Prince Igor," "Lobetanz," "Der Rosenkavalier," "Mona Lisa," "Pique

Dame," "Ariane et Barbe-Bleue," "Boris Godounoff,"
"L'Oracolo" (which provided the incomparable Antonio
Scotti with almost as fine opportunities to reveal his subtle
art of acting and singing as "Tosca"), "Saint Elizabeth,"
"La Navarraise," "Le Roi de Lahore," "Suor Angelica"
and "L'Oiseau Bleu," which brought over its composer
Albert Wolf, so that for a time New York had a first-class
Frenchman to interpret the French operas—till he was
lured back to Paris by the offer of the directorship of the
Opéra-Comique. I feel deeply grateful to the Metropolitan's manager for giving me the opportunity to hear
them. I like, also, to recall the superb new settings Gatti
gave to some of the old favorites, including "Carmen" and
"Faust." The latter was revived in the latest Parisian version at my urgent request, and William J. Guard, the
press-agent, wrote to express the hope I would be satisfied.
I was—emphatically so.

I was disappointed not to find the same compacency
when I urged the engagement of Eduard Möricke, a second Seidl, to conduct the Wagner operas at the Metropolitan in place of Artur Bodanzky, who seemed tired of them
and, anyway, conducted them too much à la Brahms, which
was unkind of him. There were in the Berlin Opera Company with which Möricke came, half a dozen singers better
than most of the Germans at the Metropolitan. And why
were not those superlative artists, Maria Ivogün and Sig-
rid Onegin at once added to the singers at that house?
It seemed to me as great a mystery as the failure to
engage Lucy Gates after her brilliant début in the little
opera "La Serva Padrona" with the Society of American
Singers.

Over the question of engaging Maurice Renaud I waged
a fierce war with Kahn and Gatti. Both admitted to me,
verbally and in letters, that there was no greater artist
on the stage, yet he was not engaged. There was always,

it seemed to me, an indisposition at this house to engage high-priced Frenchmen, like Clément (who sang only a few times), Muratore, and the great Renaud. Besides, there was Signor Amato to be considered!

Repeatedly Mr. Kahn invited me to a downtown lunch and we discussed the matter amicably, but nothing came of these peace conferences, à la Locarno.

KAHN AND GATTI AS HUMORISTS

It may not be generally known that King Gatti-Casazza and his all-powerful Prime Minister, Otto Kahn, are a pair of humorists who play into each other's hands, like Weber and Fields. One of their favorite contentions, judging by newspaper interviews, is that a smooth ensemble is preferable to all-star casts. Maybe it is, but a perfect ensemble must be the exception in an opera house where thirty or forty works have to be pitch-forked onto the stage in a few months. A man who is busy behind the scenes said to me that if he told all he knew about "rehearsals" and "ensembles" he simply wouldn't be believed. Miss Farrar informed me she couldn't get even one full rehearsal for "La Navarraise." So all this talk about ensembles is but a joke, if not a "scream." Geraldine, at nearly every appearance in a favorite rôle, had to adapt herself without a rehearsal to another tenor—including some of those awful creatures Gatti (who allowed Riccardo Martin to go) used to import from Italy. (One of these was publicly denounced at a rehearsal by Toscanini as *un porco.*)

It was in the case of Renaud, however, that I most fully realized the humorous subtleties of Otto H. Kahn and Giulio Gatti-Casazza. Whenever I tried to get a concession from the first, he protested that the directors were not allowed to interfere with the manager, while the manager in turn averred he could do nothing without the consent of the directors. So all my efforts to secure for my epicurean soul the opportunity to see and hear Renaud at the Metropolitan went for nought.

Everything done at the Metropolitan had to be O. K.'d by Otto Kahn (without whose cooperation, by the way, no musical undertaking in America seems to think it can flourish). In view of my frequent disapproval of his plans I am proud to say he generously O.K.'d me too! In a letter dated March 14, 1921, he wrote: "Though as you mention, your views and mine have not always been in full accord, may I say that I have always admired particularly three of your qualifications: your broad and profound musical (and general) culture, your courageous independence of judgment and expression, and your rare and fine capacity, after many years on the 'listening post' in concert halls and opera houses, to be thrilled by art and artists, and to command a freshness, warmth and sincerity of emotion which to most mortals is only vouchsafed, if at all, in the short years of the springtime of their lives."

This testimonial bears witness to the fact that while I deplored the disregard of the Grau traditions in the matter of casts I was always ready to enthuse in my column when Gatti gave a performance of the golden-age kind, which he often did. This is further proved by what William J. Guard, the incomparable press-agent, first of Oscar Hammerstein (who owed much of his success to him) and subsequently of the Metropolitan, wrote about me to the *Evening Post* when I retired from journalism: "There were times when he would 'pan' us but—although we had to keep a sober face—quite often he was justified, especially as he regarded our institution as occupying a position that demanded the humanly best.

"On the other hand, when we did something that was worthy of our best traditions, who among all his colleagues gave way to such enthusiasm as Henry T. Finck? That was one of his charms. Had you not known his age you might easily have exclaimed: 'There you are! See how that young fellow in the *Evening Post* lets himself go! He sure did enjoy the performance and he doesn't blush to say so.'"

As for manager Gatti, he too seemed to remember my frequent praise better than my censures, and my occasional intimation that he was giving $3 opera for $7 a seat because the house would be filled anyway by the hundred thousand visitors that come to New York every day. He continued to honor us with an occasional call at 485 Manhattan Avenue, and after I had left New York I received from him in Paris a postcard with this pleasant message: *"I piu cordiali saluti ed auguri a Mme. Finck e a voi da Giulio Gatti-Casazza."*

WAR-TIME OPERA

During the World War the Metropolitan Opera House presented for a time a ludicrously inconsistent spectacle. Richard Wagner's operas were banished, while "Martha" and "The Prophet" remained in the repertory.

See anything funny in that? You will if you know a few things about operatic history in Berlin. The composer of "Martha," Friedrich, Freiherr von Flotow, of the Archduchy of Mecklenburg, was so much liked at the Prussian Court that he was made Hofmusikintendant. The composer of "The Prophet" was a Prussian Jew who was so great a favorite of King Friedrich Wilhelm that he was appointed Generalmusikdirektor. His name was Jacob Meyerbeer.

On the other hand, Richard Wagner was never a favorite of any Prussian monarch. He was a revolutionist to the core, who pleaded for the abolition of monarchy and detested German militarism. He hated the Prussians and particularly Berlin, where he had been brutally maltreated. For twelve years he was a political exile; had he been caught on German soil he would have been imprisoned and probably shot for taking part in the revolutionary uprising of 1848. In his dislike of the Prussians, Wagner was, all his life, as much one of the Allies as if he had been a Frenchman, an Englishman or an American. In a letter to Mathilde Wesendonck he wrote: "I am much afraid I am losing all my patriotism, and being secretly delighted if the Germans receive another sound thrashing."

Yet this arch-hater of Prussia and Prussianism was kicked out of the Metropolitan when we entered the war against Prussia, while the Prussian court-pets Flotow and Meyerbeer remained. I am glad to say that Gatti and Kahn were not to blame for this absurdity and injustice. They tried to keep Wagner in the repertory, but adverse directorial and outside influences prevailed and Wagner was made the musical scapegoat for the Huns.

In the concert halls also there was much foolishness, which I combated with all my might and main. There were days during the war when, if I could have done so, I would have eagerly touched a button that would have exterminated every man in the German Empire. Yet that did not make me turn my back on the music of the Germans. "It's the best thing by far they have given the world and we can make it all our own," I argued. "In return for all the looting the Germans have done, why shouldn't we loot their music? If we avoid it, we do *them* no harm but deprive ourselves of much pleasure." And I cited the French officer who said: "We are making war on the Germans, not on their music."

To Josef Stransky belongs the honor of being the first to break the ban on Wagner in the concert halls of New

York and to Giorgio Polacco for doing the same in Chicago. I remember the extraordinary enthusiasm aroused by Stransky when he smashed the silly boycott with some Wagner pieces on his Philharmonic program. There was not a sound of disapproval.

Right here let me come to the defense of the American public, which was censured by foreigners for making war on German music whereas *they* acted rationally. As a matter of fact the American *public* had little to do with this matter. After much Sherlock Holmes detective work I concluded that the whole rumpus was caused chiefly by one woman and two men, who cowed all the musicians by swinging the "patriotic" club over their heads. When I threw the limelight of truth on this matter I received ardent letters of thanks from many musicians, including the eminent pianist and pedagog, Harold Bauer.

My story of the opera has reached its end.

The future is uncertain. Great singers are getting scarcer and scarcer and as for operas, there are no new ones that hold their own. Look at the repertories in New York, Paris, London, Berlin, Vienna, everywhere; always the same list of some twenty favorites repeated over and over again—a damnable iteration which is one reason why I gave up musical journalism. In Germany, France, England, Italy, we search in vain for a new operatic masterwork that can hold its own.

Shall we look to America for relief? Not if we judge the future by the past. But I place hope in Ernest Schelling, a master musician who has turned to this form of art after winning tremendous praise as pianist and orchestral composer, and in Deems Taylor, whose delightfully entertaining orchestral works also display Schelling's truly operatic instinct for illustrating picturesque happenings with appropriate music.

Percy Grainger

I have often wished that Percy Grainger—now an American, though he was born in Australia and came to us via England—had the operatic bee in his bonnet. But let us be grateful that we can enjoy him in our concert halls. Truth to tell, Percy is a whole opera in himself. If you have ever attended one of his recitals you will know what I mean. I shall never forget his initial recital in New York.

In appearance somewhat resembling Paderewski in his youth, he came on the stage briskly—"as if he was starting on a twenty-mile walk" as my neighbor exclaimed; and in less than half an hour he had convinced his critical audience that he belongs in the same rank as Paderewski and Kreisler, sharing their artistic ability, and yet as unique as they are—something new and *sui generis*.

England knew him before we did; it was one of the most famous London critics, John F. Runciman, who wrote: "Percy Grainger stands alone. He is the one cheerful, sunny composer living." And perhaps, as another writer has said, "it is essentially the joyous and ecstatic personality that permeates all his work (be it poetic and dreamy, or exhilarating and boisterous) to which the young Australian owes the almost unparalleled speed with which his choral, orchestral, chamber, vocal and piano compositions have attained to world-wide popularity since their first publication in 1912." England had seldom seen anything like it; his "Mock Morris" alone had some 500 orchestral performances in one year.

Following the example of Schumann when he first came across a piece by Chopin, I wrote "Hats Off! A Genius!" over my article on Percy's New York début. He began with Bach—an arrangement by Busoni (who was one of his teachers) of an organ prelude and fugue in D major. "And what a Bach!" I wrote. "The pianist made the contrapuntal network as clear to the ear of even the un-initiated as a piece of Venetian lace is to everybody's eyes. No less astonishing were the opulence and variety of his tone—his instrument seemed both piano and organ—and he showed at once, as he did in several other pieces fol-lowing this, that he can build up a climax as gradually and overwhelmingly on the piano as Anton Seidl did with his Wagnerian orchestra. The audience was stunned, be-wildered, delighted. Seldom, if ever, has a Bach fugue been so riotously applauded, and no wonder: he made it appeal to *all*—making it as real and up-to-date as the latest dance or opera."

In this quotation I have substituted *riotously* (ap-plauded) for the "profusely" I used originally. Riotously is just the word to apply to the applause Grainger gets usually, especially when he plays his own pieces, such as the "Mock Morris Dance," "One More Day," "Walking Tune," "Shepherds Hey," "Irish Tune from County Derry," "Molly on the Shore," "Country Gar-den" and the soulful "Colonial Song," which expresses the feelings aroused in the composer by Australian scenes. Its plaintive undertone suggests that it is reminiscent with a touch of homesickness. It has the tenderness and depth which we find in the songs of America's two most original melodists, Stephen Foster ("Old Folks at Home") and Edward MacDowell.

Grainger, like MacDowell, fell madly in love with Grieg's music when he was a boy, and he came personally under his influence. Grieg, in turn was infatuated with this musical genius from Australia who, as he confessed, played his Scandinavian music more idiomatically than any Scandinavian did. His untimely death prevented him from carrying out his pet project of having his concerto—the most inspired concerto ever composed—played by Grainger on an extended European tour with himself conducting the orchestra. I would rather have heard that than anything I could think of.

Grieg's influence over Percy affected his whole career to its very marrow. From him he learned how to collect folk-songs in remote places and make artistic use of them. Several hundred he collected in England; their blood courses through his musical veins. Yes, while Grainger is now an American citizen, I fear we can never claim him as an American composer. His music is English to the core. When Kurt Schindler and the Damrosch brothers first made known in New York some of his choral works I exclaimed rapturously that they were "the best things that had ever come to us from England."

But hold on! Percy Grainger is a contradictory individual. One time, when he was visiting us in Maine, I said to him: "It's a glorious morning, Percy, come into the garden with me." "No thank you, Henry," he replied. "When I am in the country I prefer to be indoors." And he sprawled on the sofa on his stomach and penned a magazine article which he had promised.

Don't imagine from this that Percy is an indoors man —heaven forbid! He loves to do things—extraordinary things—outdoors more than anywhere else in the world. Read this from an Australian letter to me dated Adelaide, July 31, 1924: "I had a glorious walk in the desert, 80 miles in 3 days, carrying 42 pounds pack and sleeping out two lovely nights. I enclose you an account of it."

The following extract from a letter written to me by his mother throws further light on this point. "After his recital at Los Angeles all the receptions given in his honor, the invitations, callers, etc., we were nearly killed with kindness and hospitality and felt quite worn out, so Percy found out this desert place, Barstow, on the map and we

came here (on the Sante Fe Railroad) on chance for five
days' rest and holiday between his recitals to find the best
hotel we have struck and the cheapest, quiet, wonderful
scenery, air and atmosphere. The sunrises and sunsets,
the coloring of the hills and the snow-clad mountains in
the distance, the queer growths, trees, shrubs, most beautiful wild flowers and grasses fill us with joy and delight. . . .

"Percy was so happy here; we motored into the hills
and he sketched the scenery, and we lay out of doors in
the blood-warm air, in the shade, for the sun was very hot.
The nights and mornings are cool. The whole thing reminded us of parts of Australia and of parts of the Riviera.
I want Percy to buy a little summer home at Santa Fé
as this is the climate for us. We can never get away from
the atmosphere we were accustomed to when young, can
we? And this is so much like the dry, hot parts of Australia; but it is grander and more strange. The tears
were in Percy's eyes when saying good-bye to me and
to our happy holiday."

All this furnishes an amusing commentary on Percy's
remark "When I am in the country I prefer to be indoors."
That remark was thoroughly characteristic: he is a bundle
of contradictions, personally and in his compositions.
From what I have said of them you would think they were
mostly of the simple mellifluous folk-music order, but
most of them are not, and many of them are as intricate
and almost as dissonantal and "futuristic" as Stravinsky's
or Scriabin's. Yet even in these ultra-modern works his
gift of popular melody does not desert him; and that
makes a fascinating combination.

As a teacher, Grainger belongs in the rank of Liszt;
and he comes right next to Liszt as an altruist, always
doing things to help other musicians on their path. Once
more, he has followed in the footsteps of Liszt in introducing in the orchestra new uses for instruments of per-

PERCY GRAINGER

cussion and even employing entirely new ones symphoni-
cally, like the American Deagan percussion instruments,
which suggest the quaintly exotic music of South Sea
Islanders that Percy loves. There are grand possibilities
along that line for the music of the future.

Some years ago one of the most enterprising New York
publishers, Alfred A. Knopf, asked me to write a book
on Percy, but I replied he was still too near the beginning
of his career; and when the time comes for such a volume
I shall be too old to write it. Therefore I vote "unani-
mously" that my friend Charles L. Buchanan, author,
critic and philosopher should do that book. Of all com-
mentators he has written the most illuminating articles on
Percy.

"What I see in Grainger," he declares, "is a new age
expressing itself. With all his partiality for what is
vague, sensuous, subtle and ingratiating in art, he is,
nevertheless, to me the incarnation of the bustle, the
activity, the cheeky, breezy, informal quality of young and
new peoples." And Buchanan does not claim too much
when he says that "Grainger's contribution to the sheerly
instrumental side of his art is obviously far and away the
most important development in contemporary symphonic
music."

As soon as Percy came to New York I began the "press-
agent" work I delight in doing when I come across a new
genius. He refers to this in a letter dated September 18,
1916: "It is too miraculous the way you manage to wedge
old P. G. into the most unpromising looking openings in
your stunning weekly writings! No matter what the subject, I soon see my name looming along, and if I fail to
become a 'household word' it will certainly not be *your*
fault! It is lucky to be one of the artists to whom your
pure and brave heart goes out. . . . I have never met any
really critical soul who at the same time has your obviously

creative mind, and that is no doubt why your word sways thousands of readers as no other writer's and why you penetrate the inner soul of a giant like Grieg in the way you do."

THREE MILLIONAIRES

After one of Grainger's early appearances in New York I met Edward J. De Coppet, the founder of the famous Flonzaley Quartet, who was all aglow with enthusiasm. "Why," he exclaimed, "he's the greatest of them all!" Then, after a pause, he added: "He plays the piano wonderfully, but, after all, with such a creative gift, should he not devote himself to that altogether?" "I wish he could," I answered, "but creative work in the musical world is, as you know, not particularly profitable."

He nodded his head significantly and not long afterwards I heard that he had offered Percy a liberal annuity if he wished to give up playing and teaching and devote himself entirely to composing. Like MacDowell under similar circumstances, he declined the generous offer, feeling no doubt that as a pianist he could much sooner get into close touch with the musical public.

Never was there a man who made more generous use of his millions than Mr. De Coppet. When I collected funds for poor demented MacDowell he contributed a large sum with the message: "If you need more, come to me again." After reading my book "Food and Flavor" he followed some of my suggestions about using flavor as an appetizer and received so much benefit from them that he sent me a check for $500 for the purpose of advertising the book so that others might be similarly benefited.

His great work was the founding of the Flonzaley Quartet and its fostering till it became one of the leading institutions in musical America. On this he spent hundreds of thousands before it became a self-supporting rival of the Kneisel Quartet.

Before this Maecenas—who reminded me of Esterhazy and the Princes who advanced the cause of music with their private bands—launched the Flonzaleys, the Kneisel Quartet was the only first-class permanent organization of its kind in America. I have already written of Kneisel, but wish to add a story. I sometimes went to his home for dinner and to listen afterwards to a rehearsal of some novelty. On one of these occasions Kneisel took me upstairs to see the twins, Franz and Fritz. "This," he said to me, "is Fritz and this is Franz." "Excuse me," said the nurse "but *this* one is Fritz and *that* one Franz."

The second of my three multimillionaires is Charles M. Schwab, the steel king, who can, among many other things, boast the distinction of having been the highest-paid employee of all time: Carnegie gave him a million dollars a year, and considered him cheap at that. Subsequently Schwab played with millions as boys play with marbles.

By great good luck he liked good music. He became interested in the Bach Festivals given in Bethlehem, Pennsylvania, under Dr. Fred Wolle, whose chorus included many employees of the steel works. Schwab's generosity made possible the engagement of the Philadelphia Orchestra for these festivals, and as the singing (after months of rehearsing) was incomparably fine, these Bach concerts drew their audiences from all states in the Union.

Busy though we New York critics were, some of us attended these festivals repeatedly. Thus came about an incident which could have happened only in America.

Having accepted the invitation to attend one of these festivals, I got a letter from Mr. Schwab asking me to make the trip to Bethlehem in his private car on the Lehigh Railroad. When I got to the car I found there two of my colleagues, Henderson of the *Sun* and Aldrich of the *Times;* also Dr. Lyman Abbott and other guests. We spent the time en route disposing of a sumptuous lunch. I narrowly escaped being put off the train because when the shad roes were passed (the season for them was about over), I referred to them as "The Last Roes of Summer."

Before we arrived, our host asked us when we would like to return to New York. Henderson said he was anxious to return that night but there was no train after the evening performance. "We'll see what we can do," said Mr. Schwab. He took us three critics to his home where, after an interesting talk about his career, we had dinner.

After the evening performance we were hustled into an auto and taken to the station. And there stood Schwab's private car with a big locomotive in front of it! In we went and off we started—there was no one else in the car but an attendant to take care of us three critics—and we made New York before one o'clock, on record time, beating even that of the Black Diamond Express.

Millionaire number three is Major Henry Lee Higginson, founder of the Boston Symphony Orchestra.

In the course of years I was honored by several letters from the Major. One of them was so peppery that it almost made me sneeze. It came about in this way: Another millionaire, Seth Low, knowing that I was an intimate friend of America's foremost composer, asked me to stop at his residence on my way uptown. There he showed me a circular asking for contributions to help MacDowell who was suffering from the brain disease which ended his life in 1905 after several years of helplessness. Mr. Low himself had put his name down for $1,000 and Andrew Carnegie had signed for another thousand. Though Mr. Low was no longer Mayor of New York he was a very busy man and so he asked me if I would take charge of the circular and get some more signatures. I said I would try, and then wrote eloquent letters to several prominent millionaires who were supposed to be interested in music.

Not one of them gave a cent. Somewhat discouraged, I determined to try Boston. Major Higginson naturally came to my mind first. I didn't tell him about my lack of success in New York but appealed to him as a well-known musical Maecenas. When I read his answer I mercifully remembered that he was a sufferer from gout and I fancy the East Wind helped to dictate that letter. The substance of it was that I ought to be ashamed of myself for appealing to him, who was already spending a fortune in behalf of music in America, when I was living in a city crammed with millionaires.

Once again I felt snubbed; but with the generous contribution of Mr. De Coppet and the invaluable aid of Victor Harris and Mr. Heffley and other good friends I succeeded nevertheless in raising the amount collected to $10,000. Many of MacDowell's pupils, after his death, went to Mr. Heffley, who was the first president of the New York MacDowell Club. Victor Harris was the most fashionable of voice teachers in New York. Seidl had paid him the compliment of choosing him as assistant conductor at the Brighton Beach Summer concerts. Afterwards he became conductor of the St. Cecilia Choir, the concerts of which I was occasionally privileged to enjoy. Nor shall I forget the dinners we had at his home whenever a friend in the South sent him some braces of red head ducks.

When Higginson brought Nikisch to Boston the orchestra had been so well-drilled by Gericke that Nikisch remarked, "All I have to do is to poetize."

And poetize he certainly did, from the very start. His début was considered so important an event that Higginson invited a bunch of us New York critics to come up to Boston for it. We went, paying our own fare. He invited us to a restaurant. As he was a millionaire, we expected to wash down with sparkling wine a lunch of choice delicatessen; but as nothing was forthcoming we ordered our own sandwiches and beer. His Puritan soul evidently shrank from the mere thought of bribing us with a lunch to praise Nikisch. But if he had treated us to white caviare, green turtle soup, broiled lobster, asparagus salad, camembert cheese, champagne and Bénédictine we could not have written more enthusiastically than we did about the new conductor; which proves that musical critics are not as black as they are painted.

Nikisch once wrote me a reproachful letter because I had told in the *Post* how, when he played Brahms's third symphony in Chickering Hall with his Boston Orchestra, the audience started an exodus which ended as a stampede. This symphony has never become a favorite but audiences have become inured to hardships; they no longer run away from it.

Philip Hale told the readers of the Boston *Herald* that whenever a Brahms symphony was played I either whiled away time by reading a book or looked for the nearest fire escape.

THREE BOSTON CRITICS

Before me lies a bundle of interesting letters which I wish I had room for in this volume, letters from the three leading Boston critics whom I had the privilege of numbering among my personal friends: Hale, Elson and

Apthorpe. Louis C. Elson's opinions almost always coincided with mine; I often wished he was on a New York paper to help fight my wars against Krehbiel and his allies. He wrote for the *Advertiser;* he was the most popular musical lecturer of the time and he taught in the New England Conservatory. From his pen came several books, the best of which makes me feel a little ashamed of myself. Doctor Van Dyck had asked me, in behalf of the Macmillan Co., to write a history of American music. I declined on the ground that there wasn't enough of it to go 'round. Then Elson was asked and he wrote a most interesting volume on the subject.

William F. Apthorpe's letters discuss all conceivable musical topics. One of them, touching on the sensualism of Jensen's song "Lean Thy Cheek Against My Cheek" (which I had included in the Ditson collection of "Fifty Mastersongs") isn't fit for print; the others are. I can not refrain from citing this delightful titbit: "One of the best things I ever heard was, when Hassard wrote back to the *Tribune,* after the first Bayreuth Festival, that 'Wagner had put the Beethoven symphony on the stage, and made it dramatic,' my friend B. J. Lang said: 'What rot! Wagner is not much like Bellini; but 'Götterdaemmerung' is a damned sight more like 'Norma' than it is like a Beethoven symphony!'"

On May 13, 1903, Philip Hale wrote me: "Apthorpe sails next week and will be in Europe two years or so for his health. I shall miss him sorely." He spent the last years of his life on the shore of Lake Geneva at Montreux where, by an odd coincidence, I am penning these words.

In the Hale letters before me nothing pleases me more than a reference to his sympathetic article on Grieg in Millet's volumes, "Music of the Modern World," with the assurance that if he wrote it again it would be "still more eulogistic."

There is so much wit and wisdom scattered about in Hale's newspaper articles that I repeatedly implored him to save some of his best things in book form. Elson had done this and Apthorpe, and his successor, Parker, why not he? But he replied: "My dear Finck, I shall not publish a book. If I could write an entertaining biography, as your Grieg or Wagner, and with your gusto, I might be tempted to make the trial; but mere collections of passing opinions, criticisms that prove stale in a day—whether they be signed by Reichardt in 1792, Hanslick in the Eighties or Krehbiel in 1908—those are tolerable neither to gods nor men. Besides, I am getting to admire the uncle of George Eliot's heroine who was 'of miscellaneous opinions and uncertain vote.'"

It was not in a personal letter but—what was better still—in the Boston *Herald* that Hale "sized me up" in a paragraph which I like so much that I hope it will be engraved, or at least pasted, on my tombstone (if I ever get one). For that purpose I herewith reprint it: "Mr. Finck has his idols—Wagner, Chopin, Grieg, Johann Strauss, Tchaikovsky, MacDowell, Jean de Reszke, Paderewski, Nordica—there are others—and he sings their praise in and out of season. He is ready to welcome a composer or singer of any nationality provided the stranger has some unusual or original characteristic. He is a sworn foe of routine. Conventional forms are to him as the abomination of desolation. His honesty is unquestioned; he is as brave as Ney; he declares his likes and dislikes, his theories and beliefs, with the bluntness of a child. He is a singular and fascinating mixture of catholicity and intolerance. His earnestness and sincerity and devotion to art command respect and wield an influence even where his deliberate opinion would seem wanton extravagance as coming from another." Thanks, Philip!

MY NEW YORK COLLEAGUES

In the course of four decades I was on friendly or intimate terms with some forty men and two women writing music criticisms for the New York newspapers. Among them were Mrs. Mary E. Bowman, Miss Emilie Frances Bauer, Albert Steinberg, Otto Floersheim, Marc A. Blumenberg, Henry Edward Krehbiel, William James Henderson, Richard Aldrich, James Gibbons Huneker, Edgar J. Levey, Willy von Sachs, Philip Gilbert Hubert, William H. Humiston, Max Smith, Leonard Liebling, Walter Kramer, Cesar Saerchinger, Carl Van Vechten, Charles L. Buchanan, Gustav Kobbé, John C. Freund, St. John Brennan, Pitts Sanborn, Reginald De Koven, Deems Taylor, Lawrence Gilman, Herbert F. Peyser, August Spanuth, Siegmund Spaeth, Edward Horsman, Clarence Lucas, Barron, William F. Chase, Olin Downs, Maurice Halperson, Ireneus Stevenson, Gilbert Gabriel, Pierre Key, Edward Ziegler, Sylvester Rawling, E. P. Jackson and Hillary Bell, or Billary Hell, as Jim Huneker used to call him.

Of several of these critics, whom I have named entirely at random without reference to rank or seniority, I have already spoken in the preceding pages. In the following thumb-nail sketches I name others at random.

On the whole the quality of the critical work done in my day was remarkably good—I do not except my own! By writing readable stories about musical events we induced the newspaper proprietors to give more space and a more conspicuous position to musical comments. I remember the time when the London *Times,* though it had a first-class critic—Doctor Francis Hueffer—printed his contributions among the market reports, or wherever else a little space could be found for them, and in the smallest type. Today that newspaper features its musical columns and sets them in large type. A similar change took place in the newspapers of New York, and for this I think my colleagues and I may fairly hold ourselves responsible.

Among my earliest critic friends was the witty Steinberg who used only one match a day for his scores of cigarets. Another pioneer was Otto Floersheim, who helped me start the Wagner propaganda. The proudest day of his life was when Paderewski played one of his compositions. He subsequently went to Germany. Having come back on a visit, I still see him standing in Carnegie Hall and, while listening to a certain conductor, moving his right hand like an organ-grinder and whispering in my ear "Immer noch die alte Geschichte!" (The same old story).

His partner Blumenberg was much dreaded and hated by musicians, whose vanity he played on. I don't know where he went when he died; perhaps he became the devil's Jester. I remember few things more funny than his printing Lambert's name in the *Musical Courier* without capitals—alexander lambert—to show his contempt when he happened to have a row with that pianist. Blumenberg was so lucky as to have Huneker on his staff. Later on Leonard Liebling became the editor of the *Courier*. Belonging to an all-round musical family he *knew* what he was writing about and everybody read—and reads—him; his inexhaustible supply of jests reminds one of Mark Twain.

John C. Freund, the founder of *Musical America,* was one of the patriarchs among New York musical journalists. Gossip, rather than criticism, was his field; nothing escaped his notice in the "Mephisto's Musings" page which Edward Ziegler had started. He had a sharp tongue, but he knew how to be pleasant too, as witness this friendly note he sent me on August 29, 1923: "Your 'Musical Progress' came to hand last Saturday with the mail about eleven o'clock in the morning. In the afternoon I started to read and became so interested that I positively forgot all about the news sent over the long distance 'phone from my house in Mt. Vernon that it had been burglarized at three A.M. and a good deal of property taken and damage done. Now when a man gets so absorbed in any book that he forgets the loss of some of the dearest of his possessions, it is a unique compliment to the author of that work."

For several years *Musical America* was the camping ground of Herbert F. Peyser and Walter Kramer, both of whom were among my intimate friends. Before Peyser became a critic he used to go to his room after returning from a concert or opera and write down his impressions which he compared the following day with what the *Evening Post* said. He often wrote for me and I valued his contributions highly. He became leading critic of Freund's paper and as such wielded a wide influence. As for Walter Kramer, he gave up criticism for composing, and for very good reasons; he is one of the coming men in the creative field.

Another follower and assistant of mine was Edgar J. Levey; but he soon deserted music and entered politics. His services as assistant Comptroller of New York were valued so highly that both the political parties retained him.

Edward Horsman also became a composer. After serving on the *Herald* a few seasons as critic he reformed, swore off, and became a dealer in imported toys—doubtless a much more profitable job. It gave him leisure to write songs, some of which became best-sellers. He was a genial and hospitable soul. Great artists like Kreisler and Safonoff were glad to be his guests. One day Horsmann and I visited a Spanish exposition in London. We came into a concert hall with a cat sitting on a chair—the only living thing in it. "What part of Spain does this suggest?" I asked. He didn't know. "Why, Catalonia," I said; yet we remained good friends.

A strange death took away my dear friend Gustav Kobbé. He was boating near his home on Long Island when a badly-managed hydroaeroplane came along and crushed the life out of him. He was a writer who knew how to prepare a Book of the Opera and other things that were popular without being superficial. We went to Bayreuth together one summer. He was very anxious to get an interview with Wagner, who refused to grant it. But an American journalist is not easily discouraged. Seeing the Master taking a walk in his park he accosted him but was told to "get out." Then he interviewed the Master's neighbors and tradespeople, who told him all they knew about his habits and opinions; and when this appeared in print it read for all the world like an interview with Wagner himself!

Van Vechten followed the wise example of Bernard Shaw, Rupert Hughes and James Huneker in becoming a literary celebrity. His books are decidedly readable. I found much truth in his scathing indictment of chamber music. St. John Brennan also was a bookman; his knowledge of Latin was astonishing. But the best thing he left behind him was two very charming daughters.

Poor Willy von Sachs practically starved to death in Vienna during the war. He was a first-class journalist; we had some good times together in Paris, where he knew all about the best restaurants.

Reginald De Koven I have spoken of before, but forgot to mention a letter from him dated September 18, 1893, in which occurs this sentence: "I should be most interested to hear from you in the way of a libretto which I hope would be rather romantic than comic." Victor Herbert and several others asked me to write librettos, but I never felt sufficiently interested to try. If I had a gift for that sort of thing I should like to provide something for Deems Taylor. I feel sure he would make the best possible use of it. No message from a colleague ever gave me more pleasure than the receipt of his clever "Through the Looking Glass" score with my name on it followed by "to whom music and I owe so much."

Two of the most competent critics ever active in New York were on the *Staats-Zeitung:* Halperson and Spanuth. Halperson can turn out more first-class copy than any critic I ever knew. Spanuth, an excellent pianist as well as writer, went to Berlin and took over one of the oldest music periodicals, *Die Signale.* When I saw him the last time at his home he was in a gay mood. He played the English national hymn, sitting down heavily on the keyboard every fourth bar to imitate the booming cannon. In Montreux (1925) I happened to come across his widow, once a distinguished opera singer (Amanda Fabbris) in company with her cousin, who was also a famous opera singer in the days of Theodore Thomas—Emma Juch.

Pierre Key left the *World* to found a unique and soon indispensable weekly, the *Musical Digest.* He has also written the official Life of Caruso, a book both reliable and readable. I was sorry when Billy Chase left the *Evening Sun* for he had a news-and-gossip column which was unlike any other; I never failed to read it. Nor did I often miss the comments of Pitts Sanborn, who has a knack of saying things in a strikingly piquant and pithy way.

Mrs. Bowman was the critic on Dana's *Sun;* she was a well-informed and racy writer, somewhat addicted to gush. She even gushed over me, a rival critic! Read these lines from a letter she wrote me about my comments on a Paderewski recital: "It was far and away the best criticism written. . . To me, your work has all the charm over other New York criticisms that a highly-finished portrait has of advantage over a cold hard photograph. You are as clever in your way as Paderewski in his."

If so, it was because his playing inspired me to super-efforts. I thank heaven that it was my privilege to help arouse enthusiasm for him throughout America. When I met him last, at Morges, in September, 1925, he referred to his next American tour and added, with a touch of sadness: "It will be the first time since I first came to New York, thirty-four years ago, that you will not be there."

The fact that Emilie Frances Bauer comes from Portland, Oregon, naturally established a bond of union between us; another was that her sister, Marion, is one of the best American song writers of the fair sex; still another, that Maurice Renaud was one of her idols, about whom she wrote as rapturously as we did. She had a gift for gathering about her the most famous artists; her "at homes" were notable.

When I left the *Evening Post* I would have voted for either William Henry Humiston or Herbert F. Peyser as my successor; but Humiston, alas, had gone to a better world. He was for many years one of my most intimate friends, and he often helped me out when I had more entertainments than I could cover. It was before the days when I signed my articles. Being a composer, he natu-rally knew more about details of scoring than I did, and he wrote not a few erudite paragraphs which helped to build up my reputation for musical scholarship.

He worshiped Bach, Wagner, Liszt, Grieg, and Mac-Dowell (who was his teacher at Columbia) as frantically as I did.

Lawrence Gilman once wrote in the *Tribune* that if he had his choice in the musical heaven he would like to sit between Bach and Wagner. Humiston ought to be sitting between them now. He knew the scores of these two masters more thoroughly than any other scholar in America, or perhaps anywhere. His shelves were filled with the various editions. Some were on the piano, some on the floor. His room was a sight. He was a bachelor who often did his own cooking. He lived not wisely but too well. Had he followed the maxims in "The Simple Life in a Nutshell" by Doctor Kellogg of Battle Creek he might have lived thirty years longer. Without being a toper he had an unholy passion for making home brews, some of them worse than the potion Mime concocted for Siegfried. I believe these brews, by irritating his kidneys, brought on the cancer which killed him.

While Krehbiel nearly reached three-score years and ten he, too, would have been good for another decade or two had he lived the Simple Life, for he was built like a Viking. No one could fail to notice those broad shoulders, that big curly head as he walked down the aisle in Carnegie Hall or at the Metropolitan. He was the Dean of the Critical Faculty, having started his career in New York a year before Henderson and me. He was naturally patriarchal and pontifical; the younger critics took refuge under his protecting wings like little chicks and with their aid he wielded a wide influence.

They looked on him with awe and veneration. Many music lovers also stood in awe of him, as was amusingly illustrated one day in Carnegie Chamber Music Hall when I heard one lady say proudly "I came up in the same elevator with Krehbiel" and her companion answered "How interesting!"

To the many tiffs Krehbiel and I had I have referred repeatedly in preceding pages. He was fiercely anti-German during the war, yet in his criticisms he was always as Teutonic as Teutonic can be. Most of our quarrels were due to the fact that he had little or no enthusiasm for non-German geniuses like Chopin, Liszt, Grieg, Tchaikovsky, Bizet, Gounod, Verdi; Liszt, indeed, he hated as the devil hates holy water, going so far as to intimate that he wasn't even much of a pianist!

My friendly relations with my distinguished colleague, in spite of our frequent scraps, are amusingly illustrated by the conclusion of one of his letters: "Yours in unspoiled good humor but a trifle belligerent H. E. Krehbiel." But we didn't always quarrel. One of the letters before me contains only six words: "Thanks for your Strauss article." Neither of us liked Richard Strauss, and as for the "futurists," compared with whom Richard Strauss is a mellifluous Bellini, we cordially applauded each other's pugilistic attacks. I shall never forget the superbly eloquent and crushing tirades he launched against these fellows who, having nothing to say, try to distract attention from their impotence by indulging in riotous orgies of dissonantal din.

His successor on the *Tribune,* Lawrence Gilman, does not indulge in these tirades; he is, in fact, a champion of the futurists—at least those of them who are sincere, like Stravinsky, his admiration for whom I share cordially; I wish I had room to print extracts from my enthusiastic articles on his music. Debussy, who is not one of the racket-makers, I do not admire as Gilman does. His infatuation for this composer is so great that when I wrote that the best thing about "Pelléas et Mélisande" was Gilman's little book about it he did not thank me for the compliment. Some people are hard to please!

As a "date-hound" (to use Huneker's apt phrase) Gilman is of the same breed as his predecessor; he keeps up the *Tribune's* reputation as a journal that takes music seriously and voluminously, and in the matter of style he is quite the equal of H. E. Krehbiel at his best. He is, in fact, the most poetic of New York's musical journalists. Read his "Nature in Music" and his book on Edward MacDowell.

When Krehbiel died the question arose "who is now the Dean?" Henderson and I discussed the matter and found that we had begun our critical career at the same time, so neither of us could lay claim to the title; which did not worry us much.

For many years Henderson and I have been good friends, calling each other by our first names. But when it came to matters of opinion we often clashed like two express trains meeting in the dark on the same track. Years ago I wrote: "I am the only man of the Harvard class of 1876 who took highest honors in philosophy. Furthermore I was awarded a fellowship which enabled me to go abroad and study psychology three more years. I have written fourteen books. Yet with all these rare advantages and opportunities for strengthening my brain powers I am unable to understand one thing. Why is it that, when our opinions clash, Henderson is invariably wrong while I am always right? It's hard luck and I really feel sorry for Willie."

Willie read this, yet he smiled amiably when next I met him. He's a great humorist, and he thought I was joking! Poor Willie! No doubt he was convinced that whenever we clashed *he* was right. That's funny too.

On the whole I think W. J. Henderson has the keenest wit of all the New York critics; I always looked for something screamingly funny in his criticisms and was seldom disappointed. Much of his wit was of the cruel kind— but—tit for tat—think how cruelly *he* had suffered listening to his victims! He could be serious, too—very, especially in his books. He's a great expert on the art of singing and its history and he has never hesitated to give his opinion of the Metropolitan's prima donnas without

undue bias in favor of clemency. In summer he has been
writing about yachts and yachting in order to qualify
himself for commenting on such nautical operas as "The
Flying Dutchman," "Tristan and Isolde" and "L'Afri-
caine," which shows how conscientiously he performs his
duty as critic.

Richard Aldrich and I differed chiefly on the duration
of musical works. He doted on the long ones, I on the
short. I often demolished him and he me in regular Kil-
kenny-cat style. In other matters we were often diametrically—I might say diabolically—opposed. But I think
I have a great advantage over him because my opinions
are brought together and preserved in my book "Musical
Progress,' while his are buried in the back numbers of
The Times. Whenever I said anything nasty about
Brahms, whose high priest he was, he retaliated by sneer-
ing at Liszt, and vice versa. In this way we had much
fun and these two composers got a lot of free advertising.

On September 24, 1924, Aldrich wrote to me: "There
have been elemental, earth-shaking changes in New York
journalism in the last year or two, and not the least is
your departure. It will indeed be strange not to read
you in the *Post,* after all these years; but you have earned
a rest, and I can now only repeat the congratulations I
sent you when I first heard of it. To sit and write quietly
in a beautiful spot of a beautiful country without having
to think of Aeolian Hall at 3 or Carnegie at 8:15, or hearing an editor call for early or any other kind of copy, will
be luxury and peace. Also to have good sound claret or
even champagne within easy call; or a Scotch high-ball;
and all the delicious things to eat."

Poor Jim Huneker had hoped to do what I did; but he
had not saved his earnings, as I had, for an annuity and
had to remain in harness. I am convinced that if he could
have lived in Europe and indulged every day in a glass or

two of the Pilsener which had become his element he would have lived years longer. Prohibition is a dangerous thing.

HUNEKER IN HIS LETTERS TO ME

When Huneker died his widow collected the letters he had written to friends and they were printed by the Scribners. She had of course asked for those addressed to me but they were scattered in a dozen boxes, mostly up in Maine, and I had no time to get at them till I sorted the whole material for my autobiography. I found twenty-two just in time for the inclusion of the more important ones in a second volume, "Intimate Letters."

Many of the letters to me were penned at the time when he was collecting the material for his volume on Liszt, which he dedicated to me. This volume involved an enormous amount of labor. He made a special pilgrimage, following the Lisztian trail to all the places made famous by the great pianist-composer. He read all his books and his countless letters and minutely studied all of his scores. "I have all Lisztiana," he wrote to me—"ask Ziegler, who weeps when he looks at my amassed material." Again and again he was appalled at his courage in undertaking so colossal a task. On August 3, 1904, he wrote:—"Hang your laziness. Think of the trouble you would have spared me if I could take down from my library shelves a volume entitled:

FRANZ LISZT
by
Henry T. Finck

He had a guilty feeling that he had no right to write a book on Liszt: "I feel that I am poaching on your legitimate preserves and if you really care to 'do' the great old man say the word. It's not too late." He thought that

after my "savage warfare for years" in a cause that had
"looked hopeless" I ought to be the one to write *the* Liszt
book. I had indeed thought of following up my "monu-
mental work on Wagner," as Jim kindly called it, by a
similar one on Liszt and had collected a heap of material,
but—well, perhaps I *was* lazy.*

Jim certainly was, with all his industry. What do you
suppose he wanted to do with regard to Liszt's songs?
He asked my permission to bodily transfer to his book (of
course with proper acknowledgment) an article of mine
on those lyrics that had appeared in the *Musical Courier!*
Unfortunately, I had transferred that article to my own
book, "Songs and Song Writers," so Jim had to content
himself with citing a few pages from it.

"You will not like it," he wrote to me about his book
when it was finished. But I did like it, on the whole, and
welcomed it as powerful aid in my Liszt propaganda. To
have a writer of his standing declare that Liszt was "a
melodic genius of the first rank" and feature the fact that
Wagner (as he himself admitted) "became harmonically
quite another fellow" after studying Liszt's symphonic
poems, was water for my mill and helped me in my fight
against H. E. Krehbiel and his allies, whose favorite sport
was throwing stones at my idol.

Huneker also shared my passionate love for Bach—the
real Bach whom I had for years tried to reveal to ignorant
pedantic musicians.

In 1905 Jim wrote to me that my "darling theories
about Bach" were incarnate in a book by Schweizer about
Bach the Romanticist, just published in Paris. "At
last Bach is placed in the right perspective, not as a manu-
facturer of dry-as-dust fugues but as a living man *writing*

---

* My chief reason for regretting the failure of my biography of Richard Strauss
(which appeared just after our entry in the World War), is that it contains the
best things I ever wrote about Liszt, whose greatness, as compared with Strauss,
I emphasized.

program music and anticipating Liszt!!! Won't H. E. Krehbiel weep?"

His conversation was as brilliant as his writings. During intermissions at opera or concert he usually had a sort of reception around his seat. Yet he was not really social; his closest friends could not persuade him to go to dinner. As he once wrote me: "I never go to dinners, public or private; I haven't the time; as for making a speech—*Mein Gott!* Heinrich, is that a little joke? I couldn't say 5 words on my hind legs."

PRESSER, COOK AND KELLEY

In a letter to W. C. Brownell, Huneker wrote: "I don't think it makes much difference whether the book is $1.50 or $2—my books don't sell anyhow." There are similar complaints in other letters; yet his books must have been profitable, else would the Scribners have been so eager to print all of them—seventeen in twenty-one years?

No—not all of them. One, the "Confessions of an Old Fogy" was issued by Theodore Presser, then the foremost music publisher in America, with a huge establishment in Philadelphia; it takes a dozen girls just to open and classify the letters received daily! Early in his career Mr. Presser started a musical monthly, *The Etude,* of which Huneker was for a time the editor. The present editor is James Francis Cooke; for him I wrote nearly all the articles gathered in my "Musical Progress." In the introduction to that volume I have written at length about Presser and Cooke.

In 1897 Apthorpe wrote to me from Boston: "Have you noticed how the magazine field has been closing for us serious musical fellows during the last few years? My show in *Scribner's* and the *Atlantic* seems to be reduced to chances for the vulgarization of the Already-Well-

Known in music and interesting details about great composers' back hair—a sort of thing for which I have neither taste nor ability. I see nothing for it but writing for 17 readers."

He should have followed my example in writing not for 17 but for the million readers of *The Etude*. I have always enjoyed writing for this musical magazine, because its editor not only tolerated jests and anecdotes in a serious article but welcomed them. I may repeat what I have said elsewhere, that Presser has, with his *Etude,* done more to educate America musically than any individual except Theodore Thomas.

His following the good old maxim that honesty is the best policy (in the long run) made him a millionaire. And he did good with his millions, as witness his splendid Home for Retired Music Teachers. With all his wealth he lived the simple life. Mr. Cooke once told me how he went down the street with his employer. They stopped for a fifteen cent lunch, then went across the street to an office where Mr. Presser signed away $750,000 for the Presser Foundation. And in his seventies he still worked as hard as any man or woman in his big building.

I used to think I was a busy man but these Philadelphians made me feel like a sloth. I grumbled when I had six letters to answer and I have become a shameless liar in explaining why I "didn't write sooner"; Cooke writes a hundred a day yet finds time for an occasional chatty epistle to me, filled with humor and fun. He has also found time to write several notable books, establishing close contact with famous musicians. In addition, he is a composer. Regarding his song "Laughing Roses" he wrote me: "Lt. Sousa was here visiting me for a little while; I showed him the proofs for his friendly advice never dreaming that he would want to use it. He pounced upon it at once and said 'this is the kind of song I have been looking for for years, because it has a great 'wallup' in the last seven measures.'"

To come back to Huneker for a moment. His best book is his Chopin, yet when he told me its sales were "negligible," I was filled with wrath at the singular stupidity of musicians.

In one of his letters to me Jim said: "Chopin as a piano writer is praised to death but Chopin the *Musician* has not had his immortal dues." It remained for Edgar Stillman Kelley to render him these immortal dues. His superb book "Chopin the Composer" shows in detail that Chopin, far from being a master "who could not master the sonata" form, improved on it wonderfully, actually increasing its formal difficulties as compared with the giants of the classical school and overcoming them triumphantly.

When, some years before the war, the leading musical magazine in Germany, *Die Musik,* asked me to write an article on the six leading American composers I began of course with MacDowell and next I placed Kelley. This, he afterwards informed me, helped him tremendously in his career. And he deserved the compliment. The fact that his works are not so well known as some others' did not deter me from placing him where I did. Schumann in his day was not rated equal to Mendelssohn. Today we all know how foolish that was. Kelley's day will come. New England has particular reason to be proud of him. His "New England Symphony" and his "Puritania" breathe a distinctive atmosphere.

Before the last-named was produced in New York, Kelley had been so imprudent as to make an enemy of Krehbiel. On Sept. 1, 1893, he wrote to me that Krehbiel had informed him by letter that "if I wished to fight, my desire should be fed fat." Nevertheless, Kelley continues, "I had not anticipated that such disastrous consequences would be the result of Krehbiel and his satellites, among whom, I am happy to be assured, you are not numbered. Since the assassination of 'Puritania' my hopes of gathering in a few hard-earned dollars have been dissipated. It is however, a source of satisfaction to read the appreciative words of yourself and those of the Boston critics which you have sent me."

Three years later Kelley asked me to recommend him among my friends as a teacher of harmony and composition. He had to have a little bread and butter, poor fellow. My article in *Die Musik* led to his getting a very desirable position at Oxford, Ohio, (and the Cincinnati Conservatory) where he taught, but had leisure to compose, too.

Early in his career, Kelley had lived in San Francisco, and while there he introduced into his compositions a new element: Chinese music, an innovation which has found imitators and which adds to American music a local color quite as delectable as the Indian and negro strains so often interwoven into our national compositions.

WHY I TOOK TO JESTING

Having given a bird's-eye view of my forty or more colleagues I wish to say a word about myself. As compared with them I labored under two great disadvantages: Most of them wrote for papers with a much larger circulation than the *Evening Post* boasted, and their papers appealed to readers of both sexes. The *Post* has always been a paper for men. Occasionally, features were introduced that it was fondly hoped would make it appeal to women too, but these bids for feminine favor were usually of the most fatuous kind, and failed dismally.

Now, imagine my situation. I was writing daily for a man's newspaper on a subject in which most men are not interested! Obviously I had to do my durndest to *make* my articles interesting, and gradually I learned that the best if not the only way to do so was to lighten and leaven my comments with the yeast of humor and jesting. That, I felt, would also make them more palatable to the few women who did read the *Evening Post,* most of them, I rather think, for the sake of the Music and Drama columns.

Did I succeed? It will be more modest to let others answer. When I resigned, Simeon Strunsky, who had been for several years the *Post's* leading editorial writer, sent me a letter in which he said: "Only to-day Ogden told me of your farewell to the *Post* and to the newspaper business, and just now I have read your swan-song in the Saturday paper. You are a greater man than the late Charles II. They said of him that nothing in his life became him so much as his leaving of it. Your own jolly *Ave atque Vale* is happily in tone with your own jolly, courageous, brilliant and scholarly career. You really belong in the Renaissance with your gift for combining knowledge and jest. . . If we had all been as alive as you are we might yet have saved the paper."

Document No. 2 is a paragraph from Winifred Katzin's review of my "Musical Laughs" in the Literary Digest's International Book Review. According to the prevailing opinion the correct style for use in critical articles "should always be magisterial, erudite and aloof, in order that artists and the general public be duly imprest with the gravity of the critic's office. But Mr. Finck didn't think so at all. On the contrary he believed that the whole musical business was taken a good deal too seriously and was badly in need of livening up. So he proceeded to do his share by sprinkling all his reviews, even the most momentous, with anecdotes and jokes, and other merry trimmings. They were a tremendous hit, and were read as much for fun as for edification. Long after the notices of his colleagues had been forgotten, Mr. Finck's witticisms, together, of course, with the judgments they pointed, were still being repeated and laughed over."

PHILHARMONIC DRIVES AND MUSICAL POLITICS

One day I was called to the telephone by Loudon Charlton, manager of the Philharmonic. He asked me what I thought of the Directors' plan to engage Josef Stransky as the next conductor of this orchestra, to succeed Mahler.

"Josef Stransky?" I echoed in astonishment. "Why, he isn't known at all over here and it has been the traditional policy of the Philharmonic to engage only men of international fame."

"Well," said the manager, "Anton Seidl also was unknown here when he was brought over, but he soon became the idol of the public. Stransky has had great success in Berlin, Prague and Hamburg both in concert hall and opera house. He is a pupil of Mahler and has been specially recommended by Paderewski and Spanuth. We shall have another meeting to-night to talk the matter over.

The next day he called me up again to tell me they had decided to engage Stransky.

"All right," I answered huffily, "it isn't *my* funeral."

It wasn't the Philharmonic's either! Stransky came, conducted, and conquered instantly. At his first concert his highly dramatic and emotional reading of Liszt's glorious "Lament and Triumph of Tasso" evoked a tornado of applause such as I had never heard at a concert except when Seidl conducted the first performance of Dvořák's "New World" Symphony. On another occasion Stransky made Grieg's orchestral version of his heavenly song, "The Last Spring," sound so rich, so warm, so euphonious that the enthralled audience simply compelled him to repeat it, contrary to the iron rule of the Philharmonic forbidding encores.

Naturally I became at once enthusiastic over a conductor who could thus make thousands share my seemingly excessive adoration of Grieg and Liszt. And when I found that Stransky was, since Seidl, the most emotional conductor of Tchaikovsky, Dvorák, Wagner and other moderns including Rimsky-Korsakoff (in the climax of whose Scheherezade—the dashing of the ship on the rocks —he raised my temperature to fever heat) I became automatically his unofficial press-agent.

As Brother Krehbiel was fond of saying: "Money talks." Instead of being the Philharmonic's funeral Stransky proved its salvation. His predecessor Mahler, though a conductor of the highest rank, did not know how to make programs to allure the public. Above all, he despised and neglected Tchaikovsky, the public's symphonic pet. The subscription suffered accordingly. Stransky's idols were the public's, and one of the things that made him popular was that he did not banish from his programs first-class compositions simply because they were popular.

To cut the story short, during the eleven years of his conductorship he doubled, trebled, and quadrupled the subscription. The sign: "All Seats Sold" came to be out at nearly every one of his concerts, an unprecedented thing in the history of the ancient and honorable Philharmonic.

Percy Grainger, in a letter to me, referred to the Philharmonic as *"perfection:* it is a nosegay of artists—each man a real soloist." Fritz Kreisler was once asked by Stransky when he could find time to rehearse. The great violinist replied: "With *you* I do not need a rehearsal." And when Paderewski had played his own concerto with the Philharmonic he brought Stransky on the stage to share with him the overwhelming applause following it, a compliment I never saw him pay any other conductor.

Yet this man, this favorite of the public and of the great artists, and this orchestra, the best in America, were the subject of perpetual jibes and sneers, and once every other year there was a regular *Philharmonic Drive.* It consisted of an obviously preconcerted attack. Dozens of letters (mostly unsigned) were printed in certain newspapers, conveying the impression that Stransky and his orchestra were seventeenth rate—a positive disgrace to the country. One of the leaders of these attacks was a man for whose compositions Stransky had found no room on his programs. But there were other reasons for these Drives.

As conductor of the best orchestra in America (not excepting the Boston Symphony) and with a salary of $30,000, Stransky had a very much-coveted position. Every other conductor in America and abroad envied him; and what more natural than that friends of these conductors should join the Drive and try to oust him? Musical politics.

He was finally ousted, though not by a Drive—these Drives were simply laughed at after I had exposed their true inwardness. But he *was ousted*—yes, Josef Stransky, who had rescued the Philharmonic by raising its subscription in ten years from $25,000 to $107,000, was ignominiously cast out. The plot by which this was accomplished was most crafty. Since Stransky's enemies could not persuade the wise directors to take him from the orchestra, it was resolved to take the orchestra away from him!

Teutonic diplomats and militarists could not have done the job more neatly. A new orchestra was created, but although astonishing sums were expended on it, and its conductor finally was no less a personage than the superbly magnetic and "live" Willem Mengelberg, it was not a success. One of the last things Huneker, whose seat was just in front of mine, whispered in my ear was: "I call this a damned bad orchestra." This was an exaggeration. It was bad, but not damned bad. Some excellent players were in it.

It was then suggested that these players be merged with the Philharmonic, which would thus be enlarged and benefited by the abandonment of the rival organization and the use of its inexhaustible financial resources. Stransky was to remain conductor during the first half of the season, while Mengelberg was to come from Amsterdam as "guest conductor" to the finish. It seemed a satisfactory arrangement; in fact Henderson exclaimed to his brethren in the press-room: "Stransky has eaten the canary."

But this was premature. In spite of the Pulitzer Fund of half a million and the enlarged Stransky subscription, the Greater Philharmonic needed more money—lots more. It was promised, on condition that Stransky be dropped, and he was dropped—in a way that was not only unjust and unbusinesslike but positively cruel.

Never shall I forget his last concert at the end of his eleventh season. *He did not know it was to be his final concert, nor did the audience.* The players knew, and so did the conspirators. The orchestra arose as Stransky came on the stage and the audience gave him ovation after ovation. Had it known the truth there would have been a riot. It was a memorable performance; the musicians were heart and soul with their beloved leader; they played like demons—thrills chased one another in squads down my medullary nerves. And poor deluded Stransky, bewildered, made a speech in which he said: "I got up from my bed to come to this concert, but nothing could have prevented me from coming to-day to tell you how much I thank you for your great kindness to me. When I come back next autumn I hope to be in better health."

There are details about this transaction which I can not tell because a man can be sued for libel for telling the truth. On the other hand I wish to say that Stransky was partly to blame for his misfortunes. He was an expert in the gentle art of making enemies. Moreover, he was by no means always at his best at these concerts. Sometimes he conducted in a slovenly way that quite justified adverse criticism. His wit also was his enemy—not always, though. One day he telephoned to ask me if I had a spare copy of my book on Strauss, which was out of print. That book, I must explain, dwells very frankly on Richard Strauss's shortcomings as man and composer. "I have one—what do you want it for?" I asked. "I want to give it to Strauss." "Does he read English?" "I hope not," was Stransky's droll answer.

Gustav Mahler in New York

In the pages on Theodore Thomas I stated that he was the first of the great Philharmonic conductors who wrote me a letter of thanks for being his champion. Stransky was the last; he "would not have remained in New York" had it not been for me. Others were Seidl, Safonoff, and Mahler. I met Mengelberg but once and he talked chiefly about Mahler, who, he tried to persuade me, was the Beethoven of our time. However that may be, he certainly was a giant among conductors. Yet when he was in New York he was so pitilessly hounded that he wrote me on the eve of his departure for Vienna, where he was idolized as few musicians ever have been: "Let me take this occasion to press your hand warmly for your repeated energetic championing of my ideals. Your sympathy and support have been among the few experiences that have made New York worth while for me."

When Liszt first heard Wagner's "Flying Dutchman"

overture he exclaimed: "It is wet! One scents the salt breeze in the air!" That was as long ago as 1843. Such music does not age. When played as it is by the Philadelphia Orchestra under Stokowsky it still sounds wet and smells of sea salt. Gericke had conducted it in a way that reminded Henderson of Mendelssohn's "Calm Sea and Prosperous Voyage." Mahler was at the opposite extreme; he made this overture even more tempestuous than Seidl did, by putting in an extra piccolo or two to whistle in the masts. It gave me a thrill I have never forgotten.

Another unforgettable thrill Mahler gave me was in the funeral march of Beethoven's "Eroica." I had heard this given by a dozen of the world's leading conductors, yet none of them had made me realize as Mahler did to what sublime heights of overwhelming, tragic grief Beethoven's colossal genius could rise. Yes, Mahler was the greatest of Beethoven conductors, and acknowledged as such abroad. Yet in New York he was persistently abused, and, strange to say, most violently by Krehbiel, the American high priest of Beethoven.

Krehbiel spent years of his life editing, completing and putting into shape for the printer Thayer's wonderful Life of Beethoven and he did it without hope of ever getting any pecuniary reward for all this toil. For this I take off my hat to him. Yet, simply because Mahler made changes here and there in Beethoven's antiquated orchestration—changes which Beethoven himself would have undoubtedly made had he lived a century later—Krehbiel jumped on him with both feet.

His assaults were so violent that they aroused the ire, among others, of the Russian pianist Ossip Gabrilowitsch, who courageously came to Mahler's rescue in a pamphlet in which he handled H. E. K. without kid gloves. No doubt, Krehbiel felt he had gone too far. He did not resent the polemics of the young Russian pianist, but continued to treat him fairly, on his merits. For that, also, I take off my hat.

Ossip, Clara, Hildegarde and John

When Gabrilowitsch made his début in New York he played, I thought, somewhat crudely and with rather excessive "storm and stress." Huneker raved over him from the start and soon I found that he had stolen a march on me; the more I heard Ossip the more I admired him, and ultimately I ranked him with the super-pianists.

He is still a super-pianist, but his heart is more in his conducting. He has given Detroit a symphony orchestra of the first rank; it has played in New York where he proved himself even greater as a conductor than as a pianist in proportion as the orchestra offers bigger opportunities for the display of interpretative genius.

Ossip's greatest triumph, however, was when he won the heart and hand of Clara Clemens, Mark Twain's beautiful daughter, whom he first met in Vienna in the class of Leschetizky. Clara had great musical ambitions from the start. Her study of the piano under Leschetizky helped to make a real musician of her but presently she decided to cultivate her voice and let Ossip play the piano for her. Their engagement was announced at Redding, Connecticut, in the big house built by young Howells for his father's great friend. Mark Twain invited David Bispham to assist Clara and Ossip in a family concert. Before it began he got up and said: "My daughter may not be as great a musician as these two men but she is much better looking."

Clara was sure of a *succès de beauté* wherever she sang. She failed to find the particular sort of teacher she needed, so it took a long time to get her voice into any sort of shape. It was naturally a voice of most agreeable quality, a genuine contralto, but none of her teachers had been able to direct her just how to shape and use it. Once I made a microscopic analysis and I offered to send it to her, at the risk of losing her friendship. She promptly sent a letter beginning: "Dear Henry. Do, *do* send me your 'diagnosis' by return mail." She received it amiably and gratefully and felt sure it would help her. She had always had moments when she displayed as gorgeous a voice as Schumann-Heink, revealing glorious possibilities.

Apart from technic, Clara was from the start an artist of the front rank. From her father she had inherited a keen intelligence which enabled her to enter into the literary and poetic spirit of art-songs in a way most of her rivals had reason to envy her, and few of them had her gift of swaying an audience emotionally and casting a spell over the hearers which was largely a matter of personal magnetism. Among the great moments at her recitals were those when she sang one of her husband's own charming songs, with himself playing the piano part.

Before the war the Gabrilowitsches lived in Munich and they had a cosy summer home in the Bavarian Highlands. When we visited them there we found also Leopold Stokowsky and his wife, the famous pianist Olga Samaroff— not a Russian, by the way, but a native of Texas. At dinner, one evening, Olga and Ossip shamelessly discussed a diabolical plan they had of playing one of the Brahms concertos on two pianos. I protested vigorously, said I'd go to bed if they did, and the calamity was averted. Ossip explained that his interest in these Brahms works was largely in their rhythmic originality. I admitted that but confessed I couldn't find much else in them.

One day in New York we were discussing vacation

plans when Clara said: "Why don't you spend the summer at Redding in the Lobster Pot?" We gladly accepted
the kind offer, and spent not one summer but two in this,
the smaller of Mark Twain's two houses.

The big house in which the humorist had lived was not
far from the Lobster Pot, up the hill. We got the key
from the guardian and explored it—but not often, for it
seemed dismal and haunted—yes, haunted; we constantly
looked around timidly as if there must be a ghost behind
us. Clara has never lived in it since her father's death.
We found his billiard table and other things as he had
left them.

Mark Twain's biographer, Albert Bigelow Payne, still
lived near by, and we had interesting chats with him.
Another entertaining neighbor was Mrs. St. Maur, the
author of several books on domestic and outdoor subjects;
she helped us out with dairy and garden products.

Another social advantage provided by Redding was
that it was a sort of Hawthorne colony. I first met Julian
Hawthorne in New York at the house of Lorenz Reich,
who loved to dine and wine celebrities; his Hungarian
wines were wonderful. Two of Julian's daughters came,
too: Beatrix, with whom I used to take long walks in
Central Park feeding the squirrels (unlike them, she could
eat peanuts shell and all) and who afterwards married
Clifford Smyth; and Hildegarde, who became my wife's
most intimate friend.

At Redding Mrs. Hawthorne's house was quite near
our temporary home. Near hers was that of her youngest
daughter, Imogen, who married Dr. Deming and whose
children, like those of Beatrix, began at an early age to
show the true intellectual Hawthorne traits. A little
farther away lived Jack and Henry Hawthorne, and
Gwen, whose husband. Mr. Mikkelson was real estate

editor of the New York *Sun*. As I have said, quite a Hawthorne colony.

Hildegarde seemed husband-proof—too busy with her books and poems and magazine stories and articles (which were always in great demand because of their brightness and humor) to think of marriage; but when she met John Oskison she ceased to be a combination of Minerva and Diana and followed the example of her sisters. We did not wonder at this when we met him. He is a man among men; an excellent novelist too.

In the winter of 1924-25 we urged the Oskisons to join us at the Cape of Antibes in the French Riviera. They came. They wrote their stories in the morning and in the afternoons we walked, or visited literary friends in the neighboring Cannes, among them Basil King and Homer Croy, the latter—a Missourian author like myself—bubbling over with fun. One day he mailed a letter addressed "To Mrs. Abbie H. Cushman, beloved wife of Henry T. Finck, Hotel du Cap, Antibes." We got it all right.

There is, we feel, only one objection to having Hildegarde near us: we then get none of her absorbingly interesting letters! Once, at a dinner, my wife was talking about these letters to the famous critic Mr. Dithmar, saying they were even more brilliant and interesting than her printed articles. "What a waste!" he exclaimed disconsolately; but they will be printed some day. Hildegarde was in Paris during its long-distance bombardment by the "Big Bertha." Her descriptions of the ensuing scenes are as vivid as Philip Gibbs's most photographic pages, if not more so.

When visiting us in Maine Hildegarde used to start out after breakfast alone and roam among the mountains and the dense forest all day long, a feminine John Muir. She has now left her teens far behind her yet one hardly suspects it, thanks to her "daily dozen" indoors and her outdoor activity. At Antibes, on the rocky shore of the Mediterranean, we often admired her lithe figure as she moved along with the airy grace of an antelope.

SUMMERS IN MAINE

On July 22, 1892, I got a letter from the eminent art critic, W. C. Brownell, then MS. reader and editor for the Scribners, containing this sentence: "I congratulate you on being able to accomplish so much at this season. I am absolutely played out myself."

I had been bombarding him with chapter after chapter of my work on Wagner (the Scribners usually began to put my books into type before they were completed) and I was able to "accomplish so much" in midsummer because I was breathing the health-giving exhilarating air of the Maine mountains. Most of my books were written there, near Bethel, where I could work hard yet improve in health every day. Friends coming there from New York or Boston "absolutely played out" would in a fortnight improve in appearance till we could hardly recognize them.

East of the Rockies, Maine is undoubtedly our most health-giving state for summer visitors. And we had been so lucky as to find a region which capped the climax climatically and—may I say it?—climbatically. Mountains, mountains everywhere, and none of them too high for climbers of even modest pretensions. We used to get up at five, drive to the foot of one of these mountains: Speckle, Saddleback, Barker, Locke and the rest of them, indulge in a feast of blueberries big as cherries, and then enjoy the grand views and the intoxicating air of the summit.

We spent fifteen summers in a farmhouse at the entrance to the picturesque Sunday River Valley, which ends in the dense mountain forest—we called it the "End of the World." The Sunday River is in spring a wild mountain torrent which brings down the thousands of logs felled during the winter by the lumbermen. We used to hear these men shouting when a log-drive was on. It was like being back in the Wild and Woolly Oregon of my boyhood days. To me these shouts were music.

In this river we bathed in summer every afternoon and so did Shep, who was really amphibious, preferring the water to the land. He belonged to Miss Locke, with whom we boarded, but she was so busy that she was glad to have me annex him as my own. He was the most pugnacious collie I have ever seen; a daily thrashing or two would not prevent him from jumping on every dog that passed the house. We had to plan special "no-dog" walks when we went out with him. But oh, what a dear he was to us, and what a beauty! When he lay curled up before me as I wrote, the mere sight of his glorious form and fur often moved me to tears. And what romps we had together!

Equally beautiful was his successor (poor Shep had to be shot because the tortures of old-age, rheumatism, kept him from sleeping). Laddie was his name, and he was as different from Shep as two dogs can be. He hated fighting, but when forced to it, knew how to take care of himself. He hated the water and never went into the river unless I ordered him. As he was mine, we took him to New York in winter. There, repeatedly, as we walked along the street, I heard a lady say: "Oh, I wish I had that dog's eyes!" They were, indeed, marvelously beautiful and expressive.

There are many, many things I would like to tell about these two dogs; I had intended to give each of them as many pages as I did to Bruno, but there isn't room now— I must leave them for some future book. A word only about Laddie's tragic death. He was bitten by a mad

dog and soon showed symptoms which made me call in a
veterinarian. "Your dog has hydrophobia," he said, and
he had to be chloroformed.

Beside the dogs and the log-drives, the mountain climbing and blueberry eating, and the writing of a new book
nearly every summer I had a garden to amuse myself with.
Our new place of abode nearer Bethel, is unfortunately
situated on a terminal moraine, bearing witness, as do
many scattered bowlders, to the fact that all this region
had once been covered by huge glaciers—two miles deep,
I have read. The soil in my garden was at first mostly
gravel, and I had to work like a beaver to get in some
humus in which plants could grow; and even then droughts
and untimely frosts and the devilish weed called witch-
grass made so much trouble that I could achieve floral
triumphs about which everybody talked and which auto
parties stopped to admire, only by using whatever brains
I had with all my might and main; and this led to my
writing the book "Gardening With Brains," which I can
honestly recommend to all who have trouble in their gardens—and who hasn't?

The climax of my floral exhibit was always a long bed of
Burbank poppies. Have you ever seen these? They have
been one of the passions of my life and in the book just
named I have given a whole chapter to a description of
their color wonders and directions for achieving the most
brilliant results. I also made a specialty of other Burbank creations and he was always glad to hear of my
success with his California novelties in the colder climate
of Maine, and the less fertile soil. The difference in this
respect is vividly shown by the fact that to raise fine sweet
peas in Maine one must change their bed every year
whereas in California they can be grown in the same spot
year after year indefinitely.

A New Psychology of Eating

It was in the bracing White Mountain atmosphere of Bethel that I wrote most of my seventeen books, not including this autobiography, which is a European product. As a musical critic I had the special advantage, not shared by other journalists, of being able to go off on a vacation for five months every year; between the first of May and the end of September there was no music worth writing about in New York. I confess that if it had not been for this, I might have hesitated to become a musical critic. My father was frankly disappointed when I wrote him about my journalistic engagement. He feared that the faculty of Harvard University would be displeased at my forsaking psychology, in which it had awarded me a fellowship. But I did not forsake psychology; the five vacation months gave me ample time to write books, and among my literary works there are four which are distinctly psychological and anthropological. They are "Romantic Love and Personal Beauty," "Primitive Love and Love Stories," "Food and Flavor" and "Girth Control," which, though semi-humorous, has a chapter on the training of the will.

To these books I attach more importance than to any of my works on musical topics, among which my favorites are the biographies of Wagner and Grieg, "Songs and Song Writers," "Musical Progress" and, the best-seller of them all, "Success in Music and How It Is Won." The most original of all my books are, undoubtedly, "Food and Flavor" and "Primitive Love." May I explain briefly and frankly, without any false modesty, why I consider them of some importance?

"Food and Flavor" contains an entirely new psychology of eating—the doctrine that *the seat of our enjoyment of food is not, as everybody has supposed, the mouth but the nose.* Taste is in the mouth, but there are only four kinds of taste: sweet, sour, bitter and salt. These are the *gustatory* flavors, but in addition to these there are thousands of *olfactory* flavors, and these are perceived and enjoyed in the nose. *To the nose we are indebted for seven-eighths of the pleasures of the table.* That's my discovery and with this alone I think I earned my Harvard Fellowship in psychology.

A more important discovery for the welfare and happiness of the human race has, I feel sure, never been made. It is surely a million times more important than Einstein's "wonderful discovery" which "marks an epoch in science," in the words of an English writer on astronomy who, however, adds cautiously that "the idea still is not proven"— the idea that light, in its flight through space, is drawn aside slightly by gravitation. To no one except an astronomer is such a detail of the slightest importance, yet books by the dozen and newspaper articles by the thousand were written about Einstein while my discovery was casually referred to in a few reviews of my book and there the matter ended. It took "Food and Flavor" ten years to reach its second edition (Harper & Bros.), carried along by the tidal wave success of its sequel, "Girth Control." Can you blame me for blowing my own horn?

Why is my discovery a million times more important than Einstein's? Because it concerns not only astronomers but every man, woman and child in the world. Everybody eats, three times a day and nearly everybody eats too much. "One third of what we eat," says Dr. Copeland, "keeps us alive; the other two-thirds keeps the doctors alive."

The sole reason, of course, for eating three times as much as is good for us, or is needed, is that we labor under the delusion that the only way to prolong the pleasures of the table is to keep on eating, gluttonously, taking a second or third helping. Some wise persons, among them Horace Fletcher, showed that eating very slowly is another way to prolong these pleasures, but they did not make many converts because they did not go to the psychological root of the matter. They did not understand the gastronomic function and importance of the nose; did not know that the nose amplifies pleasurable flavors, as a sounding-board does the tones of the piano strings or an amplifier the music in a phonograph.

All you need to do is to eat very slowly and, while doing so, *exhale* the vaporized flavors in your mouth through your nostrils. I have found it amazingly difficult to get this notion about *exhaling* food flavors through the nose, into the heads of even exceptionally intelligent persons. Smelling has always meant to them *inhaling* through the nose; and as it is not considered good form to smell of food at the table, that seemed to exclude the nose from the realm of gastronomy.

My new psychology of eating reverses matters completely, making the nose the chief seat of gastronomic enjoyment. Epicures do the right thing instinctively, but not consciously. Read the chapter "A Comedy of Errors" in my book and you will see that some writers came within an inch of anticipating my discovery, but at the critical moment all of them flopped back into the egregious error of making the sense of taste the source of food enjoyment.

Here is the gist of the matter: with one mouthful of food, crushed by teeth and tongue, you can fill your olfactory chambers a dozen times with delicious flavors and the more you do this the more you will start all the digestive forces into activity. Thus my new psychology of eating provides an antidote to dyspepsia as well as to gluttony, to both of which so many mortals succumb. Isn't this more important than the question of relativity or whether light is affected by gravitation?

My passionate insistence in "Food and Flavor" on the importance of eating only the best food attracted the attention of a man who soon became one of my most esteemed friends, Bartlett Arkell, president of the Beech Nut Company. He had a plan of buying 50,000 copies of the book and distributing them free as a help to his high-brow business, gastronomically speaking.

One of the leading French chefs in New York wrote me a letter in which he hailed me as the American Brillat-Savarin. He meant it as a great compliment and I took it as such. But as a matter of fact my book is scientifically as far ahead of that Frenchman's famous treatise on the Physiology of Taste (of olfactory flavors he knew nothing) as a Rolls-Royce is of an ox-team. This will be admitted when I am dead—while I live the college professors of psychology will continue to write text books in which not a word will be said about olfactory flavors and about my discovery. I am glad I didn't become one of them, as my father wanted me to.

From Lust To Love

In writing about Heidelberg I related how the first of my eighteen books, "Romantic Love and Personal Beauty," came to be written. At the start I had in mind nothing more elaborate than a short treatise on how to cure love and how to win it. It was to be a sort of modern Ovid in prose. Like everybody else I imagined that ancient Roman love was essentially the same as modern Romantic Love; but as I read and reread Ovid in the original, as well as the other Latin poets and then the poems and romances of the Greeks and other ancient writers, it gradually dawned on me that the infatuation

they wrote about was purely sensual and egotistic—sheer
lust and never real love as we understand the word. This
difference I found aggravated when I began to read the
references in anthropological works to the love affairs of
savages and barbarians.

A wild joy overcame me when I realized that I had
thus discovered a truth which had escaped all the his-
torians and men of science and philosophers. It *could not*
be so, I thought. Feverishly I searched in the libraries
for facts contradicting my bold theory that real love (that
is refined and altruistic love) was unknown not only to
the wild men of the woods, but to the ancient civilized
nations, including the Hebrews; but none could I find.

Here was more proof, surely, that I had earned my
Harvard Fellowship! And furthermore, I brought forward in this book the first comprehensive psychological
analysis of love. The bulk of it, however, was purely
literary—comparisons of brunettes and blondes, directions
about how to kiss, different aspects of love in America,
Germany, England, France, and so on, the whole making,
as H. W. Conn exclaimed in *Science*, "such a curious combination that we hardly know whether to set the book aside
with a laugh, or to regard it as an important contribution
to knowledge. The latter feeling, however, predominates.
. . . One can not read this discussion of romantic love without acknowledging that Mr. Finck has made out a very
strong case."

Not all the reviewers agreed with me. Some thought
my new theory simply ridiculous. They referred to such
old stories as "Hero and Leander," "Daphnis and Chloe,"
"Cupid and Psyche," "Jacob and Rachel," and "Sakun-
tala" as evidence of real romantic love among the ancients.

Evidently I had blundered—in one way. Wishing to
make my treatise on Romantic Love a book that could be
read by anybody and anywhere, I had omitted all of the

abundant evidence that love in the old times and among wild men is simply a manifestation of sexual appetite. Some of my critics, among them prominent authors, wrote in such a supercilious tone about my "exhaustive ignorance of ancient literature" that my indignation boiled over and when other critics maintained that the "noble red man" was morally and amorously superior to the white man, my wrath exploded and I wrote a second book, "Primitive Love and Love Stories"—a volume of 850 pages if you please—in which I hurled at my opponents a mass of evidence which, in the opinion of a reviewer, left their statements "very much in the condition in which a cyclone leaves a Western village."

"There is something sublime almost to the point of the grotesque," (wrote Brooklyn *Life*) "in the assurance and audacity with which Mr. Finck sets out to prove that nearly every one of any supposed authority who has written on this subject has been unable to see straight or think clearly. And the bigger the man, the keener edge does Mr. Finck put on his tomahawk and the more gleefully does he dance about his victim. This is fun for the reader, but it must be painful for the wise old philosophers whose carefully erected theories are being demolished so summarily. Especially so because Mr. Finck succeeds in making out such a good case in each instance. . . . He has produced a book which will revolutionize the sociology of love and marriage."

"All those old notions of ours about the love of Paris for Helen, of Hero for Leander, of Dido for Æneas, of Sappho for several persons, of Antony for Cleopatra, of Pericles for Aspasia—all these, not to speak of the famous affairs of numerous Dark-Age couples, and all the alleged romances of unsophisticated barbarians and savages that adorn the works of foreign missionaries and explorers, ancient and modern—all our preconceptions concerning these matters, I say, must be incontinently given up, and confessed to be apocryphal and illusion," wrote Julian Hawthorne in the Philadelphia *North American.* "None of these persons knew what real love is, much less practised it. The only thing any of them loved was himself or herself, and the gratification of his or her physical senses. Such a phenomenon as altruistic love—the love which immolates itself for the loved one, and whose only happiness is to feel as its own the happiness of the loved one—was not only not existent until quite lately but was never even conceived of. Do you believe this? Probably not now; but see what you will believe after reading Mr. Finck's book! You have never read another book like it, and I doubt if you ever will. You feel that it is original, that you are dealing with a man who is himself, taking color from no one. His book is certain to command an immense audience here and in Europe."

John Fiske said in one of three letters he wrote to me about this book, that I had made "a valuable contribution to anthropology." "The book," he added, "shows wide and accurate learning, great diligence and discrimination in the acquirement and proper use of evidence, a broad philosophical spirit and a common sense that is as refreshing as a shower-bath. It's the sort of book that I love to read, and if some little jumping-jack of a critic says it isn't original, it simply shows that he is ignorant of the literature of the subject and is trying to cover up his ignorance by putting on airs."

Some amusing things occurred while "Primitive Love" was being prepared. As usual, the Scribners began to put it into type while I was still busy writing it. It had been agreed that, while there was no intention of applying to a work of this character "an over-strict standard," I must avoid, in writing about the alleged "love" affairs of savages and Orientals, evidence that was "too broad."

This was a perplexing condition because most of this evidence was fully a yard wide. I did what I could to shrink it, but on August 21, 1897, my friend Edwin W. Morse, then manuscript reader for the Scribners, wrote me that they *must* draw the line at a certain illustration of Hindu obscenity. "I am afraid," he added, "you don't fully appreciate the effect of the constant repetition of this sort of thing even on the adult imagination. Heaven forbid this book should ever be regarded as addressed *virginibus puerisque. Your* attitude in the matter is all right. It is the unbridled sensuality and lust which saturates your citations that are turning gray my few remaining dark hairs."

The foreman of the printing-house in which the book was put into type declared he was glad when it was off his hands because his men wasted so much time reading the manuscript whenever a fresh batch of sheets arrived. Do you wonder I had visions of $100,000 in royalties?

Alas! "Primitive Love" never became a best-seller; far from it, and it was all my fault, absolutely. I failed to profit by the example of Burton, author of the interminable "Anatomy of Melancholy," who was, as he sadly wrote, "unknown to few and known to fewer still." Nobody read his book; nobody read mine. Too much anthropology. I had hugely enjoyed gathering the evidence in American and European libraries; in Boston my college friend Lindsay Swift, official at the Public Library, had turned over his own room to me for a week and I kept a boy busy bringing me books and carting them away. But in my enthusiastic and successful hunt for props for my theory I forgot that too much is too much. When readers of my book found me using six pages to prove what could have been done in one, they—well, they shut the volume and "listened in" elsewhere.

Poor Morse had to read the proofsheets. In one copious

foot-note I had referred to a certain Hindu author whose works I could not find in any language I could read. "Thank God!" he wrote on the margin.

"Primitive Love and Love Stories" is out of print. So is "Romantic Love and Personal Beauty." I have no desire to have them reprinted in their original form. Both are too long, making together some fourteen hundred pages. That's just one thousand too many in these busy days when books have so many competitors. As soon as these Memoirs are completed I shall "boil down" these 1400 pages to 400, built on a new plan and including details about medieval germs of romantic love previously overlooked.

LUTHER BURBANK AND JOHN MUIR

In writing about my Bethel garden I referred to my success in raising Burbank's California creations so far north as Maine.

In 1909 I had the pleasure of seeing him in his own garden at Santa Rosa.

While in Los Angeles we lunched with Charles F. Lummis—whose books on our Southwest have a charm equal to their lasting value and who was then head of the Public Library—in his quaint, self-built, museum-like stone residence. There we were so lucky as to meet the racy poet Charles Keeler, who was packing his valise to hurry back to San Francisco and welcome as his guest John Burroughs returning from his Hawaiian trip. He kindly invited us to join him and, in company with this famous nature writer, visit the two biggest of California's lions, Luther Burbank and John Muir.

The oil magnate H. H. Hart and his genial wife (who were building a palace largely for the entertainment of literary celebrities) took us from San Francisco in their spacious steam automobile and thus we descended upon Mr. Muir, at his home in Martinez. As he was living alone, we took along some well-filled lunch baskets to which our host added a huge basket of luscious cherries from his own trees; and thus we picnicked on the piazza, Burroughs and Muir sitting together and indulging in reminiscences of the Harriman Expedition to Alaska during which they had become such close friends that they called each other John. Then Muir took us into his house and showed us the botanic, mineral and photographic treasures he had gathered on his solitary rambles in the mountains, forests and deserts.

When I asked him if I could, at that season, visit the Hetch-Hetchy Valley from the Yosemite in two or three days, he exclaimed, "Oh muggins! You talk like a tourist!" but forgave me when I explained that I had to finish a book in a few weeks. He talked about the glories of Hetch-Hetchy, about the petrified forests of Arizona, about his wanderings in Alaska, Australia, India—every word worth printing—and showed us, among other things, a picture of a deodar tree in India which had "room in its branches for the whole Sierra Club."

As I write this I have before me a letter from Muir penned fifteen years before this visit. I had written a review for the *Nation* of his glorious book "The Mountains of California." On reading this, he wrote, "I said 'here is the only complete review of the book I have yet seen. Evidently the writer has not only read the book but heartily enjoyed it.'

"I am glad to learn," he continued, "that you are coming to the Sierra next summer. Come to my house that I may know you better and I will assist you in planning your journeys. You and your wife may easily go with animals from Lake Tahoe to Yosemite. I made that journey twice long ago without encountering the slightest difficulty. A guide will not be necessary, for every way and even no way is sure to be the right way in so fine and Godful a wilderness." This was followed by two pages of directions, ending with "but come and see me."

When we made our visit in 1909 he did not remember my name in connection with this episode. When it came back to him afterwards he wrote me an apology saying that if he had remembered he would have invited us to be his guests for a few weeks and join him in his pedestrian excursions into the mountains. That *would* have been a treat!

Owing to a previous engagement he was unfortunately unable to accompany us on our visit on the following day to Burbank at Santa Rosa, some fifty miles north of San Francisco. Here we had the pleasure of spending several hours with the man who ranked with Thomas Edison as one of America's two greatest inventors and creators of things undreamt of before them.

"I am afraid we are taking your time," said Mr. Burroughs after our host had entertained us for some time in his reception room. "On the contrary, you are giving me yours," replied Mr. Burbank; and presently he took us out into one of his experimental gardens where we saw flowers of exquisite new colors and gorgeous size that made us feel like Parsifal in the enchanted garden. We tasted fruits and berries that were more luscious than any that mortals have eaten since the Garden of Eden was destroyed, among them strawberries that seemed to be fruit and sugar and cream all in one. Here was proof on all sides that plants are, indeed, as the maker of this garden had demonstrated hundreds of times, as plastic as clay and that they can be, to use his own words, "molded into more beautiful forms and colors than any painter or sculptor can ever hope to bring forth." The Burbank plants we saw had no thorns; his cactus and his black-berry vines were as smooth as watermelons.

Like all artists, Burbank liked to know that you really saw and enjoyed what he had done; and nothing seemed to please him more than the proof my wife and I gave that we were thoroughly familiar with his creations by our comments on the improvements he had made in his crimson and crimson-and-gold California poppies and his wonderful shirleys since we last raised them, the previous summer, in our Maine garden.

Fifteen years later, on September 22, 1924, Burbank wrote to me: "Yes I had the pneumonia and was in bed, with nurse and doctor every day for forty-two days but am now just as well as I ever was and attending to all kinds of business, thousands of visitors and some of the time two thousand letters a week."

It has been so for years, and it made me realize how favored we had been to get so much of his time. In an-other letter he assured me: "for you my latch string will always be out."

He was very human, Burbank was. When I wrote to ask him, in 1919, not to take my name off his list because I had had no chance that year to have a garden, he an-swered: "You bet your life we will not take your name off the list and our seed catalog which is red hot from the printer's press goes forward to you to-day."

A number of Burbank's valuable letters to me are printed in my "Food and Flavor" and "Girth Control." Concerning fragrance in flowers, in which I am particu-larly interested, he wrote me in 1921: "Fragrance, of course, is lacking in many flowers, though I have added it to the calla, verbena and dahlia and intensified it in practically all the flowers with which I have worked. . . . Tulips can all be made to have fragrance. . . . The gladio-lus will sometime have fragrance." This prophecy was fulfilled, as I saw in the London *Times* of April 18, 1925.

Although Burbank lived to be seventy-seven years old, and his name has been in the newspapers millions of times, he is not yet really known to the public. Few of us realize what a tremendous influence he had on our gardens and markets. Take his plums, for example. Every farmer is the proud owner of a tree or two of "Burbank plums," but few know that there are at least two dozen kinds of Burbank plums, all superior to this original variety, and that they are on sale not only in all city markets but peddled in fruit wagons from village to village under such names as Santa Rosa, Duarte, Wickham, etc. If these peddlers knew they were Burbank plums and sold them as such they could dispose of five times as many.

In August, 1923, an article appeared in the newspapers intimating that Burbank was in a bad way financially, having been obliged to sell several acres of his experimental gardens at Sebastopol. Such a thing was not impossible; his expenses were enormous and a creator of new growing things can take out no patents; any one can buy a package of seed from him and ever after raise and sell it by the ton. All the same, this article made me red hot with indignation. I promptly wrote to Burbank for the exact facts and asked if I might appeal to my millionaire friends or write a stirring letter to the newspapers for help. "How much would be needed to prevent further destruction of Sebastopol? *It must not be.*"

A week later I got a consoling and amusing letter from him, in which he explained that while he had sold those acres it was because he did not need them any more. On November 28, 1925 he wrote me on the same subject a letter which has a note of pathos: "No, I am not hard up by any means, I am wealthy but can not endure the ten to fourteen hours per day physical labor that I could at one time, therefore am anxious to dispose of some of my

Sebastopol property." Referring to my remark that the first intimation I had that I was no longer young was that in my garden work I could no longer bend over with impunity, he wrote: "Yes, bending over is not good for us; I found that out long ago."

DOCTOR KELLOGG AND BATTLE CREEK

There was a time when I looked as if I had been dug out of my grave. My friends agreed, as they told me afterwards, that they gave me at most three months to live; I myself felt so wretched that I hoped all would end soon. I was suffering from an aggravated form of auto-intoxication, or self-poisoning through the alimentary canal, and didn't know it. One day, while looking over some magazines in quest of a subject for an editorial, I came across an advertisement of Battle Creek paramels and laxas. I sent for some, arrested my autointoxication and in sixteen weeks had regained sixteen pounds. I have told this story in detail in "Girth Control" and need not repeat it here. The process of rejuvenation was great fun, I assure you.

I lost no time in informing Doctor Kellogg that his books and his Battle Creek foods had saved my life. That was the beginning of a friendship which is among the happiest incidents in my life. He promptly and repeatedly invited me to come to the Sanitarium for a few weeks as his guest, so one day we took the afternoon express which takes New Yorkers overnight to the elevated town in Michigan which has become world-famed for its breakfast and health foods, and to which every doctor in America sends those of his patients that he can not do anything with.

In order to see how the wheels go round, we took the regular treatment for a few days although I told Doctor

Kellogg I would give him a dollar if his physicians found anything the matter with me. We found the Sanitarium wonderfully specialized—a department for every organ and type of illness; and saw how, after a thorough examination, each patient is assigned to the specialist he needs.

As there are from two to three thousand patients at a time (a new wing is building in 1926 at a cost of two millions), the director can not, of course, tend to all personally; but there are hours when any one may consult him. I was deeply impressed by the attitude of the patients toward Doctor Kellogg; they seemed to regard him with reverence as if he were the founder of a religion; and that, in truth, he is; a new religion of health: a medical system which has little use for medicines but relies chiefly on hydrotherapy, phototherapy, the right kind of food, and colon hygiene, for the astonishing cures effected.

The Sanitarium diet is unique—nothing like it anywhere else. Meat is never allowed on the table (because it aggravates autointoxication); but there are eggs and milk and cream and butter (the Doctor has model henneries and creameries of his own) besides vegetables in great variety and abundance. Unique are the dishes made of powdered nuts, which take the place of meat and taste surprizingly like it. Doctor Kellogg, by the way, was the inventor of the now ubiquitous peanut butter.

There is an *edition de luxe* of these viands, which we tasted at a dinner in his home—revelations of future possibilities; but we took most of our meals with the patients. Nearly every day the Doctor passed through the dining-rooms, attired in snow-white (to which he attributes special health-giving qualities), stopping here and there for a chat. From the amount of attention he paid us—he even took us out repeatedly in his auto—the patients probably got the idea that I must be the Prince of Wales or something.

Celebrities abound at the Sanitarium, and Doctor Kellogg has an irresistible way of persuading them to give little talks to the patients or in the schools annexed to the Sanitarium. We were so lucky as to hear and meet Professor Irving Fisher of Yale University of whose invaluable book "How to Live" Funk and Wagnalls have sold nearly 200,000 copies.

The Sanitarium is only one department of the Battle Creek enterprise. There are, besides, schools of domestic science, physical training, including dancing, and various other branches of education. The young girls and youths in these are enabled to meet their expenses by serving as waitresses or helping in other departments. This is one of the delights of the Sanitarium; one sees refined persons everywhere. It was pleasant to have a lovely girl say to me one day "I enjoyed your lecture very much this morning." She was running the elevator. Our waitress was the daughter of a clergyman and likely to become the wife of another one.

That Doctor Kellogg is able to look after all these branches personally, besides performing a delicate surgical operation or two every day, is one of the seven wonders of the Middle West. His activity affords astonishing proof of the value of his teachings in bestowing health and endurance. I have before me a copy of an article written some years ago by the Doctor's private secretary, Mr. R. V. Ashley, which gives almost unbelievable details concerning the stunts his employer has performed, and still performs altho he is now in his seventies.

When the Doctor lectures he talks at the rate of 185 words per minute. The secretary has to take this down and, in addition, perform so many other stunts in keeping records of his employer's dictations and doings that three girls are kept busy transcribing from machines. Another girl prepares the half-a-hundred to a hundred "personal"

letters daily for the Doctor to answer by dictation or
"skeleton suggestions." But the greatest stunts are performed when traveling. The secretary has to be ready at
a minute's notice to start for New York or anywhere else.
He has often taken notes and written answers to letters
in moving trains, interurbans, streets cars, taxicabs and
even hacks moving over roughly-paved streets. No account is taken of day or night, time for sleeping or meals.
On one occasion the secretary worked for his employer on
a train steadily for eighteen hours.

While I am 'most as poor as a churchmouse—barely
able to live in the best hotels in fashionable European
summer and winter resorts—Doctor Kellogg, a millionaire, keeps in harness. Again and again I have tried to
persuade him to follow my wise example, to quit and do
only what he enjoys most, but in vain. When I informed
him of my retirement from journalistic work, he wrote:
"I have to keep my nose on the grindstone perpetually and
very seldom get a chance to do what natural instinct would
lead me to do except that I am so much interested in promoting biologic and race betterment projects which seem
to be my mission in the world that I should not be at all
comfortable if I were not on the job every minute. There
is so much to be done and so little time in which to do it."

P. S.

A few days after writing the above, in Paris, we found
the Doctor in the Savoy Hotel, only a few doors from the
St. James et d 'Albany, where we were staying. He was
looking young and vigorous as ever. When he told me
he had come to France to stay several months I said: "At
last a vacation." But no! He had crossed the ocean to
swap ideas with Frenchmen and keep in touch with their
doings. He was busier than ever and had kept his secre-

tary at work till two in the morning, starting in again at seven.

Such superactivity on the part of a man of seventy-four seems uncanny, but it proves that brain-work does not cause breakdowns if a man's habits are all right. Doctor Kellogg's are all right; he practises everything he preaches. That's where he differs from me, I regret to say. A few weeks after we had met the Doctor, my wife was dining in a restaurant near our hotel. Opposite her sat an American lady whom we had met before. She asked where I was and was told I was sick in bed, chiefly from eating not wisely but too well. "Has he read 'Girth Control'?" said the lady and my wife replied: "Why, he wrote it," adding that I was very much ashamed at not having followed my own wise precepts. Everybody had told me I looked fifty; I felt fifty and so I ate like fifty. Particularly bad for me were the late dinners, mostly of meat, which are inevitable at all European hotels.

A man of seventy should eat no meat, eat no meal later than six oclock, if he would avoid high blood-pressure and hardening of the arteries. I had always made light of this matter. If I was told "A man is as old as his arteries" I answered flippantly "Yes, and he is as old as his liver and his bacon, or any of his other organs." That led to my downfall. I looked like a man of fifty, true, but I had the hardened arteries of an epicure of seventy who has never denied himself the pleasures of life. Then it came, like a stroke of lightning. One evening I went to bed feeling like a contented lion who has just dined on an antelope. I slept well but when I got up in the morning to close the window I couldn't reach it. My left leg was paralyzed, so was my left arm, and my speech was indistinct.

My wife hurried over to the Savoy with a note to Doctor Kellogg begging him to come and see what had hap-

pened to me. In half an hour he was there. Of course
he could not treat a patient in France but he telephoned
to Doctor Gros, head of the American Hospital, to come
and take care of me, and dropped in every other day to
see how I was getting along. It *was* blood-pressure and
hardened arteries, sure enough. *Almost* a stroke—but
not quite: still, a damaged artery, the doctor said, was
like a broken leg, and would take time to heel. Doctor
Gros had several other cases on hand just like mine—from
overdoing in various ways. His worst case was that of
an American who had been speculating frantically in
Florida real estate. The doctor was sure my collapse also
had some mental factor—worry, or something. I had to
confess that for weeks I had been daily lashed into fury by
reading in the Paris papers about Germany's secret preparations for the war which would end civilization and in
the London papers about the equally devilish plottings of
the Bolsheviks. This, combined with my gastronomic
stunts, sufficed to account for my breakdown.

The problem now confronting us was how to shorten
the period of convalescence. To remain in Paris would
have meant prolonging it indefinitely. The one thing I
needed was outdoor life and plenty of sunshine. Paris,
lying as far North as Quebec, is in winter colder than
London, and almost if not quite as sunless. Apart from
Italy, where, however, it is uncomfortably cold in winter,
with no real outdoor life, there is only one region in Europe which sports sunshine—the French Riviera, between
the Maritime Alps and the Mediterranean. Here the sky
is as blue as the ocean—it is the Côte d'Azur—the ancient
Romans already knew that and had their winter villas
where Cannes and Nice are now. To-day there are miles
upon miles of big hotels here where every Frenchman and
Englishman who can afford it spends his winters. But
the winter sunshine of the Riviera covers only about two

months; the rest of the winter it is almost as gloomy as the remainder of Europe—the dismal Continent, I feel tempted to call it. For perpetual sunshine one has to go to Southern California. "Why shouldn't I go to California?" I asked Doctor Gros. He is a Californian and approved of my suggestion cordially. It meant a trip of 6,000 miles across sea and land, but he felt sure I would be ready for it by the next sailing date of the flagship among French passenger boats, the Paris. We had a smooth midwinter trip, arriving in New York only two *hours* late. During the weeks preceding and following our crossing the storms were so violent that some of the biggest liners were delayed two *days*.

The California Limited brought us in two days from New Orleans to where I am now, writing this P. S., at Redlands, on the edge of the Mojave desert, where we started in with a whole month of daily sunshine from 8 to 5. Heliotherapy soon brought back my health and strength, in spite of my having become afflicted with what Battle Creek pronounces "the greatest of all chronic ailments," neuralgia, which makes you feel as if you had been captured by Apaches (the Apache Trail is not far from here) who were sticking daggers in between your ribs.*

Good-by to New York

That I am not a work-toper I proved by my retirement when still in full possession of all my strength and endurance. That was two years ago and I haven't for a moment

---

* When I collapsed in Paris I had nearly completed my memoirs. A few days more would have done the job. It may be of interest to state that this book has been written in nearly a dozen different places: Antibes and Nice, Venice, Tremezzo on Lake Como, Interlaken, Wengen, Mürren, Zermatt (Riffelalp) and Montreux in Switzerland, Stresa on Lago Maggiore, Paris, and Redlands, California. Luckiest of all workers is the author, who can thus carry his workshop with him wherever he wishes to go.

missed my job; all I have done in that time is to loaf and, by way of diversion, write these memoirs.

It was in the last week of May, 1924, that I sent in my resignation to the *Evening Post's* new managing editor, Mr. Merritt Bond, who replied under date of May 28 in a letter beginning with these words: "The news contained in your letter has been received with real regret by the men on the *Post*. This regret I know will be shared by the music lovers who have read your articles for so many years. I appreciated your friendly letter and will be glad to publish your valedictory, which I plan to use this Saturday." He prefaced my farewell address with this paragraph:

"The close of the music season is the close also of a career as a newspaper music critic of Henry T. Finck who has given forty-three years of distinguished service on the staff of the *Evening Post*. Mr. Finck in a 'valedictory' written in the whimsically humorous vein so characteristic of him, announces that he will devote 'the remaining twenty or thirty years of my life (I am only seventy now) to adding to the number of my books.'" Then came

MR. FINCK'S VALEDICTORY

"After having made a nuisance of myself for forty-three years to all musical mediocrities heard in New York and helping along the real artists with all my might and main, I have decided to give up musical journalism entirely and devote the remaining twenty or thirty years of my life (I am only seventy now) to adding to the number of my books (there are seventeen so far), which I can do much better in the French Riviera and Capri in winter and Switzerland in summer than I possibly could in overcrowded, noisy New York.

"Nearly half a century has elapsed since I first wrote musical criticisms for the New York *Evening Post*. I should be proud to follow the example of my highly esteemed colleague and roommate, John Ranken Towse, who has already been with this journal fifty-four years; but the lure of literature and of foreign travel, of which I used

TxU

to make a specialty, is too great. The managing editor will have no difficulty in finding a good critic to take my place and I shall be much happier than I have been these last years listening to hundreds of singers and players most of whom would be at Sing Sing if we accepted Liszt's dictum that mediocrity in music is a crime.

"Ernest Newman refers in one of his books to 'the melancholy profession of musical criticism'. It is a sad business because one has to step on so many people's toes if one is to walk the straight path. In my early years I was fearfully rude and cavemanly; but I reformed after my chief, Mr. Godkin, told me bluntly that I ought never to write a sentence about an artist—especially a woman—that I would not be willing to say to her personally. I reformed so thoroughly that repeatedly, in recent years, I have been gratified to find myself referred to as 'the most amiable of the New York critics.'

"For the countless hours of boredom patiently endured in the conscientious performance of my duty there have been many, many evenings and afternoons of superlative bliss when the world's great artists played or sang for us. Most of these I have known personally and I have many interesting anecdotes to tell about them in my autobiography, which will be my next book.

"Two of these celebrities, Jean de Reszke and Maurice Renaud, will be among my neighbors in the Riviera next winter. Perhaps I shall write about them and about the Monte Carlo Opera, second only to our Metropolitan; but I make no promise. Just at present, I confess frankly, I feel as if I would not wish to hear any music for at least forty-three years. Too much is worse than a feast.

HENRY T. FINCK."

This was followed by

MR. TOWSE'S APPRECIATION

"The retirement from active service of Henry T. Finck brings loss to the journal of which he was an ornament, to all American music lovers, and, not least, to the little circle of his fellow-workers. Of these last the writer is one of the oldest. Mr. Finck and I shared the same office for several decades, and in such continual intimacy men get to know each other pretty well. The fact that we never quarreled, altho we not infrequently differed, is a proof of the good will that existed between us. I shall miss him sorely.

"His intellectual range, the intensity of his convictions, his enthusiasms, and his contempts made him an exhilarating and delightful companion. Of his ability and authority as a critic I am not qualified to speak, but the longer I knew him the more I was impressed by the extent and minuteness of his musical knowledge. And I envied him the rapidity and facility of his composition. It was rarely that he halted for an expression, or between two opinions. He wrote with the easy, smooth and unhesitating assurance of one who had his facts and ideas at his fingers' ends. No man ever had more serene confidence in the soundness of his own judgment.

"For many of the things in which the common bulk of mankind is interested he exhibited complete indifference. Sport of every kind, except the gentle one of angling, he despised as unworthy of civilized mortals. I am afraid that he regarded my own fondness for athletics as a sign of mental degeneracy. The ordinary news gossip of the day had little charm for him. Outside music and the other subjects in which he specialized, it was with general principles rather than details with which he was concerned. But on his own favorite topics—hygiene, horticulture, travel, diet, anthropology, etc., he spoke as he wrote, with the fluent authority that springs from solid information.

"And he was always entertaining. Learned in curious directions, he is no dry pedant. He has the saving grace of humor. His writing, as his thousands of readers know, shows lightness of touch as well as incisive strokes. He has even been known to indulge in the frivolity of puns—some as bad as the worst of Theodore Hook's. That he may live to make many more is the hope of all the friends to whom he endeared himself by his kindliness, vivacity, dependability and intelligence. May health, prosperity, and happiness attend him.

J. RANKEN TOWSE."

It was an old experience for me to read *quasi* "obituaries" like Towse's and many others that appeared in newspapers all over the country, while I was still living and looking on myself as comparatively a young man; it has been shown biologically, you know, that the normal duration of a man's life should be 150 years.

Among the "obituaries" that pleased me most was one in the Chicago *Musical Leader* by Emilie Frances Bauer; I can not refrain from quoting part of it:

"His farewell brings to mind the old butler who, having

been a loved member of his employer's family for over thirty years, one day sent a bomb into camp in the form of his resignation. Unable to grasp at any reason for this he was asked: 'Have we not always treated you kindly and with consideration?' Yes, there was no cause for complaint in that direction. 'Have we not properly compensated you?' That, too, was quite as it should be. 'Then what could be the possible reason for your wanting to leave us?' was the next question, and his answer was: 'I am that sick of the whole lot of you that I can't look you in the face.'

"So Mr. Finck is tired of hearing seasoned and un-seasoned artists, tired of old music, and tired of novelties, tired of writing praises for some and abuse for others, tired of song and singers, conductors and everything ex-cept doing the thing that he wants to do. His readers are suffering a double loss for he always had the co-operation and assistance of his wife Abbie Helen Cushman Finck, who never in her own right came out of the shadow of her husband's work to shine in her own light. A scholarly musician, a woman of critical judgment, of kindly attitude to all, but first to the duty which she considered that she owed to music, Mrs. Finck's pen and her brain have helped Henry T. Finck through a career which has been covered with glory to himself, to those he served, and to the read-ers who have much education for which to thank him. With the passing of Mr. Finck there remains only W. J. Henderson of the 'old clan,' and long may his pen be spared to those who need the stabilizing effect of one whose activities and musical memories lie over a span of years which serve to link the present with the past."

From Henderson I got a characteristic letter the amusing postscript to which I must quote: "I forgot about my article on your retirement. Well, a distinguished minister, commenting on the sudden discovery of a certain

man's worth when he was dead, declared that the newspapers would have shown more intelligence, as well as
humanity, had they given him a little more taffy while he
was alive and not so much epi-taffy when he had passed
on. Them's my sentiments."

Of course I was sorry to leave New York because of
my friends there. Yet, to tell the truth, I seldom had the
time to see them that I used to have in the golden days
before elevated railways, subways and automobiles im-
peded traffic.

Things were closer together half a century ago. Food
was better and cost only half as much. My favorite lunch
used to consist of a plate of delicious oysters, but when
Alfred W. McCann described the sewage-infected bays
where bivalves were being fattened I became a total ab-
stainer.

Everything has degenerated, even the weather. Present day New York could never get up a high-brow blizzard such as we had in 1888, when all going-about (except
on foot) was stopped for two days. That *was* a blizzard!
I remember the sign-board put up by a wag in Madison
Square, when it was buried under three feet of snow:
PLEASE KEEP OFF THE GRASS. And an-
other one: THIS *WAS* 23rd. STREET.

In one way, I admit, New York has improved. I like
the skyscrapers, which have become its hall mark. Particularly the Woolworth Building. It was (and still is)
only a stone's throw from what was my window in the
Evening Post building and I often looked at it admiringly.
When it was nearly completed, Mr. Woolworth gave a
dinner on the thirtieth floor to several hundred men who
had distinguished themselves in one way or other. We
had all the caviare and terrapin and wild duck and other
luxuries we could consume, with barrels of champagne to
wash them down. And when, after the dinner, Mr. Wool-

worth got up to tell how he had built this skyscraper with the millions made in his ten-cent stores, many of the guests continued to talk and made so much noise that I could hardly hear a word though I was only twenty feet from the speaker. Pigs is pigs.

Some day, when New York traffic moves in three stories so that pedestrians can cross the street without saying a last prayer, and when the deadly soft coal smoke is banished once more, I may return to the Metropolis. In the meantime I shall spend my summers in Maine, my winters in California, the only part of the world I know where one can live in the open air always and yet be comfortable when driven indoors by an occasional cold or wet day—which is not the case in Italy. My ideal of a happy life is living in a California bungalow surrounded by flowers and orange trees.

INDEX

Abbey, H. E., 194, 203
Agassiz, L., 91
Aiken, F. G., 341
Alden, 33
Aldrich, R., 398, 412
Alvary, Max, 216
Apthorpe, W. F., 401, 415

Barrientos, Maria, 383
Bartlett, Prof., 70
Bauer, Emilie Frances, 455
Bauer, Harold, 390
Benet, W. R., 342
Bishop, J. B., 176
Blumenberg, M., 404
Bodanzky, A., 374
Bond, Merritt, 453
Bori, Lucrezia, 331, 380
Bowen, F., 99, 134
Bowman, Mrs., 407
Brandt, M., 213
Brennan, St John, 406
Bressler Gianoli, 354
Bridges, R., 341
Bristol, F. E., 240
Brownell, W. C., 346, 429
Buchanan, C. L., 395
Burbank, Luther, 8, 432, 441, 443
Burleigh, H. C., 23
Burroughs, J., 441
Bushnell, E., 240

Calvé, Emma, 217
Campanini, Cleofonte, 354
Campanini, Italo, 188
Canby, Henry Seidel, 342
Carnegie, Andrew, 255
Carreño, T., 285
Caruso, Enrico, 232, 332, 335, 376
Charlton, Loudon, 420
Chase, Wm., 407
Child, Prof., 95, 134
Clemens, Clara, 426

Conried, H., 318
Condon, 54
Cooke, J. F., 415
Croy, Homer, 429
Curtis, Cyrus H. K., 340
Curtis, George Wm., 178

Damrosch, Leopold, 195
Damrosch, Walter, 252, 319
Davies, Ben, 176
Davis, Chas. H., 348
Davis, Royal, 342
Dr. Coppet, E. J., 396
De Koven, Reginald, 371, 406
De Reszke, Edouard, 204, 205
De Reszke, Jean, 204, 206, 223, 234, 255
Destinn, Emmy, 373
Dippel, A., 365, 372
Ditson, Chas. H., 279
Doeme, Z., 235, 328
Dvorák, A., 201, 277, 280

Eames, Emma, 208
Easton, Florence, 381
Eliot, Chas. W., 73, 75, 95
Ellis, Chas., 377
Elson, L. C., 401
Emerson, R. W., 89

Fabbris, Amanda, 407
Farrar, Geraldine, 206, 222, 327-334, 376, 377, 378, 380, 386
Finck, Edward, 159
Finck, Edward J., 160
Finck, H. C., 2, 4, 5, 6, 7, 35, 40
Finck, Mrs. H. C., 3-5
Finck, Mrs. H. T., XIV, 271, 282, 333-4
Finck, J. C., 63, 120
Fischer, Emil, 216
Fischer, Kuno, 147
Fisher, Irving, 448
Fisher, Wm. Arms, 278
Fiske, John, 91, 120, 439

Flagler, H., 254
Floersheim, Otto, 404
Ford, James, 194
Fremstad, Olive, 240
Freund, J. C., 404

Gabrilowitsch, O., 425
Galli-Curci, 377, 382
Garden, Mary, 356, 362
Garrison, W. P., 164
Gates, Lucy, 284, 382
Gatti-Casazza, Giulio, 370, 376, 380, 386-9
Gavit, John, 346
Gay, E. F., 342
Gilder, R. W., 1, 207, 281
Gilibert, Chas., 364
Gilman, Lawrence, 283, 408-9
Godkin, E. L., 165, 252
Goldmark, Rubin, 278
Grainger, Percy, 316, 391
Granados, 303
Grau, Maurice, 203, 227, 242, 245, 375-6
Grieg, Edvard, 272
Gros, Dr. Emund, 451
Guard, Wm J., 387

Hale, Philip, 219, 400-1
Hall, S. Stanley, 144
Halperson, M., 407
Hammerstein, Oscar, 349
Harris, Hettie, 346
Harris, Victor, 379
Hart, H. H., 441
Hassard, J. R. G., 171
Hawthorne, Beatrix, 428
Hawthorne, Hildegarde, 428
Hawthorne, Julian, 428-439
Hearst, Phoebe, 250
Heffley, E., 399
Helmholtz, H., 141
Henderson, W. J., 317, 328, 363, 398, 411, 423, 456
Herbert, Victor, 364, 371, 406
Hertz, Alfred, 323
Higginson, H. L., 398
Hofmann, Josef, 304
Holladay, Ben, 24, 35
Holmes, O. W., 90

Holt, Hamilton, 266
Homer, Louise, 239
Horsman, E., 406
Howells, W. D., 43, 88, 120
Hubert, P. G., 300
Hughes, Rupert, 406
Humiston, W. H., 408
Humperdinck, E., 277
Huneker, James, 78, 157, 244, 316, 412, 417, 423

Ingersoll, R., 249

James, Wm., 94
Jecko, S. H., 81, 83, 113
Jeritza, Maria, 376, 377
Joseffy, R., 281
Juch, Emma, 407

Kahn, Otto H., 370, 386, 387, 389
Keil, Dr., 12, 29, 38, 40
Kelley, Edgar Stillman, 417
Kellogg, J. H., 446
Key, Pierre, 407
Kneisel, Franz, 35-6, 396
Kramer, Walter, 405
Krauss, A., 196
Kreisler, Fritz, 305, 421
Krehbiel, H. E., 146, 171, 186, 230, 356, 376, 417, 425-6
Kobbé, G., 406

Lamont, Thomas, 339
Lang, B. J., 401
Learned, J. E., 271
Lehmann, Lilli, 214, 225, 327
Levey, E. J., 209, 405
Liebling, Leonard, 404
Liszt, 123, 414
Longfellow, H. W., 84
Loveman, Amy, 342
Low, Seth, 398
Lowell, J. R., 90
Lowell, Percival, 115
Lumholtz, C., 266
Lummis, C. F., 441

McCormick, Harold, 370
MacDowell, Edward, 282, 398

MacDowell, Mrs. E., 285
MacDowell, Mrs. Thomas, 282
McKenzie, Dr. and Mrs., 86
Mahler, Gustav, 424
Mapleson, J. H., 191
Marcou, P. B., 120
Martin, Riccardo, 338
Massenet, 353
Materna, A., 157
Möricke, E., 385
Morley, Christopher, 342
Morse, E. W., 440
Muir, John, 442
Melba, Nellie, 222
Mengelberg, G., 422

Nebelung, Max, 263
Niemann, A., 215
Nikisch, A., 399
Nordica, Lillian, 224–5, 232
Norton, C. E., 71, 90
Novaes, Guiomar, 315
Noyes, A. D., 341

Ochs, A. S., 341
Ogden, Rollo, 340
Ogden, Winnifred, 359
Olmsted, J. B., 113–6, 147, 150, 167, 270
Oskison, John, 429

Paderewski, 229, 231, 287–301, 303, 408, 421
Paine, J. K., 74, 134
Palmer, G. H., 98
Patti, A., 189
Payne, A. B., 428
Peabody, Dr., A. P., 96
Peyser, H. T., 405, 408
Phelps, Wm. Lyon, 342
Polacco, Giorgio, 368, 390
Powell, John, 371
Powell, Maud, 312
Presser, T., 415

Raisa, Rosa, 368
Renaud, M., 273, 356, 385
Rodrigues, J. C., 315
Roosevelt, Theodore, 266
Rubinstein, A., 145

Sachs, Willy von, 406
Safonoff, W., 276, 310
Saint-Saëns, 145, 353
Samaroff, Olga, 427
Sanborn, Pitts, 407
Savage, H. W., 324
Sawyer, C. P., 346–9
Sawyer, Ruth, 309
Scaria, E., 215
Schelling, Ernest, 302, 390
Schumann-Heink, 236
Schott, A., 196
Schurz, Carl, 164, 169
Schwab, C. M., 397
Seidl, Anton, 177, 197–200, 215, 234, 246, 250, 255
Sembrich, Marcella, 225, 378
Sharlow, Myrna, 240
Shelley, H. R., 278
Simmons, R., 234, 236
Smith, Max, 374, 375
Smyth, Julian, 327
Sousa, J. P., 314
Spanuth, A., 199, 407
Steinway, Mrs. Frederick, 382
Steinway, Wm., 185
Stimson, F. J., 115
Stokowsky, 425, 427
Stransky, Josef, 379, 389, 420
Strauss, Johann, 155, 326
Strauss, Richard, 325, 409, 414, 424
Strobel, E., 270
Strunsky, Simeon, 342, 419
Sundelius, Marie, 240
Swift, Lindsay, 440

Taussig, Frank, 144
Taylor, Deems, XIII, 289, 390, 407
Thomas, Theodore, 173, 195
Thurber, Mrs. Jeannette M., 274, 279
Thwing, Ch. F., Dedication, 74, 82, 115
Toscanini, A., 371, 374–5
Towse, J. R., 251, 343, 454
Turner, H. G., 313
Twain, Mark, 1, 426

Van Vechten, 406
Villard, Henry, 264
Villard, Mrs. H., 266

INDEX

...ld, 267

...ner, Cosima, 200, 321
Wagner, Richard, 122, 388, 406
Wallace, H. R., 143
Waller, Henry, 278
Wellman, Frank, 116
Wheeler, A. A., 105
Wheeler, Harold, 124
White, Horace, 164

Wilhelm, Kaiser, 125
Wolf, Albert, 385
Wolf, C. W., 41-8
Wolle, Dr. F., 397
Woodberry, G. E., 110–112, 115, 133

Young, G. W., 235
Ysaye, E., 305

Zeller, E., 139
Ziegler, E., 371, 413